The Directory of

Minority Judges

of the United States

Third Edition

Defending Liberty
Pursuing Justice

Published by American Bar Association
Judicial Division
Standing Committee on Minorities in the Judiciary

The Directory of

Minority Judges

of the United States

Third Edition

First Printed in August 2001

Published by American Bar Association
Judicial Division
Standing Committee on Minorities in the Judiciary

To order a copy of this Directory or for Judicial Division membership information, please contact the ABA Service Center at (800) 285-2221 or visit our website at:
http://www.abanet.org/jd

Printed in the USA

ISBN: 1-57073-945-5
PC#:523-003201

Layout and Design: HalfLight Media Group - http://www.HalfLightMedia.com

2001 JD Standing Committee on Minorities in the Judiciary

Honorable Benjamin H. Logan II, Chair
Grand Rapids, MI

Honorable Marilyn Dolan Go
Brooklyn, NY

Mr. Gihan Fernando
Ithaca, NY

Honorable Joseph Baca
Santa Fe, NM

Honorable Charles R. Cloud
Norfolk, VA

Honorable Edward Kakita
Los Angeles, CA

Honorable Arthur L. Burnett, Sr.
Washington, DC

Honorable Ezra H. Friedlander
Indianapolis, IN

Honorable Gregory Holiday
West Bloomfield, MI

Honorable Eileen Kato
Seattle, WA

Honorable Earldean V. Robbins
San Francisco, CA

Honorable Booker T. Stephens
Welch, WV

Minority Judges by State

State	African American	Asian Pacific Island	Hispanic American	Native American	Tribal Courts	Total
Alabama	46	0	1	1	2	
Alaska	1	1	1	0	3	
Arizona	18	5	63	5	46	
Arkansas	23	0	0	0	0	
California	176	113	215	6	6	
Colorado	11	4	32	0	3	
Connecticut	23	0	6	0	3	
Delaware	15	0	0	0	0	
District of Columbia	88	2	12	0	0	
Florida	65	0	63	1	3	
Georgia	106	3	4	1	0	
Guam	0	8	0	0	0	
Hawaii	1	98	0	0	0	
Idaho	0	1	1	0	11	
Illinois	115	6	21	0	3	
Indiana	18	1	7	0	0	
Iowa	3	1	0	0	0	
Kansas	8	0	2	0	0	
Kentucky	7	0	0	1	0	
Louisiana	70	0	3	1	4	
Maine	1	0	1	0	0	
Maryland	73	2	2	0	0	
Massachusetts	27	2	7	0	0	
Michigan	135	0	4	0	19	
Minnesota	13	2	4	1	8	
Mississippi	31	0	0	0	4	
Missouri	41	0	5	1	0	
Montana	0	0	1	1	34	
Nebraska	4	1	1	0	9	
Nevada	4	0	4	2	23	
New Hampshire	0	0	0	0	0	
New Jersey	70	4	35	2	0	
New Mexico	5	1	108	3	35	
New York	130	15	64	0	4	
North Carolina	51	0	0	4	7	
North Dakota	0	0	0	1	4	
North Marianna Islands	0	7	0	0	0	
Ohio	67	1	5	0	0	
Oklahoma	10	0	0	4	8	
Oregon	3	1	4	3	22	
Pennsylvania	69	2	7	1	0	
Puerto Rico	0	0	391	0	0	
Rhode Island	2	0	0	0	0	
South Carolina	25	0	1	0	0	
South Dakota	0	0	0	0	8	
Tennessee	34	0	1	1	0	
Texas	93	14	428	7	0	
Utah	2	5	4	1	4	
Vermont	0	1	0	0	0	
Virgin Islands	11	0	0	0	0	
Virginia	56	1	5	1	0	
Washington	22	22	7	3	40	
West Virginia	7	0	0	0	0	
Wisconsin	16	0	3	3	31	
Wyoming	0	0	0	1	3	
Armed Forces	2	1	0	0	0	

PREFACE

When we published the Second Edition of The Directory of Minority Judges of the United States in May 1997, we noted that in the United States (including the Commonwealth of Puerto Rico, Guam, the Virgin Islands and the Northern Mariana Islands) there were approximately 60,000 judges. We then identified a total of 3,610 judges and judicial officers as racial or ethnic minorities. In the intervening years there has been a modest increase. We have now identified 4,045 judges and judicial officers as members of racial or ethnic minority groups, a figure which amounts to 6.75% of the total judges and judicial officers in this Nation. We have attempted to be as inclusive and as complete as possible. This Directory of Minority Judges is an effort to include all federal and state judges, administrative law judges, administrative judges, commissioners, magistrates, referees, justices of the peace, and hearing officers performing adjudication functions who have been identified as being members of racial or ethnic category groups included in this directory.

This Third Edition of the Directory of Minority Judges of the United States is the result of almost four years of effort gathering data from 2 to 4 judge representatives in each State or other jurisdiction in each category to assure completeness and accuracy as to identifying an individual as being a member of a particular racial or ethnic origin minority category. Periodic surveys were made of these designated judges by fax and e-mail to assure accuracy and constant updating of our lists for each State and jurisdiction. We canvassed every State in which there were elections involving judges in November 2000 so that this directory would reflect the impact of the last judicial elections. Further, this directory reflects judicial appointments made to March 2001 where the State representatives have brought them to our attention.

This directory was conceived as a result of requests from law schools, universities and colleges, state and local bar associations, minority mentoring organizations and entities, the National Judicial College, MCLE instructional organizations desiring to increase diversity in their faculties, and from the National minority bar associations. It is contemplated that it will serve as a means of identifying racial and ethnic category judges and judicial officers throughout the Nation for law students to seek internships and judicial clerkships. It can also serve as a resource for law professors and law students to invite minority judges to appear at their law schools as guest speakers and as moot court judges. We contemplate that the directory may also be used in universities and colleges to motivate racial and ethnic minority students to consider becoming lawyers and aspiring to become judicial law clerks and ultimately judges or judicial officers. The directory can also be used to educate and inform the media of the increasing diversity of the judicial system and to make the public aware of the extent that racial and ethnic minorities are participating in the dispensing of justice in America. Hopefully, as the numbers of racial and ethnic minority judges and judicial officers increase, and their presence affect the attitudes and perspectives of all of their judicial colleagues, this will assure all minorities in the Nation that they will receive justice in our courts from judges and judicial officers who will be culturally competent, free of biases and prejudices, and sensitive and fair in hearing and deciding all legal disputes coming before them. Eventually, we hope that this directory may also become available in public libraries throughout the Nation to inform and educate all citizens of the efforts being made to improve the quality of justice administered in this Nation by promoting the increasing diversity of the federal and state judiciary, the administrative judiciary in federal and state administrative agencies, and among all of those individuals who hear and adjudicate disputes and controversies in our legal system.

We are deeply indebted to all of the judges, judicial officers, and judicial administrators, and their support staff, in the States and in the other jurisdictions included in the directory, and in the administrative agencies who cooperated with the Editor in this collaborative effort and whose contributions make this volume the definitive work on minority judges in the United States as we embark upon the 21st Century. We are particularly indebted to the American Bar Association Judicial Division Standing Committee on Minorities in the Judiciary, which sponsored our work, to the Judicial Division Staff, and to LexisNexis in connection with the printing and publication of this Directory.

Arthur L. Burnett, Sr.
Senior Judge
Editor

May 1, 2001
Chicago, Illinois

Special Acknowledgements

This directory is truly a labor of love made possible by the contributions of substantial time and energy by many individuals who provided the necessary data on minority judges and judicial officers in their States or other jurisdictions to make this directory possible. While several hundred judges and judicial officers responded to inquiries from the Editor, those listed below deserve special recognition for the extent of their labors and the major contributions that they made.

Honorable Pamela G. Alexander, Judge
District Court, Minneapolis, Minnesota.

Honorable Haile L. Alford, Associate Judge
Superior Court, Wilmington, Delaware.

Honorable Antonio Andréu-Garcia
Chief Justice, Supreme Court of Puerto Rico
San Juan, Puerto Rico.

Honorable Lorenzo Arredondo, Judge
Lake Circuit Court, Crown Point, Indiana.

Honorable Joseph Baca, Justice, New Mexico
Supreme Court, Santa Fe, New Mexico.

Honorable Taylor L. Baker, Jr., Judge
Marion County Superior Court
Indianapolis, Indiana.

Honorable Gordon S. Baranco, Judge
Superior Court, Oakland, California.

Honorable Robert M. Bell, Chief Judge
Maryland Court of Appeals
Baltimore, Maryland.

Honorable Adolpho A. Birch, Jr.
Associate Justice, Tennessee Supreme Court
Nashville, Tennessee.

Honorable Wiley Branton, Jr., Judge
Circuit/Chancery Court, Juvenile Division
Little Rock, Arkansas.

Honorable Antonio I. Brandveen, Justice
Supreme Court, Mineola, New York.

Honorable David Briones, Judge
United States District Court, El Paso, Texas.

Honorable Dexter Brooks
Senior Resident Judge
Superior Court, Pembroke, North Carolina.

Honorable Cecilia Patricia Castellanos
Judge Superior Court, Oakland, California.

Honorable Charles R. Cloud, Judge
Norfolk General District Court, Norfolk, Virginia.

Honorable James H. Coleman, Jr. Justice
New Jersey Supreme Court, Warren, New Jersey.

Honorable William Cousins, Jr., Justice
Appellate Court of Illinois, Chicago, Illinois.

Honorable Alma S. De Leon
Administrative Law Judge, Social Security
Administration, Pittsburgh, Pennsylvania.

Honorable Marilyn Dolan-Go
United States Magistrate Judge, Eastern
District of New York, Brooklyn, New York

Honorable Carmen Elisa Espinosa, Judge
Superior Court, New Britain, Connecticut.

Honorable Aundria D. Foster, Judge
Newport News Juvenile and Domestic Relations
District Court, Newport News, Virginia.

Honorable Donald D. Haley, Judge
King County Superior Court, Seattle, Washington.

Honorable Shelvin Louise Marie Hall
Presiding Justice, Appellate Court of Illinois
Chicago, Illinois.

Honorable Patricia Lilly Harleston, Judge
Superior Court, Rockville, Connecticut.

Honorable Patrice A. Hinnant, Judge
District Court, Greensboro, North Carolina.

Honorable Gregory Holiday
Administrative Law Judge, Michigan
Department of Consumer and Industry
Services, West Bloomfield Michigan.

Honorable Deadra L. Jefferson, Judge
Family Court, Charleston, South Carolina.

Honorable Bernette Joshua Johnson
Associate Justice, Louisiana Supreme Court
New Orleans, Louisiana.

Honorable Pamela Taylor Johnson, Judge
Juvenile Court, Baton Rouge, Louisiana.

Honorable Edward Y. Kakita, Judge (Retired)
Los Angeles Superior Court
Los Angeles, California.

Honorable Eileen Kato, Judge
King County District Court, Seattle, Washington.

Honorable Ernestine Douglas Littlejohn
Administrative Law Judge, Unemployment
Insurance Appeals Board
San Diego, California.

Honorable Laura J. Livingston, Judge
District Court, Austin, Texas.

Honorable Nikki L. Marr, Associate Judge
Juvenile Court of DeKalb County
Decatur, Georgia.

Honorable Aida L. Melendez, Commissioner
Superior Court, Washington, D.C.

Honorable June C. Miles, Associate Justice
Juvenile Court, Boston, Massachusetts.

Honorable Marie Nikanishi Milks, Judge
First Circuit Court, Honolulu, Hawaii.

Honorable Susan Oki Mollway, Judge
United States District Court, Honolulu, Hawaii.

Honorable Henry E. Nieto, Judge
Colorado Court of Appeals, Denver, Colorado.

Honorable Cecil B. Patterson, Jr., Judge
Arizona Court of Appeals, Phoenix, Arizona.

Honorable Barbara Peebles, Commissioner
Drug Court, St. Louis, Missouri.

Honorable J. David Phillips, Judge
County Court at Law, Austin, Texas.

Honorable Angela Turner Quigless
Associate Judge, Circuit Court, St. Louis, Missouri.

Honorable Lillian Harris Ransom, Judge
Court of Common Pleas
Philadelphia, Pennsylvania.

Honorable Cheryl M. Rini
Administrative Law Judge, Social Security
Administration, Omaha, Nebraska.

Honorable Gregory Sampson
Master-in-Chancery. Baltimore, Maryland.

Honorable Leander J. Shaw, Jr., Justice
Florida Supreme Court, Tallahassee, Florida.

Honorable Richard Eley Scott, Judge
Justice of the Peace Court, Travis County
Austin, Texas.

Honorable George Bundy Smith, Judge
New York Court of Appeals, New York, New York.

Honorable Gregroy E. Smith, Judge
Court of Common Pleas
Philadelphia, Pennsylvania.

Honorable Patricia D. Steele, Family Judge
Territorial Court of the Virgin Islands
St. Croix, Virgin Islands.

Honorable Booker T. Stephens, Chief Judge
Circuit Court, Welch, West Virginia.

Honorable Randolph M. Subryan, Judge
Superior Court of New Jersey
Paterson, New Jersey.

Honorable Elisa M. Sukkar
U.S. Immigration Judge, Miami, Florida.

Honorable Sandra Ann Thompson, Judge
Superior Court, Torrance, California.

Honorable Bobbi Tillmon, Commissioner
Superior Court, Santa Monica, California.

Honorable Eugene R. Verin, Judge
Circuit Court, Bessemer, Alabama.

Honorable Linda T. Walker
United States Magistrate Judge
Atlanta, Georgia.

Honorable Maxine Aldridge White, Judge
Milwaukee County Circuit Court
Milwaukee, Wisconsin.

Honorable Alvin T. Wong, Judge
State Court of DeKalb County
Decatur, Georgia.

Mr. Timothy Holmes, Law Clerk to Senior
Judge Arthur L. Burnett, Sr., Superior Court
Washington, D.C.

Ms. Jessica Jackson, Law Clerk to Senior Judge Arthur L. Burnett, Sr., Superior Court Washington, D.C.

Mrs. LaJuane Braham, Secretary to Senior Judge Arthur L. Burnett, Sr., Superior Court Washington, D.C.

The Honorable Benjamin Aranda III

1940 - 1998

The Honorable Benjamin Aranda III, South Bay Municipal Court, Torrence, CA served as Chair of the ABA Judicial Division Standing Committee of Minorities in the Judiciary (1997-1998) and several other American Bar Association Committees. He co-chaired the State Bar of California's Access to Justice Committee and was co-founder the California Minority Counsel Program. His tireless work to highlight the achievements of minorities in the legal profession and commitment to ensuring that our judicial system is equally accessible and fair to all members of our society was an inspiration to members of the legal profession and every community touched by his work.

Judge Aranda's dedication to a diverse and inclusive justice system is embodied in this Directory. He updated the Directory daily and was known to travel with it just in case he learned of a new judicial appointment.

Judge Aranda dedicated his life to a judicial system capable of excellence and thoughtfulness in rendering justice for all communities. With his commitment, great intelligence and warmth, Judge Aranda influenced numerous judges and lawyers.

Contents

TOTAL JUDGES LISTED: 4,013

Section I
AFRICAN-AMERICAN (BLACK) JUDGES OF THE UNITED STATES

Prepared by
Honorable Arthur L. Burnett, Sr

ALABAMA: (46)

FEDERAL

U. W. Clemon, Chief Judge
U.S. District Court for the
Northern District of Alabama
519 Hugo L. Black United States Courthouse
1729 Fifth Avenue North
Birmingham, Alabama 35205
(205) 731-0525 FAX: (205) 278-1856

Myron H. Thompson, Judge
U.S. District Court
for the Middle District of Alabama
Post Office Box 235
Montgomery, Alabama 36101-0235
(334 223-7312 FAX: (334) 223-7800

Vanzetta Penn McPherson, Magistrate Judge
United States District Court
for the Middle District of Alabama
Frank M. Johnson, Jr..Federal Building
and United States Courthouse
15 Lee Street
Montgomery, Alabama 36104
(334) 223-7061 FAX: (334) 223-7264
E-mail:Vanzetta_McPherson@almd.uscourts.gov

James D. Smith, Administrative Law Judge
Office of Hearings & Appeals
Social Security Administration
3605 Springhill Business Park
Mobile, Alabama 36608
(334) 441-5441 FAX: (334) 441-5993

Calvin Washington, Administrative Law Judge
Office of Hearings & Appeals
Social Security Administration
381 Atlanta Highway
Montgomery, Alabama 36109
(334) 223-7503 FAX: (334) 223-7069

STATE

Supreme Court

Ralph D. Cook, Associate Justice (Retired)
300 Dexter Avenue
Montgomery, Alabama 36104-3741
(205) 325-5086

Circuit Court Judges

Houston Brown, Circuit Judge
Jefferson County Tenth Judicial Circuit
660 Jefferson County Courthouse
716 Richard Arrington, Jr. Boulevard, North
Birmingham, Alabama 35203-0035
(205) 325-5367 FAX: (205) 325-8749

Eddie Hardaway, Jr., Circuit Judge
17th Judicial Circuit
Post Office Box 605
Livingston, Alabama 35470
(205) 652-6169 FAX: (205) 652-2213

Charles Price, Presiding Circuit Judge
15th Judicial Circuit
Montgomery County Courthouse
Montgomery, Alabama 36192
(334) 832-4950, Ext. 1332 or 832-1331
FAX: (334) 265-9536

Herman Thomas, Circuit Judge
13th Judicial Circuit
205 Government Street
Mobile, Alabama 36644
(334) 690-8780 FAX: (334) 694-6637

Eugene R. Verin, Circuit Judge
10th Judicial Circuit
708 Courthouse Annex
Bessemer, Alabama 35020
(205) 481-4198
E-mail: veriner@aol.com

Marvin Wiggins, Circuit Judge
4th Judicial Circuit
1001 Main Street, Room 52
Greensboro, Alabama 36744
(334) 624-5620 FAX: (334) 624-5622

Cain J. Kennedy, Circuit Judge (Retired)
13th Judicial Circuit
4226 Golfway Drive
Eight Mile, Alabama 36613-3705
(334) 452-1401

J. Richmond Pearson, Circuit Judge (Retired)
10th Judicial Circuit
809 Bolin Street, S.W.
Birmingham, Alabama 35211
(205) 322-9910

District Judges

Michael J. Bellamy, District Judge
26th Judicial Circuit
Post Office Box 1770
Phenix City, Alabama 36868-0820
(334) 298-0931 FAX: (334) 214-9802

Eric M. Fancher, District Judge
10th Judicial Circuit
505 Courthouse Annex
Bessemer, Alabama 35020
(205) 481-4190 FAX: (205) 481-4287

Aubrey Ford, Jr., District Judge
Macon County
5th Judicial Circuit
Post Office Box 703
101 East Northside Street
Tuskegee, Alabama 36083
(334) 727-6110 FAX: (334) 724-2621
E-mail: Aurbs@MSN.Com

Tammy Montgomery, District Judge
Sumter County
17th Judicial Circuit
Post Office Box 9
Franklin Street Courthouse Square
Livingston, Alabama 35470
(205) 652-7364 FAX: (205) 652-7347

Lillie Jones Osborne, District Judge
Greene County
17th Judicial Circuit
Post Office Box 310
400 Morrow Avenue
Eutaw, Alabama 35462-0310
(205) 372-3143 FAX: (205) 372-4600

Jo Celeste Pettway, District Judge
Wilcox County
4th Judicial Circuit
Post Office Box 549
12 Waters Street
Camden, Alabama 36726
(334) 682-4619 FAX: (334) 682-9425

M. Lynn Sherrod, District Judge
Madison County
23rd Judicial Circuit
Madison County Courthouse
Huntsville, Alabama 35801
(256) 532-6990 FAX: (256) 532-6993

Nathaniel Walker, District Judge
4th Judicial Circuit
Dallas County Courthouse
105-117 Lauderdale Street
Selma, Alabama 36701
(334) 874-2529 FAX: (334) 874-2574

Municipal Court Judges

David Barnes, Presiding Judge
Municipal Court
801 17th Street, North
Birmingham, Alabama 35203
(205) 254-2930

Delores R. Boyd, Presiding Judge
Municipal Court
City of Montgomery
320 North Ripley Street
Post Office Box 2270
Montgomery, Alabama 36102
(334) 264-8005 FAX: (334) 241-2332

Albert C. Bulls, III, Judge
Municipal Court
City of Tuskegee
Post Office Box 1233
Tuskegee Institute, Alabama 36088-1233
(334) 727-1074 FAX: (334) 727-1639

Raymond Chambliss, Judge
Municipal Court - Traffic Court
801 17th Street, North
Birmingham, Alabama 35203
(205) 254-2167 FAX: (205) 254-2416

Sybil Cleveland, Judge
Municipal Court
City of Huntsville
Post Office Box 2829
Huntsville, Alabama 35804
(256) 427-7803 FAX: (256) 427-7844

Rose Evans, Presiding Judge
Municipal Court
City of Dothan
Post Office Box 2128
Dothan, Alabama 36302
(334) 793-0284
FAX: (334) 678-0901 or (334) 793-1369

Thomas H. Figures, Presiding Judge
Municipal Court
City of Prichard
Post Office Box 2645
Mobile, Alabama 36652-2645
(334) 443-0416 FAX: (334) 433-0470

Johnny Hardwick, Judge
Municipal Court
City of Montgomery
449 South McDonough Street
Montgomery, Alabama 36104
(334) 265-0117 FAX: (334) 241-2332

Willie J. Huntley, Judge
Municipal Court
City of Mobile
Post Office Box 370
Mobile, Alabama 36601-0370
(334) 434-0007 FAX: (334) 434-0086

Darlett Lucy-Dawson, Judge
Municipal Court
City of Pritchard
2257 Costarides Street
Mobile, Alabama 36617
(334) 479-0581 FAX: (334) 478-0168

Malcolm R. Newman, Judge
Municipal Court
Town of Gordon
219 Crawford Street
Dothan, Alabama 36302-6137
(334) 792-2132 FAX: (334) 671-8341

Carnella Norman, Judge
Municipal Court
Night Court
801 17th Street, North
Birmingham, Alabama 35203
(205) 254-2531

Wanda Rahman, Judge
Municipal Court
City of Mobile
Post Office Box 2446
Mobile, Alabama 36652
(334) 434-7067 FAX: (334) 208-7034

Kyra Sparks, Judge
Municipal Court
City of Selma
Post Office Box 868
Selma, Alabama 36702-0868
(334) 872-5896 FAX: (334) 872-5899

Annetta H. Verin, Judge
Municipal Court
City of Bessemer
1801 First Avenue, North
Bessemer, Alabama 35020
(205) 426-8602 Ext.253 FAX: (205) 481-4384

James D. Wilson, III, Judge
Municipal Court
City of Pritchard
Post Office Box 40425
Mobile, Alabama 36604-0425
(334) 432-1691 FAX: (334) 432-1690

Probate Court Judges

Jerry Boggan, Judge
Probate Court
Wilcox County
County Courthouse
Post Office Box 668
Camden, Alabama 36726
(334) 682-4883 FAX: (334) 682-9484

John Hulett, Judge
Probate Court
Greene County
Post Office Box 790
Eutaw, Alabama 35462
(334) 372-3340 FAX: (334) 548-5399

Earlean Isaac, Judge
Probate Court
Greene County
Post Office Box 790
Eutaw, Alabama 35462
(205) 372-3340 FAX: (205) 372-3323

Alfonza Menefee, Judge
Probate Court
Macon County
101 E. Northside Street
Tuskegee, Alabama 36083
(334) 724-2611 FAX: (205) 334-4869

Willie Pearly Watkins Rice, Judge
Probate Court
Sumter County
Post Office Box 1040
Livingston, Alabama 35470
(205) 652-7281 FAX: (205) 652-6206

Agnes Chappelle, Senior Trial Referee
Family Court
Jefferson County
120 2nd Court, North
Birmingham, Alabama 35204
(205) 325-5453 or 325-5439 FAX: (205) 325-5970

Andra Sparks, Trial Referee
Family Court
Jefferson County
120 North 2nd Court
Birmingham, Alabama 35204-4765
(205) 325-5439 FAX: (205) 325-5920

Agnes Wormley, Referee
Family Court
Jefferson County
120 2nd Court North
Birmingham, Alabama 35204
(205) 325-5453 FAX: (205) 325-5920

ALASKA: (1)

Larry D. Card, Judge
Superior Court
825 West 4th Avenue, #436
Anchorage, Alaska 99501-2083
(907) 264-0414 FAX: (907) 264-0720

ARIZONA: (18)

FEDERAL

Raner C. Collins, Judge
United States District Court
for the District of Arizona
55 East Broadway
Tucson, Arizona 85701-1719
(520) 620-7126 FAX: (520) 620-7119

Glenda E. Edmonds, Magistrate Judge
United States District Court
for the District of Arizona
55 East Broadway
Tucson, Arizona 85701-1716
(520) 620-7195 FAX: (520) 620-7197

STATE

Cecil B. Patterson, Jr., Judge
Arizona Court of Appeals
Arizona State Courts Building
1501 West Washington Street
Phoenix, Arizona 85007-2926
(602) 542-4867 FAX: (602) 542-7801
E-mail: Cpatterson@tazone.sp.state.az.us

Thomas Dunevant, III, Judge
Maricopa County Superior Court
201 West Jefferson, 4th Floor
Phoenix, Arizona 85003-2205
(602) 506-2050 FAX: (602) 506-7867

Maurice Portley, Presiding Juvenile Court Judge
Maricopa County Superior Court
Juvenile Court Center, Southeast Facility
1810 South Lewis Street
Mesa, Arizona 85210-6234
(602) 506-2306 FAX: (602) 506-4175
E-mail: MPortley@juno.com

Penny Willrich, Judge
Maricopa County Superior Court
Juvenile Court Center, Southeast Facility
1810 South Lewis Street
Mesa, Arizona 85210-6234
(602) 506-2502 FAX: (602) 506-4175

George H. Foster, Jr., Commissioner
Maricopa County Superior Court
Juvenile Court Center, Durango Facility
3125 West Durango
Phoenix, Arizona 85009-6292
(602) 506-3892 FAX: (602) 506-1372

Vernon Harris, Initial Appearance Officer
Maricopa County Superior Officer
201 West Washington Street
Phoenix, Arizona 85003-2205
(602) 506-0876 FAX: (602) 506-0856

T. Jay Cranshaw, Judge
Tuscon Municipal Court
103 East Alameda, Third Floor
Post Office Box 2893
Tuscon, Arizona 85702-2893
(520) 791-3260 FAX: (520) 791-5454
E-mail: Jcransh@ci.tucson.az.us

Lynda J. Howell, Judge
Phoenix Municipal Court
Municipal Court Center
400 North Seventh Street
Phoenix, Arizona 85006-3301
(602) 261-5741 FAX: (602) 495-0145
E-mail: LyndaHowell@azbar.org

George Logan, III, Judge
Phoenix Municipal Court
400 North Seventh Street
Phoenix, Arizona 85006-3301
(602) 261-6460 FAX: (602) 534-4779
E-mail: GeorgeLogan@azbar.org

Michelle King LueSang, Judge
Mesa Municipal Court
245 West Second Street
Mesa, Arizona 85201-6503
(480) 644-4625 FAX: (480) 644-2927

Jean F. Williams, Judge (Retired)
Phoenix Municipal Court
400 North Seventh Street
Phoenix, Arizona 85006
(602) 261-8247

Noreen L. H. Richardson
Administrative Hearing Officer
Mesa Municipal Court
245 West Second Street
Mesa, Arizona 85201-6599
(480) 644-3030 FAX: (480) 644-2927

Thomas J. Robinson, Hearing Officer
Tempe Municipal Court
140 East Fifth Street, Suite 200
Tempe, Arizona 85281-3736
(480) 350-8057 FAX: (480) 350-8681
E-mail: thomasrobinson@tempe.gov

George E. Anderson, Limited Special Magistrate
Municipal Court
Alameda Plaza - City Court Building
103 East Alameda Street, Suite 401
Tucson, Arizona 85726-7210
(520) 791-5073 FAX: (520) 791-4419

James D. Montgomery, City Magistrate
City of San Luis
Post Office Box 5
San Luis, Arizona 85349-0429
(520) 627-2020 FAX: (520) 627-2335

Pamela Gutierrez, Justice of the Peace
South Phoenix Justice Court
217 Olympic Drive
Phoenix, Arizona 85040
(602) 243-0318 FAX: (602) 243-6389

ARKANSAS:° (23)

FEDERAL

George Howard, Jr., Judge
United States District Court
for the Eastern District of Arkansas
276 United States Courthouse
600 West Capitol Avenue
Little Rock, Arkansas 72201-3325
(501) 324-6031 FAX: (501) 324-6582
E-mail: george_howard@ared.uscourts.gov

Henry L. Jones, Jr., Magistrate Judge
United States District Court
for the Eastern District of Arkansas
521 United States Courthouse
600 West Capitol Avenue
Little Rock, Arkansas 72201-3325
(501) 324-5853 FAX: (501) 324-6588
E-mail: henry_jones@ared.uscourts.gov

Administrative Law Judges

John Heck Goree, Administrative Law Judge
Office of Hearings & Appeals
Social Security Administration
2418 Federal Office Building
700 West Capitol Avenue
Little Rock, Arkansas 72201
(501) 324-6381 FAX: (501) 324-7137
E-mail: john.goree@ssa.gov

STATE

Supreme Court

Lavenski Smith, Justice
Arkansas Supreme Court
Justice Building
625 Marshall Street
Little Rock, Arkansas 72201
(501) 682-6873 FAX: (501) 682-9410
E-mail: lavenski.smith@mail.state.ar.us

Appellate Courts

Andree Layton Roaf, Judge
Arkansas Court of Appeals
Justice Building
625 Marshall Street
Little Rock, Arkansas 72201
(501) 682-7989 FAX: (501) 682-7972
E-mail: andree.roaf@mail.state.ar.us

Olly Neal, Judge
Arkansas Court of Appeals
Justice Building
625 Marshall Street
Little Rock, Arkansas 72201
(501) 682-7980 FAX: (501) 682-7972
E-mail: olly.neal@mail.state.ar.us

Wendell L. Griffen, Judge
Arkansas Court of Appeals
Justice Building
625 Marshall Street
Little Rock, Arkansas 72201
(501) 682-7987 FAX: (501) 682-7972
E-mail: wendell.griffen@mail.state.ar.us

Trial Courts

Wiley Branton, Jr., Judge
Circuit/Chancery Court, Juvenile Division
Pulaski County Juvenile Court,
Eighth Division
3001 West Roosevelt Road
Little Rock, Arkansas 72204
(501) 340-6700 FAX: (501) 340-7011

Don E. Glover, Judge
First Division Circuit Court Ashley, Bradley,
Chicot, Desha and Drew Counties
Desha County Courthouse
McGehee, Arkansas 71654
(870) 222-6885 FAX: (870) 222-4781

Marion A. Humphrey, Judge
First Division Circuit Court
Pulaski and Perry Counties
401 West Markham, Suite 420
Little Rock, Arkansas 72201
(501) 340-8590 FAX: (501) 340-6039
E-mail: mhumphrey@aristotle.net

Leon Johnson, Judge
Fifth Division Circuit Court
Pulaski County
Little Rock, Arkansas 72201
(501) 340-8557 or 340-8629, FAX: (501) 340-8465

Berlin C. Jones, Judge
First Division Circuit Court
Jefferson and Lincoln Counties
Jefferson County Courthouse
Post Office Box 8230
Pine Bluff, Arkansas 71611-8230
(870) 541-5368 FAX: (870) 536-8937

Edwin Keaton, Judge
Circuit/Chancery Court for the Thirteenth
Judicial District of Arkansas
145 Jefferson Street, Box 8
Camden, Arkansas 71701
(870) 837-2270 FAX: (870) 837-2273
E-mail: ekeaton@cei.net

Willard Proctor, Judge
Fifth Division Circuit Court
Pulaski County
Little Rock, Arkansas 72201
(501) 340-8557, FAX: (501) 340-8629

L. T. Simes, II, Judge
Circuit Court
Phillips County Courthouse
620 Cherry Street, Suite 304
Helena, Arkansas 72342
Mailing Address: Post Office Box 2775
West Helena, Arkansas 72390-2775
(870) 338-5518, FAX: (870) 338-5591
E-mail: ltsimes@hnb.com

Morris W. Thompson, Judge
Fifth Division Circuit Court
Pulaski County Courthouse
401 West Markham, Suite 410
Little Rock, Arkansas 72201
(501) 340-8550, FAX: (501) 340-8465

Samuel Turner, Jr., Judge
Sixth Division Circuit Court
Clay, Craighead, Crittenden,
Green, Mississippi and Poinsett Counties
110 East Thompson, Suite 204
Post Office Box 1043
West Memphis, Arkansas 72303-1043
(870) 735-0707 FAX: (870) 735-1567

Joyce Williams Warren, Judge
Circuit/Chancery Court, Juvenile Division
Pulaski County Juvenile Court, Tenth Division
3001 West Roosevelt Road
Little Rock, Arkansas 72204
(501) 340-6700 FAX: (501) 340-7016
E-mail: Judgewarren@aristotle.net

Kathleen Bell, Judge
Chancery Court
Cross, Lee, Monroe, Phillips,
St. Francis and Woodruff Counties
Post Office Box 3588
West Helena, Arkansas 72390-3588
(870) 338-5522 FAX: (870) 338-5595
E-mail: kbell@hnb.com

Alice S. Gray, Judge
Chancery and Probate Court
401 West Markham, Suite 350
Little Rock, Arkansas 72201
(501) 340-8530 FAX: (501) 340-6035

Leon N. Jamison, Judge
Chancery and Probate Court
Jefferson and Lincoln Counties
Post Office Box 7664
Pine Bluff, Arkansas 71611-7664
(870) 541-5383 FAX: (870) 541-5385
E-mail: subi@Seark.net

George VanHook, Jr., Judge
Municipal Court
Post Office Box 490
El Dorado, Arkansas 71730-0490
(870) 863-5119 FAX: (870) 863-5120 or 864-1955

Andrew Blood, Administrative Law Judge
Worker's Compensation Commission
Spring Plaza Building
4th & Spring Streets, Third Floor
Post Office Box 900
Little Rock, Arkansas 72203-0900
(501) 682-5090 FAX: (501) 682-2048
E-mail: ablood@awcc.state.ar.us

CALIFORNIA: (176)

FEDERAL

Saundra Brown Armstrong, Judge
U.S. District Court
for the Northern District of California
Federal Building and United States
Courthouse, Suite 400 South
1301 Clay Street
Oakland, California 94612-5212
(510) 637-3559 FAX: Call on phone first

Garland Ellis Burrell, Jr., Judge
U.S. District Court
for the Eastern District of California
501 "I" Street, Suite 4-200
Sacramento, California 95814
(916) 930-4115 FAX: (916) 930-4015

Audrey B. Collins, Judge
U.S. District Court
for the Central District of California
Roybal Federal Building - Suite 680
255 East Temple Street
Los Angeles, California 90012
(213) 894-3010 FAX: (213) 894-2735

Phyllis J. Hamilton, Judge
U. S. District Court
for the District of California
450 Golden Gate Avenue
Post Office Box 36105
San Francisco, California 94102
(415) 522-4100 FAX: (415) 522-2880

Terry J. Hatter, Jr., Chief Judge
U.S. District Court
for the Central District of California
United States Courthouse
312 North Spring Street
Los Angeles, California 90012
(213) 894-5276 FAX: (213) 894-0029

Martin Jenkins, Judge
United States District Court
for the Northern District of California
450 Golden Gate Avenue
San Francisco, California 94102
(415) 522-2123 FAX: Call on phone first

Napoleon A. Jones, Jr., Judge
United States District Court for the
Southern District of California
2125 Edward J. Schwartz
United States Courthouse
880 Front Street
San Diego, California 92101-8912
(619) 557-2993 FAX (619) 235-4704

Consuelo Bland Marshall, Judge
United States District Court for the Central
District of California
United States Courthouse
312 North Spring Street
Los Angeles, California 90012
(213) 894-5288 FAX: (213) 894-0045

James Ware, Judge
U.S. District Court for the
Northern District of California
4050 United States Courthouse
280 South First Street - Room 4050
San Jose, California 95113
(408) 535-5454 FAX: (408) 535-5464

Thelton E. Henderson, Senior Judge
U.S. District Court for the
Northern District of California
Post Office Box 36060
450 Golden Gate Avenue
San Francisco, California 94102
(415) 556-3630 FAX: (415) 522-2047

John A. Houston, Magistrate Judge
United States District Court
for the Southern District of California
880 Front Street
San Diego, California 92101
(619) 557-5716 FAX: (619) 702-9920

Maria-Elena James, Magistrate Judge
United States District Court
for the Northern District of California
United States Courthouse
450 Golden Gate Avenue
San Francisco, California 94102
(415) 522-4708 FAX: (415) 522-2140

Erithe A. Smith, Judge
United States Bankruptcy Court
United States District Court
for the Central District of California
255 East Temple Street
Los Angeles, California 90012
(213) 894-4082 FAX: (213) 894-4198

Administrative Law Judges

Homer T. Ball, Jr., Administrative Law Judge
Office of Hearings and Appeals
Social Security Administration
1301 Clay Street, Suite 200 N
Oakland, California 94612
(510) 444-1880 FAX: (510) 637-3424

James P. Berry, Administrative Law Judge
Office of Hearings and Appeals
Social Security Administration
155 East Shaw Avenue, Room 200
Shaw 41 Building
Fresno, California 93710
(559) 222-9940 FAX: (559) 222-3120

William B. Churchill, Administrative Law Judge
Office of Hearings and Appeals
Social Security Administration
301 Howard Street, 3rd Floor
San Francisco, California 94105
(415) 744-3080 FAX: (415) 744-2548

Charles L. Hall, Administrative Law Judge
Office of Hearings and Appeals
Social Security Administration
11000 Wilshire Boulevard, Suite 8200
Los Angeles, California 90024
(310) 966-4039 FAX: (310) 479-3370

Mason D. Harrell, Jr.
Chief Administrative Law Judge
Office of Hearings & Appeals
Social Security Administration
605 North Arrowhead Avenue, Room 200
San Bernandino, California 92401
(909) 383-5545 FAX: (909) 381-9288

Arthur E. Joyner, Administrative Law Judge
Office of Hearings & Appeals
Social Security Administration
Symphony Towers
750 B Street, Suite 1100
San Diego, California 92101
(619) 557-5081 FAX: (619) 557-7633

Frederick Lamont Liggett
Chief Administrative Law Judge
Office of Hearings & Appeals
Social Security Administration
2031 Howe Avenue, Suite 200
Sacramento, California 95825
(916) 566-7200 FAX: (916) 925-5014

Benjamin F. Parks
Chief Administrative Law Judge
Office of Hearings & Appeals
Social Security Administration
1301 Clay Street, 2nd Floor
Room 200 North
Oakland, California 94612
(619) 444-1880 FAX: (619) 637-3424

Earldean V. S. Robbins
Administrative Law Judge (Retired)
National Labor Relations Board 901 Market
Street - Suite # 400
San Francisco, California 94103 (415) 387-5596
FAX: (415) 387-5596 (call first)

London L. Steverson, Administrative Law Judge
Office of Hearings & Appeals
Social Security Administration
8345 Firestone Boulevard, Suite 210
Downey, California 90241
(562) 869-5889 FAX: (562) 869-8943

Jan D. Latimore
United States Immigration Judge
Executive Office for Immigration Review
606 South Oliver Street, Suite 1500
Los Angeles, California 90014
(213) 894-5165 or 894-2811 FAX: (213) 894-2812

Richard D. Walton
United States Immigration Judge
606 South Olive Street, Suite 1500
Los Angeles, California 90014
(213) 894-2811 or 894-6000 FAX: (213) 894-5196

LuNell Christina Anderson, Administrative Judge
United States Merit Systems Protection Board
250 Montgomery Street, Suite 400
San Francisco, California 94104
(415) 705-2935 FAX: (415) 705-2945
E-mail: lunell.anderson@mspb.gov

STATE

Supreme Court

Janice Rogers Brown, Justice
California Supreme Court
350 McAlister Street, 4th Floor
San Francisco, California 94102
(415) 865-7040 FAX: (415) 865-7182

Appellate Courts

Candace D. Cooper, Associate Justice
Court of Appeals
Second Appellate District, Division 2
300 South Spring Street, North Tower
Los Angeles, California 90013
(213) 830-7323 FAX: (213) 987-2430

Vance W. Raye, Justice
Court of Appeals
Third Appellate District
914 Capitol Mall - Suite #100
Sacramento, California 95814
(916) 654-0209 FAX: (916) 653-5043

Vaino Hassan Spencer, Presiding Justice
Court of Appeals
Second Appellate District, Division One
300 South Spring Street, North Tower
Los Angeles, California 90013
(213) 830-7503 FAX: (213) 897-7813

Bernard Jefferson, Presiding Justice (Retired)
Second Appellate District, Division One
4360 Don Luis Drive
Los Angeles, California 90008
(213) 292-6077

Clinton W. White, Justice (Retired)
First Appellate District, Division Three
Marathon Plaza - South Tower
303 2nd Street, Suite # 600
San Francisco, California 94107
(415) 396-9777

Arleigh Maddox Woods
Presiding Justice (Retired)
Second Appellate District, Division Four
675 South Westmoreland Avenue
Los Angeles, California 90005-3992
(213) 738-6704 FAX: (360) 687-0795

Superior Court Judges

Gordon S. Baranco, Judge
Superior Court
State of California, County of Alameda
Department 15
1221 Oak Street
Oakland, California 94612-4293
(510) 272-6124 FAX: (510) 893-4948 or 272-6072

Gail Brewster Bereola, Judge
Superior Court
State of California, County of Alameda
Oakland-Piedmont-Emeryville Judicial District
661 Washington Street
Oakland, California 94607
(510) 268-7622 FAX: (510) 268-7695

William C. Beverly, Judge
Superior Court
State of California, County of Los Angeles
Department 70
111 North Hill Street
Los Angeles, California 90012-3117
(213) 974-5791 FAX: (213) 626-7905

Glenette Blackwell, Judge
Superior Court
State of California, County of Los Angeles
210 West Temple Street
Los Angeles, California 90012-3014
(213) 974-9624 FAX: (213) 680-7804

Bob S. Bowers, Judge
Superior Court
State of California, County of Los Angeles
Compton Judicial District
200 West Compton Boulevard
Compton, California 90220
(310) 603-7724 FAX: (310) 639-8724

Diana Becton Brown-Smith, Judge
Superior Court
State of California, County of Contra Costa
100 37th Street
Richmond, California 94805
(510) 374-3163 FAX: (510) 374-1634

Irma Jean Brown, Judge
Superior Court
Compton Judicial District
State of California, County of Los Angeles
200 West Compton Boulevard
Compton, California 90220
(310) 603-7162 FAX: (310) 763-4984

Joan S. Cartwright, Judge
Superior Court
State of California, County of Alameda
1225 Fallon Street
Oakland, California 94607
(510) 272-6055 FAX: (510) 268-7695

Sharon Chatman, Judge
Superior Court
State of California, County of Santa Clara
191 North First Street
San Jose, California 95113
(408) 299-2964 FAX: (408) 292-0582

LaDoris Hazzard Cordell, Judge
Superior Court
State of California, County of Santa Clara
191 North First Street
San Jose, California 95113
(408) 299-3410 FAX: (408) 292-0582

Herbert Curtis, III, Judge
Superior Court
State of California, County of Ventura
Hall of Justice
800 South Victoria Avenue
Ventura, California 93009
(805) 654-2961 FAX: (805) 677-8714

John L. Davidson, Judge
Superior Court
State of California, County of San Diego
Juvenile Court
2851 Meadow Lark Drive
San Diego, California 92123
(619) 239-6864 FAX: (858) 694-4644

John Dearman, Judge
Superior Court
State of California, County of San Francisco
Civic Center Courthouse
400 McAllister Street
San Francisco, California 94102
(415) 554-4848 FAX: (415) 551-3840

Ellen Carol DeShazer, Judge
Superior Court
Compton Judicial District
State of California, County of Los Angeles
200 West Compton Boulevard
Compton, California 90220
(310) 603-7137 FAX: (310) 635-6623

Reginald A. Dunn, Judge
Superior Court Department 44
State of California, County of Los Angeles
111 North Hill Street
Los Angeles, California 90012-3117
(213) 974-5663 FAX: (213) 625-8536

Raymond Edwards, Jr., Judge
Superior Court
State of California, County of San Diego
South Bay Branch
500 3rd Avenue
Chula Vista, California 91910
(619) 691-4689 FAX: (619) 691-4584

Carol Williams Elswick, Judge
Superior Court
Citrus Judicial District
State of California, County of Los Angeles
1427 West Covina Parkway
West Covina, California 91790
(626) 813-3217 FAX: (626) 338-7364

Morrison C. England, Jr., Judge
Superior Court, Department 37
State of California, County of Sacramento
720 Ninth Street
Sacramento, California 95814-1398
(916) 874-5237 FAX: (916) 440-5620

Dean Farrar, Judge
Superior Court
Compton Judicial District
State of California, County of Los Angeles
Lynwood Regional Justice Center
11701 Alameda Street
Lynnwood, California 90262
(323) 357-5225 FAX: (323) 763-4984

Eudon Ferrell, Judge
Superior Court - Inglewood Judicial District
State of California, County of Los Angeles
One Regent Street
Inglewood, California 90301
(310) 419-5107 FAX: (310) 673-5931

Richard T. Fields, Judge
Superior Court
State of California, County of Riverside
Criminal Department
4100 Main Street
Riverside, California 92501-3626
(909) 955-2382 or 955-4074
FAX: (909) 955-4056 or 955-4058

Judith D. Ford, Judge
Superior Court
State of California, County of Alameda
U.S. Post Office Building
201 13th Street
Oakland, California 94612
(510) 268-7606 FAX: (510) 208-3949

Rodney G. Forneret, Judge
Superior Court
Inglewood Judicial District
State of California, County of Los Angeles
One Regent Street
Inglewood, California 90301
(310) 419-5111 FAX: (310) 673-5931

Ramona J. Garrett, Judge
Superior Court
State of California, County of Solano
600 Union Avenue
Fairfield, California 94533
(707) 421-7412 FAX: (707) 421-7828

Brenda Harbin-Forte, Judge
Superior Court
State of California, County of Alameda
County Probation Center
400 Broadway
Oakland, California 94607-3986
(510) 268-7050 FAX: (510) 268-7695

Marcelita V. Haynes, Judge
Superior Court
State of California, County of Los Angeles
Lynwood Regional Justice Center
1170 Alameda Street
Lynwood, California 90262
(323) 357-5235 FAX: (323) 249-1506

Deirdre Hill, Judge
Superior Court
State of California, County of Los Angeles
Hollywood Court
5925 Hollywood Boulevard
Hollywood, California 90028
(323) 856-5742 FAX: (323) 962-6157

Robert Bryon Hutson, Judge
Superior Court
State of California, County of Orange
Juvenile Court
700 Civic Center Drive West
Santa Ana, California 92701-4079
(714) 935-6803 FAX: (714) 935-7638

Barbara R. Johnson, Judge
Superior Court Department #117
State of California, County of Los Angeles
210 West Temple Street
Los Angeles, California 90012
(213) 974-6029 FAX: (213) 974-5749

Marion J. Johnson, Judge
Superior Court
State of California, County of Los Angeles
111 North Hill Street
Los Angeles, California 90012-3014
(213) 974-6231 FAX: (213) 680-4889

Lawrence Jones, Judge
Superior Court Department 60
State of California, County of Fresno
1100 Van Ness
Fresno, California 93724
(559) 488-3580 FAX: (559) 488-1776

Morris Bruce Jones, Judge
Superior Court
State of California, County of Los Angeles
111 North Hill Street
Los Angeles, California 90012
(213) 974-5669 FAX: (213) 617-7176

Kay T. Kingsley, Judge
Superior Court
State of California, County of Monterey
240 Church Street
Salinas, California 93901-2683
(831) 755-5050 FAX: (831) 755-5483

David Krashna, Judge
Superior Court
State of California, County of Alameda
661 Washington Street
Oakland, California 94607-3986
(510) 268-7631 FAX: (510) 269-7695

Xenophon F. Lang, Jr., Judge
Superior Court
State of California, County of Los Angeles
Compton Judicial District
200 West Compton Boulevard
Compton, California 90229
(323) 357-5215 FAX: (323) 249-1506

Joe Ervard Littlejohn, Judge
Superior Court
State of California, County of San Diego
North County Division
Vista Regional Center
325 South Melrose Drive
Vista, California 92083
(760) 806-6306 FAX: (760) 806-6345

Rudolph R. Loncke, Judge
Superior Court
State of California, County of Sacramento
720 9th Street
Sacramento, California 95814-1398
(916) 440-7561 FAX: (916) 552-8229

James L. Long, Judge
Superior Court
State of California, County of Sacramento
720 Ninth Street
Sacramento, California 95814-1398
(916) 874-7001 FAX: (916) 874-8229

Alice A. Lytle, Judge
Superior Court
State of California, County of Sacramento
720 Ninth Street
Sacramento, California 95814
(916) 874-5215 FAX: (916) 874-8229

Paula Adele Mabry, Judge
Superior Court
State of California, County of Los Angeles
210 West Temple Street
Los Angeles, California 90012
(213) 974-6057 FAX: (213) 680-7804

Robert D. Mackey, Judge
Superior Court
State of California, County of Los Angeles
110 Regent Street
Inglewood, California 90301-1274
(310) 419-5275 FAX: (310) 672-9351

Harold Craig Manson, Judge
Superior Court
State of California, County of Sacramento
B.T. Collins Juvenile Court
9601 Kiefer Boulevard
Sacramento, California 95827
(916) 874-5522 or 875-5066 FAX: (916) 874-8229

Veronica Simmons McBeth, Judge
Superior Court
State of California, County of Los Angeles
111 North Hill Street
Los Angeles, California 90012
(213) 974-5701 FAX: (213) 617-7176

Vincent J. McGraw, Judge
Superior Court Department 31
State of California, County of Fresno
1100 Van Ness
Fresno, California 93724
(559) 488-3451 or 488-3392 FAX: (599) 488-3263

Patti Jo McKay, Judge
Los Angeles Superior Court
210 West Temple Street
Los Angeles, California 90012
(213) 974-6015 FAX: (213) 680-7804

Perker L. Meeks, Jr., Judge
Superior Court
State of California, County of San Francisco
Hall of Justice
850 Bryant Street, Suite 101
San Francisco, California 94103
(415) 553-9423 FAX: (415) 553-9851

John Vernon Meigs, Judge
Superior Court
State of California, County of Los Angeles
Inglewood Judicial District
One Regent Street, Room 203
Inglewood, California 90301
(310) 419-5101 FAX: (310) 674-4862

David S. Milton, Judge
Superior Court
State of California, County of Los Angeles
400 Civic Center Plaza
Pomona, California 91766
(909) 620-3066 FAX: (909) 620-6547

Donald Mitchell, Judge
Superior Court
State of California, County of San Francisco
Civic Center Courthouse
400 McAllister Street
San Francisco, California 94102-9991
(415) 554-6064 or 551-3793 FAX: (415) 551-3687

Carl W. Morris, Judge
Superior Court
State of California, County of Alameda
County Administrative Building
1221 Oak Street
Oakland, California 94612
(510) 272-6128 FAX: (510) 271-5130

Angil P. Morris-Jones, Judge
Superior Court
State of California, County of Merced
627 West 21st Street
Merced, California 95340-3744
(209) 385-7657 FAX: (209) 725-3023

William J. Murray, Jr., Judge
Superior Court
State of California, County of San Joaquin
222 East Weber Avenue, Third Floor
Stockton, California 95202-2777
(209) 468-2827 FAX: (209) 468-0539

Henry E. Needham, Jr., Judge
Superior Court
State of California, County of Alameda
1225 Fallon Street
Oakland, California 94612-4293
(510) 272-6111 FAX: (510) 271-5130

Alban I. Niles, Judge
Superior Court
State of California, County of Los Angeles
111 North Hill Street
Los Angeles, California 90012-3014
(213) 974-6219 FAX: (213) 626-4854

L. C. Nunley, Judge
Superior Court
State of California, County of Los Angeles
111 North Hill Street
Los Angeles, California 90012-3014
(213) 974-6241 FAX: (213) 972-0172

Marla Osborne-Anderson, Judge
Superior Court
State of California, County of Monterey
240 Church Street
Salinas, California 93901-2683
(408) 755-5050 FAX: (408) 755-5483 or (831) 385-8383

Risë J. Pichon, Judge
Superior Court
State of California, County of Santa Clara
Sunnyvale Facility
605 West El Camido Real
Sunnyvale, California 94087
(408) 739-6352 or (408) 299-2074
FAX: (408) 293-1825 or 739-6749

Margaret Powers, Judge
Superior Court
State of California, County of San Bernardino
14455 Civic Drive
Victorville, California 92392
(760) 243-8648 FAX: (760) 243-8641

Gary E. Ransom, Judge
Superior Court Department 8
State of California, County of Sacramento
720 Ninth Street
Sacramento, California 95814-1398
(916) 874-5651 FAX: (916) 874-8229

Elizabeth Ann Riggs, Judge
Superior Court
State of California, County of San Diego
Juvenile Court
2851 Meadow Lark Drive
San Diego, California 92123
(858) 694-4227 FAX: (619) 441-4297

Gloria F. Rhynes, Judge
Superior Court
State of California, County of Alameda
Oakland-Piedmont-Emeryville Judicial District
661 Washington Street
Oakland, California 94607-3986
(510) 268-7635 or 268-7636 FAX: (510) 268-7695

John H. Sandoz, Judge
Superior Court
Department 60
State of California, County of Los Angeles
111 North Hill Street
Los Angeles, California 90012-3117
(213) 974-5705 FAX: (213) 625-8536

Phrasel Shelton, Sr., Judge
Superior Court Department 13
State of California, County of San Mateo
Main Courthouse
400 County Center
Redwood City, California 94063
(650) 363-4804 FAX: (415) 363-4698

Renard F. Shepard, Judge
Superior Court Department 12
State of California, County of Sacramento
720 Ninth Street
Sacramento, California 95814-1398
(916) 874-6181 FAX: (916) 874-8229

Rosemary Shumsky, Judge
Superior Court
State of California, County of Los Angeles
1633 Purdue Avenue
Los Angeles, California 90025
(310) 312-6594 FAX: (310) 312-2902

Ronald V. Skyers, Judge
Superior Court
Compton Judicial District
State of California, County of Los Angeles
200 West Compton Boulevard
Compton, California 90220-3195
(310) 635-6623 FAX: (310) 763-3964

Spurgeon E. Smith, Judge
Superior Court
State of California, County of Los Angeles
Metropolitan Court
1945 South Hill Street
Los Angeles, California 90007
(213) 744-4087 FAX: (213) 765-8463

Emily A. Stevens, Judge
Superior Court
State of California, County of Los Angeles
Department 405 - Children's Court
201 Centre Place Drive, Suite # 3
Monterey Park, California 91754-2158
(213) 526-6405 FAX: (213) 780-1003

Sandra Ann Thompson, Judge
Superior Court
State of California, County of Los Angeles
South Bay Judicial District
825 Maple Avenue
Torrance, California 90503
(310) 222-6541 FAX: (310) 328-7535

Marcus O. Tucker, Judge
Superior Court
State of California, County of Los Angeles
415 West Ocean Boulevard
Long Beach, California 90802
(562) 491-6151 FAX: (562) 435-5469

Leo Valentine, Jr., Judge
Superior Court
State of California, County of San Diego
South Bay Branch
500 Third Avenue
Chula Vista, California 91910
(619) 691-4438 FAX: (619 691-4770

Craig E. Veals, Judge
Superior Court
State of California, County of Los Angeles
210 West Temple Street
Los Angeles, California 90012-3014
(213) 974-5759 FAX: (213) 633-5025

Horace Wheatley, Judge
Superior Court
State of California, County of Alameda
Allen E. Broussard Justice Center
600 Washington Street
Oakland, California 94607-3986
(510) 268-2984 FAX: (510) 268-7695

Marshall I. Whitley, Judge
Superior Court
State of California, County of Alameda
Oakland-Piedmont-Emeryville
Judicial District - Department 6
661 Washington Street
Oakland, California 94607-3986
(510) 268-7606 or 268-7653 FAX: (510) 268-7695

Reginald Yates, Judge
Superior Court
State of California, County of Los Angeles
Pomona Judicial District
400 Civic Center Plaza
Pomona, California 91766
(909) 620-2073 FAX: (909) 622-2305

Retired Judges

Roosevelt F. Dorn, Mayor, City of Inglewood
Judge (Retired)
Superior Court
State of California, County of Los Angeles
1 Manchester Boulevard
Inglewood, California 90301
(310) 412-5300 FAX: (310) 412-8788

G. William Dunn, Judge (Retired)
Superior Court
State of California, County of Los Angeles
Long Beach Judicial District
415 West Ocean Boulevard
Long Beach, California 90802
(562) 491-6291

Sherrill D. Luke, Judge (Retired)
Superior Court
State of California, County of Los Angles
600 Commonwealth Street
Los Angeles, California 90005-4001
(213) 351-8508

Alpha Levon Montgomery, Judge (Retired)
Superior Court
State of California, County of San Diego
220 West Broadway
San Diego, California 92101
(619) 531-3842

Dion G. Morrow, Judge (Retired)
Superior Court
State of California, County of Los Angeles
5120 Bedford Avenue
Los Angeles, California 90056-1002
(310) 641-6276 FAX: (310) 348-8705

Florence T. Pickard, Judge (Retired)
Superior Court
State of California, County of Los Angeles
111 North Hill Street
Los Angeles, California 90017-3117
(213) 974-5651

Donald Pitts, Judge (Retired)
Superior Court
State of California, County of Los Angles
One Regent Street
Inglewood, California 90301
(310) 419-6707

Henry Ramsey, Jr., Judge (Retired)
Superior Court
State of California, County of Alameda
1225 Fallon Street
Oakland, California 94612
(510) 272-6360 FAX: (510) 272-6063 (Numbers are at American Arbitration Association)

Robert L. Roberson, Jr., Judge (Retired)
Superior Court
State of California, County of Los Angeles
111 North Hill Street
Los Angeles, California 90012-3117
(213) 974-5791

Charles R. Scarlett, Judge (Retired)
Superior Court
State of California, County of Los Angeles
200 West Compton Boulevard
Compton, California 90220-3194
(310) 603-7201

Sherman W. Smith, Jr., Judge (Retired)
Superior Court
State of California, County of Los Angeles
111 North Hill Street
Los Angeles, California 90012-3117
(213) 974-6995

William H. Stephens, Judge (Retired)
Superior Court
State of California, County of Marin
Hall of Justice, Civic Center
Post Office Box 4988
San Rapheal, California 94903-4988
(415) 499-6073

Benjamin Travis, Judge (Retired)
Superior Court
State of California, County of Alameda
1221 Oak Street
Oakland, California 94612-4393
(510) 272-6131

William M. Ormsby, Judge (Retired)
Los Angeles Municipal Court
Inglewood Judicial District
One Regent Street
Inglewood, California 90301
(310) 419-5105

Roosevelt Robinson, Jr., Judge (Retired)
Los Angeles Municipal Court
Inglewood Judicial District
4580 Mount Vernon Drive
Los Angeles, California 90043
(213) 296-0627

Court Commissioners

Glenda Allen-Hill, Commissioner and Referee
Superior Courts
State of California, County of Fresno
1100 Van Ness
Fresno, California 93721-2059
(559) 488-3957 or (559) 488-3345
FAX: (559) 488-3423

Claudette Brooks, Commissioner
Superior Court
State of California, County of Alameda
and Referee, Juvenile Division
2200 Fairmont Drive
San Leandro, California 94578
(510) 667-4910 FAX: (510) 667-4919

Ulysses Burns, Commissioner
Superior Court
State of California, County of Los Angeles
Inglewood Judicial District
One Regent Street
Inglewood, California 90301
(310) 419-5115 FAX: (310) 674-4862

Geoffrey Carter, Commissioner
Superior Court
State of California, County of Alameda
Oakland-Piedmont-Emeryville
Judicial District - Department 15
600 Washington Street
Oakland, California 94607-3986
(510) 268-7294 FAX: (510) 268-7695

Deborah Christian, Commissioner
Superior Court
State of California, County of Los Angeles
Inglewood Judicial District
One Regent Street
Inglewood, California 90301
(310) 419-5115 FAX: (310) 674-4862

George Patton Colbert, Commissioner
Superior Court
State of California, County of San Francisco
Hall of Justice
850 Bryant Street
San Francisco, California 94103
(415) 553-9382 or 553-9384 FAX: (415) 553-7939

Beverly Daniels-Greenberg, Commissioner
Superior Court
State of California, County of Alameda
Hayward Hall of Justice
24405 Amador Street
Hayward, California 94544
(510) 670-5906 FAX: (510) 670-5687

Wayne Denton, Commissioner
Superior Court
State of California, County of Los Angeles
Inglewood Juvenile Court
110 Regent Street
Inglewood, California 90301
(310) 419-5273 FAX: (310) 398-8605

John T. Doyle, Commissioner
Superior Court
State of California, County of Los Angeles
Compton Judicial District
200 West Compton Boulevard
Compton, California 90220
(310) 603-7151 FAX: (310) 635-6623

Kelvin Filer, Commissioner
Superior Court
State of California, County of Los Angeles
Compton Judicial District
200 Compton Boulevard
Compton, California 90220
(310) 603-7158 FAX: (310) 763-4984

John R. Johnson, Commissioner
Superior Court
State of California, County of Los Angeles
Compton Judicial District
200 Compton Boulevard
Compton, California 90220
(310) 603-7660 FAX: (310) 635-6623

H. Kirkland Jones, Commissioner
Superior Court
State of California, County of Los Angeles
David V. Kenyon Juvenile Justice Center
7625 South Central Avenue
Los Angeles, California 90001-2999
(323) 586-6051 FAX: (323) 582-2212

Kristi Lousteau, Commissioner
Superior Court
State of California, County of Los Angeles
Central Arraignment Courts
429 Bauchet Street
Los Angeles, California 90012
(213) 974-6087 FAX: (213) 680-7804

Lonzo Lucas, Commissioner
Superior Court
State of California, County of Los Angeles
Southeast Judicial District
8640 California Avenue
South Gate, California 90280-3074
(213) 563-4001 FAX: (213) 569-4840

Beverly E. Mosley, Commissioner
Superior Court
State of California, County of Los Angeles
1945 South Hill Street
Los Angeles, California 90007
(213) 744-4061 FAX: (213) 746-6218

Kenneth Eugene Norman, Commissioner
Superior Court
State of California, County of Alameda
Oakland-Piedmont-Emeryville
Judicial District - Department 1
660 Washington Street
Oakland, California 94607-3986
(510) 268-2778 FAX: (510) 268-7695

Thomas Parrott, Commissioner
Superior Court
State of California, County of Los Angeles
415 West Ocean Boulevard
Long Beach, California 90802
(562) 491-6157 FAX: (562) 495-3814

Raoul M. Thorbourne, Commissioner
Superior Court
State of California, County of Sacramento
301 Bicentennial Circle
Sacramento, California 95826-2881
(916) 875-7718 FAX: (916) 874-5347

Bobbi Tillmon, Commissioner
Superior Court
State of California, County of Los Angeles
1725 Main Street
Santa Monica, California 90401
(310) 260-3609 FAX: (310) 394-1983

Allen Webster, Jr., Commissioner
Superior Court
State of California, County of Los Angeles
Compton Judicial District
200 West Compton Boulevard
Compton, California 92200
(310) 603-7750 FAX: (310) 632-4966

Referees

Natalie S. Lindsey, Referee
Superior Court
State of California, County of Sacramento
William R. Ridgeway Family Relations Court
3341 Power Inn Road
Sacramento, California 95826
(916) 875-2539 and (916) 874-5487
FAX: (916) 874-5347

Marilyn H. Mackel, Referee
Los Angeles Superior Court
Department 402
201 Center Plaza Drive # 3
Monterey Park, California 91754-2158
(323) 526-6402 FAX: (323) 881-3794

Stephanie Thornton, Juvenile Hearing Officer
San Diego Superior Court
Post Office Box 23599
San Diego, California
(619) 694-4204 FAX: (619) 694-4773

Administrative Law Judges

Francis B. Beckwith, Administrative Law Judge
Unemployment Insurance Appeals Board
9800 La Cienega Boulevard, # 901
Inglewood, California 90301
(310) 337-4302 FAX: (310) 337-4395

Patricia Ann Bennett, Administrative Law Judge
State Public Utilities Commission
505 Van Ness Avenue, Suite 5016
San Francisco, California 94102
(415) 703-2271 FAX: (415) 703-1723

Otis Benning, Administrative Law Judge
Disability Hearings Bureau
Administrative Adjudications Division
California Department of Social Services
744 P Street, MS 19-66
Sacramento, California 95814
(916) 229-4187 FAX: (916) 387-4807

Desiree A. Bruce-Lyle, Administrative Law Judge
Workers' Compensation Appeals Board
San Diego District Office
1350 Front Street, Room 3047
San Diego, California 92101
(619) 525-4780 FAX: (619) 286-6560

Donald Gayden, Administrative Law Judge
Unemployment Insurance Appeals Board
1515 Clay Street, Suite 902
Oakland, California 94612
(510) 286-0695 FAX: (510) 622-3929

Cynthia F. George, Administrative Law Judge
Unemployment Insurance Appeals Board
770 East Shaw Avenue, Suite 222
Fresno, California 93710
(559) 248-2520 FAX: (559) 248-2546

Kathy Gilmore, Administrative Law Judge
Unemployment Insurance Appeals Board
San Diego Office of Appeals
3517 Camino del Rio South, Suite 310
San Diego, California 92108-4027
(619) 521-3300 FAX: (619) 521-3334

Janet B. Henley, Administrative Law Judge
Unemployment Insurance Appeals Board
9800 La Cienega Boulevard, #901
Inglewood, California 90301
(310) 337-4302 FAX: (310) 337-4395

Charles Hollis, Administrative Law Judge
Sacramento Regional Office
Administrative Adjudications Division
California Department of Social Services
744 P Street, MS 19-44
Sacramento, California 95814
(916) 229-4187 FAX: (916) 387-4803

Joy E. Johnson, Administrative Law Judge
Unemployment Insurance Appeals Board
2550 Mariposa Street, Room 4067
Fresno, California 93721-2281
(559) 445-5363 FAX: (559) 248-2546

Vallera J. Johnson, Administrative Law Judge
State of California Office of
Administrative Hearings
San Diego Office
1350 Front Street, Room 6022
San Diego, California 92101
(619) 525-4475 FAX: (619) 525-4419

Catherine Leslie, Administrative Law Judge
Unemployment Insurance Appeals Board
9655 Arrow Route, Building # 19, Suite A
Post Office Box 3100
Rancho Cucamonga, California 91729
(909) 987-2212 FAX: (909) 481-5779

Ernestine Douglas Littlejohn
Administrative Law Judge
Unemployment Insurance Appeals Board
3517 Camino del Rio South, Suite #310
San Diego, California 92108-4027
(619) 521-3300 FAX: (619) 521-3334

Elaine Mallette, Administrative Law Judge
Unemployment Insurance Appeals Board
9800 La Cienega Boulevard, Suite #901
Inglewood, California 90301
(310) 426-2157 FAX: (310) 337-4395

Sandra K. Mitchell, Administrative Law Judge
Unemployment Insurance Appeals Board
9800 La Cienega Boulevard, # 901
Inglewood, California 90301
(310) 337-4302 FAX: (310) 337-4395

Carolyn Richardson Owens
Administrative Law Judge
1877 Olmeda Place
San Diego, California 92128
(858) 485-1462 FAX: (858) 485-1572

Scipio Porter, Administrative Law Judge
Unemployment Insurance Appeals Board
1515 Clay Street, Suite #902
Oakland, California 94612-3505
(510) 286-0695 FAX: (510) 662-3929

Rochelle S. Ramsey, Administrative Law Judge
California Unemployment Insurance
Appeals Board
2499 Ventura Oaks Way, Suite 300
Sacramento, California 95833
(916) 464-3520 FAX: (916) 263-6765

Jacqueline Reed, Administrative Law Judge
California State Public Utilities Commission
505 Van Ness Avenue - Suite 5117
San Francisco, California 94102
(415) 703-2935 FAX: (415) 703-1723

Harold V. Rucker, Administrative Law Judge
Unemployment Insurance Appeals Board
San Diego Office of Appeals
3517 Camino del Rio South, Suite # 310
San Diego, California 92108-4027
(619) 521-3300 FAX: (619) 521-3334

Jo Anne Sawyer, Administrative Law Judge
San Diego Regional Office
Administrative Adjudication Division
California Department of Social Services
355 West Grand Avenue, Suite 4
Escondido, California 92025-2649
(760) 735-5070 FAX: (760) 735-5084

Betty Jo Smith, Administrative Law Judge
Unemployment Insurance Appeals Board
Post Office Box 944275
Sacramento, California 94280-0000
(916) 255-3320 FAX: (916) 255-3337

Charles Stanley Snead
Administrative Law Judge
Unemployment Insurance Appeals Board
1515 Clay Street, Suite # 902
Oakland, California 94612-3505
(510) 286-0695 FAX: (510) 622-3929

John H. Stewart, Administrative Law Judge
Unemployment Insurance Appeals Board
6 Centerpointe Drive, Fourth Floor
La Palma, California 90623
(714) 562-5560 FAX: (714) 562-5592

Gregory H. Tomlin, Administrative Law Judge
Unemployment Insurance Appeals Board
1515 Clay Street, Suite # 902
Oakland, California 94612
(510) 622-3900 FAX: (510) 622-3929

Jacqueline Walker, Administrative Law Judge
Unemployment Insurance Appeals Board
San Diego Office of Appeals
3517 Camino del Rio South, Suite # 310
San Diego, California 92108-4027
(619) 521-3300 FAX: (619) 521-3334

Deborah L. Walton, Administrative Law Judge
Unemployment Insurance Appeals Board
2400 Ventura Oaks Way, Suite #100
Sacramento, California 95833
(916) 263-6706 FAX: (916) 263-6765

Dorothy L. Washington
Administrative Law Judge
Unemployment Insurance Appeals Board
433 North Fair Oaks Avenue, Suite # 200
Pasadena, California 91103
(626) 304-7962 FAX: (626) 304-7981

Daniel Weber, Administrative Law Judge
Unemployment Insurance Appeals Board
San Diego Office of Appeals
3517 Camino del Rio South, Suite #310
San Diego, California 92108
(619) 521-3300 FAX: (619) 521-3334

Reba M. Zachery, Administrative Law Judge
Unemployment Insurance Appeals Board
433 North Fair Oaks Avenue, Suite #200
Pasedena, California 91103
(626) 304-7962 FAX: (626) 304-7981

COLORADO: (11)

FEDERAL

Wiley Y. Daniel, Judge
U. S. District Court
for the District of Colorado
C-218 Byron G. Rogers
U. S. Courthouse
1929 Stout Street
Denver, Colorado 80294
(303) 844-2170 FAX: (303) 844-3035

STATE

Gregory Kellam Scott, Justice
Colorado Supreme Court
Colorado State Judicial Building
2 East 14th Avenue
Denver, Colorado 80203-2116
(303) 861-1111 Ext. 256 FAX: (303) 861-7429

Raymond Dean Jones, Judge
Colorado Court of Appeals
Colorado State Judicial Building
2 East 14th Avenue
Denver, Colorado 80203
(303) 861-1111 or 837-3785
FAX: (303) 837-3702

R. Michael Mullins, Judge
Denver District Court, City and County Building
1437 Bannock Street - Room 466
Denver, Colorado 80202
(303) 640-3089 FAX: (303) 640-2089

Larry J. Naves, Judge
Denver District Court, City and County Building
1437 Bannock Street, Room 259
Denver, Colorado 80202
(303) 640-5709 FAX: (303) 640-3375

Alfred C. Harrell, Judge Denver County Court
City and County Building
1437 Bannock Street
Denver, Colorado 80202
(303) 640-3802 FAX: (303) 640-2089
E-mail: aharrell@ci.denver.co.us

Claudia J. Jordan, Judge
Denver County Court City and County Building
1437 Bannock Street
Denver, Colorado 80202
(303) 640-2054 FAX: (303) 640-1065

Robert L. Patterson, Presiding Judge
Denver County Court, City and County Building
1437 Bannock Street
Denver, Colorado 80202
(303) 640-2651 FAX: (303) 640-1065

Robert H. Russell, II, Judge
Arapahoe District Court
7325 South Potomac
Englewood, Colorado 80012
(303) 649-6202 FAX: (303) 649-6371

Karen Ashby, Judge
Denver Juvenile Court
Room 159
1437 Bannock Street
Denver, Colorado 80202
(303) 640-2868 FAX: (303) 640-3410

T. J. Cole, Magistrate
Boulder Justice Center
Post Office Box 4249
1777 Sixth Street
Boulder, Colorado 80306-4249
(303) 441-4758 FAX: (303) 441-1695

CONNECTICUT: (23)

FEDERAL

Alvin W. Thompson, Judge
U. S. District Court
for the District of Connecticut
Federal Building and U. S. Courthouse
450 Main Street
Hartford, Connecticut 06103
(860) 240-3224 FAX: (860) 240-3465

James Garrett, Chief Administrative Law Judge
Office of Hearings and Appeals
Social Security Administration
Connecticut Financial Center
157 Church Street, 22nd Floor
New Haven, Connecticut 06510
(203) 787-7771 FAX: (203) 787-7771
E-mail: james.garrett@ssa.govt.

STATE

Flemming L. Norcott, Jr., Justice
Supreme Court of Connecticut
231 Capital Avenue
Hartford, Connecticut 06106
(860) 757-2113 FAX: (860) 757-2214

E. Eugene Spear, Judge
State of Connecticut Court of Appeals
95 Washington Street
Hartford, Connecticut 06106
(860) 548-2828 FAX: (860) 548-2870

Vanessa L. Bryant, Judge
Superior Court, GA 14
101 Lafayette Street
Hartford, Connecticut 06016
(860) 566-1630 FAX: (860) 566-1983

E. Curtissa R. Cofield, Judge
Superior Court
Waterbury Judicial District
400 Grand Street
Waterbury, Connecticut 06702
(203) 236-8200 FAX: (203) 236-8205

Juliett L. Crawford, Judge
Superior Court, G.A. 14
101 Lafayette Street
Hartford, Connecticut 06106
(860) 566-3861 FAX: (860) 566-6977

Patricia Lilly Harleston, Judge
Superior Court
Juvenile Matters
20 Park Street
Rockville, Connecticut 06066
(860) 872-7143 FAX: (860) 871-1802
E-mail: patricia.harleston@jud.state.ct.us

Lubbie Harper, Jr., Judge
Superior Court, G.A. 6 & 8
121 Elm Street
New Haven, Connecticut 06510
(203) 789-7461 or (203) 789-7478
FAX: (203) 789-6455

William Holden, Judge
Superior Court
Danbury Judicial District
146 White Street
Danbury, Connecticut 06810
(203) 207-8690 FAX: (203) 207-8689

Clarence J. Jones, Judge
Superior Court
New Haven Judicial District
235 Church Street
New Haven, Connecticut 06510
(203) 789-7922 or 503-6830
FAX: (203) 789-6826

L. Scott Melville, Judge
Superior Court
Bridgeport Judicial District
1061 Main Street
Bridgeport, Connecticut 06604
(203) 579-6540 FAX: (203) 579-6928

Sheridan Moore, Judge
Superior Court
Waterbury Judicial District
400 Grand Street
Waterbury, Connecticut 06702
(203) 236-8200 FAX: (860) 236-8205

Earl B. Richards, III, Judge
Superior Court
Juvenile Matters
239 Whalley Avenue
New Haven, Connecticut 06511
(203) 786-0337 FAX: (203) 786-0327

Angela C. Robinson, Judge
Superior Court, GA 7
54 West Main Street
Meriden, Connecticut 06451
(203) 238-6130 or 238-6137
FAX: (203) 238-6322 or 238-6423

Barry K. Stevens, Judge
Superior Court, GA 2
172 Golden Hill Street
Bridgeport, Connecticut 06604
(203) 579-6568 FAX: (203) 382-8408

Bruce Thompson, Judge
Superior Court, GA 6 & 8
121 Elm Street
New Haven, Connecticut 06510
(203) 789-7461 FAX: (203) 789-6455

John Turner, Judge
Superior Court, G.A. 14
101 Lafayette Street
Hartford Connecticut 06106
(860) 566-1630 or 566-3861
FAX: (860) 556-1983 or 566-6977

Thomas G. West, Judge
Superior Court
Waterbury Judicial District
300 Grand Street
Waterbury, Connecticut 06702
(203) 596-4033 FAX: (203) 236-8205 or 596-4488

Gary J. White, Judge
Superior Court
Judicial District of Danbury
146 White Street
Danbury, Connecticut 06810
(203) 207-8690 FAX: (203) 207-8689

Denese C. Langley, Magistrate
Family Support
Hartford Superior Court
95 Washington Street
Hartford, Connecticut 06106
(860) 548-2700 FAX: (860) 548-2783

Robert D. Glass, State Trial Referee
Superior Court
300 Grand Street
Waterbury, Connecticut 06702
(203) 596-4033 FAX: (203) 596-4488

William Beale Ramsey, State Referee
Superior Court
235 Church Street
New Haven, Connecticut 06510
(203) 789-7922 FAX: (203) 789-6424

DELAWARE: (15)

FEDERAL

Gregory M. Sleet, Judge
U. S. District Court for the District of Delaware
J. Caleb Boggs Federal Building - Lockbox 19
844 North King Street
Wilmington, Delaware 19801-3570
(302) 573-6475 and 573-6470 FAX: (302) 573-6472

STATE

Haile L. Alford, Associate Judge
Superior Court of Delaware
Daniel L. Herrmann Courthouse
1020 King Street
Wilmington, Delaware 19801
(302) 577-2400 Ext. 205 FAX: (302) 577-3835

Charles H. Toliver, IV, Associate Judge
Superior Court of Delaware
Daniel L. Herrmann Courthouse
1020 King Street
Wilmington, Delaware 19801
(302) 577-2400, Ext. 216 FAX: (302) 577-3835

Alex J. Smalls, Chief Judge
Court of Common Pleas
Daniel L. Herrmann Courthouse
1000 North King Street, 3rd Floor
Wilmington, Delaware 19801
(302) 577-2430, Ext. 239 FAX: (302) 577-5889

William L. Chapman, Jr., Associate Judge
Family Court of the State of Delaware
900 King Street
Wilmington, Delaware 19801
(302) 577-2200, Ext. 3122 FAX: (302) 577-3407

Aida Waserstein, Associate Judge
Family Court of the State of Delaware
900 King Street
Wilmington, Delaware 19801
(302) 577-2200, Ext. 3169 FAX: (302) 577-6022

Leonard L. Williams, Judge (Retired)
Municipal Court
1214 King Street
Wilmington, Delaware 19801
(302) 652-3141

Arlene Minus Coppadge, Commissioner
Court of Common Pleas
1000 North King Street, 3rd Floor
Wilmington, Delaware 19801
(302) 577-2430, Ext. 203 FAX: (302) 577-2450

Clarence Bennett, Justice of the Peace
Court #13
820 North French Street, 2nd Floor
Wilmington, Delaware 19801
(302) 577-2552 FAX: (302) 577-2526

Bonita N. Lee, Justice of the Peace
Court #18
1301 East 12th Street
Wilmington, Delaware 19809
(302) 429-7740 FAX: (302) 577-6140

Marcealeate S. Ruffin, Justice of the Peace Court #3
17 Shortly Road
Post Office Box 605
Georgetown, Delaware 19947
(302) 856-1445 FAX: (302) 856-5923

Vernon Taylor, Justice of the Peace Court# 20
Public Safety Building
300 North Walnut Street
Wilmington, Delaware 19801
(302) 577-7234 FAX: (302) 577-7237

Rosalind Toulson, Justice of the Peace Court #18
1301 East 12th Street
Wilmington, Delaware 19801
(302) 429-7740 FAX: (302) 577-6140

Relief Judges

Katherine Ross, Justice of the Peace Court
1030 Boxwood Road
Wilmington, Delaware 19804
(302) 429-7740 FAX: (302) 577-6140

Terry Smith, Justice of the Peace Court
2603 Skylark Road
Wilmington, Delaware 19808
(302) 429-7740 FAX: (302) 577-6140

[illegible]

FEDERAL

U. S. Supreme Court

Clarence Thomas, Associate Justice
Supreme Court of the U. S. 1 First Street, N.E.
Washington, D.C. 20543
(202) 479-3000 FAX: Call on phone first

U. S. Court of Appeals

Harry T. Edwards, Chief Judge
U. S. Court of Appeals for the District of Columbia Circuit
E. Barrett Prettyman, U. S. Courthouse
333 Constitution Avenue, N.W.
Washington, D.C. 20001-2866
(202) 216-0380 FAX: (202) 216-0119

Judith W. Rogers, Judge
U. S. Court of Appeals for the District of Columbia Circuit
E. Barrett Prettyman, U. S. Courthouse
333 Constitution Avenue, N.W.
Washington, D.C. 20001-2866
(202) 216-7260 FAX: (202) 482-2546

U. S. Court of Appeals for Veterans Claims

William P. Greene, Jr., Judge
U. S. Court of Appeals
for Veterans Claims
625 Indiana Avenue, N.W., Suite #900
Washington, D.C. 20004
(202) 501-5890 FAX: (202) 501-5849

U. S. District Court

Norma H. Johnson, Chief Judge
U.S. District Court for the District of Columbia
E. Barrett Prettyman
U. S. Courthouse - Room 2315
333 Constitution Avenue, N.W.
Washington, D.C. 20001-2802
(202) 354-3500 FAX: (202) 354-3412

Henry H. Kennedy, Jr., Judge
U. S. District Court for the District of Columbia
E. Barrett Prettyman
U. S. Courthouse - Room 4317
333 Constitution Avenue, N.W.
Washington, D.C. 20001-2802
(202) 354-3350 FAX: (202) 354-3352

Richard W. Roberts, Judge
U. S. District Court for the District of Columbia
E. Barrett Prettyman
U. S. Courthouse, Room 4329
333 Constitution Avenue, N.W.
Washington, D.C. 20001-2801
(202) 354-3400 or 354-3401 FAX: (202) 354-3256

Emmet G. Sullivan, Judge
U. S. District Court for the District of Columbia
E. Barrett Prettyman
U. S. Courthouse - Room 2114
333 Constitution Avenue, N.W.
Washington, D.C. 20001-2866
(202) 354-3260 FAX: (202) 273-0093

William B. Bryant, Senior Judge
U. S. District Court for the District of Columbia
E. Barrett Prettyman
U. S. Courthouse - Room 6309
333 Constitution Avenue, N.W.
Washington, D.C. 20001-2802
(202) 354-3480 FAX: (202) 354-3482

John Garrett Penn, Senior Judge
U.S. District Court for the District of Columbia
E. Barrett Prettyman
U. S. Courthouse - Room 6327
333 Constitution Avenue, N.W.
Washington, D.C. 20001-2802
(202) 354-3450 FAX: (202) 354-3452

Deborah A. Robinson, Magistrate Judge
U.S. District Court for the District of Columbia
E. Barrett Prettyman
U. S. Courthouse - Room 1114
333 Constitution Avenue, N.W.
Washington, D.C. 20001-2802
(202) 354-3070 FAX: (202) 273-0064

U. S. Court of Federal Claims

Lynn J. Bush, Judge
U. S. Court of Federal Claims
717 Madison Place, N.W.
Suite 602
Washington, D.C. 20005
(202) 219-1269 FAX: (202) 219-1275

Reginald W. Gibson, Senior Judge
U.S. Court of Federal Claims
717 Madison Place, N.W.
Washington, D.C. 20005
(202) 219-9578 FAX: (202) 219-9538

U. S. Tax Court

John F. Dean, Special Judge
U. S. Tax Court
400 Second Street, N.W.
Washington, D.C. 20217
(202) 874-6083 FAX: Call on phone first

Maurice Foley, Judge
U. S. Tax Court
400 Second Street, N.W. - Room 396
Washington, D.C. 20217
(202) 606-8800 FAX: Call on phone first

Administrative Law Judges

Larry Banks, Administrative Law Judge
Office of Hearings and Appeals
Social Security Administration
Union Center Plaza
820 First Avenue, N.E.- 8th Floor
Washington, D.C. 20002-4205
(202) 523-0408 FAX: (202) 408-8995

Michael O. DeMouy, Administrative Law Judge
Office of Hearings and Appeals
Social Security Administration
Union Center Plaza
820 First Avenue, N.E. - 8th Floor
Washington, D.C. 20002-4205
(202) 523-0408 Ext. 3033 FAX: (202) 408-8995

William E. Fowler, Jr.
Chief Administrative Law Judge
National Transportation Safety Board
490 L'Enfant Plaza East, S.W.
Washington, D.C. 20594-2000
(202) 314-6150 FAX: (202) 382-0658
E-mail: fowlerw@ntsb.gov or aliyvett@ntsb.gov

Lillian A. McEwen, Administrative Law Judge
Securities and Exchange Commission
450 Fifth Street, N.W.
Washington, D.C. 20549
(202) 942-0399 FAX: (202) 942-8088

Mollie W. Neal, Administrative Law Judge
U.S. Department of Labor
800 K Street, N.W., Suite 400
Washington, D.C. 20001
(202) 219-5000 FAX: (202) 633-0325

Constance O'Bryant, Administrative Law Judge
U.S. Department of Housing and
Urban Development
409 3rd Street, S.W., Suite #320
Washington, D.C. 20024
(202) 708-4806 Ext. 118 FAX: (202) 708-5014

Covette Rooney, Administrative Law Judge
Occupational, Safety & Health Administration
1 Lafayette Centre
1120 20th Street, N.W.
Washington, D.C. 20036
(202) 606-5405 FAX: (202) 606-5409

Earl Ellison Shamwell, Jr.
Administrative Law Judge
National Labor Relations Board
1099 14th Street, N.W., Suite 5400E
Washington, D.C. 20011
(202) 501-8636 FAX: (202) 501-8606

Julius Johnson, Administrative Law Judge
(Retired)
U.S. Department of Labor
2760 Unicorn Lane, N.W.
Washington, D.C. 20015

Contract Appeals Boards Administrative Judges

David T. Anderson, Chief Administrative Judge
Board of Contract Appeals
U.S. Department of Housing and
Urban Development
1707 H Street, N.W., 11th Floor
Washington, D.C. 20006
(202) 254-0000 FAX: (202) 254-0011

Jerome Drummond, Administrative Judge
Board of Contract Appeals
U.S. Department of Housing and
Urban Development
1707 H Street, N.W., 11th Floor
Washington, D.C. 20006
(202) 254-0000 FAX: (202) 254-0011

Beryl Sansom Gilmore, Administrative Judge
Board of Contract Appeals
U. S. Department of Energy
HC-50, Building 950
1000 Independence Avenue, S.W.
Washington, D.C. 20585-0116
(202) 426-9316 FAX: (202) 426-0215

Administrative Judges

Evelyn M. Gunn, Administrative Judge
U. S. Equal Employment
Opportunity Commission
1400 L Street, N.W., Suite 200
Washington, D.C. 20005
(202) 275-7377 FAX: (202) 275-6834 or 275-0025

Varice Ted Henry, Administrative Judge
U. S. Equal Employment
Opportunity Commission
1400 L Street, N.W., Suite 200
Washington, D.C. 20005
(202) 275-7377 FAX: (202) 275-6834

A. Tonya Ellington Odom
Administrative Judge
U. S. Equal Employment
Opportunity Commission
1400 L Street, N.W., Suite 200
Washington, D.C. 20005
(202) 275-7377 FAX: (202) 275-6834

Veronica Venture, Administrative Judge
U. S. Equal Employment
Opportunity Commission
1400 L Street, N.W., Suite 200
Washington, D.C. 20005
(202) 275-7377 FAX: (202) 275-0076

Thaddeus V. Ware, Chief Administrative Judge
U.S. Department of Transportation
Room 5101
400 7th Street, S.W.
Washington, D.C. 20590
(202) 366-4305 FAX: (202) 366-1025

District of Columbia

Inez Smith-Reid, Associate Judge
District of Columbia Court of Appeals
500 Indiana Avenue, N.W.
Washington, D.C. 20001
(202) 879-2726 or 879-2727 FAX: (202) 626-8802

Annice M. Wagner, Chief Judge
District of Columbia Court of Appeals
500 Indiana Avenue, N. W. - Room 6000
Washington, D.C. 20001
(202) 879-2770 or (202) 879-2771
FAX: (202) 626-8841

Eric T. Washington, Associate Judge
District of Columbia Court of Appeals
500 Indiana Avenue, N.W.
Washington, D.C. 20001
(202) 879-2750 FAX: (202) 824-8580

Julia Cooper Mack, Senior Judge
District of Columbia Court of Appeals
500 Indiana Avenue, N.W. - 6th Floor
Washington, D.C. 20001
(202) 879-2765 FAX: (202) 626-8869

Theodore R. Newman, Jr., Senior Judge
District of Columbia Court of Appeals
500 Indiana Avenue, N.W. - Room 5510
Washington, D.C. 20001
(202) 879-2739 FAX: (202) 626-8876

William C. Pryor, Senior Judge
District of Columbia Court of Appeals
500 Indiana Avenue, N.W. - Room 5510
Washington, D.C. 20001
(202) 879-2745 FAX: (202) 626-8876

Trial Court Judges

Anna Blackburne-Rigsby, Associate Judge
Superior Court of the District of Columbia
500 Indiana Avenue, N.W. - Room JM-610
Washington, D.C. 20001
(202) 879-0055 FAX: (202) 879-0041
E-mail: blackba@dcsc.gov

Shellie F. Bowers, Associate Judge
Superior Court of the District of Columbia
500 Indiana Avenue, N.W. - Room 3000
Washington, D.C. 20001
(202) 879-1288 or 879-1289 FAX: (202) 879-0109
E-mail: bowerssf@dcsc.gov

Zoe Bush, Associate Judge
Superior Court of the District of Columbia
500 Indiana Avenue, N.W. - Room 2520
Washington, D.C. 20001
(202) 879-0023 or 879-0025 FAX: (202) 879-0173
E-mail: bushz@dcsc.gov

Kaye K. Christian, Associate Judge
Superior Court of the District of Columbia
500 Indiana Avenue, N.W. - Room 2510
Washington, D.C. 20001
(202) 879-1668 or 879-1673 FAX: (202) 879-0092
E-mail: christkk@dcsc.gov

Harold L. Cushenberry, Jr., Associate Judge
Superior Court of the District of Columbia
500 Indiana Avenue, N.W. - Room 5610
Washington, D.C. 20001
(202) 879-4866 or 879-4867 FAX: (202) 879-0130
E-mail: cushenhl@dcsc.gov

Herbert B. Dixon, Jr., Associate Judge
Superior Court of the District of Columbia
500 Indiana Avenue, N.W. - Room 2530
Washington, D.C. 20001
(202) 879-4808 or 879-4809 FAX: (202) 879-0127
E-mail: dixonhb@dcsc.gov

Frederick D. Dorsey, Associate Judge
Superior Court of the District of Columbia
500 Indiana Avenue, N.W. - Room 1440
Washington, D.C. 20001
(202) 879-7837 or 879-7838 FAX: (202) 879-0138
E-mail: dorseyfd@dcsc.gov

Wendell P. Gardner, Jr., Associate Judge
Superior Court of the District of Columbia
500 Indiana Avenue, N.W. - Room 1420
Washington, D.C. 20001
(202) 879-1810 or 879-1812 FAX: (202) 879-0148
E-mail: gardnewp@dcsc.gov

Natalia Combs Greene, Associate Judge
Superior Court of the District of Columbia
500 Indiana Avenue, N.W. - Room JM-660
Washington, D.C. 20001
(202) 879-8350 FAX: (202) 879-8363
E-mail: combsgn@dcsc.gov

William M. Jackson, Associate Judge
Superior Court of the District of Columbia
500 Indiana Avenue, N.W. - Room 2630
Washington, D.C. 20001
(202) 879-1909 or 879-1911 FAX: (202) 879-0191
E-mail: jacksowm@dcsc.gov

Anita Josey-Herring, Associate Judge
Superior Court of the District of Columbia
500 Indiana Avenue, N.W. - Room 2640
Washington, D.C. 20001
(202) 879-1574 or 879-1576 FAX: (202) 879-0107
E-mail: herringa@dcsc.gov

Cheryl M. Long, Associate Judge
Superior Court of the District of Columbia
500 Indiana Avenue, N.W. - Room 1630
Washington, D.C. 20001
(202) 879-1200 or 879-1199 FAX: (202) 879-0134
E-mail: longcm@dcsc.gov

George W. Mitchell, Associate Judge
Superior Court of the District of Columbia
500 Indiana Avenue, N.W. - Room 3540
Washington, D.C. 20001
(202) 879-1277 or 879-1278 FAX: 879-0114
E-mail: mitchegw@dcsc.gov

Zinora M. Mitchell-Rankin, Associate Judge
Superior Court of the District of Columbia
500 Indiana Avenue, N.W. - Room 2420
Washington, D.C. 20001
(202) 879-7846 or 879-7847 FAX: 879-0136
E-mail: mitchezm@dcsc.gov

Thomas John Motley, Associate Judge
Superior Court of the District of Columbia
500 Indiana Avenue, N.W. - Room 1430
Washington, D.C. 20001
(202) 879-8377 FAX: (202) 879-8357
E-mail: motleytj@dcsc.gov

Evelyn E. Queen, Associate Judge
Superior Court of the District of Columbia
500 Indiana Avenue, N.W. - Room 1510
Washington, D.C. 20001
(202) 879-4886 or 879-4887 FAX: (202) 879-0121
E-mail: queenee@dcsc.gov

Michael L. Rankin, Associate Judge
Superior Court of the District of Columbia
500 Indiana Avenue, N.W. - Room 2620
Washington, D.C. 20001
(202) 879-1220 or 879-1436 FAX: (202) 879-0129
E-mail: rankinml@dcsc.gov

Lee F. Satterfield, Associate Judge
Superior Court of the District of Columbia
500 Indiana Avenue, N.W. - Room 1530
Washington, D.C. 20001
(202) 879-1918 or 879-1919 FAX: (202) 879-0159
E-mail: satterlf@dcsc.gov

Mary A. Gooden Terrell, Associate Judge
Superior Court of the District of Columbia
500 Indiana Avenue, N.W. - Room JM-670
Washington, D.C. 20001
(202) 879-1639 or 879-1640 FAX: 879-1642
E-mail: terrelma@dcsc.gov

Linda D. Turner, Associate Judge
Superior Court of the District of Columbia
500 Indiana Avenue, N. W. - Room 2000
Washington, D.C. 20001
(202) 879-1819 or 879-1821 FAX: (202) 879-0147
E-mail: hamiltlt@dcsc.gov

Reggie B. Walton, Associate Judge
Superior Court of the District of Columbia
500 Indiana Avenue, N.W. - Room 5630
Washington, D.C. 20001
(202) 879-1815 or 879-1817 FAX: (202) 879-0199
E-mail: waltonrb@dcsc.gov

Susan R. Winfield, Associate Judge
Superior Court of the District of Columbia
500 Indiana Avenue, N.W. - Room 3510
Washington, D.C. 20001
(202) 879-1272 or 879-1273 FAX: (202) 879-0126
E-mail: winfiesr@dcsc.gov

Rhonda Reid Winston, Associate Judge
Superior Court of the District of Columbia
500 Indiana Avenue, N.W. - Room 1620
Washington, D.C. 20001
(202) 879-4750 or 879-4761 FAX: (202) 879-0172
E-mail: winstorr@dcsc.gov

Melvin R. Wright, Associate Judge
Superior Court of the District of Columbia
500 Indiana Avenue, N.W. - Room JM-650
Washington, D.C. 20001
(202) 879-8336 FAX: (202) 879-8339
E-mail: wrightmr@dcsc.gov

Patricia A. Wynn, Associate Judge
Superior Court of the District of Columbia
500 Indiana Avenue, N.W. - Room 3640
Washington, D.C. 20001
(202) 879-4630 or 879-4631 FAX: (202) 879-0140
E-mail: wynnpa@dcsc.gov

Iraline G. Barnes, Senior Judge
Superior Court of the District of Columbia
500 Indiana Avenue, N.W. - Room 2440
Washington, D.C. 20001
(202) 879-1570 FAX: (202) 879-0179
e-mail: barnesig@dcsc.gov

Arthur L. Burnett, Sr., Senior Judge
Superior Court of the District of Columbia
500 Indiana Avenue, N.W. - Room JM-680B
Washington, D.C. 20001
(202) 879-4627 or 879-4883 FAX: (202) 879-7821
E-mail: Albsr2alb@aol.com or burnetta@dcsc.gov

Eugene N. Hamilton, Senior Judge
Superior Court of the District of Columbia
500 Indiana Avenue, N.W. - Room 5520
(202) 879-1727 FAX: (202) 879-0178
E-mail: hamilten@dcsc.gov

Margaret A. Haywood, Senior Judge
Superior Court of the District of Columbia
500 Indiana Avenue, N.W. - Room 5520
Washington, D.C. 20001
(202) 879-4633 FAX: (202) 879-0178
E-mail: haywooma@dcsc.gov

Robert S. Tignor, Senior Judge
Superior Court of the District of Columbia
500 Indiana Avenue, N.W. - Room JM-680A
Washington, D.C. 20001
(202) 879-1252 FAX: (202) 879-7821
E-mail: tignorrs@dcsc.gov

Paul R. Webber, III, Senior Judge
Superior Court of the District of Columbia
500 Indiana Avenue, N.W. - Room 2440
Washington, D.C. 20001
(202) 879-1426 FAX: (202) 879-0179
E-mail: webberpr@dcsc.gov

Commissioners

Jerry S. Byrd, Commissioner
Superior Court of the District of Columbia
500 Indiana Avenue, N.W. - Room 4450
Washington, D.C. 20001
(202) 879-4797 FAX: (202) 879-4855
E-mail: byrdjs@dcsc.gov

Pamela Young Diaz, Commissioner
Superior Court of the District of Columbia
500 Indiana Avenue, N.W. - Room 4450
Washington, D.C. 20001
(202) 879-4853 FAX: (202) 393-6738
E-mail: diazpy@dcsc.gov

John W. King, Commissioner
Superior Court of the District of Columbia
500 Indiana Avenue, N.W. - Room 4450
Washington, D.C. 20001
(202) 879-1169 FAX: (202) 393-6738
E-mail: kingjw@dcsc.gov

Milton C. Lee, Commissioner
Superior Court of the District of Columbia
500 Indiana Avenue, N.W. - Room 4450
Washington, D.C. 20001
(202) 879-4793 FAX: (202) 393-6738
E-mail: leemc@dcsc.gov

Arlene L. Robinson, Commissioner
Superior Court of the District of Columbia
500 Indiana Avenue, N.W. - Room 4450
Washington, D.C. 20001
(202) 879-1327 or 879-1333 FAX: (202) 393-6738
E-mail: robinsoa@dcsc.gov

Fern L. R. Saddler, Commissioner
Superior Court of the District of Columbia
500 Indiana Avenue, N.W. - Room 4450
Washington, D.C. 20001
(202) 879-4854 FAX: (202) 393-6738
E-mail: flanagf@dcsc.gov

District of Columbia Administrative Judges

Valerie V. Ali, Hearing Examiner
Administrative Law Judge
District of Columbia, Dept. of Motor Vehicles
Traffic Adjudication
55 K Street, N.E.
Washington, D.C. 20002
(202) 535-1510 FAX: (202) 727-3768

Sylvia Anderson, Chief Hearing Examiner
Administrative Law Judge
District of Columbia, Dept. of Human Services
441 4th Street, N.W., Suite 870 North
Washington, D.C. 20001
(202) 724-5477 FAX: (202) 724-4129
E-mail: seanderso@yahoo.com

Ruth R. Banks, Commissioner (Chairperson)
Administrative Judge District of Columbia
Rental Housing Commission
941 North Capital Street, N.E., Suite 9200
Washington, D.C. 20002
(202) 442-8949 FAX: (202) 442-9446
E-mail: rbanks@DCRA.dcgov.org

Sylvia Goldsberry-Adams, Hearing Examiner
Administrative Judge District of Columbia
Dept. of Human Services
441 4th Street, N.W., Suite 870 North
Washington, D.C. 20001
(202) 724-5431 FAX: (202) 724-4129
E-mail: sgddsberryadams@yahoo.com

Phyllis W. Jackson, Administrative Judge
District of Columbia
Contract Appeals Board
717 14th Street, N.W., Suite 430
Washington, D.C. 20005
(202) 727-6597 FAX: (202) 727-3993
E-mail: pjackson/cab@dcgov.org

Wanda Jackson, Administrative Judge
District of Columbia
Office of Employee Appeals
717 14th Street, N.W. 3rd Floor
Washington, D.C. 20005
(202) 727-0004 FAX: (202) 727-5631
E-mail: wjackson - oea@dcgov.org

Jennifer M. Long, Commissioner
Administrative Judge
District of Columbia, Rental Housing Commission
941 North Capital Street, N.E., Suite 9200
Washington, D.C. 20002
(202) 442-8949 FAX: (202) 442-9446
E-mail: longjen@hotmail.com

Roe Quander, Administrative Judge
District of Columbia Dept. of Consumer
and Regulatory Affairs
Office of Adjudication
941 North Capital Street, N.E., Suite 9100
Washington, D.C. 20002
(202) 442-8170 FAX: (202) 442-9451
E-mail: rquander@DCRA.dcgov.org

Deborah Reeves, Administrative Judge
District of Columbia, Office of Employee Appeals
717 14th Street, N.W., 3rd Floor
Washington, D.C. 20005
(202) 727-0009 FAX: (202) 727-5631
E-mail: reevesdeborah@hotmail.com

Lorilyn E. Simkins, Chief Administrative Judge
District of Columbia, Contract Appeals Board
717 14th Street, N.W., Suite 430
Washington, D.C. 20005
(202) 727-6597 FAX: (202) 727-3993
E-mail: lsimkins/cab@dcgov.org

Pamela Washington, Hearing Examiner
Administrative Judge
District of Columbia, Dept. of Motor Vehicles
Traffic Adjudication
55 K Street, N.E.
Washington, D.C. 20002
(202) 535-1510 FAX: (202) 727-3768

Denise Wilson-Taylor, Hearing Examiner
Administrative Judge
District of Columbia
Dept. of Employment Services
500 C Street, N.W., Suite 509
Washington, D.C. 20001
(202) 724-7481 FAX: (202) 724-7486
E-mail: denisetaylor@hotmail.com

Ronald Young, Commissioner,
Administrative Judge
District of Columbia, Rental Housing Commission
941 North Capital Street, N.E., Suite 9200
Washington, D.C. 20002
(202) 442-8949 FAX: (202) 442-9446
E-mail: ryoung@DCRA.dcgov.org

FLORIDA: (65)

FEDERAL

Charles R. Wilson, Judge
U. S. Court of Appeals
for the Eleventh Circuit
801 North Florida Avenue #14B
Tampa, Florida 33602-4511
(813) 301-5650 FAX: (813) 301-5659

Henry Lee Adams, Jr., Judge
U. S. District Court for
the Middle District of Florida
223 U. S. Courthouse
801 North Florida Avenue
Tampa, Florida 33602-3800
(813) 301-5880 FAX: (813) 225-2765

Wilkie D. Ferguson, Jr., Judge
U. S. District Court for
the Southern District of Florida
U. S. Courthouse - Suite 207B
299 East Broward Boulevard
Ft. Lauderdale, Florida 33301
(954) 769-5470 FAX: (954) 356-7884

Donald L. Graham, Judge
U. S. District Court
for the Southern District
James Lawrence King
Federal Justice Building - Suite 1067
99 Northeast Fourth Street
Miami, Florida 33132
(305) 523-5130 FAX: (305) 523-5139

Stephan P. Mickle, Judge
U. S. District Court
for the Northern District of Florida
401 S.E. First Avenue - Suite 367
Gainesville, Florida 32601-6897
(352) 380-2742 FAX: (352) Call on phone first

Administrative Law Judges

Theodore S. Haynes, Administrative Law Judge
Office of Hearings and Appeals
Social Security Administration
Glenridge Building - Suite 300
3505 Lake Lynda Drive
Orlando, Florida 32817
(407) 380-2345 Ext. 3063 FAX: (380) 3658

Dwight Evans, Administrative Law Judge
Office of Hearings and Appeals
Social Security Administration
New River Center, Suite 1550
200 E. Las Olas Boulevard
Ft. Lauderdale, Florida 33301
(954) 356-7385 FAX: (954) 356-7901

STATE

Supreme Court

Leander J. Shaw, Jr., Justice
Supreme Court of Florida
Supreme Court Building
500 South Duval Street
Tallahassee, Florida 32399-1925
(850) 488-0208 FAX: (850) 487-2823

Peggy A. Quince, Justice
Supreme Court of Florida
Supreme Court Building
Tallahassee, Florida 32399-1925
(850) 922-5624 FAX: (850) 487-2823

Courts of Appeal

Melvia B. Green, Judge
Third District Court of Appeal
2001 S.W. 117th Avenue
Post Office Box 65030
Miami, Florida 33175-1716
(305) 229-3200 FAX: (305) 229-3206

Joseph Lewis, Judge
First District Court of Appeals
301 South Martin Luther King Boulevard
Tallahassee, Florida 32301
(850) 487-1000 FAX: (850) 488-7989

Matthew W. Stevenson, Judge
Fourth District Court of Appeal
1525 Palm Beach Lakes Boulevard
Post Office Box 3315
West Palm Beach, Florida 33402-3315
(561) 697-7206 FAX: (561) 697-7227

Thomas Stringer, Sr., Judge
Second District Court of Appeal
Post Office Box 327
Lakeland, Florida 33802
(941) 499-2290 FAX: (941) 499-2277

Carole Y. Taylor, Judge
Fourth District Court of Appeal
Post Office Box 3315
West Palm Beach, Florida 33402-3315
(561) 242-2073 FAX: (561) 242-2095

Emerson R. Thompson, Jr., Chief Judge
Fifth District Court of Appeal
300 South Beach Street
Daytona Beach, Florida 32114-5097
(904) 947-1576 FAX: (904) 947-1562

Circuit Court Judges

Isaac Anderson, Jr., Judge
Circuit Court
20th Judicial District
Lee County Justice Center
Court Administrator's Office - #3112
1700 Monroe Street, Third Floor
Ft. Myers, Florida 33901
(941) 335-2412 FAX: (941) 335-2387 or 477-2069

Jerald Bagley, Judge
Circuit Court
11th Judicial Circuit
Richard E. Gerstein Building
1351 N.W. 12th Street - Room 217
Miami, Florida 33125
(305) 547-7898 FAX: (305) 325-8641

Moses Baker, Jr., Judge
Circuit Court
15th Judicial Circuit
205 North Dixie Highway
West Palm Beach, Florida 33401
(561) 355-4622 FAX: (561) 355-6048

Theotis Bronson, Judge
Circuit Court
9th Judicial Circuit
Orange County Courthouse
425 North Orange Avenue
Orlando, Florida 32801
(407) 836-2229 FAX: (407) 836-2310

Catherine M. Brunson, Judge
Circuit Court
15th Judicial Circuit
205 North Dixie Highway
West Palm Beach, Florida 33401
(561) 355-2595 FAX: (561) 355-1616

Michael B. Chavies, Judge
Circuit Court
11th Judicial Circuit
1915 Courthouse Center
175 Northwest 1st Avenue
Miami, Florida 33128
(305) 349-5735 FAX: (305) 349-6171

Nikki Ann Clark, Judge
Circuit Court
2nd Judicial Circuit
365-F Leon County Courthouse
301 South Monroe Street
Tallahassee, Florida 32301
(850) 922-0691 FAX: (850) 922-0327

Marva L. Crehshaw, Judge
Circuit Court
10th Judicial Circuit
800 East Kennedy Boulevard, Suite #201
Tampa, Florida 33602
(813) 272-5809 FAX: (813) 276-8015

Brian J. Davis, Judge
Circuit Court
4th Judicial Circuit
206 Duval County Courthouse
330 East Bay Street
Jacksonville, Florida 32202
(904) 630-2583 FAX: (904) 630-2879

Henry E. Davis, Judge
Circuit Court
4th Judicial Circuit
200 Duval County Courthouse
330 East Bay Street
Jacksonville, Florida 32202
(904) 630-2530 FAX: (904) 630-2979

Sandra Edwards-Stephens, Judge
Circuit Court
5th Judicial Circuit
Marion County Judicial Center, Suite 3030
110 Northwest First Avenue
Ocala, Florida 34475
(352) 620-3540 FAX: (352) 620-3560

Hubert Grimes, Judge
Circuit Court
7th Judicial Circuit
120 West Indiana Avenue, Suite 300
Deland, Florida 32720
(904) 822-5744 FAX: (904) 740-5128

Ilona M. Holmes, Judge
Circuit Court
17th Judicial Circuit
Broward County Courthouse
201 Southeast 6th Street
Ft. Lauderdale, Florida 33301
(954) 831-7797 FAX: (954) 831-5533

William Johnson, Judge
Circuit Court
11th Judicial Circuit
3300 N.W. 27th Avenue, Suite #210
Miami, Florida 33142
(305) 638-6229 FAX: (305) 638-6355

Perry A. Little, Judge
Circuit Court
East Division, 13th Judicial Circuit
437 Hillsborough County Courthouse Annex
801 East Twiggs Street
Tampa, Florida 33602-3554
(813) 272-5775 FAX: (813) 276-2079

Belvin Perry, Jr., Chief Judge
Circuit Court
9th Judicial Circuit
Orange County Courthouse
425 North Orange Avenue
Orlando, Florida 32801
(407) 836-2008 FAX: (407) 836-2006

James E. C. Perry, Judge
Circuit Court
18th Judicial Circuit
Seminole County Courthouse
301 North Park Avenue
Sanford, Florida 32771-1292
(407) 665-5341 FAX: (407) 665-5349

Daryl E. Trawick, Judge
Circuit Court
11th Judicial Circuit
Richard E. Gerstein Justice Building
1351 N.W. 12th Street, Room 711
Miami, Florida 33125
(305) 548-5110 FAX: (305) 325-8641

Reginald K. Whitehead, Sr., Judge
Circuit Court
9th Judicial Circuit
Osceola County Courthouse
12 South Vernon Street
Kissimmee, Florida 34741
(407) 343-2495 FAX: (407) 847-1256

Charles E. Williams, Judge
Circuit Court
12th Judicial Circuit
1115 Manatee Avenue West
Post Office Box 1000
Bradenton, Florida 34206
(941) 749-7139 FAX: (941) 742-5957

Kenneth L. Williams, Judge
Circuit Court
1st Judicial Circuit
M.C. Blanchard Judicial Building
190 Governmental Center
Pensacola, Florida 32501
(850) 595-4465 FAX: (805) 595-4466

County Court Judges

James R. Adams, County Court Judge
Lee County
Twentieth Judicial Circuit
Lee County Justice Center
1700 Monroe Street
Fort Myers, Florida 33901
(941) 335-2954 FAX: (941) 477-2069

Alphonso Leo Adderly, County Court Judge
Dade County
Eleventh Judicial Circuit
1017 Dade County Courthouse
73 West Flagler Street
Miami, Florida 33130
(305) 375-2857 FAX: (305) 375-5815

Augustus D. Aikens, County Court Judge
Leon County
Second Judicial Circuit
Leon County Courthouse
301 South Monroe Street
Tallahassee, Florida 32301
(850) 488-6298 FAX: (850) 922-0070

Michael F. Andrews, County Court Judge
Pinellas County
Sixth Judicial Circuit
Criminal Justice Center
14250 49th Street North
Clearwater, Florida 33762
(727) 464-6470 FAX: (727) 464-6484

Cathleen B. Clarke, County Court Judge
Melbourne County
18th Judicial Circuit
Brevard County Courthouse
50 S. Nieman Avenue, Suite 130
Melbourne, Florida 32901-1261
(321) 952-4702 FAX: (321) 952-4704

Timothy Coon, County Court Judge
Polk County
Tenth Judicial Circuit
Polk County Courthouse
Post Office Box 9000, Drawer J-140
Bartow, Florida 33831-9000
(863) 534-7780 FAX: (863) 534-7723

Sheree D. Cunningham, County Court Judge
Palm Beach County
Fifteenth Judicial Circuit
Criminal Justice Complex
3228 Gun Club Road
West Palm Beach, Florida 33406
(561) 688-4600 FAX: (561) 688-4597

Karen Francis-Mills, County Court Judge
Dade County
Eleventh Judicial Circuit
Civic Park Plaza
1469 Northwest 13 Terrace
Miami, Florida 33125
(305) 324-2900 FAX: Call on phone first

Wendell M. Graham, County Court Judge
Dade County
Eleventh Judicial Circuit
1-5 Coral Gables Branch Court
3100 Ponce de Leon Boulevard
Coral Gables, Florida 33134
(305) 569-2518 FAX: (305) 569-2558

Judith Hawkins, County Court Judge
Leon County
Second Judicial Circuit
265-H Leon County Courthouse
301 South Monroe Street
Tallahassee, Florida 32301
(850) 488-5374 FAX: (850) 922-0070

Eric William Hendon, County Court Judge
Dade County
Eleventh Judicial Circuit
Richard Gerstein Building, Room 505
1351 Northwest 12th Street
Miami, Florida 33125
(305) 545-3498 FAX: (305) 545-3534

Pauline M. Ingram-Drayton, County Judge
Duval County
Fourth Judicial Circuit
324 Duval County Courthouse
300 East Bay Street
Jacksonville, Florida 32202
(904) 630-2581 FAX: (904) 630-2957

Phyllis D. Kotey, County Court Judge
Alachua County
Sixth Judicial Circuit
205 Alachua County Courthouse
201 East University Avenue
Gainesville, Florida 32601
(352) 337-6130 FAX: (352) 374-5238

Alli Baksh Majeed, County Court Judge
Brevard County
Eighteenth Judicial Circuit
The Moore Justice Center
2825 Judge Fran Jamieson Way
Viera, Florida 32940
(321) 617-7270 FAX: (321) 617-7278

Myra Scott McNary, County Court Judge
Pinella County, Sixth Judicial Circuit
324 South Fort Harrison Avenue
Clearwater, Florida 33756
(727) 464-3034 FAX: (727) 464-5484

Eric Renard Myers, County Court Judge
Hillsborough County
Thirteenth Judicial Cirucit
800 East Kennedy Boulevard - Office 201
Tampa, Florida 33602-4146
(813) 272-5809 FAX: (813) 276-8015

Orlando Alberto Prescott, County Court Judge
Dade County
Eleventh Judicial Circuit
Caleb Center, Room 242
5400 Northwest 22nd Avenue
Miami, Florida 33142
(305) 636-2262 FAX: (305) 636-2287

Mary Rudd Robinson, County Court Judge
Broward County
Seventeenth Judicial Circuit
329 Broward County Courthouse
201 Southeast Sixth Street
Fort Lauderdale, Florida 33301
(954) 831-7039 FAX: (954) 831-5572

James A. Ruth, County Court Judge
Duval County
Fourth Judicial Circuit
301 Duval County Courthouse
330 East Bay Street
Jacksonville, Florida 32202
(904) 630-2568 FAX: (904) 630-2979

Elijah Smiley, County Court Judge
Bay County Fourteenth Judicial Circuit
Bay County Courthouse
300 East 4th Street
Post Office Box 2269
Panama City, Florida 32401
(850) 747-5205 FAX: (850) 747-5629

Dedra Moses Stephens, County Court Judge
Palm Beach County
Fifteenth Judicial Circuit
9.2203 Palm Beach County Courthouse
205 North Dixie Highway
West Palm Beach, Florida 33401
(561) 355-2534 FAX: (561) 355-3841

Teretha Lundy Thomas, County Court Judge
Dade County
Eleventh Judicial Circuit
610 Richard E. Gerstein Justice Building
1351 Northwest 12th Street
Miami, Florida 33125
(305) 548-5350 FAX: (305) 548-5332

Freddie J. Worthen, County Court Judge
Volusia County
Seventh Judicial Circuit
Volusia County Courthouse
206 Courthouse Annex
125 East Orange Avenue
Daytona Beach, Florida 32114
(904) 257-6070 FAX: (904) 257-6094

Karla Foreman Wright, County Court Judge
Polk County
Tenth Judicial Circuit
Post Office Box 9000
Drawer J-147
Bartow, Florida 33831
(863) 534-5820 FAX: (863) 534-5382

Zebedee W. Wright, County Court Judge
Broward County
Seventeenth Judicial Circuit
310 Broward County Courthouse
201 Southeast Sixth Street
Fort Lauderdale, Florida 33301
(954) 831-7841 FAX: (954) 831-5572

Administrative Law Judges

Fred Buckine, Administrative Law Judge
Division of Administrative Hearings
State of Florida
The DeSoto Building
1230 Apalachee Parkway
Tallahassee, Florida 32399-3060
(850) 488-9675 FAX: (850) 488-5366

Carolyn Holifield, Administrative Law Judge
Division of Administrative Hearings
State of Florida
The DeSoto Building
1230 Apalachee Parkway
Tallahassee, Florida 32399-3060
(850) 488-9675 FAX: (850) 488-5366

Eleanor M. Hunter, Administrative Law Judge
Division of Administrative Hearings
State of Florida
The DeSoto Building
1230 Apalachee Parkway
Tallahassee, Florida 32399-3060
(850) 488-9675 FAX: (850) 488-5366

Errol H. Powell, Administrative Law Judge
Division of Administrative Hearings
State of Florida
The DeSoto Building
1230 Apalachee Parkway
Tallahassee, Florida 32399-3060
(850) 488-9675 FAX: (850) 488-5366

GEORGIA: (106)

FEDERAL

Clarence Cooper, Judge
U. S. District Court
for the Northern District of Georgia
1721 Richard B. Russell Federal Building
and U. S. Courthouse
75 Spring Street, S.W.
Atlanta, Georgia 30303-3361
(404) 331-0558 FAX: (404) 331-0579
E-mail: clarence_cooper@gand.uscourts.gov

W. Louis Sands, Judge
U. S. District Court
for the Middle District of Georgia
Post Office Box 1705
Albany, Georgia 31702-1705
(912) 430-8553 FAX: (912) 430-8559
E-mail: Louis_Sands@gand.uscourts.gov

Horace T. Ward, Senior Judge
U. S. District Court
for the Middle District of Georgia
2388 Richard B. Russell Federal Building
and U. S. Courthouse
75 Spring Street, S.W.
Atlanta, Georgia 30303-3361
(404) 215-1330 FAX: (404) 215-1326
E-mail: Sharon_Lane@gand.uscourts.gov

Linda T. Walker, Magistrate Judge
U. S. District Court
for the Northern District of Georgia
1629 Richard B. Russell Federal Building
and U. S. Courthouse 75 Spring Street, S.W.
Atlanta, Georgia 30303
(404) 215-1370 FAX: (404)215-1586 or 215-1370
E-mail: linda_t_walker@gand.uscourts.gov

C. Ray Mullins, Judge
U. S. Bankruptcy Court
for the Northern District of Georgia
1270 Richard B. Russell Federal Building
and U. S. Courthouse
75 Spring Street, S.W.
Atlanta, Georgia 30303-3361
(404) 215-1002 FAX: (404) 215-1117
E-mail: ray_mullins@gand.uscourts.gov

Administrative Law Judges

William L. Akers, Administrative Law Judge
Office of Hearings and Appeals
Social Security Administration
60 Forsyth Street, S.W.
Suite 2M15
Atlanta, Georgia 30303
(404) 562-5570 FAX: (404) 562-0989
E-mail: william.akers@ssa.gov

Glenn M. Embree
Chief Administrative Law Judge
Office of Hearings & Appeals
Social Security Administration
60 Forsyth Street, S.W.
Suite 2M15
Atlanta, Georgia 30303
(404) 562-5570 FAX: (404) 562-5599 or 562-0989
E-mail: glenn.embree@ssa.gov

Robert T. Jackson, Administrative Law Judge
Office of Hearings and Appeals
Social Security Administration
60 Forsyth Street, S.W.
Suite 2M15
Atlanta, Georgia 30303
(404) 562-5570 FAX: (404) 562-5599 or 562-0989
E-mail: robert.jackson@ssa.gov

Henry G. Watkins
Regional Chief Administrative Law Judge
Office of Hearings and Appeals
Social Security Administration
61 Forsyth Street, S.W.- Suite 20T40
Atlanta, Georgia 30303
(404) 562-1182 FAX: (404) 562-1151

Paul L. Brady, Administrative Law Judge (Retired)
Occupational Safety & Health
Review Commission
1185 Niskey Lake Road, S.W.
Atlanta, Georgia 30331
(404) 344-5816

Administrative Judges

Anthony Wayne Cummings
Administrative Judge
U. S. Merit Systems Protection Board
401 West Peachtree Street, N.W.
Suite # 1050
Atlanta, Georgia 30309
(404) 730-2751 FAX: (404) 730-2767
E-mail: anthony.cummings@mspb.gov

Pamela Jackson, Administrative Judge
U. S. Merit Systems Protection Board
401 West Peachtree Street, N.W.
Suite # 1050
Atlanta, Georgia 30309
(404) 730-7251 FAX: (404) 730-2767
E-mail: pamela.jackson@mspb.gov

STATE

Supreme Court

Robert Benham, Chief Justice
Supreme Court of Georgia
507 State Judicial Building
Atlanta, Georgia 30334
(404) 656-3476 FAX: (404) 657-4329

Leah Ward-Sears, Associate Justice
Supreme Court of Georgia
501 State Judicial Building
Atlanta, Georgia 30334
(404) 656-3474 FAX: (404) 657-6997

Court of Appeals

M. Yvette Miller, Judge
Georgia Court of Appeals
334 State Judicial Building
Atlanta, Georgia 30304
(404) 463-3032 FAX: (404) 463-3027
E-mail: millery@appeals.courts.state.ga.us

Herbert E. Phipps, Judge
Georgia Court of Appeals
435 State Judicial Building
Atlanta, Georgia 30334
(404) 656-3457 FAX: (404) 651-8139
E-mail: phippsh@appeals.courts.state.ga.us

John H. Ruffin, Jr., Judge
Georgia Court of Appeals
40 Capitol Square, Suite 412
Atlanta, Georgia 30334
(404) 656-3458 FAX: (404) 651-8139
E-mail: ruffini@appeals.courts.state.ga.us

Court Judges

William H. Alexander, Judge
Superior Court of Fulton County
160 Pryor Street, S.W., Room C210
Atlanta, Georgia 30303
(404) 730-4195 FAX: (404) 730-4565

John D. Allen, Judge
Superior Court of Muscogee County
Post Office Box 1340
Columbus, Georgia 31902
(706) 653-4277 FAX: (706) 653-4275

James F. Bass, Jr., Judge
Superior Court
Eastern Judicial Circuit
421 Chatham County Courthouse
133 Montgomery Street
Savannah, Georgia 31401
(912) 652-7154 FAX: (912) 652-3527
E-mail: jbass10295@aol.com

Carl C. Brown, Jr., Judge
Superior Court
Augusta Judicial District
320 City-County Building
530 Greene Street
Augusta, Georgia 30911
(706) 821-2347 FAX: (706) 721-4476

Alford J. Dempsey, Jr., Judge
Superior Court of Fulton County
T-4955 Justice Center Tower
185 Central Avenue, S.W.
Atlanta, Georgia 30303-3643
(404) 302-8527 FAX: (404) 335-2862
E-mail: alford.dempsey@fultoncourt.org

Michael E. Hancock, Judge
Superior Court
Stone Mountain Judicial Circuit
403 DeKalb County Courthouse
556 North McDonough Street
Decatur, Georgia 30030-3356
(404) 371-2344 FAX: (404) 371-2002

Linda Warren Hunter, Judge
Superior Court
Stone Mountain Judicial Circuit
505 DeKalb County Courthouse
556 North McDonough Street
Decatur, Georgia 30030-3643
(404) 371-2501 FAX: (404) 371-4754

Isaac Jenrette, Judge
Superior Court of Fulton County
T-8905 Justice Center Tower
185 Central Avenue, S.W.
Atlanta, Georgia 30303-3643
(404) 730-4335 FAX: (404) 335-2863

Steve C. Jones, Judge Superior Court
Western Judicial Circuit
Post Office Box 1623
Athens, Georgia 30603
(706) 613-3780 FAX: (706) 613-3782
E-mail: stevejones.cscj@hotoffice.net

Bensonetta Tipton Lane, Judge
Superior Court of Fulton County
T-1955 Justice Center Tower
185 Central Avenue, S.W.
Atlanta, Georgia 30303-3643
(404) 302-8535 FAX: (404) 335-2864
E-mail: bensonetta.lane@fultoncourt.org

Willie Lockette, Judge
Superior Court of Doughtery County
Post Office Box 1827
Albany, Georgia 31702-1827
(912) 431-2186 FAX: (912) 431-2174

John E. Morse, Jr., Judge
Superior Court of Chatham County
213 Chatham County Courthouse
133 Montgomery Street
Savannah, Georgia 31401-3239
(912) 652-7236 FAX: (912) 652-7361
E-mail: jemorse@wpo.co.chatham.ga.us

Thelma Wyatt Cummings Moore, Judge
Superior Court of Fulton County
T-4905 Justice Center Tower
185 Central Avenue, S.W.
Atlanta, Georgia 30303-3643
(404) 730-4305 FAX: (404) 730-0162
E-mail: thelma.moore@fultoncourt.org

Constance C. Russell, Judge
Superior Court of Fulton County
T-8755 Justice Center Tower
185 Central Avenue, S.W.
Atlanta, Georgia 30303-3643
(404) 335-2803
FAX: Call on phone first

Gail S. Tusan, Judge
Superior Court of Fulton County
Family Division
T-8955 Justice Center Tower
185 Central Avenue, S.W.
Atlanta, Georgia 30303-3643
(404) 302-8520 FAX: (404) 302-8524
E-mail: gail.tusan@fultoncourt.org

State Court Judges

M. Gino Brogdon, Judge
State Court of Fulton County
T-3855 Justice Center Tower
185 Central Avenue, S.W.
Atlanta, Georgia 30303-3643
(404) 730-7760 FAX: (404) 224-0572
E-mail: brothaman@mindspring.com

Bridgette Jean Campbell, Judge
State Court of Cobb County - Division II
12 East Park Square
Suite 4-D
Marietta, Georgia 30090
(770) 423-6800 FAX: (770) 528-1788 or 423-6804

Myra H. Dixon, Judge
State Court of Fulton County
T-3655 Justice Center Tower
185 Central Avenue, S.W.
Atlanta, Georgia 30303
(404) 730-4295 FAX: (404) 224-0573
E-mail: myra.dixon@cjisful.net

Orion L. Douglass, Judge
State Court of Glynn County
Post Office Box 879
Brunswick, Georgia 31521
(912) 267-5675 FAX: (912) 267-5642
E-mail: odoug@gate.net

Denise L. Majette, Judge
State Court of DeKalb County
556 North McDonough Street, Room 804
Decatur, Georgia 30030
(404) 371-2350 FAX: (404) 371-2014
E-mail: dmajette@randomc.com

Patsy Porter, Judge
State Court of Fulton County
T-2855 Justice Center Tower
185 Central Avenue, S.W.
Atlanta, Georgia 30303-3643
(404) 730-4345 FAX: (404) 224-0575

Penny Brown Reynolds, Judge
State Court of Fulton County
T-3705 Justice Center Tower
185 Central Avenue, S.W.
Atlanta, Georgia 30303
(404) 730-4430 FAX: (404) 225-0570

Albert L. Thompson, Chief Judge
State Court of Fulton County
T-3955 Justice Center Tower
185 Central Avenue, S.W.
Atlanta, Georgia 30303-3643
(404) 730-4497 FAX: (404) 730-7179

Civil Court Judge

William C. "Billy" Randall, Judge
Bibb County Civil Court
Room 111 Bibb County Courthouse
601 Mulberry Street
Macon, Georgia 31201
(478) 749-6338 FAX: (478) 749-6470

Juvenile Court Judges

Gregory A. Adams, Chief Presiding Judge
Juvenile Court of DeKalb County
3631 Camp Circle
Decatur, Georgia 30032-1308
(404) 294-2727 FAX: (404) 294-2981
E-mail: g.adams@usa.net

Nina R. Hickson, Judge
Juvenile Court of Fulton County
160 Pryor Street, S.W.
Suite J-241
Atlanta, Georgia 30303
(404) 730-1128 and 730-1130 FAX: (404) 335-2732
E-mail: nrhickson4@hotmail.com

David Getachew-Smith, Judge
Juvenile Court of Fulton County
160 Pryor Street, S.W.
Suite J-233
Atlanta, Georgia 30303
(404) 335-2728 FAX: (404) 335-2739

Genet McIntosh Hopewell, Judge
Juvenile Court of DeKalb County
4283 Memorial Drive, Suite 1
Decatur, Georgia 30032-1219
(404) 299-9697 FAX: (404) 299-9755

Associate Judges

Karen Baynes-Galvin, Associate Judge
Juvenile Court of Fulton County
160 Pryor Street, S.W.
Atlanta, Georgia 30303
(404) 730-6882 FAX: (404) 730-7357
E-mail: kgalvin@mindspring.com

Quintress J. Gilbert, Associate Judge
Juvenile Court of Bibb County
505 Bibb County Courthouse
Macon, Georgia 31201
(912) 749-6448 FAX: (912) 749-6482
E-mail: msnquintress@msn.com

Charles G. Hodges, Associate Judge
Juvenile Court of Fulton County
445 Capitol Avenue, S.W.
Atlanta, Georgia 30312-2899
(404) 730-1123 or 730-1044 FAX: (404) 730-1120

Nikki L. Marr, Associate Judge
Juvenile Court of DeKalb County
3631 Camp Circle
Decatur, Georgia 30032-1308
(404) 294-2916
FAX: (404) 294-2702 or 294-2956
E-mail: lomarr@usa.net

Desiree Sutton Peagler, Associate Judge
Juvenile Court of DeKalb County
3631 Camp Circle
Decatur, Georgia 30032-1308
(404) 297-3842 FAX: (404) 294-2702
E-mail: dpeagler@usa.net

George Geiger, Associate Judge (Retired)
Juvenile Court of Fulton County
1480 New Hope Road, S.W.
Atlanta, Georgia 30331-7401
(404) 344-1614

Probate Court

Roberta Cross-Davenport, Judge
Probate Court of Emanuel County
Post Office Drawer 70
Swainsboro, Georgia 30401
(912) 237-7091 FAX: (912) 237-2633

Edith J. Ingram, f/k/a **Edith Ingram-Grant**
Judge Probate Court of Hancock County
Courthouse Square
Sparta, Georgia 31087
(706) 444-5343 FAX: (706) 444-8024

Pinkie Toomer, Judge
Probate Court of Fulton County
136 Pryor Street, S.W., Suite 230-C
Atlanta, Georgia 30303
(404) 730-4660 FAX: (404) 730-8283

City Court Judges

Edward L. Baety, Chief Judge
City Court of Atlanta
104 Trinity Avenue, S.W.
Atlanta, Georgia 30335
(404) 658-6919 FAX: (404) 658-7125

Elaine Lynn Carlisle, Judge
City of Atlanta Municipal Court
170 Garnett Street, S.W.
Atlanta, Georgia 30335
(404) 865-8103 FAX: (404) 658-6805
E-mail: ecarlisle@mindspring.com

James F. Council, Jr., Judge
Valdosta Municipal Court &
Morven Municipal Court
301 Webster Street
Post Office Box 1201
Valdosta, Georgia 31603-1201
(912) 242-5362 FAX: (912) 242-5375
E-mail: council@datasys.com

Clinton Deveaux, Judge
Atlanta Municipal Court
170 Garnett Street, S.W.
Atlanta, Georgia 30303
(404) 865-8104 FAX: (404) 658-6805
E-mail: cedeveaux@ci.atlanta.ga.us
E-mail: judgeclint@aol.com

Calvin S. Graves, Judge
City Court of Atlanta
104 Trinity Avenue, S.W.
Atlanta, Georgia 30335
(404) 658-7049 FAX: (404) 658-7125
E-mail: cgraves@ci.atlanta.ga.us

Andrew J. Hairston, Judge
City Court of Atlanta
104 Trinity Avenue, S.W.
Atlanta, Georgia 30335
(404) 658-6919 FAX: (404) 658-7125
E-mail: ahairston@ci.atlanta.ga.us

Barbara A. Harris, Chief Judge
Atlanta Municipal Court
170 Garnett Street, S.W.
Atlanta, Georgia 30335
(404) 865-8102 FAX: (404) 658-6805
E-mail: Honharr@hotmail.com

Lenwood A. Jackson, Judge
City Court of Atlanta
104 Trinity Avenue, S.W.
Atlanta, Georgia 30335
(404) 658-7048 FAX: (404) 658-6508
E-mail: lajackson@ci.atlanta.ga.us

Howard R. Johnson, Judge
Atlanta Municipal Court
170 Garnett Street, S.W.
Atlanta, Georgia 30335
(404) 865-8105 FAX: (404) 658-6805

Rhathelia Stroud, Judge
City of Pine Lake Municipal Court
Associate Judge City of Decatur
Post Office Box 2877
Decatur, Georgia 30031-2877
(404) 377-5540 FAX: (404) 377-5539
E-mail: rstroud@stsi.net

Julie M. T. Walker, Judge
City Court of Atlanta
104 Trinity Avenue, S.W.
Atlanta, Georgia 30335
(404) 658-6919 FAX: 658-7053
E-mail: jmtwalker@ci.atlanta.ga.us

Pro Hac Vice Judges

Jacqueline D. Bennett, Pro Hac Vice Judge
Atlanta Municipal Court
170 Garnett Street, S.W.
Atlanta, Georgia 30303
(404) 865-8100 FAX: (404) 658-6805

Linda Y. Bratton-Haynes, Pro Hac Vice Judge
Juvenile Court of DeKalb County
1947 East Gate Drive
Stone Mountain, Georgia 30087-6018
(404) 638-1736 FAX: (770) 638-1737
E-mail: lbhaynes@bellsouth.com

Myra Dickson, Pro Hac Vice Judge
Traffic Court
City Court of Atlanta
104 Trinity Avenue
Atlanta, Georgia 30335
(404) 865-6919 FAX: (404) 658-7125

Wesley M. Mathews, Pro Hac Vice Judge
Atlanta Municipal Court
170 Garnett Street, S.W.
Atlanta, Georgia 30335
(404) 865-8100 FAX: (404) 658-6805

A. Kenneth Secret, Pro Hac Vice Judge
City Court of Atlanta
Axam, Adams & Secret
1280 W. Peachtree Street, Suite 310
Atlanta, Georgia 30309
(404) 872-9800 FAX: (404) 897-1376
E-mail: akilesq@aol.com

Benjamin Spalding, Pro Hac Vice Judge
Atlanta Municipal Court
& Magistrate Judge
Magistrate Court of Fulton County
3480 Greenbriar Parkway, Suite 206A
Atlanta, Georgia 30331-3123
(404) 349-2121 FAX: (404) 349-2121

County Recorders Court Judges

Joyce M. Averlis, Chief Judge
Recorders Court of DeKalb County
3630 Camp Circle
Decatur, Georgia 30032
(404) 294-2635 FAX: (404) 294-2148
E-mail: SMTP:JMAVERIL@co.dekalb.ga.us

LeRoy Burke, III, Judge
Recorders Court of Chatham County
133 Montgomery Street, Room 104
Savannah, Georgia 31401
(912) 652-7429 FAX: (912) 525-1654
E-mail: lburke@ci.savannah.ga.us

Angela T. Butts, Judge
Recorders Court of DeKalb County
3630 Camp Circle
Decatur, Georgia 30032-1394
(404) 294-2635 FAX: (404) 294-2148

Lester B. Johnson, III, Judge
Recorders Court of Chatham County
Post Office Box 8285
Savannah, Georgia 31412-8285
(912) 238-5100 FAX: (912) 238-5378

Magistrate Court Judges

JoAnn Bayneum,Chief Magistrate Judge
Magistrate Court of Fulton County
Fulton County Courthouse, Suite C-669
136 Pryor Street, S.W.
Atlanta, Georgia 30303-4565
(404) 730-4552 FAX: (404) 893-2683

Winston P. Bethel, Chief Magistrate Judge
Magistrate Court of DeKalb County
807 KeKalb County Courthouse
556 North McDonough Street
Decatur, Georgia 30030
(404) 371-4766 FAX: (404) 371-2986
E-mail: wpbethel@co.dekalb.ga.us

Jimmy R. Bomar, Magistrate Judge
Magistrate Court of Liberty County
Post Office Box 912
Hinesville, Georgia 31310
(912) 876-2343 FAX: (912) 876-2474

Robert L. Burton, Magistrate Judge
Magistrate Court of Hancock County
Route 1, Box 478
Sparta, Georgia 31087
(706) 444-6234 FAX: (706) 444-6221

Barbara H. Caldwell, Magistrate Judge
Magistrate Court of Douglas County
8700 Hospital Drive
Douglasville, Georgia 30134
(770) 949-2000

Vivian L. Cummings, Magistrate Judge
Magistrate Court of Wilkinson County
Post Office Box 201
Irwinton, Georgia 31042-0201
(912) 946-2222 FAX: (912) 946-1497

Fred C. Eady, Magistrate Judge
Magistrate Court of Fulton County
526 Flint Trail
Jonesboro, Georgia 30236
(770) 603-2714 FAX: (770) 603-2715
E-mail: eadylaw@aol.com

Ronald J. Freeman, Magistrate Judge
Magistrate Court of Fulton County
1069 Spring Street, N.W.
Atlanta, Georgia 30309
(404) 873-0093 FAX: (404) 873-2311
E-mail: attyrif@aol.com

Ural Glanville, Magistrate Judge
Magistrate Court of Fulton County
T-2755 Justice Center Tower
185 Central Avenue, S.W.
Atlanta, Georgia 30303
(404) 730-4362 FAX: (404) 224-0579
E-mail: ural.glanville@cjisful.net

Divida Gude, Magistrate Judge
Magistrate Court of Fulton County
70 Fairlie Street, N.W., Suite 410
Atlanta, Georgia 30303
(404) 688-5548 FAX: (404) 522-0076
E-mail: dividag@aol.com

Henry C. Johnson, Jr., Magistrate Judge
Magistrate Court of DeKalb County
4319 Covington Highway, Suite 117-A
Decatur, Georgia 30035
(404) 534-9166 FAX: (404) 534-9160

George O. Lawson, Sr., Magistrate Judge
Magistrate Court of Fulton County
970 Martin Luther King, Jr. Drive, S.W., Suite 202
Atlanta, Georgia 30314
(404) 522-6964 FAX: (404) 522-6972
E-mail: geolawson@mindspring.com

Charles W. Manning, Magistrate Judge
Magistrate Court of Laurens County
Post Office Box 1008
400 Hester Drive
Dublin, Georgia 31040-1008
(912) 272-3786 FAX: (912) 277-2913

Sue McWaters, Magistrate Judge
Magistrate Court of Troup County
119 Ridley Avenue
LaGrange, Georgia 30240
(706) 882-5235 FAX: (706) 883-1623

Dorothy Pertilla, Magistrate Judge
Magistrate Court of Bibb County
100 Bibb County Courthouse
Macon, Georgia 31201
(912) 749-6505 FAX: (912) 722-5862

Gail Sims, Magistrate Judge
Magistrate Court of Crisp County
318 West 26th Avenue
Cordele, Georgia 31015
(912) 276-2618 FAX: (912) 276-2675

Linwood Slayton, Magistrate Judge
Superior Court of Fulton County
Post Office Box 55557
Atlanta, Georgia 30308
(404) 888-9602 FAX: (404) 888-9444
E-mail: linwood@africana.com

Benjamin W. Spaulding, Magistrate
Fulton County
Magistrate Court of Fulton County
5480 Greenbriar Parkway, Suite 250
Atlanta, Georgia 30331-3123
(404) 349-2121 FAX: (404) 658-6805

Cornell Stevens, Magistrate Judge
Magistrate Court of DeKalb County
4400 Camp Circle
Decatur, Georgia 30340
(404) 294-2150 FAX: (404) 294-2145

Alma Young Tuff, Magistrate Judge
Magistrate Court of Burke County
Post Office Box 401
Waynesboro, Georgia 30830-0401
(706) 554-4281 FAX: (706) 554-8772

R. David Ware, Magistrate Judge
Magistrate Court of Fulton County
230 Peachtree Street, Suite 2400
Atlanta, Georgia 30303-1557
(404) 525-8622 FAX: (404) 525-6955
E-mail: rdware@aol.com

Ethel P. Douse f/k/a **Ethel P. Woodward**
Magistrate Judge
Magistrate Court of Burke County
Post Office Box 401
Waynesboro, Georgia 30830-0401
(706) 554-4281 FAX: 9706) 554-8772

Administrative Law Judges

Noreen Banks-Ware, Administrative Law Judge
Office of State Administrative Hearings
3636 Panola Road
Lithonia, Georgia 30038
(770) 593-9849 FAX: (770) 593-9851
E-mail: nbwlaw@mindspring.com

Patrice Brown, Administrative Law Judge
Office of State Board Administrative Hearings
235 Peachtree Street, N.E., Suite 700
Atlanta, Georgia 30303-1299
(404) 657-2800 FAX: (404) 651-7845
E-mail: pbrown@osah.state.ga.us

William Churchill, Administrative Law Judge
Office of State Board Administrative Hearings
235 Peachtree Street, N.E., Suite 700
Atlanta, Georgia 30303-1299
(404) 657-2800 FAX: (404) 651-7845
E-mail: wchurchill@osah.state.ga.us

Donald Dotson, Administrative Law Judge
Office of State Board Administrative Hearings
235 Peachtree Street, N.E., Suite 700
Atlanta, Georgia 30303-1299
(404) 657-2800 FAX: (404) 651-7845
E-mail: ddotson@osah.state.ga.us

Viola Drew, Chief Administrative Law Judge
State Board of Workers' Compensation
270 Peachtree Street
Atlanta, Georgia 30303-1299
(404) 656-7772 FAX: (404) 657-6018

Phillip Jackson, Administrative Law Judge
Office of State Board Administrative Hearings
235 Peachtree Street, N.E., Suite 700
Atlanta, Georgia 30303-1299
(404) 657-2800 FAX: (404) 651-7845
E-mail: pjackson@osah.state.ga.us

Johnny W. Mason, Jr.
Chief Administrative Law Judge
Office of State Administrative Hearings
235 Peachtree Street, N.E., Suite 700
Atlanta, Georgia 30303-1299
(404) 656-3508 FAX: (404) 651-7845

Carol Walker-Russell, Administrative Law Judge
Office of State Board Administrative Hearings
235 Peachtree Street, N.E., Suite 700
Atlanta, Georgia 30303-1299
(404) 657-2800 FAX: (404) 651-7845
E-mail: crussell@osah.state.ga.us

Albert W. Thompson
Administrative Law Judge (Retired)
Post Office Box 587
Columbus, Georgia 31902
(706) 649-7372

GUAM: (0)

HAWAII: (1)

Sandra A. Simms
Circuit Court of the First Circuit
Post Office Box 619
Honolulu, Hawaii 96813
(808) 538-5236 FAX: (808) 538-5118

IDAHO: (0)

ILLINOIS: (115)

FEDERAL

Ann Claire Williams, Judge
U. S. Court of Appeals
for the Seventh Circuit
Everett McKinley Dirksen
U. S. Courthouse
219 South Dearborn Street
Chicago, Illinois 60604
(312) 435-5532 FAX: (312) 408-5141

David H. Coar, Judge
U. S. District Court
for the Northern District of Illinois
Everett McKinley Dirksen
U. S. Courthouse - Suite 1478
219 South Dearborn Street
Chicago, Illinois 60604
(312) 435-5648 FAX: (312) 554-8572

William J. Hibbler, Judge
U. S. District Court
for the Northern District of Illinois
Everett McKinley Dirksen
U. S. Courthouse - Suite 1746
219 South Dearborn Street
Chicago, Illinois 60604
(312) 435-5613 FAX: (312) 554-8469

Blanche M. Manning, Judge
U. S. District Court
for the Northern District of Illinois
Everett McKinley Dirksen
U. S. Courthouse - Suite 2156
219 South Dearborn Street
Chicago, Illinois 60604
(312) 435-7608 FAX: (312) 554-8512

Joe Billy McDade, Chief Judge
U. S. District Court
for the Central District of Illinois
122 Federal Building
100 N.E. Monroe Street - #122
Peoria, Illinois 61602
(309) 671-7821 FAX: (309) 671-7120

Arlander Keys, Presiding Magistrate Judge
U. S. District Court
for the Northern District of Illinois
Everett McKinley Dirksen
U. S. Courthouse - Room 2578
219 South Dearborn Street
Chicago, Illinois 60604
(312) 435-5630 FAX: (312) 554-8546

W. Thomas Rosemond, Jr., Magistrate Judge
U. S. District Court
for the Northern District of Illinois
Everett McKinley Dirksen
U. S. Courthouse - Room 2240
219 South Dearborn Street
Chicago, Illinois 60604
(312) 435-5638 FAX: (312) 554-8541

Administrative Law Judges

Alfred G. Burton, Jr., Administrative Law Judge
Office of Hearings & Appeals
Social Security Administration
55 West Monroe Street, Suite 700
Chicago, Illinois 60603
(312) 353-7754 or 353-1873 FAX: (312) 750-9108
E-mail: Alfred.Burton@ssa.gov

Percival Harmon, Administrative Law Judge
Office of Hearings & Appeals
Social Security Administration
55 West Monroe Street, Suite 700
Chicago, Illinois 60603
(312) 353-8377 or 353-1873 FAX: (312) 750-9108

Christine Holtz, Administrative Law Judge
Office of Hearings and Appeals
Social Security Administration
55 West Monroe Street, Suite #700
Chicago, Illinois 60603
(312) 353-8377, 353-1873 or 353-5856
FAX: (312) 750-9108

STATE

Supreme Court

Charles E. Freeman, Justice
Supreme Court of Illinois
160 North LaSalle Street - 20th Floor
Chicago, Illinois 60601
(312) 793-5480 FAX: (312) 793-4578

Courts of Appeals

Calvin C. Campbell, Presiding Justice
Appellate Court of Illinois
1st Judicial District - 6th Division
160 North LaSalle Street - Suite S1508
Chicago, Illinois 60601
(312) 793-5442 FAX: (312) 793-2616

William Cousins, Jr., Justice
Appellate Court of Illinois
1st Judicial District - 2nd Division
160 North LaSalle Street - Suite S-1905
Chicago, Illinois 60601
(312) 793-5424, 793-5426 or (773) 374-0910
FAX: (312) 793-2596

Shelvin Louise Marie Hall, Presiding Justice
Appellate Court of Illinois
1st Judicial District - 3rd Division
160 North LaSalle Street - Suite 1910
Chicago, Illinois 60601
(312) 793-5438 FAX: (312) 793-2596
E-mail: slmhall@dellnet.com

Ellis E. Reid, Justice
Appellate Court of Illinois
1st Judicial District
160 North LaSalle Street - Suite N 1506
Chicago, Illinois 60608
(312) 793-4403 FAX: (312) 793-2622

Leslie E. South, Justice
Appellate Court of Illinois
1st Judicial District - 4th Division
160 North LaSalle Street - Suite N-1607
Chicago, Illinois 60601
(312) 793-5450 FAX: (312) 793-2599

Glenn T. Johnson, Justice (Retired)
Appellate Court of Illinois
5050 Lake Shore Drive, Suite 2203-5
Chicago, Illinois 60615
(773) 493-1628

Carl McCormick, Justice (Retired)
Appellate Court of Illinois
Now Chief Attorney
Cook County Forest Preserve District
69 West Washington Street - Suite 2220
Chicago, Illinois 60602
(312) 603-0200 FAX: (312) 603-9850

R. Eugene Pincham, Justice (Retired)
Appellate Court of Illinois
1st Judicial District
9316 South Michigan Avenue
Chicago, Illinois 60619
(773) 568-7927 FAX: (773) 568-7938

Circuit Court Judges

Patricia Banks, Judge
Circuit Court of Cook County
3004 Richard J. Daley Center
50 West Washington Street
Chicago, Illinois 60602
(312) 603-4605 FAX: (312) 603-5199
or (312) 808-0017

Cynthia Brim, Judge
Circuit Court of Cook County
10221 South 76th Avenue, Room 109A
Chicago, Illinois 60455
(708) 974-6542 FAX: (708) 974-6021

Rodney Hughes Brooks, Judge
Circuit Court of Cook County
1100 South Hamilton, Room 365
Chicago, Illinois 60612
(312) 433-4757 FAX: (312) 433-4515

F. Keith Brown, Judge
Circuit Court of Kane County
37 W777 Route 38, Suite 400B
St. Charles, Illinois 60175
(630) 232-5820 FAX: (630) 406-7123 or 406-7121

Bernetta D. Bush, Judge
Circuit Court of Cook County
2008 Richard J. Daley Center
50 West Washington Street
Chicago, Illinois 60602
(312) 603-5926 FAX: (312) 603-4351

Evelyn B. Clay, Judge
Circuit Court of Cook County
2600 South California Avenue, Room 305
Chicago, Illinois 60608
(773) 869-7443 FAX: (773) 869-4440

Sharon Johnson Coleman, Judge
Circuit Court of Cook County
1100 South Hamilton Avenue, Room 6021
Chicago, Illinois 60612
(312) 603-6020 FAX: (312) 603-4351

Jacqueline P. Cox, Presiding Judge
1st Municipal District
Circuit Court of Cook County
Presiding Judge of First Municipal District
1303 Richard J. Daley Center
50 West Washington Street
Chicago, Illinois 60602
(312) 603-6132 FAX: (312) 629-6622

Wilbur E. Crooks, Judge
Circuit Court of Cook County
2600 South California Avenue - Room 101
Chicago, Illinois 60608
(773) 869-3049 FAX: (773) 869-4440

Loretta Daniels, Judge
Circuit Court of Cook County
Richard J. Daley Center
50 West Washington Street
Chicago, Illinois 60602
(312) 822-3530 FAX: (312) 822-3640

Timothy C. Evans, Judge
Circuit Court of Cook County
1901 Richard J. Daley Center
50 West Washington Street
Chicago, Illinois 60602
(312) 603-6556 FAX: (312) 603-6453

Donna Felton, Judge
Circuit Court of Cook County
Richard J. Daley Center
50 West Washington Street
Chicago, Illinois 60602
(312) 822-3530 FAX: (312) 822-3640

Raymond Funderburk, Judge
Circuit Court of Cook County
1102 Richard J. Daley Center
50 West Washington Street
Chicago, Illinois 60602
(312) 603-4545 FAX: (312) 603-4211

Llwellyn Greene-Thapedi, Judge
Circuit Court of Cook County
1106 Richard J. Daley Center
50 West Washington Street
Chicago, Illinois 60602
(312) 603-4548 FAX: (312) 603-4211

Sophia H. Hall, Judge
Circuit Court of Cook County
1407 Richard J. Daley Center
50 West Washington Street
Chicago, Illinois 60602
(312) 603-3733 FAX: (312) 603-5576

R. Morgan Hamilton, Judge
Circuit Court of Cook County
1508 Richard J. Daley Center
50 West Washington Street
Chicago, Illinois 60602
(312) 603-4808 FAX: (312) 603-4351

LeQuietta J. Hardy, Judge
Circuit Court of Cook County
3006 Richard J. Daley Center
Chicago, Illinois 60602
(312) 603-6417 FAX: (312) 603-5199

Marsha D. Hayes, Judge
Circuit Court of Cook County
1711 Richard J. Daley Center
50 West Washington Street
Chicago, Illinois 61612
(312) 603-5113 or 603-7547 FAX: (312) 603-4351

Curtis Heaston, Presiding Judge
Juvenile Justice Division
Circuit Court of Cook County
1100 South Hamilton Avenue
Chicago, Illinois 60612
(312) 443-4757 FAX: (312) 433-6591

Leo E. Holt, Judge
Circuit Court of Cook County
2600 South California, Room 201
Chicago, Illinois 60608
(773) 869-7431 FAX: (773) 869-4440

Vanessa A. Hopkins, Judge
Circuit Court of Cook County
1302 Richard J. Daley Center
50 West Washington Street
Chicago, Illinois 60602
(312) 603-4805 FAX: (312) 603-4351

Nathaniel R. Howse, Jr., Judge
Circuit Court of Cook County
1401 Richard J. Daley Center
Chicago, Illinois 60612
(312) 603-4371 FAX: (312) 603-5576

Arnette R. Hubbard, Judge
Circuit Court of Cook County
1106 Richard J. Daley Center
Chicago, Illinois 60602
(312) 603-4548 FAX: (312) 603-4211

Cheyrl D. Ingram, Judge
Circuit Court of Cook County
1500 Maybrook Drive, Room 139
Maywood, Illinois 60153
(708) 865-6060 FAX: (708) 865-4952

Dorothy F. Jones, Judge
Circuit Court of Cook County
1308 Richard J. Daley Center
50 West Washington Street
Chicago, Illinois 60602
(312) 603-3484 FAX: (603) 603-4351

Rickey Jones, Judge
Circuit Court of Cook County
2600 South California Avenue - Room 303
Chicago, Illinois 60605
(773) 869-3323 FAX: (773) 869-4440

Sidney A. Jones, III, Judge
Circuit Court of Cook County
2301 Richard J. Daley Center
50 West Washington Street
Chicago, Illinois 60602
(312) 603-7996 FAX: (312) 603-6787

Bertina E. Lampkin, Judge
Circuit Court of Cook County
2600 South California Avenue - Room 506
Chicago, Illinois 60608
(773) 869-3196 FAX: (773) 869-4440

Marjorie C. Laws, Judge
Circuit Court of Cook County
2600 South California Avenue, Room 303
Chicago, Illinois 60608
(773) 869-3049 FAX: (773) 433-4515 or 433-6591

Gay Lloyd Lott, Judge
Circuit Court of Cook County
32 West Randolph Street, Room 1401R
Chicago, Illinois 60602
(312) 609-3790 FAX: (312) 609-3779

Patricia M. Martin-Bishop, Presiding Judge
Child Protection Division
Circuit Court of Cook County
1100 South Hamilton Avenue
Chicago, Illinois 60612
(312) 433-4756 FAX: (312) 603-4351

Janice R. McGaughey, Judge
Circuit Court of Cook County
1303 Richard J. Daley Center
50 West Washington Street
Chicago, Illinois 60602
(312) 603-7959 FAX: (312) 603-4351

Judy I. Mitchell-Davis, Judge
Circuit Court of Cook County
1500 Maybrook Drive, Room 299
Chicago, Illinois 60153
(708) 865-6060 FAX: (708) 865-4952

Elliott Muse, Jr., Judge
Circuit Court of Cook County
16501 South Kedzie Parkway, Room 203
Markham, Illinois 60426
(708) 210-4170 FAX: (708) 210-4441

Raymond Myles, Judge
Circuit Court of Cook County
1100 South Hamilton Avenue - Room G025
Chicago, Illinois 60612
(312) 433-4756 FAX: (312) 603-4351

P. Scott Neville, Jr., Judge
Circuit Court of Cook County
1101 Richard J. Daley Center
50 West Washington Street, Suite 2600
Chicago, Illinois 60602
(312) 603-4415 FAX: (312) 603-5366

William D. O'Neal, Judge
Circuit Court of Cook County
16501 South Kedzie Parkway, Room 204
Markham, Illinois 60426
(708) 210-4170 FAX: (708) 210-4441

James L. Rhodes, Judge
Circuit Court of Cook County
16501 South Kedzie Parkway - Room 107
Markham, Illinois 60426
(708) 210-4170 FAX: (708) 210-4441

Ronald C. Riley, Presiding Judge
6th Municipal District
Circuit Court of Cook County
16501 South Kedzie Parkway
Markham, Illinois 60426
(708) 210-4170 FAX: (708) 210-4441

Drella C. Savage, Judge
Circuit Court of Cook County
32 West Randolph, Room 1402
Chicago, Illinois 60602
(312) 609-3790 FAX: (312) 609-3779

Cheryl A. Hillard Starks, Judge
Circuit Court of Cook County
2103 Richard J. Daley Center
Chicago, Illinois 60602
(312) 603-4183 FAX: (312) 433-5199

John O. Steele, Judge
Circuit Court of Cook County
Richard J. Daley Center
50 West Washington Street, Suite 1603
Chicago, Illinois 60602
(312) 603-5938 FAX: (312) 603-4351

Victoria A. Stewart, Judge
Circuit Court of Cook County
727 East 111th Street
Chicago, Illinois 60628
(773) 660-0346 FAX: (312) 264-3997

Jane Louise Stuart, Judge
Circuit Court of Cook County
1406 Richard J. Daley Center
50 West Washington Street
Chicago, Illinois 60602
(312) 603-4867 FAX: (312) 603-4351

Michael W. Stuttley, Judge
Circuit Court of Cook County Juvenile Division
Markham County Courthouse
16501 South Kedzie Parkway, Room 099
Markham, Illinois 60426
(708) 210-4170 FAX: (708) 210-4689

Bill Taylor, Judge
Circuit Court of Cook County
2010 Richard J. Daley Center
50 West Washington Street
Chicago, Illinois 60602
(312) 603-5932 FAX: (312) 603-4211

Lawrence Terrell, Judge
Circuit Court of Cook County
1500 Maybrook Drive, Room 128
Maywood, Illinois 60153
(708) 865-6060 FAX: (708) 865-4952

Mary Maxwell Thomas, Judge
Circuit Court of Cook County
2600 South California Avenue, Room 604
Chicago, Illinois 60608
(773) 869-3183 or 869-4965
FAX: (773) 869-3147 or 869-4965

Amanda S. Toney, Judge
Circuit Court of Cook County
1304 Richard J. Daley Center
50 West Washington Street
Chicago, Illinois 60602
(312) 603-5007 FAX: (312) 603-4211

Edna M. Turkington, Judge
Circuit Court of Cook County
1410 Richard J. Daley Center
50 West Washington Street
Chicago, Illinois 60602
(312) 603-4871 FAX: (312) 603-4211

John D. Turner, Jr., Judge
Circuit Court of Cook County
16501 South Kedzie Parkway - Room 207
Markham, Illinois 60426
(708) 210-4170 FAX: (708) 210-4441

Milton S. Wharton, Judge
Circuit Court of St. Clair County
10 Public Square
Belleville, Illinois 62220
(618) 277-7325 FAX: (618) 277-1398

Willie M. Whiting, Judge
Circuit Court of Cook County
1408 Richard J. Daley Center
50 West Washington Street
Chicago, Illinois 60602
(312) 603-4869 FAX: (312) 603-4211

Shelli D. Williams-Hayes, Judge
Circuit Court of Cook County
1707A Richard J. Daley Center
50 West Washington Street
Chicago, Illinois 60602
(312) 603-7559 FAX: (312) 603-4351

Camille E. Willis, Judge
Circuit Court of Cook County
16501 South Kedzie Parkway, Room 101
Markham, Illinois 60612
(708) 210-4170 FAX: (708) 210-4441

E. Kenneth Wright, Jr., Judge
Circuit Court of Cook County
1808 Richard J. Daley Center
50 West Washington Street
Chicago, Illinois 60602
(312) 603-6466 FAX: (312) 603-4351

Anthony L. Young, Judge
Circuit Court of Cook County
1601 Richard J. Daley Center
Chicago, Illinois 60602
(312) 603-4845 FAX: (312) 603-5199

Circuit Court Associate Judges

Reginald H. Baker, Associate Judge
Circuit Court of Cook County
16501 South Kedzie Parkway - Room 103
Markham, Illinois 60426
(708) 210-4170 FAX: (708) 210-4441

Adam Donald Bourgeois, Jr., Associate Judge
Circuit Court of Cook County
155 West 51st Street
Chicago, Illinois 60609

Preston L. Bowie, Jr., Associate Judge
Circuit Court of Cook County
2600 South California, Room 203
Chicago, Illinois 60602
(773) 869-7413 FAX: (773) 869-3147

William Stewart Boyd, Associate Judge
Circuit Court of Cook County
1605 Richard J. Daley Center
Chicago, Illinois 60602
(312) 603-4836 FAX: (312) 603-4351

Michael Brown, Associate Judge
Circuit Court of Cook County
1100 South Hamilton Avenue - Room C019
Chicago, Illinois 60612
(312) 433-4756 FAX: (312) 603-4351

Wilbur E. Crooks, Associate Judge
Circuit Court of Cook County
2600 South California Avenue, Room 308
Chicago, Illinois 60608
(773) 869-3049 FAX: (773) 869-3147

Abishi C. Cunningham, Associate Judge
Circuit Court of Cook County
1108 Richard J. Daley Center
Chicago, Illinois 60602
(312) 603-4635 FAX: (312) 603-4211

Ellar Duff-Williams, Associate Judge
Circuit Court, 3rd Judicial Court
Madison County Courthouse
Edwardville, Illinois 62025
(618) 692-7040 Ext. 4416 FAX: (618) 692-0676

Marvin E. Gavin, Associate Judge
Circuit Court of Cook County
16501 South Kedzie Parkway, Room 104T
Markham, Illinois 60426
(708) 210-4170 FAX: (708) 210-4441

Patricia Brown Holmes, Associate Judge
Circuit Court of Cook County
1100 South Hamilton Avenue - Room G013
Chicago, Illinois 60612
(312) 433-4758 FAX: (312) 433-4515

Marianne Jackson, Associate Judge
Circuit Court of Cook County
1100 South Hamilton Avenue - Room G032
Chicago, Illinois 60612
(312) 433-4757 FAX: (312) 433-4515

Sandi G. Johnson-Speh, Associate Judge
Circuit Court of Cook County
10220 South 76th Avenue, Room 103A
Bridgeview, Illinois 60455
(708) 974-6534 FAX: (708) 974-6021

Theodis P. Lewis, Associate Judge
Sangamon County Circuit Court
200 South Ninth Street, Room 616
Springfield, Illinois 62701
(217) 753-6392 FAX: (217) 753-6357

Charles M. May, Associate Judge
Circuit Court of Cook County, Juvenile Division
1100 South Hamilton Avenue, Room G-18N
Chicago, Illinois 60612
(312) 433-4756 or 433-4757 FAX: (312) 433-4515

Alexis Diane Otis-Lewis, Associate Judge
Circuit Court, 20th Judicial Circuit
10 Public Square
Belleville, Illinois 62220
(618) 277-7325 FAX: (618) 277-1398

Marcus R. Salone, Associate Judge
Circuit Court of Cook County
2600 South California Avenue - Room 308
Chicago, Illinois 60608
(773) 869-7434 FAX: (773) 869-3147

Oliver M. Spurlock, Associate Judge
Circuit Court of Cook County
1303 Richard J. Daley Center
Chicago, Illinois 60602
(312) 603-4623 FAX: (312) 603-4351

Eddie A. Stephens, Associate Judge
Circuit Court of Cook County
1100 South Hamilton Avenue - Room C031
Chicago, Illinois 60612
(312) 433-4758 FAX: (312) 433-4515

Thomas Sumner, Associate Judge
Circuit Court of Cook County
2600 South California Avenue, Room 206
Chicago, Illinois 60608
(773) 869-7416 FAX: (773) 869-3147

LaBrenda E. White, Associate Judge
Circuit Court of Cook County
10220 South 76th Avenue - Room 030A
Bridgeview, Illinois 60455
(708) 974-6295 FAX: (708) 974-6868

Walter Williams, Associate Judge
Circuit Court of Cook County
1303 Richard J. Daley Center
Chicago, Illinois 60602
(312) 603-7959 FAX: (312) 603-4351

William S. Wood, Associate Judge
Circuit Court of Cook County
2600 South California - Room 101
Chicago, Illinois 60608
(773) 869-3160 FAX: (773) 869-3147

Hearing Officer

Sybil Thomas, Hearing Officer
Child Protection Division
Circuit Court of Cook County
2245 West Ogden Avenue
Chicago, Illinois 60612
(312) 433-7827 FAX: (312) 433-7829

Retired Judges

Everette A. Braden, Judge (Retired)
Circuit Court of Cook County
8948 South Jeffrey
Chicago, Illinois 60617
(773) 721-8508

Clarence Bryant, Judge (Retired)
Circuit Court of Cook County
104[illegible] South King Drive
Chicago, Illinois 60628
(773) [illegible]-0346 FAX: (773) 264-3997

[illegible] Hamilton, Judge (Retired)
Circuit Court of Cook County
[illegible] South Michigan Avenue
Chicago, Illinois 60619
(773) [illegible]-3290

[illegible] Harris, Judge (Retired)
Circuit Court of Cook County
[illegible] South Rhodes Avenue
Chicago, Illinois 60619
(773) [illegible]-4103

[illegible] C. Johnson, Judge (Retired)
Circuit Court of Cook County
90[illegible] South Oakley Avenue
Chicago, Illinois 60620
(773) 233-1192 FAX: (773) 133-1192 #1

[illegible] Nicholson, Judge (Retired)
4940 East End Avenue
Chicago, Illinois 60615
(773) 643-5285

Albert S. Porter, Judge (Retired)
155 North Michigan Avenue, Suite 700
Chicago, Illinois 60601
(312) 946-1555 FAX: (312) 946-1556

D. Adolphus Rivers, Judge (Retired)
Circuit Court of Cook County
6947 South Cregier
Chicago, Illinois 60649
(773) 493-2780

John W. Rogers, Judge (Retired)
4800 South Chicago Beach, Apt. 1470N
Chicago, Illinois 60615

Earl E. Strayhorn, Judge (Retired)
Circuit Court of Cook County
2725 South Michigan
Chicago, Illinois 60616

Lucia T. Thomas, Judge (Retired)
Circuit Court of Cook County
737 East 93rd Street
Chicago, Illinois 60619-7703

Garland Watt, Judge (Retired)
Circuit Court of Cook County
Watt and Sawyer
53 West Jackson, Suite 1120
Chicago, Illinois 60604
(312) 663-1440 FAX: (312) 663-1410

James H. Williams, Judge (Retired)
Circuit Court of Cook County
2231 East 67th Street
Chicago, Illinois 60649
(773) 324-3998

Lawrence W. Carroll, Associate Judge (Retired)
Circuit Court of Cook County
16501 South Kedzie Parkway
Markham, Illinois 60427
(708) 210-4170

Calvin H. Hall, Associate Judge (Retired)
Circuit Court of Cook County
1735 East 91st Street
Chicago, Illinois 60617
(773) 731-3168

Wendell P. Marbly, Associate Judge (Retired)
Circuit Court of Cook County
155 W. 51st. Street
Chicago, Illinois 60609
(773) 373-8878

INDIANA: (18)

FEDERAL

Christine E. Dibble, Administrative Judge
U. S. Equal Employment Opportunity Commission
Indianapolis District Office
101 West Ohio Street, Suite 1900
Indianapolis, Indiana 46204-2403
(317) 226-7952 FAX: (317) 226-5571

STATE

Robert D. Rucker, Jr., Associate Justice
Indiana Supreme Court
312 State House
200 West Washington Street
Indianapolis, Indiana 46204-2732
(317) 232-2544 FAX: (317) 232-8372

Carr L. Darden, Judge
Indiana Court of Appeals
Merchants Plaza - 1270 South Tower
115 West Washington Street
Indianapolis, Indiana 46204-3419
(317) 232-6900 FAX: (317) 233-4627

Cynthia J. Ayers, Judge
Marion County Superior Court
Civil Division Room IV,
City-County Building - W442
200 East Washington Street
Indianapolis, Indiana 46204-3338
(317) 327-5084 FAX: (317) 327-4740

Taylor L. Baker, Jr., Judge
Marion Superior Court
Criminal Division 19
Center Tower, Room T442
200 East Washington Street
Indianapolis, Indiana 46204-3307
(317) 327-3885 FAX: (317) 327-4474

Clarence D. Bolden, Judge
Marion County Superior Court
Criminal Division 8
E-643 City-County Building
200 East Washington Street
Indianapolis, Indiana 46204
(317) 327-3202 FAX: (317) 327-3844

William L. Briggs, Judge
Allen County Superior Court - Room 208
715 South Calhoun Street
Fort Wayne, Indiana 46802-1805
(219) 428-7258 FAX: (219) 449-7432

William E. Davis, Judge
Lake Superior Court
Civil Division, Room II
3711 Main Street
East Chicago, Indiana 46312-2299
(219) 398-2443 FAX: (219) 392-0047

Z. Mae Jimison, Judge
Marion County Superior Court
Criminal Division 14
T-441 City-County Building
200 East Washington Street
Indianapolis, Indiana 46204-3307
(317) 327-5363 or 327-5365 FAX: (317) 327-3220
E-mail: Zjimison@Indygov.org

Sheila M. Moss, Judge
Lake Superior Court, Room Two
2293 North Main Street
Crown Point, Indiana 46307-1854
(219) 755-3580 FAX: (219) 755-3588

Viola J. Taliaferro, Judge
Monroe Circuit Court, Division VII
301 North College Avenue
Bloomington, Indiana 47404-3865
(812) 349-2629 FAX: (812) 349-2791

Tanya Walton-Pratt, Judge
Marion County Superior Court
Room #1 - W-202 City-County Building
200 East Washington Street
Indianapolis, Indiana 46204
(317) 327-4289 FAX: (317) 327-7835

Webster L. Brewer, Senior Judge
Marion County Superior Court 2
W-241 City-County Building
200 East Washington Street
Indianapolis, Indiana 46202
(317) 464-1463 FAX: (317) 632-1671

Gregory A. Gillis, Magistrate
Title IV-D Court
Lake Superior Court, Juvenile Division
400 Broadway, Room 107
Gary, Indiana 46402-1284
(219) 881-6053 FAX: (219) 881-6004

Jeffrey Miller, Magistrate
Lake County Superior Court
Juvenile Division, Second Floor
400 Broadway
Gary, Indiana 46402-1284
(219) 881-6133 FAX: (219) 881-6133

Lori K. Morgan, Magistrate
Allen Superior Court
715 South Calhoun Street, Room 208
Fort Wayne, Indiana 46802
(219) 499-4777 FAX: (219) 449-7432

Clarence D. Murray, Magistrate
Lake Superior Court
County Division II
2293 North Main Street
Crown Point, Indiana 46307
(219) 755-3580 FAX: (219) 755-3588

David A. Shaheed, Magistrate
Marion County Superior Court
W542 City-County Building
200 East Washington Street
Indianapolis, Indiana 46204
(317) 327-3870 FAX: (317) 327-3876

IOWA: (3)

George L. Stigler, Judge
First Judicial District
Black Hawk County Courthouse
316 East 5th Street
Waterloo, Iowa 50703-4774
(319) 291-2489 FAX: (312) 232-9934

Dennis J. Stovall, Judge
Fifth Judicial District of Iowa
Polk County Courthouse
5th & Mulberry Street
Des Moines, Iowa 50309-4238
(515) 286-3905 FAX: (515) 286-3858
E-mail: DJStovall@jb.state.ia.us

Jeffrey Harris, District Associate Judge
Grundy County Courthouse
700 G Avenue
Grundy Center, Iowa 50638
(319) 824-5244 FAX: (319) 824-3447

KANSAS: (8)

FEDERAL

Julie A. Robinson, Judge
U.S. Bankruptcy Court for the District of Kansas
225 U. S. Courthouse
444 Southeast Quincy
Topeka, Kansas 66683
(913) 295-2646 FAX: (913) 295-2964

Evelyn M. Gunn, Administrative Judge
U. S. Equal Employment Opportunity Commission
Kansas City Area Office, Gateway Tower II
400 State Avenue, Room 905
Kansas City, Kansas 66101
(913) 551-5844 FAX: (913) 551-6957

STATE

Court of Appeals

Henry W. Green, Jr., Judge
Kansas Court of Appeals
301 West 10th Street
Topeka, Kansas 66612-1507
(913) 296-5409 FAX: (913) 296-7079

Trial Court Judges

J. Dexter Burdette, Judge
District Court of Kansas
29th Judicial District, Division 5
Wyandotte County Courthouse
710 North 7th Street
Kansas City, Kansas 66101
(913) 573-2967 FAX: (913) 573-8105

Jennifer L. Jones, Judge
District Court of Kansas
18th Judicial District
Juvenile Dept. of the District Court
1015 South Minnesota Street
Wichita, Kansas 67211-2730
(316) 383-7487 FAX: (316) 383-8000

Cordell D. Meeks, Jr., Judge
District Court of Kansas
29th Judicial District, Division 6
Wyandotte County Courthouse
710 North 7th Street
Kansas City, Kansas 66101
(913) 573-2926 FAX: (913) 573-4134

Gregory L. Waller, Judge
District Court of Kansas
18th Judicial District
Sedgwick County Courthouse
525 North Main Street
Wichita, Kansas 67203-3790
(316) 383-7641 FAX: (316) 383-7560

Administrative Law Judge

Nelsonna Potts-Barnes
Administrative Law Judge
Workers' Compensation Court
110 E. Waterman
Wichita, Kansas 67202
(316) 264-0220 FAX: (316) 264-0687

KENTUCKY: (7)

STATE

Court of Appeals

William E. McAnuity, Jr., Judge
Kentucky Court of Appeals
700 West Jefferson Street
Division L - Suite 1010
Louisville, Kentucky 40202
(502) 595-3430 FAX: (502) 595-3432
E-mail: WilliamMcAnulty@mail.aoc.state.ky.us

Trial Court Judges

Gary D. Payne, Judge
Circuit Court 2nd Division
22nd Judicial District
215 West Main Street
Lexington, Kentucky 40507
(859) 246-2214 FAX: (859) 246-2139
E-mail: GaryP@mail.aoc.state.ky.us

Denise Clayton, Judge
Jefferson Family Court Division 7
13th Judicial District
Jefferson County Judicial Center
Hall of Justice
700 West Jefferson Street
Louisville, Kentucky 40202
(502) 595-4993 FAX: (502) 595-3495
E-mail: DeniseC@mail.aoc.state.ky.us

Pamela R. Goodwine, Judge
Fayette District Court
1st Division
22nd Judicial District
136 Martin Luther King Boulevard - Suite #300
Lexington, Kentucky 40507
(606) 246-2247 FAX: (606) 246-2614
E-mail: pgoodwine@mail.aoc.state.ky.us

Janice R. Martin, Judge
Jefferson District Court
13th Judicial District
600 West Jefferson Street
Louisville, Kentucky 40202
(502) 595-4999 FAX: (502) 595-3270
E-mail: JaniceM@mail.aoc.state.ky.us

Joan A. "Toni" Stringer, Judge
Jefferson District Court
30th Judicial District
Hall of Justice
600 West Jefferson Street
Louisville, Kentucky 40202
(502) 595-4960 FAX: (502) 595-3270
E-mail:JoanStringer@mail.aoc.ky.us

Ernest Jasmin, Judge (Retired)
Jefferson Circuit Court, Division 1
Hall of Justice
700 West Jefferson Street
Louisville, Kentucky 40202

LOUISIANA: (70)

FEDERAL

Carl E. Stewart, Judge
U. S. Court of Appeals for the Fifth Circuit
U. S. Courthouse - Suite 2299
300 Fannin Street
Shreveport, Louisiana 71101-3074
(318) 676-3765 FAX: (318) 676-3768

Ivan L. R. Lemelle, Judge
U. S. District Court
for the Eastern District of Louisiana
C525 U. S. Courthouse
500 Camp Street
New Orleans, Louisiana 70130-3318
(504) 589-7555 FAX: (504) 589-7623

Ralph Tyson, Judge
U. S. District Court
for the Middle District of Louisiana
777 Florida Street, Room 301
Baton Rouge, Louisiana 70801
(225) 389-3634 FAX: (225) 389-3501

Louis Moore, Jr., Magistrate Judge
U. S. District Court
for the Eastern District of Louisiana
B-409 Hale Boggs Federal Building
501 Magazine Street
New Orleans, Louisiana 70130
(504) 589-7625 FAX: (504) 589-7628

STATE

Supreme Court

Bernette Joshua Johnson
Associate Justice, Supreme Court
301 Loyola Avenue
New Orleans, Louisiana 70112
(504) 568-8062 or 568-5707 FAX: (504) 599-1120

Court of Appeals

Joan Bernard Armstrong, Judge
Fourth Circuit Court of Appeal
1515 Poydras Street - Seventh Floor
New Orleans, Louisiana 70112
(504) 568-4707 FAX: (504) 568-4730

Dennis R. Bagneris, Sr., Judge
Fourth Circuit Court of Appeal
1515 Poydras Street - Seventh Floor
New Orleans, Louisiana 70112
(504) 592-0901 FAX: (504) 568-4730
E-mail: drb@4thcir-app.state.La.us

Sylvia R. Cooks, Judge
Third Circuit Court of Appeal
Post Office Box 3841
Lafayette, Louisiana 70502-3841
(318) 235-2196 FAX: (318) 235-0026

John Guidry, Judge
First Circuit Court of Appeal
1600 North Third Street
Baton Rouge, Louisiana 70802
(225) 342-1065 FAX: (225) 342-8942
E-mail: jguidry@La.fcca.org

Charles R. Jones, Judge
Fourth Circuit Court of Appeal
1515 Poydras Street - Seventh Floor
New Orleans, Louisiana 70112
(504) 592-0917 FAX: (504) 592-0996
E-mail:crj@4thcir-app.state.La.us

Terri Fleming Love, Judge
Fourth Circuit Court of Appeals
1515 Poydras Street
New Orleans, Louisiana 70112
(504) 592-0921 FAX: (504) 568-4730
E-mail: tfl@4thcir-app.state.La.us

James Stewart, Judge
Second Circuit Court of Appeal
430 Fannin Street
Shreveport, Louisiana 71101
(318) 227-3740 FAX: (318) 227-3708

Ulysses Gene Thibodeaux, Judge
Third Circuit Court of Appeal
Post Office Box 16577
Lake Charles, Louisiana 70602-6577
(318) 433-9403 FAX: (318) 491-2830

Felicia Toney Williams, Judge
Second Circuit Court of Appeal
430 Fannin Street
Shreveport, Louisiana 71101
(318) 227-3744 FAX: (318) 227-3774
E-mail: fwilliams@Lasccoa.state.La.us

Trial Court Judges

Curtis A. Calloway, Judge
District Court
Nineteenth Judicial District
222 St. Louis Street - Suite 831
Baton Rouge, Louisiana 70801
(225) 389-4737 FAX: (225) 389-8616

Wilfred D. Carter, Judge
District Court
Fourteenth Judicial District
Post Office Box 3210
Lake Charles, Louisiana 70602-3210
(318) 437-3530 FAX: (318) 437-3332

Janice Clark, Judge
District Court
Nineteenth Judicial District
222 St. Louis Street - Suite 816
Baton Rouge, Louisiana 70802
(225) 389-5012 FAX: (225) 389-8780

Randy E. Collins, Judge
District Court
First Judicial District
1230 Texas Avenue, Room J1
Shreveport, Louisiana 71101
(318) 673-5879 FAX: (318) 773-5813

Jules D. Edwards, III, Judge
District Court
Fifteenth Judicial District
Post Office Drawer 3568
Lafayette, Louisiana 70502-3568
(318) 269-5708 FAX: (318) 269-5726

Leon Emanuel III, Judge
District Court
First Judicial District
501 Texas Street, Suite 300-A
Shreveport, Louisiana 71101
(318) 226-6812 FAX: (318) 429-7615

Ramona Emanuel, Judge
District Court
First Judicial District
501 Texas Street, Room 300-A
Shreveport, Louisiana 71101
(318) 226-6812 FAX: (318) 429-7615

Alcide J. Gray, Judge
District Court
Fourteenth Judicial District
Post Office Box 3210
Lake Charles, Louisiana 70602
(318) 437-3530 FAX: (318) 437-3332

Alan J. Green, Judge
District Court
Twenty-Fourth Judicial District
Second and Derbigny Street
Gretna, Louisiana 70053
(504) 364-3866 FAX: (504) 365-3383
E-mail: alang@24jdc.co.jefferson.La.us

Alonzo Harris, Sr., Judge
District Court
Twenty-Seventh Judicial District Courthouse
Post Office Box 473
Opelousas, Louisiana 70571
(337) 948-0584 FAX: (337) 948-0583
E-mail: ah27thjda@aol.com

Sarah Harris, Judge
District Court
Eighteenth Judicial District
Post Office Box 426
Iberville Parish Courthouse
Plaquemine, Louisiana 70765-0426
(504) 687-5230 FAX: (504) 687-1225
Point Coupee Office: (504) 627-4548
Baton Rouge Office: (504) 389-8765
E-mail: judgesh@eatel.net

Bonnie Jackson, Judge
District Court
Nineteenth Judicial District
222 St. Louis Street - Suite 683
Baton Rouge, Louisiana 70801
(225) 398-4755 FAX: (225) 389-4856

Madeline Jasmine, Judge
District Court
Fortieth Judicial District- Division A Courthouse
Post Office Box 277
Edgard, Louisiana 70049
(504) 497-3315 FAX: (504) 497-5399

Don Johnson, Judge
District Court
Nineteenth Judicial District
222 St. Louis Street - Suite 623
Baton Rouge, Louisiana 70802
(225) 389-4717 FAX: (225) 389-8941

Donald T. Johnson, Judge
District Court
Fourth Judicial District - Division A
Rapides Parish Courthouse
700 Murray Street
Alexandria, Louisiana 71309
(318) 443-6893 FAX: (318) 484-2704

Benjamin Jones, Judge
Fourth Judicial District
300 St. John Street
Monroe, Louisiana 71201
(318) 361-2250 FAX: (318) 361-2273
E-mail: bjonesjd@4jdc.com

George C. Metoyer, Jr., Judge
District Court
Fourth Judicial District
Rapides Parish Courthouse
701 Murray Street
Alexandria, Louisiana 71301
(318) 473-6893 FAX: (318) 484-2704

John D. Mosely, Jr., Judge
District Court
First Judicial District
Texas Street, Suite 620
Shreveport, Louisiana 71101
(318) 226-6966 FAX: (318) 226-6538

Charles Porter, Judge
District Court
Sixteenth Judicial District
210 Courthouse, Suite 210
300 Iberia Street
New Iberia, Louisiana 70560
(318) 369-4410 FAX: (318) 369-4456
E-mail: judgeporter@aisp.net

Edward Rubin, Judge
District Court
Fifteenth Judicial District
Post Office Drawer 3568
Lafayette, Louisiana 70502-3568
(318) 232-8211 FAX: (318) 269-5746

Alvin Sharp, Judge
District Court
Fourth Judicial District
300 St. John Street - Division 1
Monroe, Louisiana 71201
(318) 361-2273 FAX: (318) 361-2273
E-mail: asharp@4jdc.com

Carl Van Sharp, Judge
District Court
Fourth Judicial District
300 St. John Street
Monroe, Louisiana 71201
(318) 361-2250 FAX: (318) 361-2273
E-mail: csharp@4jdc.com

Alvin Turner, Jr., Judge
District Court
Twenty-Third Judicial District
828-202 South Irma Boulevard
Gonzales, Louisiana 70737
(225) 621-8500 FAX: (225) 647-9975
E-mail: courthse@eatel.net

Michael Walker, Judge
District Court
First Judicial District
501 Texas Street, Room 300-C
Shreveport, Louisiana 71101
(318) 226-6823 FAX: (318) 424-3725

Carl J. Williams, Judge
District Court
Sixteenth Judicial District
Post Office Box 626
St. Martinville, Louisiana 70582
(318) 394-2253 FAX: (318) 394-2225
E-mail: cwilliams@aisp.net

Melvin C. Zeno, Judge
District Court
Twenty-Fourth Judicial District
Courthouse Annex
Second and Derbigny Street
Gretna, Louisiana 70053
(504) 364-3975 FAX: (504) 365-3380

Marie A. Bookman, Judge
Criminal District Court of Orleans Parish
2700 Tulane Avenue, M-2
New Orleans, Louisiana 70119
(504) 827-3440 FAX: (504) 826-5599

Charles Elloie, Judge
Criminal District Court of Orleans Parish
2700 Tulane Avenue
New Orleans, Louisiana 70119
(504) 827-3490 FAX: (504) 827-3497

Arthur L. Hunter, Jr., Judge
Criminal District Court of Orleans Parish
2700 Tulane Avenue
New Orleans, Louisiana 70119
(504) 826-5503 FAX: (504) 826-5501

Sharon K. Hunter, Judge
Criminal District Court of Orleans Parish
2700 Tulane Avenue
New Orleans, Louisiana 70119
(504) 827-3434 FAX: (504) 826-2988

Calvin Johnson, Judge
Criminal District Court of Orleans Parish
2700 Tulane Avenue
New Orleans, Louisiana 70119
(504) 827-3482 FAX: (504) 826-5152
E-mail: fourwakes@aol.com

Julian Parker, Judge
Criminal District Court
of Orleans Parish
2700 Tulane Avenue
New Orleans, Louisiana 70119
(504) 827-3462 FAX: (504) 826-5167

Michael Bagneris, Judge
Civil District Court
of Orleans Parish
421 Loyola Avenue - Suite 304
New Orleans, Louisiana 70112
(504) 592-9337 FAX: (504) 552-5820
E-mail: bagneris@acadiacom.net

Carolyn Gill-Jefferson, Judge
Civil District Court of Orleans Parish
421 Loyola Avenue - Suite 303
New Orleans, Louisiana 70112
(504) 592-9200 FAX: (504) 558-9342
E-mail: gilljeff@acadiacom.net

Ethel Simms Julien, Judge
Civil District
Court of Orleans Parish
421 Loyola Avenue - Suite 312
New Orleans, Louisiana 70112
(504) 592-9254 FAX: (504) 558-9038
E-mail: julien@acadiacom.net

C. Hunter King, Judge
Civil District
Court of Orleans Parish
Division M
421 Loyola Avenue
New Orleans, Louisiana 70112
(504) 592-9250 FAX: (504) 558-0257

Rose Ledet, Judge
Civil District Court of Orleans Parish
Division B
421 Loyola Avenue
New Orleans, Louisiana 70112
(504) 592-9204 FAX: (504) 522-3552

Yada T. Magee, Judge
Civil District Court of Orleans Parish
421 Loyola Avenue - Suite 302
New Orleans, Louisiana 70112
(504) 592-9216 FAX: (504) 522-2660
E-mail: ymagee@acadiacom.net

Lloyd J. Medley, Jr., Judge
Civil District Court of Orleans Parish
421 Loyola Avenue
New Orleans, Louisiana 70112
(504) 592-9222 FAX: (504) 558-0060
E-mail: lj@acadiacom.net

Nadine Ramsey, Judge
Civil District Court of Orleans Parish
421 Loyola Avenue
New Orleans, Louisiana 70112
(504) 592-9230 FAX: (504) 680-8427
E-mail: nramsey@acadiacom.net

Luke A. LaVergne, Judge
Family Court of East Baton Rouge Parish
222 St. Louis Street, Room 948
Baton Rouge, Louisiana 70801
(225) 389-7657 FAX: (225) 389-8368
E-mail: Lavi938@aol.com

Juvenile Court Judges

Vernon Claville, Judge
Juvenile Court of Caddo Parish
1835 Spring Street
Shreveport, Louisiana 71101-4298
(318) 226-6751 FAX: (318) 226-6942

Ernestine Steward Gray, Judge
Juvenile Court of the Parish of Orleans
421 Loyola Avenue
New Orleans, Louisiana 70112
(504) 565-7326 FAX: (504) 565-6078
E-mail: egsteward@aol.com

Yvonne Hughes, Judge
Juvenile Court of the Parish of Orleans
421 Loyola Avenue - Section C
New Orleans, Louisiana 70112
(504) 565-7351 FAX: (504) 565-7391

Pamela Taylor Johnson, Judge
Juvenile Court of East Baton Rouge Parish
8333 Veterans Memorial Boulevard
Baton Rouge, Louisiana 70807
(225) 354-1250 FAX: (225) 354-1305

C. Hearn Taylor, Judge
Juvenile Court of the Parish of Orleans
421 Loyola Avenue
New Orleans, Louisiana 70112
(504) 565-7315 FAX: (504) 565-7391

City Court Judges

Yvette M. Alexander, Judge
City Court of Baton Rouge
233 St. Louis Street
Baton Rouge, Louisiana 70821-3438
(225) 389-5006 FAX: (225) 389-3104

LaLeshia Walker Alford, Judge
City Court of Shreveport
1244 Texas Avenue
Shreveport, Louisiana 71101
(318) 673-5890 FAX: (318) 673-5874

Angelique Reed, Judge
First City Court of New Orleans
421 Loyola Avenue
New Orleans, Louisiana 70112
(504) 592-9243 FAX: (504) 484-2704

James Garland Smith, Judge
City Court of Monroe
Post Office Box 777
Monroe, Louisiana 71203
(318) 329-2580 FAX: (318) 329-2622

Sonja Spears, Judge
First City Court of New Orleans
421 Loyola Avenue
New Orleans, Louisiana 70112
(504) 592-9247 FAX: (504) 525-3637

Trudy M. White, Judge
Baton Rouge City Court
233 St. Louis Street
Baton Rouge, Louisiana 70801
(225) 389-3025 FAX: (225) 389-7814

Bobby Jones, Judge
Municipal Court of the City of New Orleans
727 South Broad Street
New Orleans, Louisiana 70119
(504) 827-5095 FAX: (504) 826-5811

Bruce J. McConduit, Judge
Municipal Court of the City of New Orleans
727 South Broad Street, Room 105
New Orleans, Louisiana 70119
(504) 827-5081 or 827-5085 FAX: (504) 826-5811

Ronald J. Sholes, Judge
Traffic Court of New Orleans
727 South Broad Street
New Orleans, Louisiana 70119
(504) 827-9250 FAX: (504) 826-5099

Dennis Dannel, Judge
Traffic Court of New Orleans, Division A
727 South Broad Street
New Orleans, Louisiana 70119
(504) 827-5000 FAX: (504) 827-5081

MAINE: (1)

Rick E. Lawrence, Judge
Maine District Court
Post Office Box 412
Portland, Maine 04112-0412
(207) 822-4269
Superior Court FAX: (207) 822-4136

MARYLAND: (73)

FEDERAL

Andre M. Davis, Judge
U. S. District Court for the District of Maryland
U. S. Courthouse - Suite 5B
101 West Lombard Street
Baltimore, Maryland 21201
(410) 962-0801 FAX: (410) 962-0820

Alexander Williams, Jr., Judge
U. S. District Court for the District of Maryland
Southern Division
U. S. Courthouse - Room 445A
6500 Cherrywood Lane
Greenbelt, Maryland 20770
(301) 344-0637 FAX: (301) 344-0672

Charles B. Day, Magistrate Judge
U.S. District Court for the District of Maryland
235A U. S. Courthouse
6500 Cherrywood Lane
Greenbelt, Maryland 20770
(301) 344-0393 FAX: (301) 344-0394

Administrative Law Judges

David C. Harty, Administrative Law Judge
Appeals Council
Office of Hearings and Appeals
Social Security Administration
The Rotunda - Room 415
West 40th Street
Baltimore, Maryland 21211
(410) 962-3361 FAX: (410) 889-5968

Shirley Watts, Chief Administrative Law Judge
Office of Hearings and Appeals
Social Security Administration
The Rotunda - Room 415
West 40th Street
Baltimore, Maryland 21211
(410) 962-3361 FAX: (410) 889-5968

STATE

Court of Appeal

Robert M. Bell, Chief Judge
Maryland Court of Appeals
634 Courthouse East
111 North Calvert Street
Baltimore, Maryland 21202
(410) 333-6396 FAX: (410) 347-3908

Special Court of Appeals

Arrie W. Davis, Associate Judge
Maryland Court of Special Appeals
630 Courthouse East
111 North Calvert Street, Suite 630
Baltimore, Maryland 21202
(410) 233-3200 FAX: (410) 783-9879

Trial Court Judges

DeLawrence Beard, Chief Judge
Circuit Court for Montgomery County
50 Courthouse Square
Rockville, Maryland 20850
(301) 217-7515 FAX: (301) 217-7732

Roger W. Brown, Associate Judge
Circuit Court for Baltimore City
330 Courthouse East
111 North Calvert Street
Baltimore, Maryland 21202
(410) 396-5054 FAX: (410) 545-7312

Evelyn O. Cannon, Associate Judge
Circuit Court for Baltimore City
245 Clarence M. Mitchell, Jr. Courthouse
110 North Calvert Street
Baltimore, Maryland 21202
(410) 545-6235 FAX: (410) 545-6237

Toni E. Clarke, Associate Judge
Circuit Court for Prince George's County
Courthouse
Upper Marlboro, Maryland 20772
(301) 952-4988 FAX: (301) 952-4555

Bonita L. Dancy, Associate Judge
Circuit Court for Baltimore City
343 Courthouse East
111 North Calvert Street
Baltimore, Maryland 21202
(410) 396-5102 FAX: (410) 545-3181

Herman Dawson, Associate Judge
Circuit Court for Prince George's County
308 D Courthouse
14735 Main Street
Upper Marlboro, Maryland 20772
(301) 952-3676 FAX: (301) 780-6666

Clayton Greene, Jr., Administrative Judge
Circuit Court for Anne Arundel County
Courthouse, Post Office Box 2395
Annapolis, Maryland 21401
(410) 222-1375 FAX: (410) 222-1890

Clifton J. Gordy, Jr., Associate Judge
Circuit Court for Baltimore City
531 Courthouse East
111 North Calvert Street
Baltimore, Maryland 21202
(410) 396-5062 FAX: (410) 752-5274

Wanda Keyes Heard, Associate Judge
Circuit Court for Baltimore City
343 Courthouse East
111 North Calvert Street
Baltimore, Maryland 21202
(410) 396-4918 FAX: (410) 545-7318

Marcella A. Holland, Associate Judge
Circuit Court for Baltimore City
417 Clarence Mitchell Courthouse
110 North Calvert Street
Baltimore, Maryland 21202
(410) 396-3836 FAX: (410) 545-0180
E-mail: JMAHOLL@aol.com

Mitchele D. Hotten, Associate Judge
Circuit Court for Prince George's County
14735 Main Street
Upper Marlboro, Maryland 20772
(301) 952-3788 FAX: (301) 952-5837

Dwight Jackson, Associate Judge
Circuit Court for Prince George's County
14735 Main Street
Upper Marlboro, Maryland 20772
(301) 952-4342 FAX: (301) 952-5837

Eric M. Johnson, Associate Judge
Circuit Court for Montgomery County
Judicial Center, Room 911
50 Maryland Avenue
Rockville, Maryland 20850
(301) 777-9197 FAX: (240) 777-9203

G. R. Hovey Johnson, Associate Judge
Circuit Court for Prince George's County
Courthouse, Duvall Wing, Suite #2280
14735 Main Street
Upper Marlboro, Maryland 20772-1600
(301) 952-3808 FAX: (310) 952-5533

Kenneth Lavon Johnson, Associate Judge
Circuit Court for Baltimore City
214 Courthouse East
111 North Calvert Street
Baltimore, Maryland 21202
(410) 396-5066 FAX: (410) 545-7314

Larnzell D. Martin, Jr., Associate Judge
Circuit Court for Prince George's County
Courthouse, Marbury Wing, Suite # #144M
14735 Main Street
Upper Marlboro, Maryland 20772
(301) 952-3489 FAX: (301) 952-5837

William D. Missouri, Administrative Judge
Circuit Court for Prince George's County
Courthouse, Marbury Wing, Suite 244M
14735 Main Street
Upper Marlboro, Maryland 20772
(301) 952-3728 FAX: (301) 952-3204

David B. Mitchell, Associate Judge
Circuit Court for Baltimore City
Division for Juvenile Causes
252 Courthouse East
111 North Calvert Street
Baltimore, Maryland 21202
(410) 396-5052 FAX: (410) 545-7322

Alfred Nance, Associate Judge
Circuit Court for Baltimore City
226 Clarence Mitchell Courthouse
110 North Calvert Street
Baltimore, Maryland 21202
(410) 396-4020 FAX: (410) 545-7332

Thomas Edward Noel, Associate Judge
Circuit Court for Baltimore City
561 Courthouse East
111 North Calvert Street
Baltimore, Maryland 21202
(410) 396-5112 FAX: (410) 545-7321

William D. Quarles, Associate Judge
Circuit Court for Baltimore City
408 Clarence Mitchell Courthouse
110 North Calvert Street
Baltimore, Maryland 21202
(410) 545-3766 FAX: (410) 545-3768

Paul A. Smith, Associate Judge
Circuit Court for Baltimore City
251 Clarence Mitchell Courthouse
110 North Calvert Street
Baltimore, Maryland 21202
(410) 396-5677 FAX: (410) 545-7315

Sheila R. Tillerson-Adams, Associate Judge
Circuit Court
for Prince George's County Courthouse
14735 Main Street
Upper Marlboro, Maryland 20772
(301) 952-3766 FAX: (301) 952-3101

Martin Welch, Associate Judge
Circuit Court for Baltimore City
17 Clarence Mitchell Courthouse
110 North Calvert Street
Baltimore, Maryland 21202
(410) 396-4930 FAX: (410) 545-7317

Alexander Wright, Jr., Associate Judge
Circuit Court for Baltimore County
120 East Chesapeake Avenue
Towson, Maryland 21286
(410) 887-6531 FAX: (410) 887-4160

David W. Young, Associate Judge
Circuit Court for Baltimore City
636 Clarence Mitchell Courthouse
110 North Calvert Street
Baltimore, Maryland 21202
(410) 396-5076 FAX: (410) 545-7316

Mabel Hubbard, Associate Judge (Retired)
Circuit Court for Baltimore City
111 North Calvert Street
Baltimore, Maryland 21202

Bradley O. Bailey, Master
Circuit Court for Baltimore City
Clarence Mitchell Courthouse Building
100 North Calvert Street - Room 130
Baltimore, Maryland 21202
(410) 396-1381 FAX: (410) 545-6135

Brenda Clark, Master
Circuit Court for Baltimore City
111 North Calvert Street
Baltimore, Maryland 21202
(410) 396-1919 FAX: (410) 752-5274

Zakia Mahasa, Master
Circuit Court for Baltimore City
111 North Calvert Street - Room 113-E
Baltimore, Maryland 21202
(410) 545-3653 FAX: (410) 545-6135

Claudette McDonald-Brown, Master
Circuit Court for Baltimore City
Clarence Mitchell Courthouse Building
111 North Calvert Street - Room 146
Baltimore, Maryland 21202
(410) 545-6378 FAX: (410) 545-6135

Gregory Sampson, Master-in-Chancery
Circuit Court for Baltimore City
100 North Calvert Street, Room 101
Baltimore, Maryland 21202
(410) 396-5050 FAX: (410) 545-6135

Orphans' Court Judges

George Ames, Jr., Judge
Orphans Court for Dorchester County
Post Office Box 263
Cambridge, Maryland 21613
(410) 228-4181 FAX: (410) 228-4988

Norma Lee Barkley, Chief Judge
Orphans Court for Wicomico County
Post Office Box 787
Salisbury, Maryland 21803-0707
(410) 543-6635 FAX: (410) 334-3440

Joyce M. Baylor-Thompson, Associate Judge
Orphans' Court for Baltimore City
311 Courthouse East
111 North Calvert Street
Baltimore, Maryland 21202
(410) 396-9539 FAX: (410) 545-7363

Fannie Burkett, Judge
Orphans' Court of Worcester County
The Charlotte Cathell
Register of Wills
36 Pinehurst Road
Berlin, Maryland 21811
(410) 632-2097 or 632-1529 FAX: (410) 632-5600

Lewyn S. Garrett, Associate Judge
Orphans' Court for Baltimore City
311 Courthouse East
111 North Calvert Street
Baltimore, Maryland 21202
(410) 396-4597 FAX: (410) 545-7363

Sherae M. McNeal, Judge
Orphans' Court of Howard CountyCourthouse
8360 Court Avenue
Ellicott City, Maryland 21043
(410) 313-2133 FAX: (410) 313-3409

Lucy B. Warr, Chief Judge
Orphans' Court for Prince George's County
Post Office Box 368
Upper Marlboro, Maryland 20772
(301) 952-3790 FAX: (410) 952-4489

State District Court Judges

Emanuel Brown, Associate Judge
District Court of Maryland for Baltimore City
5800 Wabash Avenue
Baltimore, Maryland 21215
(410) 878-8540 FAX: (410) 878-8551

Alice Gail Pollard Clark, Associate Judge
District Court of Maryland for Howard County
341 Courthouse Drive
Ellicott City, Maryland 21043
(410) 461-0113 FAX: (410) 461-0220

Ben C. Clyburn, Associate Judge
District Court of Maryland for Baltimore City
5800 Wabash Avenue
Baltimore, Maryland 21215
(410) 764-4210 FAX: (410) 554-5770

Angela Eaves, Associate Judge
District Court of Maryland for Harford County
2 Smith Bond Street
Bel Air, Maryland 21014-3737
(410) 836-4510 FAX: (410) 877-3074

Hassan El-Amin, Associate Judge
District Court of Maryland for
Prince George's County
14735 Main Street, Room 173B
Upper Marlboro, Maryland 20772
(301) 952-4011 FAX: (301) 952-5561

Askew W. Gatewood, Jr., Associate Judge
District Court of Maryland for Baltimore City
1400 East North Avenue
Baltimore, Maryland 21213
(410) 764-8969 FAX: (410) 358-7637

John R. Hargrove, Jr., Associate Judge
District Court of Maryland for Baltimore City
5800 Wabash Avenue
Baltimore, Maryland 21215
(410) 764-8714 FAX: (410) 358-7637

C. Yvonne Holt-Stone, Associate Judge
District Court of Maryland for Baltimore City
5800 Wabash Avenue
Baltimore, Maryland 21215
(410) 764-8714 FAX: (410) 358-7637

Miriam Hutchins, Associate Judge
District Court of Maryland for Baltimore City
501 East Fayette Street
Baltimore, Maryland 21202
(410) 878-8901 FAX: (410) 878-8910

Norman E. Johnson, Jr., Associate Judge
District Court for Maryland for Baltimore City
5800 Wabash Avenue
Baltimore, Maryland 21215
(410) 764-8714 FAX: (410) 358-7637

Keith E. Matthews, Administrative Judge
District Court for Maryland for Baltimore City
5800 Wabash Avenue
Baltimore, Maryland 21215
(410) 764-8714 FAX: (410) 358-7637

Michael McCampbell, Administrative Judge
District Court of Maryland
for Baltimore County
120 Chesapeake Avenue
Towson, Maryland 21204
(410) 321-3884 FAX: (410) 321-3529

Thurman H. Rhodes, Associate Judge
District Court of Maryland
for Prince George's County
Courthouse, Room 150B
14757 Main Street
Upper Marlboro, Maryland 20772
(301) 952-5309 FAX: (301) 952-5561

Esson V. Ricks, Jr., Associate Judge
District Court for Maryland
for Anne Arundel County
The Robert F. Sweeney District Court Building
251 Rowe Boulevard
Annapolis, Maryland 21401
(410) 260-1362 FAX: (410) 260-1312

Melanie M. Shaw-Geter, Associate Judge
District Court for Maryland
for Prince George's County
Courthouse, Room 173B
14735 Main Street
Upper Marlboro, Maryland 20772
(301) 952-4021 FAX: (301) 952-5561

Vicki Watts, Associate Judge
District Court of Maryland
for Baltimore County
120 East Chesapeake Avenue
Towson, Maryland 21286
(410) 512-2121 FAX: (410) 512-2063

Beverly Woodward, Associate Judge
District Court of Maryland
for Prince George's County
Upper Marlboro, Maryland 20772
(301) 952-4021 FAX: (301) 574-5282

Administrative Law Judges

Wayne Brooks, Judge
Office of Administrative Hearings
11101 Gilroy Road
Hunt Valley, Maryland 21301-1301
(410) 229-4181 FAX: (410) 229-4111

James Carroll, Judge
Office of Administrative Hearings
11101 Gilroy Road
Hunt Valley, Maryland 21301-1301
(410) 229-4184 FAX: (410) 229-4111

Thomas Curtis, Judge
Office of Administrative Hearings
11101 Gilroy Road
Hunt Valley, Maryland 21301-1301
(410) 229-4172 FAX: (410) 229-4111

Charles Davis, Judge
Office of Administrative Hearings
11101 Gilroy Road
Hunt Valley, Maryland 21301-1301
(410) 229-4234 FAX: (410) 229-4111

William England, Judge
Office of Administrative Hearings
11101 Gilroy Road
Hunt Valley, Maryland 21301-1301
(410) 229-4197 FAX: (410) 229-4111

Cornelia Bright Gordon, Judge
Office of Administrative Hearings
11101 Gilroy Road
Hunt Valley, Maryland 21301-1301
(410) 229-4160 FAX: (410) 229-4111

Merry Hudson, Judge
Office of Administrative Hearings
11101 Gilroy Road
Hunt Valley, Maryland 21301-1301
(410) 229-4195 FAX: (410) 229-4111

Sara Louise Moreland, Hearing Examiner
Maryland Dept. of Labor
Licensing and Regulation
1505 Northgate Road
Baltimore, Maryland 21218
(410) 767-2421 FAX: (410) 767-2532

Sondra Mackel Spencer
Office of Administrative Hearings
11101 Gilroy Road
Hunt Valley, Maryland 21301-1301
(410) 229-4219 FAX: (410) 229-4111

Edward Walker
Office of Administrative Hearings
11101 Gilroy Road
Hunt Valley, Maryland 21301-1301
(410) 229-4198 FAX: (410) 229-4111

MASSACHUSETTS: (27)

FEDERAL

Reginald C. Lindsey, Judge
U. S. District Court
for the District of Massachusetts
Room 5130, One Courthouse Way
Boston, Massachusetts 02110
(617) 748-4829 FAX: (617) 748-9096

Joyce London Alexander, U. S. Magistrate Judge
U. S. District Court for the
District of Massachusetts
Room 7410, One Courthouse Way
Boston, Massachusetts 02110
(617) 748-9236 FAX: (617) 748-9096

Administrative Law Judge

Thurman E. Anderson, Regional Chief
Administrative Law Judge
Office of Hearings and Appeals
Social Security Administration
O'Neill Federal Office Building
10 Causeway Street, Room 417
Boston, Massachusetts 02222-1091
(617) 565-5050 FAX: (617) 248-0978

STATE

Supreme Court

Roderick L. Ireland, Associate Justice
Supreme Judicial Court of Massachusetts
New Court House
Pemberton Square
Boston, Massachusetts 02108
(617) 557-1000 FAX: (617) 723-3577

Court of Appeals

Frederick L. Brown, Associate Justice
Appeals Court
New Court House - 15th Floor
Pemberton Square
Boston, Massachusetts 02108
(617) 725-8090 FAX: (617) 523-2845

Trial Court Judges

Julian Houston, Associate Justice
Superior Court
U. S. Post Office and Court House
90 Devonshire Street, Room 1417
Boston, Massachusetts 02109
(617) 788-8130 FAX: (617) 788-8137

James D. McDaniel, Jr., Associate Justice
Superior Court
U. S. Post Office and Court House
90 Devonshire Street, Room 1417
Boston, Massachusetts 02109
(617) 788-8130 FAX: (617) 788-8137

Tina S. Page, Associate Justice
Superior Court
50 State Street
Post Office Box 559
Springfield, Massachusetts 01102-0559
(413) 748-8600 FAX: (413) 737-1611

Herman J. Smith, Jr., Associate Justice
Superior Court
U. S. Post Office and Court House
90 Devonshire Street, Room 1417
Boston, Massachusetts 02109
(617) 788-8130 FAX: (617) 788-8137

Charles T. Spurlock, Associate Justice
Superior Court
U. S. Post Office and Court House
90 Devonshire Street, Room 1417
Boston, Massachusetts 02109
(617) 788-8130 FAX: (617) 788-8137

Judith Nelson Dilday, Associate Justice
Probate and Family Court
Middlesex Division
208 Cambridge Street
Post Office Box 410480
East Cambridge, Massachusetts 02141-0005
(617) 494-4560 or 494-4295 FAX: (617) 494-6710

Annette Forde, Associate Justice
Boston Municipal Court
380 Old Court House
Pemberton Square
Boston, Massachusetts 02108
(617) 725-8000 FAX: (617) 725-8395

Marjory A.C. German, Justice
Administrative Office, Juvenile Court
20 - 24 New Chardon Street
Post Office Box 9664
Boston, Massachusetts 02114
(617) 788-6550 FAX: (617) 788-8965

Ronald D. Harper, Presiding Justice
Juvenile Court, Bristol County
75 North Sixth Street
New Bedford, Massachusetts 02740
(508) 999-9700 FAX: (508) 999-2917

Leslie E. Harris, Associate Justice
Boston Juvenile Court
20-24 New Chardon Street
Boston, Massachusetts 02114
(617) 788-8542 FAX: (617) 788-8982
E-mail: honharris@aol.com

Marie Jackson-Thompson, 1st Justice
District Court - Woburn Division
Dept. of the Trial Court
Cambridge Division
Court House
30 Pleasant Street
Woburn, Massachusetts 01801-4184
(781) 935-4000 FAX: (781) 938-7942

Charles R. Johnson, Associate Justice
Boston Municipal Court
380 Old Court House
Pemberton Square
Boston, Massachusetts 02108
(617) 725-8000 FAX: (617) 725-8395

Jacques C. Leroy, Justice
District Court
Springfield Division
50 State Street
Post Office Box 2421
Springfield, Massachusetts 01103
(413) 747-8646 FAX: (413) 739-5579

Paul L. McGill, 1st Justice
District Court
Concord Division
305 Walden Street
Concord, Massachusetts 01742-3616
(978) 369-0500 FAX: (978) 371-9919

June C. Miles, Associate Justice
Juvenile Court Boston Division
380 Old Court House
174 Pemberton Square
Boston, Massachusetts 02108
(617) 788-8542 FAX: (617) 788-8978

Gregory L. Phillips, 1st Justice
District Court
Roxbury Division
85 Warren Street
Roxbury, Massachusetts 02119
(617) 427-7000 FAX: (617) 442-0615

Edward R. Redd, Justice
District Court
Roxbury Division
85 Warren Street
Roxbury, Massachusetts 02119
(617) 427-7000 FAX: (617) 541-0286

Severlin B. Singleton, Justice
District Court
Cambridge Division
40 Thorndike Street
Post Office Box 338
East Cambridge, Massachusetts 02141
(617) 494-4350 FAX: (617) 494-4357

Mark Hart Summerville, Associate Justice
Boston Municipal Court
380 Old Court House
Pemberton Square
Boston, Massachusetts 02108
(617) 725-8000 FAX: (617) 725-8395

Gwendolyn R. Tyre, Associate Justice
Juvenile Court
Middlesex County Division
40 Thorndike Street, Room 3-33
Cambridge, Massachusetts 02141
(617) 494-4100 FAX: (617) 577-9278

Joseph M. Walker, III, Justice
District Court
Dorchester Division
510 Washington Street
Dorchester, Massachusetts 02124
(617) 288-9500 FAX: (617) 436-8250

Milton L. Wright, Jr., Justice
District Court
Roxbury Division
85 Warren Street
Roxbury, Massachusetts 02119
(617) 427-7000 FAX: (617) 422-0615

MICHIGAN: (135)

FEDERAL

Appellate Judges

Eric L. Clay, Judge
U. S. Court of Appeals
for the Sixth Circuit
619 Theodore Levin U. S.Courthouse
231 West Lafayette Boulevard
Detroit, Michigan 48226
(313) 234-5260 FAX: (313) 234-5398

Damon J. Keith, Senior Judge
U. S. Court of Appeals for the Sixth Circuit
240 Theodore Levin U. S. Courthouse
231 West Lafayette Boulevard, Room 240
Detroit, Michigan 48226
(313) 234-5245 FAX: (313) 234-5382

U. S. District Court Judges

Denise Page Hood, Judge
U. S. District Court
for the Eastern District of Michigan
235 Theodore Levin U. S. Courthouse
231 West Lafayette Boulevard
Detroit, Michigan 48226
(313) 234-5165 FAX: (313) 226-5358

Victoria A. Roberts, Judge
U. S. District Court
for the Eastern District of Michigan
123 Theodore Levin U. S. Courthouse
231 West Lafayette Boulevard, Room 123
Detroit, Michigan 48226
(313) 234-5230 FAX: (313) 234-5493
E-mail: victoria-roberts@ck6.uscourts.gov

Anna Diggs Taylor, Senior Judge
U. S. District Court
for the Eastern District of Michigan
740 Theodore Levin U. S. Courthouse
231 Lafayette Boulevard
Detroit, Michigan 48226-2791
(313) 234-5105 FAX: (313) 234-5588
E-mail: ataylorck@uscourts.gov

Julian Abele Cook, Jr., Senior Judge
U. S. District Court
for the Eastern District of Michigan
718 Theodore Levin U. S. Courthouse
231 West Lafayette Boulevard
Detroit, Michigan 48226
(313) 234-5100 FAX: (313) 234-5352

Benjamin F. Gibson, Judge (Retired)
U. S. District Court
for the Western District of Michigan
616 Federal Building
110 Michigan Avenue, N.W.
Grand Rapids, Michigan 49503-2363

Wallace Capel, Jr., Magistrate Judge
U. S. District Court for the
Eastern District of Michigan
600 Church Street, Room 112
Flint, Michigan 48502
(810) 341-7850 FAX: (810) 341-7854

Lynn V. Hooe, Jr., Magistrate Judge (Recalled)
U. S. District Court
for the Eastern District of Michigan
Theodore Levin U. S. Courthouse
231 West Lafayette Boulevard
Detroit, Michigan 48226
(248 848-0562

Ray Reynolds Graves, Judge
U. S. Bankruptcy Court
for the Eastern District of Michigan
211 West Fort Street, Suite 1900
Detroit, Michigan 48226
(313) 234-0030 FAX: (313) 226-2211

Administrative Law Judges

Ethel M. Revels, Administrative Law Judge
Office of Hearings and Appeals
Social Security Administration
Patrick J. McNamara Federal Building
477 Michigan Avenue, Rooms 430 - 449
Detroit, Michigan 48226
(313) 226-6008 or 226-6180 FAX: (313) 226-3625
E-mail: ethel.revels@ssa.gov

STATE

Supreme Court

Robert P. Young, Jr., Justice
Michigan Supreme Court
500 Woodward Avenue, Suite 2000
Detroit, Michigan 48226
(313) 256-9145 FAX: (313) 256-9168
E-mail: ryoung@jud.state.mi.us

Court of Judges

Jeffrey G. Collins, Judge
Court of Appeals
900 First Federal Building
Detroit, Michigan 48226
(313) 256-9291 FAX: (313) 256-9807
E-mail: jcollins@jud.state.mi.us

Harold Hood, Judge
Court of Appeals
900 First Federal Building
Detroit, Michigan 48226
(313) 256-9223 FAX: (313) 256-9807
E-mail: hhood@jud.state.mi.us

Kurtis T. Wilder, Judge
Court of Appeals
900 First Federal Building
Detroit, Michigan 48226
(313) 256-9285 FAX: (313) 256-9168
E-mail: kwilder@jud.state.mi.us

Circuit Court Judges

Wendy M. Baxter, Judge
3rd Circuit Court of Michigan
Civil Division
1501 Coleman A. Young Municipal Center
Detroit, Michigan 48226
(313) 224-2427 FAX: (313) 224-6070

June Blackwell-Hatcher, Judge
Wayne County Probate Court
1399 Coleman A Young Municipal Center
Detroit, Michigan 48226
(313) 224-5676 FAX: (313) 224-8097

Ulysses W. Boykin, Judge
3rd Circuit Court of Michigan
Criminal Division
1441 St. Antoine Street, Room 810
Detroit, Michigan 48226
(313) 224-2275 FAX: (313) 224-2786

Margie R. Braxton, Judge
3rd Circuit Court of Michigan
Criminal Division
1441 St. Antoine Street, Room 1821
Detroit, Michigan 48226
(313) 224-2477 FAX: (313) 224-7286

Helen E. Brown, Judge
3rd Circuit Court of Michigan
Family Division
1441 St. Antoine Street, Room 1821
Detroit, Michigan 48226
(313) 224-2441 FAX: (313) 224-2786

Freddie G. Burton, Jr., Judge
3rd Circuit Court of Michigan
Family Division, Juvenile Section
1269 Coleman A. Young Municipal Center
Detroit, Michigan 48226
(313) 224-5686 FAX: (313) 224-5407

George W. Crockett, III, Judge
3rd Circuit Court of Michigan
Criminal Division
1441 St. Antoine Street, Room 402
Detroit, Michigan 48226
(313) 224-2467 FAX: (313) 224-2786

Daphne Means Curtis, Judge
3rd Circuit Court of Michigan
Civil Division
1007 Coleman A. Young Municipal Center
Detroit, Michigan 48226
(313) 224-2240 FAX: (313) 224-6070

Gershwin Allen Drain, Judge
3rd Circuit Court of Michigan
Criminal Division
1441 St. Antoine Street, Room 202
Detroit, Michigan 48226
(313) 224-2474 FAX: (313) 224-2786
E-mail: Paul12449@aol.com

Maggie Drake, Judge
3rd Circuit Court of Michigan
Criminal Division
1441 St. Antoine Street, Room 703
Detroit, Michigan 48226
(313) 224-2481 FAX: (313) 224-2786

Prentis Edwards, Judge
3rd Circuit Court of Michigan
Criminal Division
1441 St. Antoine Street, Room 503
Detroit, Michigan 48226
(313) 224-0250 FAX: (313) 224-2786

Robert L. Evans, Judge
3rd Circuit Court of Michigan
Criminal Division
1441 St. Antoine Street, Room 303
Detroit, Michigan 48226
(313) 224-2464 FAX: (313) 224-2786

Vonda R. Evans, Judge
3rd Circuit Court of Michigan
Criminal Division
1441 St. Antoine Street, Room 602
Detroit, Michigan 48226
(313) 224-5440 FAX: (313) 224-2786

Nancy Cornelia Francis, Judge
Washtenaw County Probate Court
2270 Platt Road
Ann Arbor, Michigan 48104-5197
(734) 971-2240 FAX: (734) 971-5084

Cynthia Gray Hathaway, Judge
3rd Circuit Court of Michigan
Criminal Division
1441 St. Antoine Street, Room 801
Detroit, Michigan 48226
(313) 224-2120 FAX: (313) 224-2786

Karen Fort Hood, Presiding Judge
3rd Circuit Court of Michigan
Criminal Division
1441 St. Antoine Street, Room 302
Detroit, Michigan 48226
(313) 224-2477 FAX: (313) 224-2786

Thomas Edward Jackson, Judge
3rd Circuit Court of Michigan
Criminal Division
1441 St. Antoine Street, Room G-1
Detroit, Michigan 48226
(313) 224-5435 FAX: (313) 224-2786

Vera Massey Jones, Judge
3rd Circuit Court of Michigan
Criminal Division
1441 St. Antoine Street, Room G-2
Detroit, Michigan 48226
(313) 224-2487 FAX: (313) 224-2786

Denise Langford-Morris, Judge
6th Circuit Court of Michigan
Oakland County
1200 North Telegraph Road
Pontiac, Michigan 48341-1043
(248) 858-0363 FAX: (248) 975-9791

William Lucas, Judge
3rd Circuit Court of Michigan
Family Division
1201 Coleman A. Young Municipal Center
Detroit, Michigan 48226
(313) 224-5216 FAX: (313) 224-6070

Sheila Gibson Manning, Judge
3rd Circuit Court of Michigan
Family Division
1907 Coleman A. Young Municipal Center
Detroit, Michigan 48226
(313) 224-2471 FAX: (313) 224-6070

Mabel Johnson Mayfield, Judge
Berrien County Probate Court Courthouse
811 Port Street
St. Joseph, Michigan 49085
(616) 983-7111 Ext. 8450 FAX: (616) 982-8697

Warfield Moore, Jr., Judge
3rd Circuit Court of Michigan
Criminal Division
1441 St. Antoine Street, Room 404
Detroit, Michigan 48226
(313) 224-2430 FAX: (313) 224-2786

Bruce U. Morrow, Judge
3rd Circuit Court of Michigan
Criminal Division
1441 St. Antoine Street, Room 403
Detroit, Michigan 48226
(313) 224-0415 FAX: (313) 224-2786

John A. Murphy, Judge
3rd Circuit Court of Michigan, Civil Division
901 Coleman A. Young Municipal Center
Detroit, Michigan 48226
(313) 224-0142 FAX: (313) 224-6070

Gregory Pittman, Judge
Muskegon County Probate Court
990 Terrace Street
Muskegon, Michigan 49442-3377
(616) 724-6530 or 724-6241 FAX: (616) 724-6232

Frances Pitts, Judge
3rd Circuit Court of Michigan
Family Division, Juvenile Section
1025 East Forest Avenue
Detroit, Michigan 48207
(313) 833-0667 FAX: (313) 833-0670

Louis F. Simmons, Jr., Judge
3rd Circuit Court of Michigan, Civil Division
1921 Coleman A. Young Municipal Center
Detroit, Michigan 48226
(313) 224-5234 FAX: (313) 224-6070

Cynthia D. Stephens, Chief Judge Pro Tem
3rd Circuit Court of Michigan
1719 Coleman A. Young Municipal Center
Detroit, Michigan 48226
(313) 224-2451 FAX: (313) 224-6070

Craig S. Strong, Judge
3rd Circuit Court of Michigan, Criminal Division
1441 St. Antoine Street, Room 803
Detroit, Michigan 48226
(313) 224-2484 FAX: (313) 224-2786

Deborah A. Thomas, Judge
3rd Circuit Court of Michigan, Civil Division
802 Coleman A. Young Municipal Center
Detroit, Michigan 48226
(313) 224-5210 FAX: (313) 224-6070

Edward M. Thomas, Judge
3rd Circuit Court of Michigan, Civil Division
913 Coleman A. Young Municipal Center
Detroit, Michigan 48226
(313) 224-5246 (FAX) (313) 224-6070

Leonard Townsend, Judge
3rd Circuit Court of Michigan, Criminal Division
1441 St. Antoine Street, Room 702
Detroit, Michigan 48226
(313) 224-2437 FAX: (313) 224-2786

Carolyn H. Williams, Presiding Judge
9th Circuit Court of Michigan
Kalamazoo County Probate Court
1400 Gull Road
Kalamazoo, Michigan 49001
(616) 385-6001 FAX: (616) 385-8588
E-mail: chwill@kalcounty.com

Kym L. Worthy, Judge
3rd Circuit Court of Michigan, Criminal Division
1441 St. Antoine Street, Room 502
Detroit, Michigan 48226
(313) 224-2520 FAX: (313) 224-2786

Geraldine Bledsoe Ford, Judge (Retired)
3rd Circuit Court of Michigan, Criminal Division
1947 Hyde Park
Detroit, Michigan 48207
(313) 939-3859

Claudia House Morcum, Judge (Retired)
3rd Circuit Court of Michigan, Civil Division
9000 East Jefferson, Suite 1410
Detroit, Michigan 48213
(313) 331-0692

Dalton Roberson, Judge (Retired)
3rd Circuit Court of Michigan, Criminal Division
640 Apelehama
Diamond Head, Mississippi 39525
(228) 255-6027

Lucille Watts, Judge (Retired)
3rd Circuit Court of Michigan, Civil Division
16929 Wyoming Avenue
Detroit, Michigan 48221
(313) 341-7200

District Court Judges

Deborah Ross Adams, Judge
District Court
36th Judicial District
421 Madison Avenue, Suite 3075
Detroit, Michigan 48226
(313) 965-4694 FAX: (313) 965-3951

Trudy DunCombe Archer, Judge
District Court
36th Judicial District
421 Madison Avenue, Suite 3074
Detroit, Michigan 48226
(313) 965-8726 FAX: (313) 965-3951

Marylin E. Atkins, Chief Judge
District Court
36th Judicial District
421 Madison Avenue, Suite 5028
Detroit, Michigan 48226
(313) 965-8738 FAX: (313) 965-2211

Joseph N. Baltimore, Judge
District Court
36th Judicial District
421 Madison Avenue, Suite 3073
Detroit, Michigan 48226
(313) 965-8740 FAX: (313) 965-3951

William F. Bledsoe, Chief Judge Pro Tem
District Court
30th Judicial District
28 Gerald Avenue
Highland Park, Michigan 48203
(313) 252-0241 FAX: (313) 865-1115

Nancy McCaughan Blount, Judge
District Court
36th Judicial District
421 Madison Avenue, Suite 4070
Detroit, Michigan 48226
(313) 965-8715 FAX: (313) 965-39

Leo Bowman, Chief Judge
District Court
50th Judicial District
70 North Saginaw
Pontiac, Michigan 48342
(248) 857-8007 FAX: (248) 857-6028

David Martin Bradfield, Judge
District Court
36th Judicial District
421 Madison Avenue, Suite 4072
Detroit, Michigan 48226
(313) 965-8737 FAX: (313) 965-3951

Vanesa Jones Bradley, Judge
District Court
36th Judicial District
421 Madison Avenue, Suite 5066
Detroit, Michigan 48226
(313) 965-8708 FAX: (313) 965-3951

Izetta F. Bright, Judge
District Court
36th Judicial District
421 Madison Avenue, Suite 5069
Detroit, Michigan 48226
(313) 965-4070 FAX: (313) 965-3951

Christopher C. Brown, Chief Judge Pro Tem
District Court
50th Judicial District
70 North Saginaw Street
Pontiac, Michigan 48342
(248) 857-8059 FAX: (248) 857-6028

Terry L. Clark, Chief Judge
District Court
70th Judicial District
111 South Michigan Avenue
Saginaw, Michigan 48602
(517) 790-5371 FAX: (517) 790-5589

Donald Coleman, Judge
District Court
36th Judicial District
421 Madison Avenue, Suite 4066
Detroit, Michigan 48226
(313) 965-8712 FAX: (313) 965-3951

Wendy Cooley, Judge
District Court
36th Judicial District
421 Madison Avenue, Suite 5072
Post Office Box 07189
Detroit, Michigan 48207
(313) 833-8180 FAX: (313) 832-2799

William H. Crawford II, Chief Judge
District Court
68th Judicial District
630 South Saginaw Street
Flint, Michigan 48502
(810) 766-8981 FAX: (810) 766-8967

Theresa Doss, Judge
District Court
36th Judicial District
421 Madison Avenue, Suite 4069
Detroit, Michigan 48226
(313) 965-8722 FAX: (313) 965-3951

Norma Y. Dotson, Judge
District Court
36th Judicial District
421 Madison Avenue, Suite 3070
Detroit, Michigan 48226
(313) 965-8728 FAX: (313) 965-3951

Nancy A. Farmer, Chief Judge Pro Tem
District Court
36th Judicial District
421 Madison Avenue, Suite 4071
Detroit, Michigan 48226
(313) 965-8720 FAX: (313) 965-3951

Ruth Garrett, Judge
District Court
36th Judicial District
421 Madison Avenue
Detroit, Michigan 48226
(313) 965-8710 FAX: (313) 965-3951

Jimmylee Gray, Judge
District Court
36th Judicial District
421 Madison Avenue, Suite 5067
Detroit, Michigan 48226
(313) 965-8742 FAX: (313) 965-3951

L. Kim Hoagland, Chief Judge
District Court
30th Judicial District
28 Gerald Avenue
Highland Park, Michigan 48203
(313) 252-0244 FAX: (313) 865-1115

Paula G. Humphries, Judge
District Court
36th Judicial District
421 Madison Avenue, Suite 5074
Detroit, Michigan 48226
(313) 965-8622 FAX: (313) 965-3951

Sylvia A. James, Chief Judge
District Court
22nd Judicial District
27331 South River Park Drive
Inkster, Michigan 48141
(313) 277-8200 FAX: (313) 277-8206

Patricia L. Jefferson, Judge
District Court
36th Judicial District
421 Madison Avenue, Suite 4075
Detroit, Michigan 48226
(313) 965-8745 FAX: (313) 965-3951

Deborah Lewis-Langston, Judge
District Court
36th Judicial District
421 Madison Avenue, Suite 4068
Detroit, Michigan 48226
(313) 965-8717 FAX: (313) 965-3951

Willie G. Lipscomb, Jr., Judge
District Court
36th Judicial District
421 Madison Avenue, Suite 3069
Detroit, Michigan 48226
(313) 965-8730. FAX: (313) 965-3951

Leona L. Lloyd, Judge
District Court
36th Judicial District
421 Madison Avenue, Suite 3067
Detroit, Michigan 48226
(313) 965-8727 FAX: (313) 965-3951

Leonia J. Lloyd, Judge
District Court
36th Judicial District
421 Madison Avenue, Suite 3066
Detroit, Michigan 48226
(313) 965-8741 FAX: (313) 965-3951

Benjamin H. Logan, II, Judge
District Court
61st Judicial District
333 Monroe Street, N.W.
Grand Rapids, Michigan 49503
(616) 456-3802 FAX: (616) 456-3311

Herman Marable, Judge
District Court
68th Judicial District
630 South Saginaw Street
Flint, Michigan 48502
(810) 766-8979 FAX: (810) 766-8967

B. Martin-Clark, Judge
District Court
36th Judicial District
421 Madison Avenue, Suite 5074
Detroit, Michigan 48226
(313) 965-8734 FAX: (313) 965-3951

Wade Harper McCree, Jr., Judge
District Court
36th Judicial District
421 Madison Avenue, Suite 5071
Detroit, Michigan 48226
(313) 965-8731 FAX: (313) 965-3951

Donna Robinson Millhouse, Judge
District Court
36th Judicial District
421 Madison Avenue, Suite 3072
Detroit, Michigan 48226
(313) 965-8714 FAX: (313) 965-3951

Marion A. Moore, Judge
District Court
36th Judicial District
421 Madison Avenue, Suite 3071
Detroit, Michigan 48226
(313) 965-8732 FAX: (313) 965-3951

Lydia Nance-Adams, Judge
District Court
36th Judicial District
421 Madison Avenue, Suite 4074
Detroit, Michigan 48226
(313) 965-8716 FAX: (313) 965-3951

Beverly Nettles-Nickerson, Judge
District Court
54-A Judicial District
124 West Michigan Avenue
Lansing, Michigan 48933
(517) 483-4441 FAX: (517) 483-4108
E-mail: jbnn@ci.lansing.mi.us

Jeanette O'Banner-Owens, Judge
District Court
36th Judicial District
421 Madison Avenue, Suite 3068
Detroit, Michigan 48226
(313) 965-8724 FAX: (313) 965-3951

John R. Perry, Presiding Judge
District Court
36th Judicial District
421 Madison Avenue, Suite 4067
Detroit, Michigan 48226
(313) 965-8735 FAX: (313) 965-3951

Nathaniel C. Perry, III, Judge
District Court
68th Judicial District
630 South Saginaw Street
Flint, Michigan 48502
(810) 766-8987 FAX: (810) 257-2607

Ramona M. Roberts, Judge
District Court
68th Judicial District
630 South Saginaw Street
Flint, Michigan 48502
(810) 766-8989 or 766-8990
FAX: (810) 766-8967 or 232-6368

C. Lorene Royster, Judge
District Court
36th Judicial District
421 Madison Avenue, Suite 5073
Detroit, Michigan 48226
(313) 965-8743 FAX: (313) 965-3951

Chris E. Stith, Judge
District Court
36th Judicial District
421 Madison Avenue, Suite 5068
Detroit, Michigan 48226
(313) 965-8739 FAX: (313) 965-3951

Preston G. Thomas, Judge
District Court
50th Judicial District
70 North Saginaw
Pontiac, Michigan 48342
(248) 857-8081 FAX: (248) 857-6028

Theodore C. Wallace, Judge
District Court
36th Judicial District
421 Madison Avenue, Suite 4073
Detroit, Michigan 48226
(313) 965-8713 FAX: (313) 965-3951

William Waterman, Judge
District Court
50th Judicial District
70 North Saginaw Street
Pontiac, Michigan 48342
(248) 857-8081 FAX: (248) 857-6028

Magistrates

Charles W. Anderson, III, Magistrate
District Court
36th Judicial District
421 Madison Avenue, Suite 1051
Detroit, Michigan 48226
(313) 965-8723 FAX: (313) 965-3951

Margaret E. Baylor, Magistrate
District Court
36th Judicial District
421 Madison Avenue, Suite 2027
Detroit, Michigan 48226
(313) 965-5025 FAX: (313) 965-3951

Irma J. Chenevert-Bragg, Magistrate
District Court
36th Judicial District
421 Madison Avenue, Suite 1063
Detroit, Michigan 48226
(313) 965-5220 FAX: (313) 965-3951

Judith Gracey, Magistrate
District Court
48th Judicial District
4280 Telegraph Road
Bloomfield Hills, Michigan 48302
(248) 647-1141 FAX: (248) 569-5045

Gerry K. Hearn, Magistrate
District Court
22nd Judicial District
27331 South River Park Drive
Inkster, Detroit 48141
(313) 277-8200 FAX: (313) 277-8206

B. Penny Millender, Magistrate
District Court
36th Judicial District
421 Madison Avenue, Suite 2028
Detroit, Michigan 48226
(313) 965-8729 FAX: (313) 965-3951

William Mitchell, III, Magistrate
District Court
45-B Judicial District
13600 Oak Park Boulevard
Oak Park, Michigan 48237
(248) 542-7042 FAX: (248) 691-7159

Andra Richardson, Magistrate
District Court
52-1st District Court
48150 Grand River
Novi, Michigan 48374
(248) 305-6120 FAX: (248) 305-6118

Thomas J. Shannon, Chief Magistrate
District Court
36th Judicial District
421 Madison Avenue, Suite 2029
Detroit, Michigan 48226
(313) 965-8744 FAX: (313) 965-3951

A. Kay Stanfield-Brown, Magistrate
District Court
46th Judicial District
26000 Evergreen Road
Southfield, Michigan 48076
(248) 354-9509
E-mail: aksbrown@sherbowlaw.com

Referees

Deborah Autman, Referee
17th Circuit Court of Michigan
Family Division
1501 Cedar Street, N.E.
Grand Rapids, Michigan 49503
(616) 458-2298 FAX: (616) 336-3349

Catherine Gardner, Referee
3rd Circuit Court of Michigan
Family Division, Juvenile Section
1025 East Forest
Detroit, Michigan 48207
(313) 833-0596 FAX: (313) 833-2235

Harriet E. Harris, Referee
Wayne County Friend of the Court
Penobscot Building, 3rd Floor
645 Griswold Street
Detroit, Michigan 48226
(313) 224-5272 FAX: (313) 967-3533

David Perkins, Referee
3rd Circuit Court of Michigan
Family Division, Juvenile Section
1025 East Forest
Detroit, Michigan 48207
(313) 833-0165 FAX: (313) 387-0192

Richard B. Smart, III, Referee
3rd Circuit Court of Michigan
Family Division, Juvenile Section
1025 East Forest
Detroit, Michigan 48207
(313) 833-0148 FAX: (313) 833-2235

C. Jane Varner, Chief Referee
3rd Circuit Court of Michigan
Family Division, Juvenile Section
1025 East Forest
Detroit, Michigan 18207
(313) 833-4777 FAX: (313) 833-1787

Clinton Carter, Retired Referee
3rd Circuit Court of Michigan
Family Division
601 North Piper Court
Detroit, Michigan 48215
(313) 822-4106

Administrative Law Judges

Tessema Berga, Administrative Law Judge
Dept. of Education - Office of Administrative Law
608 West Allegan
Post Office Box 30008
Lansing, Michigan 48909-0008
(517) 373-8369 FAX: (517) 373-9238

Rhonda P. Craig, Administrative Law Judge
Family Independence Agency
1200 6th Street, Suite 540
Detroit, Michigan 48226
(313) 256-2810 FAX: (313) 256-1569
E-mail: craigr2@state.mi.us

William Bly Edwards, Administrative Law Judge
Dept. of Community Health
Post Office Box 30195
Lansing, Michigan 48909-0195
(517) 335-9384 FAX: (517) 335-9180
E-mail: edwardsw@state.mi.us

Cheryl T. Fischre, Hearing Officer
Dept. of Consumer and Industry Services
Bureau of Hearings
Post Office Box 30695
Lansing, Michigan 48909
(517) 335-2484 FAX: (517) 335-6696
E-mail: cheryl.t.fischre@cis.state.mi.us

Andrew Foster, Administrative Law Judge
Dept. of Consumer and Industry Services
Bureau of Hearings
1200 Sixth Street, 8th Floor
Detroit, Michigan 48226
(313) 256-3511 FAX: (313) 256-3090

Carol Guyton, Magistrate
Worker's Compensation Board of Magistrates
1200 Sixth Street, 12th Floor, North Tower
Detroit, Michigan 48226
(313) 256-2770 FAX: (313) 256-1110

LaNita R. Haith, Magistrate
Worker's Compensation Board of Magistrates
28 North Saginaw Street, Suite 1310
Pontiac, Michigan 48342
(248) 334-2497 FAX: (248) 334-5256

Gregory Holiday, Administrative Law Judge
Dept. of Consumer and Industry Services
Bureau of Hearings
1200 Sixth Street, 8th Floor, North Tower
Detroit, Michigan 48226
(313) 256-2300 FAX: (313) 256-3497
E-mail: gregory.holiday@cis.state.mi.us

Barbara Kai Lanier-Jones
Administrative Law Judge
Dept. of State-Driver License, Appeal Division
17117 West Nine Mile Road, 7th Floor
Southfield, Michigan 48075
(313) 256-9032 FAX: (248) 569-1341
E-mail: Lanier-JonesK@state.mi.us

Carroll D. Little, Administrative Law Judge
Michigan Employment Security Agency
7310 Woodward Avenue, Suite 4
Detroit, Michigan 48202
(313) 876-5222 FAX: (313) 876-5722

John R. Mayfield, Jr., Administrative Law Judge
Dept. of State-Driver License
Appeal Division
428 Bradford Drive
Benton Harbor, Michigan 49022
(616) 459-3080 E-mail: mayfield@state.mi.us

Robert Mourning, Administrative Law Judge
Dept. of Consumer and Industry Services
Bureau of Hearings
Post Office Box 30695
Lansing, Michigan 48909
(517) 241-1466 FAX: (517) 335-6696
E-mail: robert.h.mourning@cis.state.mi.us

Marya Nelson-Davis, Administrative Law Judge
Family Independence Agency
Grand Tower, 7th Floor
Lansing, Michigan 48933
(517) 373-0722 FAX: (517) 335-6088
E-mail: nelson.davism@state.mi.us

Daniel E. Nickerson, Administrative Law Judge
Dept. of Consumer and Industry Services
Public Service Commission
Post Office Box 30221
Lansing, Michigan 48909
(517) 334-6374 FAX: (517) 334-6398
E-mail: daniel.e.nickerson@cis.state.mi.us

Renee A. Ozburn, Administrative Law Judge
Dept. of Consumer and Industry Services,
Bureau of Hearings
Post Office Box 30695
Lansing, Michigan 48909
(517) 335-2087 FAX: (517) 335-6696
E-mail: renee.ozburn@cis.state.mi.us

Roy L. Roulhac, Administrative Law Judge
Michigan Employment Relations Commission
1200 6th Street, 14th Floor
Detroit, Michigan 48202
(313) 256-3519 FAX: (313) 256-3090

Sharon Smith, Magistrate
Workers' Compensation Board of Magistrates
1200 Sixth Street - 12th Floor, North Tower
Detroit, Michigan 48226
(313) 256-2770 FAX: (313) 256-1110

Howard T. Spence, Administrative Law Judge
Dept. of Consumer and Industry Services
Bureau of Hearings
Post Office Box 30695
Lansing, Michigan 48909
(517) 373-6529 FAX: (517) 335-6696
E-mail: htspence@mindspring.com

Erick Williams, Administrative Law Judge
Dept. of Consumer and Industry Services
Bureau of Hearings
Post Office Box 30695
Lansing, Michigan 48909
(517) 355-2085 FAX: (517) 335-6696
E-mail: erick.williams@cis.state.mi.us

MINNESOTA: (13)

FEDERAL

Michael J. Davis, Judge
U. S. District Court
for the District of Minnesota
14E U. S. Courthouse
300 South 4th Street
Minneapolis, Minnesota 55415
(612) 664-5070 FAX: (612) 664-5077

Administrative Law Judge

David Washington, Administrative Law Judge
Office of Hearings and Appeals
Social Security Administration
Towle Building, Suite 650
330 Second Avenue South
Minneapolis, Minnesota 55401
(612) 348-1230 FAX: (612) 348-1255

STATE

Supreme Court

Alan C. Page, Justice
Minnesota Supreme Court
427 Judicial Center
25 Constitution Avenue
St. Paul, Minnesota 55155
(651) 296-6615 FAX: (651) 222-6250

Court of Appeals

Edward Toussaint, Jr., Chief Judge
Minnesota Court of Appeals
314 Judicial Center
25 Constitution Avenue
St. Paul, Minnesota 55155
(651) 297-1006 FAX: (651) 297-8779

Trial Court Judges

Pamela G. Alexander, Judge
District Court
1251-C Government Center
300 South 6th Street
Minneapolis, Minnesota 55487
(612) 348-5558 FAX: (612) 348-2131

Tanya Bransford, Judge
District Court
4th Judicial District, Juvenile Division
1053-C Government Center
Minneapolis, Minnesota 55487
(612) 348-3771 FAX: (612) 348-2131

James Clarke, Judge
District Court
2nd Judicial District
Ramsey County Courthouse
15 West Kellogg Boulevard
St. Paul, Minnesota 55102
(651) 266-5156 FAX: (651) 266-5277

Harry S. Crump, Judge
District Court
4th Judicial District
Hennepin County Government Center
Minneapolis, Minnesota 55487
(612) 348-5474 FAX: (612) 348-2131

LaJune Thomas Lange, Judge
District Court
4th Judicial District
1251-C Government Center
300 South 6th Street
Minneapolis, Minnesota 55487
(612) 348-5474 FAX: (612) 348-2131

Edward S. Wilson, Judge
District Court
2nd Judicial District
1570 Ramsey County Courthouse
15 West Kellogg Boulevard
St. Paul, Minnesota 55102
(651) 266-8297 FAX: (651) 266-8311

Milton G. Dunham, Referee
Family Court
4th Judicial District
552-C Government Center
Minneapolis, Minnesota 55487
(612) 348-4229 FAX: (612) 348-2131

Charles H. Williams, Referee
District Court
2nd Judicial District
Ramsey County Courthouse
15 West Kellogg Boulevard, Suite 845
St. Paul, Minnesota 55102
(651) 266-2829 FAX: (651) 266-2850

Administrative Law Judge

James F. Cannon, Administrative Law Judge
Office of Administrative Hearings
Worker's Compensation Court
380 East Lafayette Frontage Road
St. Paul, Minnesota 55107
(651) 296-8049 FAX: (651) 282-5404

MISSISSIPPI: (31)

FEDERAL

Henry T. Wingate, Judge
U. S. District Court
for the Southern District of Mississippi
109 James O. Eastland U. S. Courthouse
245 East Capitol Street
Jackson, Mississippi 39201
(601) 965-4042 FAX: (601) 965-4935

Administrative Law Judge

Willie Rose, Administrative Law Judge
Office of Hearings and Appeals
Social Security Administration
McCoy Federal Building, Suite 1014
100 West Capitol Street
Jackson, Mississippi 39269
(601) 965-4650 FAX: (601) 965-5267

STATE

Fred L. Banks, Jr., Associate Justice
Supreme Court of Mississippi
Carroll Gartin Justice Building
450 High Street
Post Office Box 117
Jackson, Mississippi 39205-0117
(601) 359-2096 or (601) 359-3697
FAX: (601) 354-7524 or (601) 359-2443
E-mail: jbanks@mssc.state.ms.us

Tyree Irving, Judge
Court of Appeals
656 High Street
Post Office Box 22847
Jackson, Mississippi 39225-2847
(601) 354-7427 or 354-6218 FAX: (601) 354-7472
E-mail: jirving@mssc.state.ms.us

Leslie D. King, Presiding Judge
Court of Appeals
656 High Street
Post Office Box 22847
Jackson, Mississippi 39205
(601) 354-7441 or 354-7435 FAX: (601) 354-7472
E-mail: jking@mssc.state.ms.us

Circuit Court Judges

Margaret Carey-McCray, Judge
Circuit Court 4th Judicial District
Post Office Box 1775
Greenville, Mississippi 38702-1775
(601) 334-2797 FAX: (601) 334-2716

James Graves, Judge
Circuit Court
7th Judicial District
Post Office Box 327
Jackson, Mississippi 39205
(601) 968-6677 or 968-6688 FAX: (601) 973-5541

Tomie T. Green, Judge
Circuit Court
7th Judicial District
Post Office Box 327
Jackson, Mississippi 39205
(601) 968-6658 FAX: (601) 973-5541

Jannie M. Lewis, Judge
Circuit Court
21st Judicial District
Post Office Box 605
Lexington, Mississippi 39095
(601) 834-1452 FAX: (601) 834-1481
E-mail: JudgeLewis@Sprintmail.com

Isadore W. Patrick, Judge
Circuit Court
9th Judicial District
New Courthouse
Post Office Box 351
Vicksburg, Mississippi 39181
(601) 634-8042 FAX: (601) 634-8049
E-mail: IPatrick@Magnolia.net

Betty W. Sanders, Judge
Circuit Court
4th Judicial District
Post Office Box 244
Greenwood, Mississippi 38930-0244
(601) 455-7946 FAX: (601) 455-7959
E-mail: Judge@netdoor.com

Lillie Blackmon Sanders, Judge
Circuit Court
6th Judicial District
Post Office Box 1384
Natchez, Mississippi 39121
(601) 445-7933 or 445-7938 FAX: (601) 445-2369

Kenneth L. Thomas, Judge
Circuit Court
11th Judicial District
Post Office Box 548
Cleveland, Mississippi 38732
(601) 846-2939 FAX: 846-6280 or 846-2937
E-mail: klthomas@clarsdale.com

John Whitfield, Judge
Circuit Court
2nd Judicial District
Post Office Box 351
Biloxi, Mississippi 39533-0351
(228) 865-4104 FAX: (228) 865-4099
E-mail: JHWhitfield@goldinc.com

Chancery Court Judges

Vicki Roach Barnes, Judge
Chancery Court
9th Judicial District
Post Office Box 351
Vicksburg, Mississippi 39181
(601) 636-8327 FAX: (601) 630-8021

Dorothy W. Colom, Judge
Chancery Court
14th Judicial District
Post Office Box 708
Columbus, Mississippi 39703-0708
(601) 329-5844 FAX: (601) 241-1913
E-mail: DWC@ebicom.net

Ceola James, Judge
Chancery Court
9th Judicial District
Post Office Box 1762
Greenville, Mississippi 38702-1762
(601) 334-2685 FAX: (601) 334-2782

Kennie E. Middleton, Judge
Chancery Court
17th Judicial District
Post Office Box 10
Fayette, Mississippi 39069
(601) 786-6123 FAX: (601) 786-6130
E-mail: Kmiddle@aol.com

Denise Owens, Judge
Chancery Court
5th Judicial District
Post Office Box 686
Jackson, Mississippi 39205
(601) 973-5542 FAX: (601) 968-6794
E-mail: dowens43@yahoo.com

Gail Shaw-Pierson, Judge
Chancery Court
11th Judicial District
Post Office Box 39
Lexington, Mississippi 39095
(601) 834-2599 FAX: (601) 834-043

Johnny Lee Williams, Judge
Chancery Court
10th Judicial District
Post Office Box 1664
Hattiesburg, Mississippi 39403
(601) 545-6032 or 545-6037 FAX:(601) 545-6038

Patricia D. Wise, Judge
Chancery Court
5th Judicial District
Chancery Court Building
Post Office Box 686
Jackson, Mississippi 39205
(601) 968-6521 FAX: (601) 968-6794
E-mail: pwise@metamall.com

County Court Judges

Vernita King Johnson, Judge
County Court
Washington County
Post Office Box 816
Greenville, Mississippi 38702-0816
(601) 334-2654 or 334-2657 FAX: (601) 334-2796

Robin Alfred Midcalf, Judge
County Court Harrison County
Post Office Box 1889
Gulfport, Mississippi 39502
(228) 865-4026 FAX: (228) 865-6523

Houston J. Patton, Judge
County Court
Hinds County
Post Office Box 327
Jackson, Mississippi 39205
(601) 968-6663 FAX: (601) 973-5575

Municipal Court Judges

Lewis Burke, Judge
Municipal Court
City of Vicksburg
820 Veto Street
Vicksburg, Mississippi 39180
(601) 636-2511

Henry Clay, Judge
Municipal Court
City of Jackson
327 East Pascagoula Street
Jackson, Mississippi 39205
(601) 957-0093 FAX: (601) 957-2895

Gail Lowery, Judge
Municipal Court
City of Jackson
327 East Pascaguola Street
Jackson, Mississippi 39205
(601) 366-4739

Oran C. Page, Judge
Municipal Court
City of Jackson
327 East Pascagoula Street
Jackson, Mississippi 39205
(601) 355-2477

State Administrative Law Judges

Melba Dixon, Administrative Law Judge
Mississippi Workers' Compensation Commission
1428 Lakeland Drive
Post Office Box 5300
Jackson, Mississippi 39296-5300
(601) 987-4264 or 987-4273 FAX: (601) 987-4233

Roosevelt Daniels, Hearing Officer
Mississippi Employee Appeals Board
301 North Lamar Street, Suite 100
Jackson, Mississippi 39201
(601) 359-2708 FAX: (601) 359-2729

MISSOURI: (41)

FEDERAL

Theodore McMillan, Judge
U. S. Court of Appeals for the Eighth Circuit
526 U.S. Court & Custom House
1114 Market Street
St. Louis, Missouri 63101
(314) 539-3601 FAX: (314) (314) 539-3632

Fernando J. Gaitan, Jr., Judge
U. S. District Court
for the Western District of Missouri
400 East Ninth Street, Room 7552
Kansas City, Missouri 64106
(816) 512-5630 FAX: (816) 512-5643

Carol E. Jackson, Judge
U. S. District Court
for the Eastern District of Missouri
812 U. S. Court and Custom House
1114 Market Street
St. Louis, Missouri 63101
(314) 539-2368 FAX: (314) 539-7875

Charles A. Shaw, Judge
U. S. District Court
for the Eastern District of Missouri
828 U. S. Court and Custom House
1114 Market Street
St. Louis, Missouri 63101
(314) 539-6926 FAX: (314) 539-3514

Clyde Cahill, Senior Judge
U. S. District Court
for the Eastern District of Missouri
812 U. S. Court and Custom House
1114 Market Street
St. Louis, Missouri 63101
(314) 539-6225

Administrative Law Judges

Jesse H. Butler, Regional Chief Administrative Law Judge
Office of Hearings and Appeals
Social Security Administration
1100 Main Street, Suite 1700
Kansas City, Missouri 64105
(816) 426-5246 FAX: (816) 426-2552

Eve M. Riley, Chief Administrative Law Judge
Office of Hearings and Appeals
Social Security Administration
Old Post Office Building
815 Olive Street, Room 220
St. Louis, Missouri 63101-9933
(314) 539-2804 or 588-7534 FAX: (314) 539-3758

Harvey L. McCormick
Administrative Law Judge (Retired)
Social Security Administration
5613 North Tullis Drive
Kansas City, Missouri 64119
(816) 453-6037

STATE

Supreme Court

Ronnie L. White, Associate Justice
Supreme Court
Supreme Court Building
Post Office Box 150
Jefferson County, Missouri 65102
(573) 751-9652 FAX: (573) 751-7359

Courts of Appeal

George W. Draper, III, Judge
Court of Appeals
Eastern District
111 South 7th Street
St. Louis, Missouri 63101
(314) 340-6932 FAX: (314) 340-6960

Thomas H. Newton, Judge
Court of Appeals
Western District
1300 Oak Street
Kansas City, Missouri 64106
(816) 889-3600 FAX: (816) 889-3599

Trial Court Judges

Henry Edward Autrey, Judge
Circuit Court
22nd Judicial Circuit
Civil Courts Building
10 North Tucker Street
St. Louis, Missouri 63101
(314) 622-4322 FAX: (314) 622-4524

Evelyn Marie Baker, Judge
Circuit Court
22nd Judicial Circuit
Civil Courts Building
10 North Tucker Street
St. Louis, Missouri 63101
(314) 622-3789 FAX: (314) 622-4524

Nannette A. Baker, Judge
Circuit Court
22nd Judicial Circuit
10 North Tucker Street
St. Louis, Missouri 63101
(314) 622-4503 FAX: (314) 622-4524

Michael B. Calvin, Judge
Circuit Court
22nd Judicial Circuit
Civil Courts Building
10 North Tucker Street
St. Louis, Missouri 63101
(314) 622-4311 FAX: (314) 622-4524

Jimmie M. Edwards, Judge
Circuit Court
22nd Judicial Circuit
Civil Courts Building
10 North Tucker Street
St. Louis, Missouri 63101
(314) 622-4376 FAX: (314) 622-4524

Jon R. Gray, Judge
Circuit Court
16th Judicial Circuit - Division 18
Jackson County Courthouse
415 East 12th Street
Kansas City, Missouri 64106
(816) 881-3618 FAX: (816) 881-3950
E-mail: jgray@osca.state.mo.us

Lisa White Hardwick, Judge
Circuit Court
16th Judicial Circuit
Jackson County Courthouse
415 East 12th Street - Division 14
Kansas City, Missouri 64106
(816) 881-3614 FAX: (816) 881-3225

David C. Mason, Judge
Circuit Court
22nd Judicial Circuit
10 North Tucker Street
St. Louis, Missouri 63101
(314) 622-4691 FAX: (314) 622-4524

Donald L. McCullin, Judge
Circuit Court
22nd Judicial Circuit
10 North Tucker Street
St. Louis, Missouri 63101
(314) 622-4819 FAX: (314) 662-4519

Booker T. Shaw, Judge
Circuit Court
22nd Judicial Circuit
Civil Courts Building
10 North Tucker Street
St. Louis, Missouri 63101
(314) 622-4401 FAX: (314) 622-4524

Daniel T. Tillman, Senior Judge
Circuit Court
22nd Judicial Circuit
Civil Courts Building
10 North Tucker Street
St. Louis, Missouri 63101
(314) 622-4331 FAX: (314) 662-4524

David L. Vincent III, Judge
Circuit Court
21st Judicial Circuit
St. Louis County Court Building
7900 Carondelet Avenue
Clayton, Missouri 63105
(314) 615-1509 FAX: (314) 615-7658

Sandra Farragut-Hemphill, Associate Judge
Circuit Court
21st Judicial Circuit
St. Louis County Court Building
7900 Carondelet Avenue
Clayton, Missouri 63105
(314) 889-3062 FAX: (314) 854-6280

Iris Ferguson, Associate Judge
Circuit Court
22nd Judicial Circuit
10 North Tucker Street
St. Louis, Missouri 63101
(314) 622-4555 FAX: (314) 622-4524

Michael Jamison, Associate Judge
Circuit Court
21st Judicial Circuit
St. Louis County Court Building
7900 Carondelet Avenue
Clayton, Missouri 63105
(314) 615-1543 FAX: (314) 854-6280

Brenda Stith Loftin, Associate Judge
Circuit Court
21st Judicial Circuit
St. Louis County Court Building
7900 Carondelet Avenue
Clayton, Missouri 63105
(314) 615-3047 FAX: (314) 854-6280

Angela Turner Quigless, Associate Judge
Circuit Court
22nd Judicial Circuit
Civil Courts Building
10 North Tucker Street
St. Louis, Missouri 63101
(314) 622-4687 FAX: (314) 622-4524

Leonard S. Hughes, III, Judge
Municipal Court of Kansas City
1101 Locust Street
Kansas City, Missouri 64106
(816) 513-1068 FAX: (816) 513-3905

William J. McHugh, Judge
Municipal Court of St. Louis
1430 Olive
St. Louis, Missouri 63103
(314) 622-4701 FAX: (314) 622-3223

Deboral Neal, Judge
Municipal Court of Kansas City
1101 Locust Street
Kansas City, Missouri 64106
(816) 513-1068 FAX: (816) 513-3905

James M. Reed II, Judge
Municipal Court of Kansas City
1101 Locust Street
Kansas City, Missouri 64106
(816) 513-1068 FAX: 513-3905

Lisl Williams, Judge
Municipal Court of St. Louis
1430 Olive
St. Louis, Missouri 63103
(314) 622-4601 FAX: (314) 622-3223

Andrew Mosby, Police Judge
108 West Francis Street
Howardville, Missouri 63839
(314) 688-2370

Anne-Marie Clarke, Commissioner
Family Court
920 North Vandeventer
St. Louis, Missouri 63108
(314) 552-2030 FAX: (314) 552-2260

Gregory B. Gillis, Commissioner
Drug Court
Jackson County, Courthouse
415 East 12th Street
Kansas City, Missouri 64106
(816) 881-3304 FAX: (816) 881-3894

John F. Payne, Commissioner
Family Court
625 East 26th Street
Kansas City, Missouri 64108
(816) 435-4710 FAX (816) 435-4792

Barbara Peebles, Commissioner
Drug Court
Municipal Court Building
1320 Market
St. Louis, Missouri 63103
(314) 613-7184 FAX: (314) 552-7667

Administrative Law Judges

Karen Bosley, Administrative Law Judge
Dept. of Labor and Industrial Relations
Division of Workers' Compensation
St Louis City
111 North 7th Street, Room 250
St. Louis, Missouri 63101
(314) 340-6865 or 340-6866 FAX: (314) 340-6915

Leslie H. Brown, Chief Administrative Law Judge
Dept. of Labor and Industrial Relations
Division of Workers' Compensation
3737 Harry S. Truman Boulevard, Suite 300
St. Charles, Missouri 63301
(314) 940-3326 or 940-1284 FAX: (314) 940-3331

Kenneth J. Cain, Administrative Law Judge
Dept. of Labor and Industrial Relations
Division of Workers' Compensation
1805 Grand Avenue # 400
Kansas City, Missouri 64108
(816) 889-2481 FAX: (816) 889-2489

MONTANA: (0)

NEBRASKA: (4)

Edna R. Atkins, Judge
County Court
Douglas County
1701 Farnam Street
Omaha, Nebraska 68183-0001
(402) 444-4230 FAX: (402) 444-6890

Darryl R. Lowe, Judge
County Court
Douglas County
1701 Farnam Street
Omaha, Nebraska 68183
(402) 444-6828 FAX: (402) 444-6787

Wadie Thomas, Jr., Judge
The Separate Juvenile Court of Douglas County
Hall of Justice - Room 600
1600 Farnam Street
Omaha, Nebraska 68183-0001
(402) 444-7889 or 444-4539 FAX: (402) 444-3444

Administrative Law Judge

Brenda J. Council, Judge
Commission of Industrial Relations
Kutak Rock
1650 Farnam Street
Omaha, Nebraska 68102
(402) 346-6000 FAX: (402) 346-1148

NEVADA: (4)

FEDERAL

Johnnie Rawlinson, Judge
U. S. Court of Appeals
for the Ninth Circuit
U. S. Courthouse
333 Los Vegas Boulevard South - Room 7072
Las Vegas, Nevada 89101
(702) 464-5670 FAX: (702) 464-5671

STATE

Michael L. Douglas, District Court Judge
Dept. 11
Eighth Judicial District Court
Clark County Courthouse
200 South Third Street
Las Vegas, Nevada 89155
(702) 455-4527 FAX: (702) 455-0058

Lee A. Gates, Chief Judge
District Court Judge Dept. 8
Eighth Judicial District Court
Clark County Courthouse
200 South Third Street
Las Vegas, Nevada 89155-0001
(702) 455-4681 FAX: (702) 382-1015

Lizzie R. Hatcher, Coroner's Inquest Master
Eighth Judicial District Court
of the State of Nevada
302 East Carson Street, Suite # 930
Las Vegas, Nevada 89155
(702) 386-2988 FAX: (702) 386-8066

NEW HAMPSHIRE: (0)

NEW JERSEY: (70)

FEDERAL

Joseph A. Greenaway, Jr., Judge
U. S. District Court for the District of New Jersey
Martin Luther King, Jr. Federal Building
and U. S. Courthouse
50 Walnut Street - Rm. 4040
Post Office Box 999
Newark, New Jersey 07101-0999
(973) 622-4828 FAX: (973) 622-4803

Anne E. Thompson, Chief Judge
U. S. District Court
for the District of New Jersey
4000 Clarkson S. Fisher Federal Building
and U. S. Courthouse
402 East State Street
Trenton, New Jersey 08608
(609) 989-2123 FAX: (609)989-2187 or 989-2007

William H. Walls, Judge
U. S. District Court
for the District of New Jersey
Martin Luther King, Jr. Federal Building
and U. S. Courthouse
50 Walnut Street - Rm. 4046
Post Office Box 999
Newark, New Jersey 07101-0999
(973) 645-2564 FAX: (973) 645-6467 or 645-3436

Susan D. Davis Wiggenton, Magistrate Judge
U. S. District Court
for the District of New Jersey
Martin Luther King, Jr. Federal Building
and U. S. Courthouse
50 Walnut Street
Newark, New Jersey 07101
(973 645-5903 FAX: (973) 645-3843

STATE

Supreme Court

James H. Coleman, Jr., Justice
New Jersey Supreme Court
99 Mount Bethel Road
Warren, New Jersey 07059
(908) 769-9011 FAX: (908) 769-5624

Courts of Appeals

Dennis J. Braithwaite, Judge
Appellate Division,
Superior Court of New Jersey
1201 Bacharach Boulevard
Atlantic City, New Jersey 08401
(609) 441-3330 FAX: (609) 345-1355

John E. Wallace, Jr., Judge
Appellate Division
Superior Court of New Jersey
216 Haddon Avenue, Suite #700
Westmont, New Jersey 08108-2815
(856) 858-8636 FAX: (609) 858-9243
E-mail: Sheila_Silva@judiciary.state.nj.us

Superior Court Judges

Christine Allen-Jackson, Judge
Superior Court of New Jersey
Cumberland County
Cumberland County Courthouse, Room A215
Broad Street & Fayette Street
Bridgeton, New Jersey 08302
(856) 453-4690 FAX: (856) 453-4592

Frances L. Antonin, Judge
Superior Court of New Jersey
Hudson County
Administration Building - Room 213
595 Newark Avenue
Jersey City, New Jersey 07206-2392
(201) 795-6622 FAX: (201) 795-0725 or 217-5288
E-mail: Frances_Antonin@judiciary.state.nj.us
E-mail: Antonins@peoplepc.com

Marie White Bell, Judge
Superior Court of New Jersey
Burlington County
Courts Facility - Room 601
49 Rancocas Road
Post Office Box 6555
Mt. Holly, New Jersey 08060-6555
(609) 518-2720 FAX: (609) 702-5643
E-mail: Marie_Bell@judiciary.state.nu.us

Audrey Peyton Blackburn, Judge
Superior Court of New Jersey
Mercer County Courthouse
175 South Broad Street
Trenton, New Jersey 08650-0068
(609) 278-7197 FAX: (609) 633-0746
E-mail: Audrey_Blackburn@judiciary.state.nj.us

Thomas A. Brown, Jr., Judge
Superior Court of New Jersey
Camden County - Hall of Justice - Room 370
101 South 5th Street
Camden, New Jersey 08103-4001
(856) 225-5007 FAX: (856) 756-2276
E-mail: Thomas_Brown@judiciary.state.nj.us

Rudy B. Coleman, Judge
Superior Court of New Jersey, Union County
2 Broad Street
Elizabeth, New Jersey 07207
(908) 659-4143 FAX: (908) 659-3880
E-mail: Judge_R_Coleman@judiciary.state.nj.us

Gerald J. Council, Judge
Superior Court of New Jersey
Mercer County Courthouse
209 South Broad Street
Post Office Box 8068
Trenton, New Jersey 08650-0068
(609) 989-6239 FAX: (609) 278-2705

Wendel E. Daniels, Judge
Superior Court of New Jersey
118 Washington Street
Toms River, New Jersey 08754
(732) 929-2006 FAX: (732) 506-5087
E-mail: Wendel_Daniels@judiciary.state.nj.us

Theodore Z. Davis, Presiding Judge
General Equity, Superior Court of New Jersey
Camden County Court House - Hall of Justice
101 South 5th Street, Suite 640
Camden, New Jersey 08103-4001
(856) 225-7013 FAX: (856) 580-5391
E-mail: Judge_Davis@judiciary.state.nj.us

Travis L. Francis, Judge
Superior Court of New Jersey
Middlesex County Courthouse
1 J. F. Kennedy Square
Post Office Box 964
New Brunswick, New Jersey 08903-0964
(732) 981-3216 FAX: (732) 981-3216
E-mail: Judge_T_Francis@judiciary.state.nj.us

Ronald J. Freeman, Judge
Superior Court of New Jersey
Camden County Courthouse
Hall of Justice - Suite 260
101 South 5th Street
Camden, New Jersey 08103
(856) 225-7025 FAX: (856) 365-8256

Harold C. Fullilove, Presiding Judge
Criminal Division
Superior Court of New Jersey
Essex County Courthouse
New Courts Building - Room 608
50 West Market Street
Newark, New Jersey 07102
(973) 693-5862 FAX: (973) 693-5851
E-mail: Judge_Fullilove@judiciary.state.nj.us

F. Michael Giles, Judge
Superior Court of New Jersey
Essex County Courthouse
New Courts Building - Room 706
50 West Market Street
Newark, New Jersey 07102
(973) 693-5864 or 693-5865
FAX: (973) 693-5851 or 693-5963
E-mail: Judge_M_Giles@judiciary.state.nj.us

Glenn A. Grant, Judge
Superior Court of New Jersey
212 Washington Street
Gibraltar Building, 13th Floor
Newark, New Jersey 07102
(973) 693-6814 FAX: (973) 693-6636
E-mail: Judge_G_Grants@judiciary.state.nj.us

Michelle Hollar Gregory, Judge
Superior Court of New Jersey
Hall of Records - Room 420
465 Dr. Martin Luther King, Jr. Boulevard
Newark, New Jersey 07102
(973) 693-6703 FAX: (973) 693-6636
E-mail: Judge_HollarGregory@judiciary.state.nj.us

Rudolph N. Hawkins, Jr., Judge
Superior Court of New Jersey
Union County Courthouse
2 Broad Street
Elizabeth, New Jersey 07207
(908) 659-3415 FAX: (908) 659-3350 or 820-3239
E-mail: Judge_R_Hawkins@judiciary.state.nj.us

Mac D. Hunter, Judge
Superior Court of New Jersey
Hudson County Courthouse
Administration Building
595 Newark Avenue
Jersey City, New Jersey 07306-2392
(201) 795-6912 FAX: (201) 459-2010
E-mail: Mac_Hunter@judiciary.state.nj.us

James L. Jackson, Judge
Superior Court of New Jersey
Atlantic County Courthouse
1201 Bacharach Boulevard
Atlantic City, New Jersey 08401
(609) 345-6700, Ext. 3258 FAX: (609) 343-2238
E-mail: Judge_J_Jackson@judiciary.state.nj.us

Lawrence M. Lawson, Assignment Judge
Superior Court of New Jersey
Monmouth County Courthouse
Court and Monument Streets, Room 301
Post Office Box 1266
Freehold, New Jersey 07728-1266
(732) 431-7128 FAX: (732) 431-1147
E-mail: Judge_Lawson@judiciary.state.nj.us

Betty J. Lester, Judge
Superior Court of New Jersey
Essex County Courthouse
New Courts Building - Room 1206
50 West Market Street
Newark, New Jersey 07102
(973) 693-5872 FAX: (973) 424-2421
E-mail: Judge_B_Lester@judiciary.state.nj.us

Elijah L. Miller, Jr., Judge
Superior Court of New Jersey
Bergen County Justice Center
10 Main Street, Room 401
Hackensack, New Jersey 07601
(201) 646-3581 FAX: (201) 646-6791
E-mail: Elijah_Miller@judiciary.state.nj.us

Michael J. Nelson, Judge
Superior Court of New Jersey
Essex County Courthouse
New Courts Building - Room 1218
50 West Market Street
Newark, New Jersey 07102
(973) 693-6794 FAX: (973) 424-2424
E-mail: Judge-M_Nelson@judiciary.state.nj.us

Lorraine Pullen, Judge
Superior Court of New Jersey, Family Division
Middlesex County Courthouse - Room 102
120 New Street
New Brunswick, New Jersey 08903-2691
(732) 981-3031 FAX: (732) 565-2937
E-mail: Judge_L_Pullen@judiciary.state.nj.us

Paulette M. Sapp-Peterson, Judge
Superior Court of New Jersey
Mercer County Civil Courts
175 South Broad Street
Post Office Box 8068
Trenton, New Jersey 08650-0068
(609) 989-6823 FAX: (609) 392-1720

Thomas S. Smith, Jr., Judge
Superior Court of New Jersey
Burlington County
49 Rancocas Road
Post Office Box 6555
Mount Holly, New Jersey 08060-6555
(609) 518-2700 FAX: (609) 702-5647
E-mail: Thomas_Smith@judiciary.state.nj.us

Shirley A. Tolentino, Judge
Superior Court of New Jersey
Hudson County Courthouse
Administrative Building
595 Newark Avenue, Room 911
Jersey City, New Jersey 07306-2392
(201) 795-6668 FAX: (201) 795-6766

Renee Jones Weeks, Judge
Superior Court of New Jersey
Gibraltar Building, 13th Floor
212 Washington Street
Newark, New Jersey 07102
(973) 693-5891 FAX: (973) 693-6658 or 693-6727

Stephen H. Womack, Judge
Superior Court of New Jersey—Passaic County
County Administration Building, Room 944
401 Grand Street
Paterson, New Jersey 07505
(973) 247-8452 FAX: (973) 754-6951
E-mail: Judge_S_Womack@judiciary.state.nj.us

Municipal Courts

Caryl Mills Amana, Judge
Lawnside (Boro) Municipal Court
4 Douglas Avenue - Boro Hall
Lawnside, New Jersey 08045
(856) 573-6209 FAX: (856) 546-3232

Esther Canty Barnes, Judge
Irvington Municipal Court—Civic Square
Irvington, New Jersey 07111
(973) 399-0004 FAX: (973) 399-6746

Clarence Barry-Austin, Judge
South Orange Municipal Court
201 South Orange Avenue
South Orange,New Jersey 07079
(973) 378-7805 FAX: (973) 378-9322
E-mail: CBARRYAUST@AOL.COM

Ernest R. Booker, Judge
East Orange Municipal Court
221 Freeway Drive East
East Orange, New Jersey 07018
(973) 266-5300
and, Judge Montclair Township Municipal Court
647 Bloomfield Avenue
Montclair, New Jersey 07042
(973) 509-4774 FAX: (973) 744-6902

Alison Brown-Jones, Judge
Newark City Municipal Court
Brennan/Marshall Court Complex
31 Green Street
Newark, New Jersey 07102
(973) 733-6520 FAX: (973) 733-8533

Rosalyn Cary Charles, Judge
Irvington Municipal Court
Public Safety Building - Civic Square
Irvington, New Jersey 07111
(973) 399-6671 or 399-6674 FAX: (973) 399-6746

Joseph M. Clark, Judge
Englewood Municipal Court
73 South Van Brundt Street
Englewood, New Jersey 07631-0228
(201) 569-0255 FAX: (201) 567-7083

Claude M. Coleman, Judge
Newark Municipal Court
31 Green Street
Newark, New Jersey 07102
(973) 733-8905 FAX: (973) 733-8533

Harry L. Cornish, Judge
Paterson Municipal Court
111 Broadway
Paterson, New Jersey 07514
(973) 881-6876 FAX: (973) 357-1765

Charles Craig, Judge
Plainfield City Municipal Court
325 Watchung Avenue
Plainfield, New Jersey 07061
(908) 753-3064 FAX: (908) 753-3030

James W. Faison, III, Judge
Camden Municipal Court
City Hall
Sixth and Market Streets
Post Office Box 95120
Camden, New Jersey 08101
(856) 757-7100 FAX: (856) 541-5326
E-mail: WF3CJMC@AOL.com

Horatious Green, Judge
Orange Municipal Court
29 Park Street
Orange, New Jersey 07050-2015
(973) 266-4161 FAX: (973) 674-8865

Joan Robinson Gross, Presiding Judge
Plainfield Municipal Court
325 Watchung Avenue
Plainfield, New Jersey 07061
(908) 753-3064 FAX: (908) 753-3030

Karimu Hill-Harvey, Judge
East Orange Municipal Court
221 Freeway Drive East
East Orange, New Jersey 07018
(973) 266-5300 FAX: (973) 266-5249

Jason Holt, Judge
Orange Municipal Court
593 Lincoln Avenue
Orange, New Jersey 07050
(973) 266-4161 FAX: (973) 672-5233

James A. Key, Jr., Judge
Plainfield Municipal Court
325 Watchung Avenue
Plainfield, New Jersey 07061
(908) 753-3064 FAX: (908) 753-3065

Carl Marshall, Judge
Elizabeth Municipal Court
One Police Plaza
Elizabeth, New Jersey 07201-2397
(908) 527-6550 FAX: (908) 558-1503

Lawson McElroy, Judge
Trenton Municipal Court
227 North Clinton Avenue
Trenton, New Jersey 0869
(609) 989-3700 FAX: (609) 989-4247

Paul McLemore, Judge
Trenton Municipal Court
225 North Clinton Avenue
Trenton, New Jersey 08609
(609) 989-3700 FAX: (609) 989-4247

Lewis Stephenson McRae, Judge
Jersey City Municipal Court
769 Montgomery Street
Jersey City, New Jersey 07306
(201) 547-4326 FAX: (201) 547-4984

Billie J. Moore, Judge
Pleasantville Municipal Court
18 North First Street
Pleasantville, New Jersey 08232
(609) 484-3663 FAX: (609) 484-8641

Dan Solomon Smith, Judge
Orange Municipal Court
439 Lincoln Avenue
Civic Square
Orange, New Jersey 07111
(973) 266-4164 FAX: (973) 672-5233

Theodore N. Stephens, II, Judge
East Orange Municipal Court
221 Freeway Drive East
East Orange, New Jersey 07018
(973) 266-5300 FAX: (973) 266-5249

Shaka Taylor, Judge
Newark Municipal Court
31 Green Street
Newark, New Jersey 07102
(973) 733-6520 FAX: (973) 733-6147

Lisa Thornton, Judge
Neptune Township Municipal Court
25 Neptune Boulevard
Neptune, New Jersey 07753
(732) 988-5200 FAX: (732) 988-3128

Sheila A. Venable, Judge
Jersey City Municipal Court
769 Montgomery Street
Jersey City, New Jersey 07306
(201) 547-4326 FAX: (201) 574-4984

Sharon Wade-Spearman, Judge
Irvington Municipal Court
Civic Square
Irvington, New Jersey 07111
(973) 399-6674 FAX: (973) 399-6746

John H. Watson, Jr., Judge
East Orange Municipal Court
221 Freeway, New Jersey 07018
(973) 266-5300 FAX: (973) 266-5249

Bruce F. Weekes, Jr., Judge
Atlantic City Municipal Court
3200 Fairmount Avenue
Atlantic City, New Jersey 08401
(609) 347-5560 or 347-5470 FAX: (609) 347-5450

Marilyn E. Williams, Judge
Newark Municipal Court
31 Green Street
Newark, New Jersey 07102
(973) 733-6520 FAX: (973) 733-8533

E. Ronald Wright, Judge
New Brunswick Municipal Court
Memorial Parkway, Route 18 N
Post Office Box 265
New Brunswick, New Jersey 08903
(732) 745-5089 FAX: (732) 745-5180

James E. Young, Jr., Judge
Teaneck Municipal Court
818 Teaneck Road
Teaneck, New Jersey 07666
(201) 837-4850 or 837-0851 FAX: (201) 833-8047

Administrative Law Judges

Mumtaz Bari-Brown
State Administrative Law Judge
185 Washington Street
Newark, New Jersey 07102
(973) 648-6051 FAX: (973) 648-6124

Irene Jones, State Administrative Law Judge
185 Washington Street
Newark, New Jersey 07102
(973) 648-6015 FAX: (973) 648-6124

Phillip N. Gumbs
Supervising Administrative Judge
Workers' Compensation
954 Route 166
Toms River, New Jersey 08753-7331
(732) 349-9592 FAX: (732) 349-7348

NEW MEXICO: (5)

Tommy Jewell, Presiding Children's Court Judge
Division III
5100 Second Street N.W.
Albuquerque, New Mexico 87107
(505) 841-7392 FAX: (505) 841-5915
E-mail: albdtej@nmcourts.com

Angela Jewell, Presiding Judge
Domestic Violence Division
Division XXI
Post Office Box 488
Albuquerque, New Mexico 87103
(505) 841-6748 FAX: (505) 841-7446
E-mail: albdajj@nmcourts.com

Kisha Shantee, Judge
Metropolitan Court
Division VI
Post Office Box 133
Albuquerque, New Mexico 87103
(505) 841-8289 FAX: (505) 841-8192

Frederick Arnold, Judge
Municipal Court
1700N. Boxton
Portalas, New Mexico 88130
(505) 356-4923 FAX: (505) 356-1490

Stan Whittaker
Domestic Violence Hearing Officer
Second Judicial District Court
Post Office Box 488
Albuquerque, New Mexico 87103
(505) 841-6731 FAX: (505) 841-7446

NEW YORK: (130)

Amalya Lyle Kearse, Judge
U. S. Court of Appeals for the Second Circuit
U. S. Courthouse
40 Foley Square
New York, New York 10007-1507
(212) 857-2250 or (212) 857-2259

Deborah A. Batts, Judge
U.S. District Court
for the Southern District of New York
2510 U. S. Courthouse - Foley Square
500 Pearl Street
New York, New York 10007-1501
(212) 805-0186 or 805-0187 FAX: (212) 805-7902

George B. Daniels, Judge
U. S. District Court
for the Southern District of New York
410 U. S. Courthouse
New York, New York 10007
(212) 463-6976 FAX: (212) 805-6737
E-mail: george_daniels@nysd.uscourts.gov

Kevin N. Fox, Judge
U. S. District Court
for the Southern District of New York
40 Centre Street
New York, New York 10007-1507
(212) 805-6705 FAX: (212) 805-6712

Sterling Johnson, Jr., Judge
U. S. District Court
for the Eastern Distict of New York
5162 U. S. Courthouse
225 Cadman Plaza East
Brooklyn, New York 11201-1818
(718) 260-2465 FAX: (718) 260-2467

Barrington D. Parker, Jr., Judge
U. S. District Court
for the Southern District of New York
U. S. Courthouse
300 Quarropas Street
White Plains, New York 10601-4150
(914) 390-4177 FAX: (914) 390-4179

Laura Taylor Swain, Judge
U. S. District Court
for the Southern District of New York
U. S. Courthouse
40 Foley Square
New York, New York 10007
(212) 805-0417 FAX: (212) 805-8426
E-mail: ltswain@juno.com

Robert L. Carter, Senior Judge
U. S. District Court
for the Southern District of New York
2220 U. S. Courthouse
500 Pearl Street
New York, New York 10007-1501
(212) 805-0196 FAX: (212) 805-7904

Constance Baker Motley, Senior Judge
U. S. District Court
for the Southern District of New York
2540 U. S. Courthouse
500 Pearl Street
New York, New York 10007-1501
(212) 805-0231, 805-0232 or 805-0233
FAX: (212) 805-7916

James L. Watson, Senior Judge
U.S. Court of International Trade
1 Federal Plaza
New York, New York 10278-0001
(212) 264-2877 FAX: (212) 264-7568
E-mail: ziks@aol.com

Cornelius Blackshear, Judge
U.S. Bankruptcy Court
One Bowling Green
New York, New York 10004-1408
(212) 668-5632 FAX: (212)-668-3186

Ronald L. Ellis, Magistrate Judge
U. S. District Court for the Southern District of New York
740 U. S. Courthouse
40 Foley Square
New York, New York 10007-1507
(212) 805-0242 FAX: (212) 805-7929

Hugh B. Scott, Magistrate Judge
U. S. District Court
for the Western District of New York
414 U. S. Courthouse
68 Court Street
Buffalo, New York 14202
(716) 551-4010 FAX: (716) 551-3011

George A. Yanthis, Magistrate Judge
U. S. District Court
for the Southern District of New York
U. S. Courthouse
300 Quarropas Street
White Plains, New York 10601-4150
(914) 390-4088 FAX: (914) 390-4095
E-mail: george_a_yanthis@nysd.uscourts.gov

STATE

Court of Appeals

George Bundy Smith, Judge
State of New York Court of Appeals
61 Broadway - Room 2900
New York, New York 10006-2704
(212) 363-5990 or (518) 455-7710
FAX: (212) 344-3958 or (518) 463-8782
E-mail: :GBSmithG@netscape.net

Intermediate Appellate Courts

William J. Davis, New York Appellate Division
1st Department
Supreme Court of the State of New York
Hall of Justice - 60 Centre Street
New York, New York 10007-1474
(212) 374-4502 FAX: (212) 748-5928
E-mail: wdavis@courts.state.nys_us

Marquette L. Floyd, Justice
Appellate Term
2nd Department
400 Carleton Avenue
Central Islip, New York 11722-9070
(516) 853-4537 FAX: (516) 853-4543
E-mail: mfloyd@courts.state.ny.us

Samuel L. Green
New York State Appellate Division
4th Department
Supreme Court of the State of New York
501 Hall of Justice Civic Center Plaza
Rochester, New York 14614
(716) 851-3415 FAX: (716) 852-6367

Daniel W. Joy
New York State Appellate Division
2nd Department
Supreme Court of the State of New York
88-11 Sutphin Boulevard
Jamaica, New York 11435-3792
(718) 520-3722
FAX: (718) 657-9865 or (718) 520-2458

Michelle Weston Patterson, Judge
Appellate Term, 2nd Department
360 Adams Street
Brooklyn, New York 11201-3712
(718) 643-7074 FAX: (718) 643-7250
E-mail: kellecp@aol.com

William C. Thompson
New York State Appellate Division
2nd Department
Supreme Court of the State of New York
45 Monroe Place
Brooklyn, New York 11202-2695
(718) 722-6351 FAX: (718) 722-6302

Milton L. Williams
New York State Appellate Division
1st Department
Supreme Court of the State of New York
27 Madison Avenue & 25th Street
New York, New York 10010-2295
(212) 340-0430 FAX: (212) 889-4412
E-mail: mwilliam@courts.state.ny.us

Trial Court Judges

Sheila Abdus-Salaam, Justice
New York State Supreme Court
71 Thomas Street
New York, New York 10013-3821
(212) 815-0878 or 815-0880 FAX: (212) 815-0892)
E-mail: sabdussa@courts.state.ny.us

Laura D. Blackburne, Justice
New York State Supreme Court
125-01 Queens Boulevard E-387
Kew Gardens, New York 11415-3791
(718) 520-4584 FAX: (718) 520-4661
E-mail: lbackburn@courts.state.ny.us

Janice L. Bowman, Justice
New York State Supreme Court
851 Grand Concourse
Bronx, New York 10451-2978
(718) 590-3794 FAX: (718) 590-8914

Antonio I. Brandveen, Justice
New York State Supreme Court
Nassau County Courthouse
262 Old Country Road
Mineola, New York 11501-4212
(516) 571-2628 FAX: (516) 571-2160
E-mail: abrandve@courts.state.ny.us

Cheryl E. Chambers, Justice
New York State Supreme Court
360 Adams Street
Brooklyn, New York 11201-3712
(718) 643-4407 FAX: (718) 643-3549
E-mail: cchambe@courts.state.ny.us

Barry A. Cozier, Justice
New York State Supreme Court
60 Centre Street
New York, New York 10007-1474
(212) 374-8515 FAX: (212) 374-7256
E-mail: bcozier@courts.state.nys_us

Dorothy A. Cropper, Justice
New York State Supreme Court
100 Centre Street
New York, New York 10013-4386
(212) 374-5258 FAX: (212) 374-3003
E-mail: dcroppe@courts.state.ny.us

Gloria M. Dabiri, Justice
New York State Supreme Court
360 Adams Street - Room 717
Brooklyn, New York 11201-3712
(718) 643-6246 FAX: (718) 643-4994
E-mail: gdabiri@courts.state.nys_us

Leland G. DeGrasse, Justice
New York State Supreme Court
60 Centre Street
New York, New York 10007-1474
(212) 374-4735 FAX: (212) 374-3326
E-mail: idegrass@courts.state.ny.us

Lewis L. Douglass, Justice
New York State Supreme Court
360 Adams Street
Brooklyn, New York 11201-3712
(718) 643-5086 FAX: (718) 643-3549
E-mail: douglas@courts.state.ny.us

Deborah A. Dowling, Justice
New York State Supreme Court
360 Adams Street
Brooklyn, New York 11201-3712
(718) 643-5340 FAX: (718) 643-4995
E-mail: ddowlin@courts.state.ny.us

Luther V. Dye, Justice
New York State Supreme Court
88-11 Sutphin Boulevard
Jamaica, New York 11435-3792
(718) 520-3025 FAX: (718) 520-6611
E-mail: idye@courts.state.ny.us

Simeon Golar, Justice
New York State Supreme Court
88-11 Sutphin Boulevard
Jamaica, New York 11435-3792
(718) 520-2599 FAX: (718) 520-6433
E-mail: sgolar@courts.state.ny.us

Priscilla L. Hall, Justice
New York State Supreme Court
360 Adams Street
Brooklyn, New York 11201-3712
(718) 643-5121 FAX: (718) 643-7934
E-mail: phall@courts.state.ny.us

Carol E. Huff, Justice
New York State Supreme Court
60 Centre Street
New York, New York 10007-1474
(212) 374-8369 FAX: (212) 374-3326
E-mail: chuff@courts.state.ny.us

Alexander W. Hunter, Jr., Justice
New York State Supreme Court
851 Grand Concourse
Bronx, New York 10451-2978
(718) 590-3779 FAX: (718) 590-7302
E-mail: sct324@aol.com

James W. Hutcherson, Justice
New York State Supreme Court
360 Adams Street
Brooklyn, New York 11201-3712
(718) 643-8094 FAX: (718) 643-7020
E-mail: jhutcher@courts.state.ny.us

Randolph Jackson, Justice
New York State Supreme Court
360 Adams Street
Brooklyn, New York 11201-3712
(718) 643-2116 FAX: (718) 643-2044
E-mail: rjackson@courts.state.ny.us

Theodore T. Jones, Jr., Justice
New York State Supreme Court
360 Adams Street
Brooklyn, New York 11201-3712
(718) 643-5880 FAX: (718) 643-4222
E-mail: tjones@courts.state.ny.us

Leslie G. Leach, Justice
New York State Supreme Court
125-01 Queens Boulevard
Kew Gardens, New York 11415-3791
(718) 520-2218 FAX: (718) 520-2494
E-mail: lleach@courts.state.ny.us

Daniel Lewis, Justice
New York State Supreme Court
125-01 Queens Boulevard
Kew Gardens, New York 11415-3791
(718) 520-4662 FAX: (718) 520-2494
E-mail:dlewis@courts.state.ny.us

Yvonne Lewis, Justice
New York State Supreme Court
360 Adams Street
Brooklyn, New York 11201-3712
(718) 643-3191 FAX: (718) 643-4995
E-mail: ylewis@courts.state.ny.us

Plummer E. Lott, Justice
New York State Supreme Court
360 Adams Street
Brooklyn, New York 11201-3712
(718) 643-5349 FAX: (718) 643-7934
E-mail: plott@courts.state.ny.us

Richard B. Lowe III, Justice
New York State Supreme Court
100 Centre Street
New York, New York 10013-4386
(212) 374-8151 FAX: (212) 748-5089
E-mail: rlowe@courts.state.ny.us

La Tia Martin, Justice
New York State Supreme Court
851 Grand Concourse
Bronx, New York 10451
(718) 590-3632 FAX: (718) 590-7837
E-mail: lmartin@courts.state.ny.us

Larry D. Martin, Justice
New York State Supreme Court
360 Adams Street
Brooklyn, New York 11201-3712
(718) 643-3985 FAX: (718) 743-4993
E-mail: lmartin@courts.state.ny.us

Reynold N. Mason, Justice
New York State Supreme Court
360 Adams Street
Brooklyn, New York 11201-3712
(718) 643-8038 FAX: (718) 643-7934
E-mail: rmason@courts.state.ny.us

Donna M. Mills, Justice
New York State Supreme Court
111 Centre Street
New York, New York 10013-4389
(212) 374-8463 FAX: (212) 374-0402
E-mail: dmills@courts.state.ny.us

Juanita Bing Newton, Deputy Chief Administrative Judge for Justice Initiatives
New York State Supreme Court
25 Beaver Street
New York, New York 10004
(212) 428-2130 FAX: (212) 428-2192
E-mail: jbnewton@courts.state.ny.us

Kibbie F. Payne, Justice
New York State Supreme Court
111 Centre Street
New York, New York 10013-4389
(212) 374-8497 FAX: (212) 374-0402
E-mail: kpayne@courts.state.ny.us

Frederick D. R. Sampson, Justice
New York State Supreme Court
25-10 Court Square
Long Island City, New York 11101
(718) 520-3903 FAX: (718) 520-2539

Patricia P. Satterfield, Justice
New York State Supreme Court
88-11 Sutphin Boulevard
Jamaica, New York 11435-3792
(718) 520-3732 FAX: (718) 520-6683
E-mail: psatterf@courts.state.ny.us

Rose H. Sconiers, Justice
New York State Supreme Court
Erie County Hall
Buffalo, New York 14202
(716) 851-3404 FAX: (716) 851-3292
E-mail: rsconier@courts.state.ny.us

Mark H. Spires, Justice
New York State Supreme Court
125-01 Queens Boulevard
Kew Gardens, New York 11415-3791
(718) 520-6737 or 520-4873 FAX: (718) 261-6240
E-mail: mspires@courts.state.ny.us

Janice A. Taylor, Justice
New York State Supreme Court
88-11 Sutphin Boulevard
Jamaica, New York 11435-3792
(718) 520-3159 FAX: (718) 520-6406
E-mail: jtaylor@courts.state.ny.us

Kenneth L. Thompson, Jr., Justice
New York State Supreme Court
851 Grand Concourse
Bronx, New York 10451-2978
(718) 590-3967 FAX: (718) 590-8914

Sandra L. Townes, Justice
New York Supreme Court
Onondaga County Court House, Suite 405
401 Montgomery Street, Room 405
Syracuse, New York 13202-2126
(315) 435-2485 FAX: (315) 435-3393
E-mail: stownes@courts.state.ny.us

Troy K. Webber, Justice
New York State Supreme Court
851 Grand Concourse
Bronx, New York 10451
(718) 590-3744 FAX: (718) 590-8899
E-mail: twebber@courts.state.ny.us

Lottie E. Wilkins, Justice
New York State Supreme Court
71 Thomas Street
New York, New York 10013-3821
(212) 815-0883 or 815-0884 FAX: (212) 815-0892

Patricia Anne Williams, Justice
New York State Supreme Court-Criminal Term
851 Grand Concourse
Bronx, New York 10451-2978
(718) 590-3792 FAX: (718) 590-7837

**Retired Judges without telephone numbers listed may be contacted through the Administrative Judge of the New York State Supreme Court system.*

Howard E. Bell, Justice (Retired)
(Judicial Hearing Officer)*
New York State Supreme Court
100 Centre Street
New York, New York 10013.

Edward R. Dudley, Justice (Retired)
New York State Supreme Court
100 Centre Street
New York, New York 10013

Thomas R. Jones, Justice (Retired)
New York State Supreme Court
100 Centre Street
New York, New York 10013

Edith Miller, Justice (Retired)
New York State Supreme Court
100 Centre Street
New York, New York 10013

Alfred S. Robbins, Justice (Retired)
(Judicial Hearing Officer)
New York State Supreme Court
McCabe, Collins, McGeough & Fowler, LLP
114 Old Country Road
Mineola, New York 11501
(516) 741-6266 FAX: (516) 873-9496

Jawn A. Sandifer, Justice (Retired)
New York State Supreme Court
100 Centre Street
New York, New York 10013

Clifford Scott, Justice (Retired)
New York State Supreme Court
100 Centre Street
New York, New York 10013

James H. Shaw, Jr., Justice (Retired)
New York State Supreme Court
360 Adams Street
Brooklyn, New York 11201-3712
(718) 643-7020 FAX: (718) 643-4993
E-mail: jshaw@courts.state.ny.us

George E. Wade, Jr., Justice (Retired)
New York State Supreme Court
360 Adams Street
Brooklyn, New York 11201-3712
(718) 643-3656 FAX: (718) 643-7934
E-mail: gwade2@courts.state.ny.us

William Wallace, Justice (Retired)
(Judicial Hearing Officer)
New York State Supreme Court
100 Centre Street
New York, New York 10013

Harold L. Wood, Justice (Retired)
New York State Supreme Court
100 Centre Street
New York, New York 10013

Bruce McM. Wright, Justice (Retired)
New York State Supreme Court
100 Centre Street
New York, New York 10013

Special Court Judges

Civil Court Judges

Maxine L. Archer, Judge
New York City Civil Court
141 Livingston Street
Brooklyn, New York 11201
(718) 643-8474 FAX: (718) 643-3733

Bernadette Baynes, Judge
New York City Civil Court
927 Castleton Avenue
Staten Island, New York 10310
(718) 390-5427 FAX: (718) 390-8108
E-mail: bfbayne@courts.state.ny.us

Johnny L. Baynes, Judge
New York City Civil Court – Housing Part
141 Livingston Street
Brooklyn, New York 11201
(718) 643-0848 FAX: (718) 643-3733

Pam B. Jackman Brown, Judge
New York City Civil Court – Housing Part
89-17 Sutphin Boulevard
Jamaica, New York 11435
(718) 262-7387 FAX: (718) 262-7291
E-mail: pjackman@courts.state.ny.us

Bert A. Bunyan, Judge
New York City Civil Court
141 Livingston Street
Brooklyn, New York 11201
(718) 643-5060 FAX: (718) 643-3733

Laura Douglas, Supervising Judge
Bronx County Civil Court
851 Grand Concourse
Bronx, New York 10451-2978
(718) 590-3677 FAX: (718) 590-7292
E-mail: ldouglas@courts.state.ny.us

Fern Fisher-Brandveen, Administrative Judge
New York City Civil Court
111 Centre Street
New York, New York 10013-4389
(212) 374-8082 FAX: (212) 374-5709
E-mail: fbrandve@courts.state.ny.us

Duane A. Hart, Judge
New York City Civil Court
89-17 Sutphin Boulevard
Jamaica, New York 11435
(718) 262-7379 FAX: (718) 262-7107
E-mail: dhart@courts.state.ny.us

Ronald D. Hollie, Judge
New York City Civil Court
89-17 Sutphin Boulevard
Jamaica, New York 11435
(718) 262-7357 FAX: (718) 262-7341

Debra A. James, Judge
New York City Civil Court
111 Centre Street
New York, New York 10013-4389
(212) 374-8499 FAX: (212) 374-0402
E-mail: djames@courts.state.ny.us

Diana Johnson, Judge
New York City Civil Court
141 Livingston Street
Brooklyn, New York 11201
(718) 643-8421 FAX: (718) 643-3733

Ulysses Bernard Leverett, Judge
New York City Civil Court – Housing Part
89-17 Sutphin Boulevard
Jamaica, New York 11438
(718) 262-7359 FAX: (718) 262-7341

Eardell J. Rashford, Judge
New York City Civil Court – Housing Part
1118 Grand Concourse
Bronx, New York 10451
(718) 466-3175 FAX: (718) 466-3006
E-mail: erashfo@courts.state.ny.us

Dianne T. Renwick, Judge
New York City Civil Court
851 Grand Concourse
Bronx, New York 10451-2978
(718) 590-2682 FAX: (718) 590-7294
E-mail: drenwick@courts.state.ny.us

Kathryn Montgomery Smith, Judge
New York City Civil Court
141 Livingston Street
Brooklyn, New York 11201
(718) 643-5012 FAX: (718) 643-3733
E-mail: ksmith@courts.state.ny.us

Brenda S. Spears, Judge
New York City Civil Court – Housing Part
111 Centre Street
New York, New York 10013-4389
(212) 374-8154 FAX: (212) 374-8053
E-mail: bspears@courts.state.ny.us

Delores J. Thomas, Judge
New York City Civil Court – Housing Part
141 Livingston Street
Brooklyn, New York 11201
(718) 643-8318 FAX: 643-3733
E-mail: dthomas@courts.state.ny.us

Milton L. Tingling, Jr., Judge
New York City Civil Court
111 Centre Street
New York, New York 10013-4389
(212) 374-8458 or (212) 374-8459
FAX: (212) 374-0402 or (212) 374-2579
E-mail: mtinglin@courts.state.ny.us

Pierre B. Turner, Judge
New York City Civil Court – Housing Part
1118 Grand Concourse
Bronx, New York 10451
(718) 466-3120 FAX: (718) 466-3006
E-mail: pturner@courts.state.ny.us

Deighton Waithe, Judge
New York City Civil Court – Housing Part
111 Centre Street
New York, New York 10013-4389
(212) 374-4521 FAX: (212) 374-0402
E-mail: dwaithe@courts.state.ny.us

Dolores L. Waltrous, Judge
New York City Civil Court
141 Livingston Street
Brooklyn, New York 11201
(718) 643-8826 FAX: (718) 643-3733
E-mail: dwaltrou@courts.state.ny.us

Geoffrey D. Wright, Judge
New York City Civil Court
141 Livingston Street
Brooklyn, New York 11201
(718) 643-2866 FAX: (718) 643-3537

Criminal Court Judges

John W. Carter, Judge
New York City Criminal Court
120 Schmerhorn Street
Brooklyn, New York 11201
(718) 643-4381 Fax: (718) 643-3538

Darcel D. Clark, Judge
New York City Criminal Court
215 East 161 Street
Bronx, New York 10451
(718) 590-0888 FAX: (718) 590-7297
E-mail: ddclark@courts.state.ny.us

Carol R. Edmead, Judge
New York City Criminal Court
111 Centre Street
New York, New York 10013
(212) 374-8478 FAX: (212) 374-2579

Pauline A. Mullings, Judge
New York City Criminal Court
125-01 Queens Boulevard
Kew Gardens, New York 11415-3791
(718) 520-3646 FAX: (718) 520-2494
E-mail: bbb@uno.com

Eugene Oliver, Jr., Supervising Judge
New York City Criminal Court
215 East 161 Street
Bronx, New York 10451
(718) 590-2945 FAX: (718) 590-7297
E-mail: eoliver@courts.state.ny.us

Larry R. C. Stephen, Judge
New York City Criminal Court
215 East 161st Street
Bronx, New York 10451
(212) 590-6094 FAX: (212) 590-7297
E-mail: lstephen@courts.state.ny.us

James P. Sullivan, Judge
New York City Criminal Court
100 Centre Street
New York, New York 10013-4386
(212) 374-3398 FAX: (212) 374-2579
E-mail: jsulliva@courts.state.ny.us

Family Court Judges

Michael A. Battle, Judge
New York State Family Court
25 Delaware Avenue
Buffalo, New York 14202-3903
(716) 858-8079 FAX: (716) 858-8432
E-mail: mbattle@courts.state.ny.us

Tandra L. Dawson, Judge
New York State Family Court
900 Sheridan Avenue
Bronx, New York 10451-3308
(718) 590-3376 or 590-3383 FAX: (718) 590-7305
E-mail: tdawson@courts.state.ny.us

Carnell T. Foskey, Judge
New York State Family Court
1200 Old Country Road
Westbury, New York 11590
(516) 571-9022 FAX: (516) 571-9335
E-mail: cfoskey@courts.state.ny.us

Paul H. Grosvenor, Judge
New York State Family Court
283 Adams Street
Brooklyn, New York 11201-2899
(718) 643-5686 FAX: (718) 643-5103

Claire T. Pearce, Judge
New York State Family Court
283 Adams Street
Brooklyn, New York 11201-2899
(718) 643-8032 FAX: (718) 643-5103
E-mail: cpearce@courts.state.ny.us

Clark V. Richardson, Supervising Judge
New York State Family Court
900 Sheridan Avenue
Bronx, New York 10451-3308
(718) 590-3389 FAX: (718) 590-7305
E-mail: crichard@courts.state.ny.us

Gayle P. Roberts, Judge
New York State Family Court
900 Sheridan Avenue
Bronx, New York 10451-3308
(718) 590-3388 FAX: (718) 590-7305
E-mail: grobert@courts.state.ny.us

Betty E. Staton, Judge
New York State Family Court
283 Adams Street
Brooklyn, New York 11201-2899
(718) 643-2849 FAX: (718) 643-5103
E-mail: bstaton@courts.state.ny.us

Bruce E. Tolbert, Judge
New York State Family Court
111 Grove Street
White Plains, New York 10601-2595
(914) 285-3615
FAX: (914) 285-4110 or (914) 285-4468
E-mail: btolbert@courts.state.ny.us

Other Special Courts

Alton R. Waldon, Judge
New York State Court of Claims
Five World Trade Center, Suite 8399
New York, New York 10048
(212) 775-0100 FAX: (212) 432-5602

Dennis Edwards Jr., Judge (Retired)
New York State Court of Claims
(Judicial Hearing Officer)
New York State Supreme Court
100 Centre Street
New York, New York 10013

City Court Judges

Brenda L. Dowery-Rodriguez, Judge
City Court of Mount Vernon
Municipal Building – Roosevelt Square
Mount Vernon, New York 10550-2019
(914) 665-2418 FAX: (914) 699-1230
E-mail: bdowery@courts.state.ny.us

Teresa D. Johnson, Judge
City Court of Rochester
One Hall of Justice
Rochester, New York 14614
(716) 428-2096 FAX: (716) 428-4265
E-mail: tjohnson@courts.state.ny.us

Barbara Leak, Judge
City Court of White Plains
77 South Lexington Avenue
White Plains, New York 10601
(914) 422-6050 FAX: (914) 422-6058
E-mail: bleak@courts.state.ny.us

Langston C. McKinney, Judge
City Court of Syracuse
511 South State Street
Public Safety Building
Syracuse, New York 13202-2126
(315) 477-2766 FAX: (315) 474-2601
E-mail: lmckinne@courts.state.ny.us

James A. W. McLeod, Judge
City Court of Buffalo
50 Delaware Avenue
Buffalo, New York 14202-3898
(716) 847-8257 FAX: (716) 847-8271
E-mail: jmcleod@courts.state.ny.us

E. Jeanette Ogden, Judge
City Court of Buffalo
50 Delaware Avenue
Buffalo, New York 14202-3803
(716) 847-8240 FAX: (716) 856-4670
E-mail: eogden@courts.state.ny.us

Gail B. Rice, Judge
City Court of New Rochelle
90 Beaufort Place
New Rochelle, New York 10801
(914) 654-2286 FAX: (914) 633-9291
E-mail: grice@courts.state.ny.us

Robert T. Russell, Jr., Judge
City Court of Buffalo
50 Delaware Avenue - Suite 200
Buffalo, New York 14202
(716) 847-8231 FAX: (716) 856-4670
E-mail: rrussell@courts.state.ny.us

Shirley Troutman, Judge
City of Buffalo
50 Delaware Avenue
Buffalo, New York 14202-3803
(716) 847-8242 FAX: (716) 856-4670
E-mail: stroutma@courts.state.ny.us

Sam Walker, Judge
City Court of Mount Vernon
Municipal Building – Roosevelt Square
Mount Vernon, New York 10550-2019
(914) 665-2419 FAX: (914) 699-1230
E-mail: swalker@courts.state.ny.us

Roseanna Washington, Judge
City Court of White Plains
77 South Lexington Avenue
White Plains, New York 10601
(914) 683-6691 FAX: (914) 422-6058
E-mail: rwashing@courts.state.ny.us

Other Courts

Jerald S. Carter, Judge
Nassau County District Court
262 Old Country Road
Mineola, New York 11501-4212
(516) 571-3560 FAX: (516) 571-1121
E-mail: jcarter@courts.state.ny.us

Alfred Cooper, Sr., Judge
Nassau County District Court
99 Main Street – Room JC-21
Hempstead, New York 11550
(516) 572-2121 FAX: (516) 572-2536 or 572-2507

William K. Nelson, Judge
Rockland County Court
Courthouse
New City, New York 10956
(914) 638-5336 FAX: (914) 638-5312
E-mail: wnelson@courts.state.ny.us
or n2ggq@aol.com

Joseph K. West, Judge
Westchester County Court
111 Dr. Martin Luther King, Jr. Blvd.
White Plains, New York 10601-2595
(914) 285-4305 FAX: (914) 285-4547
E-mail: jwest@courts.state.ny.us

Cynthia Diaz-Wilson, Judge
Hempstead Village Court
Assistant Provost - Hofstra University
113 Hofstra University - Gallon Wing - Room 132
Hempstead, New York 11550-1090
(516) 463-6976 FAX: (516 463-5139
E-mail: noacdw@hofstra.edu

NORTH CAROLINA: (51)

FEDERAL

James A. Beaty, Jr., Judge
U. S. District Court
for the Middle District of North Carolina
248 Federal Building
251 North Main Street
Winston-Salem, North Carolina 27101-3914
(336) 631-5195 FAX: (919) 631-5004

Richard C. Erwin, Sr. Judge
U.S. District Court
for the Middle District of North Carolina
223-A Federal Building
251 North Main Street
Winston-Salem, North Carolina 27101-3194
(336) 631-5007 FAX: (919) 631-5004

William Webb, Magistrate Judge
U. S. District Court
for the Eastern District of North Carolina
Terry Sanford Federal Building, Room 222
310 New Bern Avenue
Raleigh, North Carolina 27601
(919) 856-4370 FAX: (919) 856-4160 or 4462

Administrative Law Judges

Emanuel Clabon Edwards
Administrative Law Judge
Office of Hearings and Appeals
Social Security Administration
101 South Edgeworth, Suite 300
Greensboro, North Carolina 27401
(336) 333-5382 FAX: (336) 333-5435

Helen O. Evans, Administrative Law Judge
Office of Hearings and Appeals
Social Security Administration
101 South Edgeworth Street, Suite 300
Greensboro, North Carolina 27401
(336) 333-5382 FAX: (336) 333-5433

State

Supreme Court

Henry E. Frye, Chief Justice (Retired)
Brooks, Pierce, McLendon, Humphrey & Leonard, L.L.P.
Post Office Box 26000
Greensboro, North Carolina 27420
(336) 373-8850 FAX: (336) 378-1001
hfrye@brookspierce.com

Court of Appeals

Patricia Timmons Goodson, Judge
Court of Appeals of North Carolina
Post Office Box 888
Raleigh, North Carolina 27602-0888
(919) 733-6185 FAX: (919) 733-8003

James A. Wynn, Jr., Judge
Court of Appeals of North Carolina
Post Office Box 888
Raleigh, North Carolina 27602-0888
(919) 733-6185 FAX: (919) 733-8003

Superior Court Judges

Ola Mose-El Lewis Bray, Judge
Superior Court
399 North Shore Drive
Southport, North Carolina 28461
(910) 253-8107 or 641-3070 FAX: (910) 641-3077

L. Todd Burke, Judge
Superior Court
P.O. Box 20099
Winston-Salem, North Carolina
(336) 761-2420 FAX: (336) 761-2089

G. K. Butterfield, Jr., Judge
Superior Court
Judicial District 7B
Post Office Box 2445
Wilson, North Carolina 27894-2445
(919) 399-0008 FAX: (919) 291-8635

Stafford G. Bullock, Judge
Superior Court
Judicial District 10
Wake County Courthouse
Post Office Box 351
Raleigh, North Carolina 27602
(919) 755-4101 FAX: (919) 715-4064

Henry E. Frye, Jr., Judge
Superior Court
18th Judicial District
Guilford County Courthouse
Post Office Box 3008
Greensboro, North Carolina 27402
(336) 574-4300 FAX: (336) 574-4396

Ernest B. Fullwood, Judge
Superior Court
Judicial District 5
P.O. Box 1557
New Hanover County Judicial Building, Suite 519
Wilmington, North Carolina 28402-1557
(919) 341-4415 FAX: (919) 341-4071

Shirley L. Fulton, Judge
Superior Court
Judicial District 26
Mecklenburg County Courthouse
700 E. Fourth Street
Charlotte, North Carolina 28202
(704) 347-7800 FAX: (704) 347-7867

Cy Anthony Grant, Sr., Judge
Superior Court
Judicial District 6B
Bertie County Courthouse
Post Office Box 489
Windsor, North Carolina 27983
(252) 794-9406 FAX: (252) 794-2482

Orlando F. Hudson, Jr., Judge
Superior Court
Judicial District 14
Durham County Judicial Building, Sixth Floor
Durham, North Carolina 22701
(919) 560-6814 FAX: (919) 560-5414

Marcus L. Johnson, Judge
Superior Court
Judicial District 26
Mecklenburg County Courthouse
Charlotte, North Carolina 28202
(704) 347-7800 FAX: (704) 347-7867

Abraham Penn Jones, Judge
Superior Court
Judicial District 10
Wake County Courthouse
Post Office Box 351
Raleigh, North Carolina 27602
(919) 755-4100 FAX: (919) 715-4064

A. Leon Stanback, Jr., Judge
Superior Court
Judicial District 14
Durham County Judicial Building – Sixth Floor
Durham, North Carolina 27701
(919) 560-6814 FAX: (919) 560-5414

Quentin T. Sumner, Judge
Superior Court
Judicial District 7A
Post Office Box 1215
Rocky Mount, North Carolina 27802-1215
(252) 459-4707 FAX: (252) 459-4509

Gregory A. Weeks, Judge
Superior Court
Judicial District 12
Cumberland County Courthouse
Post Office Box 363
Fayetteville, North Carolina 28301-0363
(919) 678-2900 FAX: (919) 678-2975

Jerry Braswell, Special Superior Court Judge
Post Office Box 253
Goldsboro, North Carolina 27533
(919) 736-4262 FAX: (919) 736-4347

Paul L. Jones
Senior Resident Superior Court Judge
District 8A
Lenoir County Courthouse
Post Office Box 68
Kinston, North Carolina 28501
(252) 527-2629 FAX: (252) 523-2084

District Court Judges

Robert L. Anderson, Sr., Judge
District Court
District 11
238 Pineland Avenue
Clayton, North Carolina 27520
(919) 708-4440 FAX: (919) 708-4472

J. Henry Banks, Judge
District Court
Post Office Box 1482
Henderson, North Carolina 27536
(252) 492-4015 or (919) 693-5193
FAX: (919) 690-8330

Cheri Beasley, Judge
District Court
Cumberland County Courthouse
Post Office Box 363
Fayetteville, North Carolina 28302
(910) 678-2901 FAX: (910) 486-8555

Kevin M. Bridges, Judge
District Court
1520 Springhaven Circle (H)
Albermarle, North Carolina 28001
(704) 982-3095 FAX: (704) 984-6119

John Carter, Judge
District Court
Judicial District 16B
Robeson County Courthouse, Box 18
Lumberton, North Carolina 28358
(910) 671-3355 FAX: (910) 671-3113

J. Carlton Cole, Judge
District Court
Post Office Box 400
Hertford, North Carolina 27944
(252) 331-4750 FAX: (252) 331-4814

Craig Croom, Judge
District Court
Judicial District 10
Wake County Courthouse
Fayetteville Street Mall
Post Office Box 351
Raleigh, North Carolina 27602-0351
(919) 755-4101 FAX: (919) 715-4064

Yvonne Mims Evans, Judge
District Court
700 East Fourth Street, Suite 3304
Charlotte, North Carolina 28202-3304
(704) 347-7801 FAX: (704) 342-6321

Paul A. Hardison, Judge
District Court
Post Office Box 1101
Jacksonville, North Carolina 28541
(910) 455-6285 FAX: (910) 455-6285

Robert Harrell, Emergency Judge
District Court
Buncombe County, North Carolina
(704) 255-4701

Roland B. Hayes, Judge
District Court
Forsyth County Hall of Justice
Post Office Box 20099
Winston-Salem, North Carolina 27120-0099
(336) 761-2478 FAX: (336) 761-2018

Patrice A. Hinnant, Judge
District Court
Judicial District 18
Post Office Box 3008
Greensboro, North Carolina 27402-3008
(336) 574-4301 FAX: (336) 335-3401

Carol Jones, Judge
District Court
Judicial District 4
113 Sarah Jones Lane
Kenansville, North Carolina 28349
(910) 455-8008 FAX: Call on phone first

Alfred W. Kwasikpui, Chief Judge
District Court
Post Office Box 643
Jackson, North Carolina 27845
(919) 534-1785 FAX: (919) 534-1308

W. Rob Lewis, II, Judge
District Court
Judicial District 6B
Route 3, Box 17H
Akoskie, North Carolina 27910
(252) 534-1785 FAX: (252) 534-1308

Lawrence C. McSwain, Chief Judge
District Court
Judicial District 18
Post Office Box 3008
Greensboro, North Carolina 27402
(336) 574-4301 FAX: (336) 335-3401

Regan A. Miller, Judge
District Court
Judicial District 26
Criminal Courts Building
700 East Fourth Street, Suite 3304
Charlotte North Carolina 28202
(704) 347-7801 FAX: (704) 347-6321

Rickye Mitchell, Judge
District Court
700 E. Fourth Street, Suite 3304
Charlotte, North Carolina 28202
(704) 347-7801 FAX: (704) 347-6321

Michael Rivers Morgan, Judge
District Court
Judicial District 10 – Wake County Courthouse
Fayetteville Street Mall
Post Office Box 351
Raleigh, North Carolina 27602-0351
(919) 755-4101 FAX: (919) 715-4064

Elaine M. O'Neal, Judge
District Court
Judicial District 14
Durham County Judicial Building, 6th Floor
210 East Main Street
Durham, North Carolina 27701
(919) 560-6807 FAX: (919) 560-6877

Edward Pone, Judge
District Court
Cumberland County Courthouse
Post Office Box 363
Fayetteville, North Carolina 28302
(910) 678-2901 FAX: (910) 486-8555

Herbert L. Richardson, Chief Judge
District Court
Judicial District 16B
Robeson County Courthouse, Box 18
Lumberton, North Carolina 28358
(910) 671-3355 FAX: (910) 671-3113

Cheryl L. Spencer, Judge
District Court
Judicial District 3B
302 Broad Street
New Bern, North Carolina 28560
(252) 514-4782 FAX: (252) 514-4891

Teresa Vincent, Judge
District Court
Judicial District 18
Post Office Box 3008
Greensboro, North Carolina 27042
(336) 574-4301 FAX: (336) 335-3401

Administrative Law Judges

Brenda B. Becton, Administrative Law Judge
Office of Administrative Hearings
Post Office Drawer 27447
Raleigh, North Carolina 27611-7447
(919) 733-2698 FAX: (919) 733-3478

Sammie Chess, Administrative Law Judge
Office of Administrative Hearings
Post Office Drawer 27447
Raleigh, North Carolina 27611-7447
(919) 733-2698 FAX: (919) 733-3478

Beryl Wade, Administrative Law Judge
Office of Administrative hearings
Post Office Drawer 27447
Raleigh, North Carolina 27611-7447
(919) 733-2698 FAX: (919) 733-3478

NORTH DAKOTA: (0)

NORTH MARIANNA ISLANDS: (0)

OHIO: (67)

FEDERAL

Court of Appeals

Ramsey Guy Cole, Jr., Judge
U. S. Court of Appeals for the Sixth Circuit
127 U. S. Courthouse
85 Marconi Boulevard
Columbus, Ohio 43215
(614) 719-3350 FAX: (614) 469-6973
E-mail: judge_cole@ck6.uscourts.gov

Nathaniel R. Jones, Sr. Judge
U. S. Court of Appeals for the Sixth Circuit
432 Potter Stewart U. S. Courthouse
Post Office Building
100 East Fifth Street
Cincinnati, Ohio 45202
(513) 564-7400 FAX: (513) 564-7403

Trial Court Judges

Algenon L. Marbley, Judge
U. S. District Court
for the Southern District of Ohio
85 Marconi Boulevard
Columbus, Ohio 43215
(614) 719-3260 FAX: (614) 469-5908
E-mail: algenon_marbley@ck6.uscourts.gov

Solomon Oliver, Jr., Judge
U. S. District Court
for the Northern District of Ohio
250 Howard M. Metzenbaum
U. S. Courthouse
201 Superior Avenue East
Cleveland, Ohio 44114-1201
(216) 522-7955 FAX: (216) 522-7951

Randolph Baxter, Judge
U. S. Bankruptcy Court
for the Northern District of Ohio
127 Public Square
Key Tower, 32nd Floor
Cleveland, Ohio 44114-1309
(216) 522-4373 Ext. 3063 FAX: (216) 522-4791

Charles M. Caldwell, Judge
U. S. Bankruptcy Court
for the Southern District of Ohio
137 U. S. Courthouse
85 Marconi Boulevard
Columbus, Ohio 43215
(614) 469-2053 or 469-6638, Ext. 260
FAX: (614) 469-2478

Jeffery P. Hopkins, Judge
U. S. Bankruptcy Court
for the Southern District of Ohio
Atrium Two, Suite 800
221 East Fourth Street
Cincinnati, Ohio 45202
(513) 684-2572, Ext. 131 FAX: (513) 684-6727

Vernelis K. Armstrong, Magistrate Judge
U. S. District Court
for the Northern District of Ohio
318 U. S. Courthouse
1716 Spielbusch Avenue
Toledo, Ohio 43624
(419) 259-6217 FAX: (419) 259-3728

Jack Sherman, Jr., Magistrate Judge
U. S. District Court
for the Southern District of Ohio
716 Potter Stewart U. S. Courthouse
100 East 5th Street
Cincinnati, Ohio 45202
(513) 564-7640 FAX: (513) 564-7644

Administrative Law Judge

Richard D. Letts, Administrative Law Judge
Office of Hearings and Appeals
Social Security Administration
Two Nation Wide Plaza
280 North High Street, Room 300
Columbus, Ohio 43215
(614) 469-7404 FAX: (614) 469-6786

STATE

Court of Appeals

Patricia Ann Blackmon, Court of Appeals
8th Appellate District
1 Lakeside Avenue
Cleveland, Ohio 44113
(216) 443-6358 FAX: (216) 443-2044
E-mail: PB1702@aol.com

Sara J. Harper, Judge (Retired)
Court of Appeals
13807 Drexmore Road
Cleveland, Ohio 44120
(216) 991-9122

Trial Court - Court of Common Pleas

Janet E. Burney, Judge
Cuyahoga County Court of Common Pleas
Juvenile Court Division
2163 East 22nd Street
Cleveland, Ohio 44115
(216) 443-8411 FAX: (216) 443-3386 or 443-3413

Charles J. Doneghy, Judge
Lucas County Court of Common Pleas
700 Adams Street
Toledo, Ohio 43624
(419) 213-4570 FAX: (419) 213-4181

Lillian J. Greene, Judge
Cuyahoga County Court of Common Pleas
1200 Ontario Street
Cleveland, Ohio 44113-1664
(216) 443-8681 FAX: (216) 348-4038

Yvette McGee-Brown, Judge
Franklin County Court of Common Pleas
Domestic Relations Division, Juvenile Branch
373 South High Street
Columbus, Ohio 43215-4598
(614) 462-4444 FAX: (614) 462-7440
E-mail: ymmcgeeb@co.franklin.oh.us

Melba D. Marsh, Judge
Hamilton County Court of Common Pleas
1000 Main Street
Cincinnati, Ohio 45202
(513) 946-5866 FAX: (513) 946-5868

Michael B. Murphy, Judge
Montgomery County Court of Common Pleas
Juvenile Court Division
303 West 2nd Street
Dayton, Ohio 45422
(937) 225-4780 FAX: (937) 496-7756

Adele Riley, Judge
Montgomery County Court of Common Pleas
41 North Perry Street
Dayton, Ohio 45422-2150
(937) 225-4448 FAX: (937) 225-5406
E-mail: rileya@jud.mccpc.oh.net

Shirley Strickland Saffold, Judge
Cuyahoga County Court of Common Pleas
1200 Ontario Street
Cleveland, Ohio 44113-1678
(216) 443-8735 FAX: (216) 443-5424

James R. Williams, Judge
Summit County Court of Common Pleas
209 South High Street
Akron, Ohio 44308
(216) 643-2241 FAX: (216) 643-2045

Carl J. Character, Judge (Retired)
Cuyahoga County Court of Common Pleas
3055 Ludlow Road
Shaker Heights, Ohio 44120-2812
(216) 752-4986 FAX: (216) 752-4986

Court of Common Pleas Referees and Magistrates

Wanda Birch, Magistrate
Cuyahoga County Court of Common Pleas
Probate Division
1 Lakeside Avenue, N.W.
Cleveland, Ohio 44113
(216) 443-8780 FAX: (216) 443-4943

Carole Bugg, Magistrate
Cuyahoga County Court of Common Pleas
Juvenile Division
2163 East 22nd Street
Cleveland, Ohio 44115
(216) 443-3425 FAX: (216) 443-5826

Kim Wilson Burke, Magistrate
Hamilton County Juvenile Court
800 Broadway
Cincinnati, Ohio 45202-1225
(513) 852-8600 or 852-8944 FAX: (513) 852-4608

Dana Chavers, Magistrate
Cuyahoga County Court of Common Pleas
Juvenile Court Division
2163 East 22nd Street
Cleveland, Ohio 44115
(216) 443-3535 FAX: (216) 443-3913

Odella Lampkin Crafter, Magistrate
Franklin County Court of Common Pleas
Juvenile Division
373 South High Street, 5th Floor
Columbus, Ohio 43215
(614) 462-4496 FAX: (614) 462-7440

Sharon Dennis, Magistrate
Summit County Court of Common Pleas
Domestic Relations Court
209 South High Street
Akron, Ohio 44308-1610
(330) 643-2372 FAX: (330) 643-2126

Woodrow Hudson, Magistrate
Franklin County Court of Common Pleas
Juvenile Court Division
373 South High Street, 5th Floor
Columbus, Ohio 43215
(614) 462-5295 FAX: (614) 462-7440

William Hutcheson, Magistrate
Lucas County Court of Common Pleas
Juvenile Court Division
Lucas County Family Court Center
429 North Michigan Street
Toledo, Ohio 43624-1688
(419) 213-6685 FAX: (419) 249-6898

Garlandine Jones, Magistrate
Cuyahoga County Court of Common Pleas
Domestic Relations Division
1 Lakeside Avenue, N.W.
Cleveland, Ohio 44113
(216) 443-8826 FAX: (216) 443-4943

Alison Nelson-Floyd, Magistrate
Cuyahoga County Court of Common Pleas
Domestic Relations Division
1 Lakeside Avenue, N.W.
Cleveland, Ohio 44113
(216) 443-8856 FAX: (216) 443-4943

Larry Smith, Magistrate
Cuyahoga County Court of Common Pleas
Juvenile Court Division
2163 East 22nd Street
Cleveland, Ohio 44115
(216) 443-3425 or 443-8400 FAX: (216) 443-3913

James Tanner, Jr., Magistrate
Cuyahoga County Court of Common Pleas
Domestic Relations Division
1 Lakeside Avenue, N.W.
Cleveland, Ohio 44113
(216) 443-8800 FAX: (216) 443-4943

Joyce Ann Woods, Magistrate
Lucas County Court of Common Pleas
Juvenile Court Division
Lucas County Family Court Center
429 North Michigan Street
Toledo, Ohio 43624
(419) 249-6685 FAX: (419) 213-6898

Municipal Court

Ronald B. Adrine, Judge
Cleveland Municipal Court
1200 Ontario Street
Cleveland, Ohio 44113-1669
(216) 664-4974 FAX: (216) 664-4283
E-mail: longpencil@msn.com

Nadine L. Allen, Judge
Hamilton County Municipal Court
1000 Main Street, Room 170
Cincinnati, Ohio 45202
(513) 946-5154 FAX: (513) 946-5157

James F. Cannon, Judge
Dayton Municipal Court
301 West Third Street
Dayton, Ohio 45402-1424
(937) 443-4367 FAX: (937) 443-4494
E-mail: jcannon331@prodigy.com

C. Ellen Connally, Judge
Cleveland Municipal Court
1200 Ontario Street
Cleveland, Ohio 44113-1669
(216) 664-4972 FAX: (216) 664-4283
E-mail: cellenc@aol.com

Robert A. Douglas, Jr., Judge
Youngstown Municipal Court
26 South Phelps Street
Youngstown, Ohio 44503
(330) 742-8857 FAX: (330) 742-8845

Cheryl D. Grant, Judge
Hamilton County Municipal Court
1000 Main Street
Cincinnati, Ohio 45202
(513) 946-5165 FAX: (513) 946-5167
E-mail: cgrant@mscc06.hamilton-co.org

James E. Green, Judge
Franklin County Municipal Court
375 South High Street, Room 14C
Columbus, Ohio 43215
(614) 645-8295 FAX: (614) 645-7802

Mable M. Jasper, Judge
Cleveland Municipal Court
1200 Ontario Street
Cleveland, Ohio 44113-1669
(216) 664-4978 FAX: (216) 664-4283

Larry A. Jones, Judge
Cleveland Municipal Court
1200 Ontario Street
Cleveland, Ohio 44113-1669
(216) 664-4996 FAX: (216) 664-4283

Una H. R. Keenon, Judge
East Cleveland Municipal Court
14340 Euclid Avenue
East Cleveland, Ohio 44112
(216) 681-2214 FAX: (216) 681-2197
E-mail: JUDGEU@amerited.net

William C. Littlejohn, Judge
Dayton Municipal Court
301 West 3rd Street, Room 313
Dayton, Ohio 45402-1424
(937) 443-4369 FAX: (937) 443-4496

William L. Mallory, Jr., Judge
Hamilton County Municipal Court
Hamilton County Courthouse
1000 Main Street
Cincinnati, Ohio 45202
(513) 946-5112 FAX: (513) 946-5114

W. Dwayne Maynard, Judge
Franklin County Municipal Court
375 South High Street
Columbus, Ohio 43215
(614) 645-8286 FAX: (614) 645-7802

Alice O. McCollum, Judge
Dayton Municipal Court
301 West Third Street
Dayton, Ohio 45402-1424
(937) 443-4362 FAX: (937) 443-0124

C. Allen McConnell, Judge
Toledo Municipal Court Housing Division
555 North Erie Street
Toledo, Ohio 43624-1391
(419) 245-1946 FAX: (419) 245-1802

Carla D. Moore, Judge
Akron Municipal Court
217 South High Street, Room 917
Akron, Ohio 44308-1611
(330) 375-2053 FAX: (330) 375-2303

Jeff Payton, Judge
Mansfield Municipal Court
30 North Diamond
Mansfield, Ohio 1702
(419) 755-9616 FAX: (419) 755-9650

Angela R. Stokes, Judge
Cleveland Municipal Court
1200 Ontario Street
Cleveland, Ohio 44113-1669
(216) 664-4986 FAX: (216) 664-4283

Lynn C. Toler, Judge
Cleveland Heights Municipal Court
40 Severance Circle
Cleveland Heights, Ohio 44118
(216) 291-3418 FAX: (216) 291-2459

Andrew West, Judge
Hamilton County Municipal Court
1000 Main Street
Cincinnati, Ohio 45202
(513) 946-5122 FAX: (513) 946-5124

Robert Penn, Judge (Retired)
Toledo Municipal Court
4034 Marlaine Drive
Toledo, Ohio 43606
(419) 474-1944

George W. Trumbo, Judge (Retired)
Cleveland Municipal Court
13807 Drexmore Road
Cleveland, Ohio 44120
(216) 991-9122

Municipal Court Magistrates

Gayle A. Belcher, Magistrate
Cleveland Municipal Court
1200 Ontario Street
Cleveland, Ohio 44113-1669
(216) 664-4959 FAX: (216) 664-4949

Cynthia Bowers, Magistrate
Cleveland Municipal Court
1200 Ontario Street
Cleveland, Ohio 44113-1669
(216) 664-4958 FAX: (216) 664-4949

Gregory Clifford, Deputy Chief Magistrate
Cleveland Municipal Court
1200 Ontario Street
Cleveland, Ohio 44113-1669
(216) 664-4957 FAX: (216) 664-4283

Carl Henderson, Magistrate
Dayton Municipal Court
301 West 3rd Street
Dayton, Ohio 45402-1424
(937) 443-4450 FAX: (937) 443-4494

Warner Jackson, Magistrate
East Cleveland Municipal Court
14340 Euclid Avenue
East Cleveland, Ohio 44112
(216) 681-5020 FAX: (216) 681-2217

Bobette S. Ousley, Magistrate
Cleveland Municipal Court
1200 Ontario Street
Cleveland, Ohio 44113-1669
(216) 664-4969 FAX: (216) 664-4283 or 664-4949

Ruben E. Pope, III, Magistrate
Cleveland Municipal Court Housing Division
1200 Ontario Street
Cleveland, Ohio 44113-1669
(216) 664-4760 FAX: (216) 664-6103

Franzetta D. Turner, Magistrate
Cleveland Municipal Court
1200 Ontario Street
Cleveland, Ohio 44113-1669
(216) 664-4942 FAX: (216) 664-4283 or 664-4949

Scherazade Washington, Magistrate
Hamilton County Juvenile Court
800 Broadway
Cincinnati, Ohio 45202-1225
(513) 852-8944 FAX: (513) 852-4608

Paul Tuffin, Magistrate (Retired)
Cleveland Municipal Court, Housing Division
3637 Sutherland Road
Shaker Heights, Ohio 44122
(216) 561-0566

OKLAHOMA: (10)

FEDERAL

Vicki Miles-LaGrange, Judge
U. S. District Court
for the Western District of Oklahoma
5011 U. S. Courthouse
200 Northwest Fourth Street
Oklahoma City, Oklahoma 73102
(405) 231-4518 FAX: (405) 231-4522

STATE

Tammy Bass-Jones, Judge
District Court
Oklahoma County Courthouse
321 Park Avenue, Room 722
Oklahoma City, Oklahoma 73102
(405) 713-1426 FAX: (405) 713-1437

Susan Bragg, Judge
District Court
Oklahoma County Courthouse
321 Park Avenue, Room 223
Oklahoma City, Oklahoma 73102
(405) 713-1456 FAX: (405) 713-1852

Jesse S. Harris, Judge
District Court
14th Judicial District
Tulsa County Courthouse - Room 509
500 South Denver
Tulsa, Oklahoma 74103-3832
(918) 596-5320 Library FAX: (918) 596-4509

Philippa C. James, Judge
Oklahoma City Municipal Court
700 Couch Drive
Oklahoma City, Oklahoma 73102
(405) 297-2701
Administrative Office FAX: 297-3641

Carlos J. Chappelle, Special District Judge
14th Judicial District, State of Oklahoma
Tulsa County District Court
500 South Denver Avenue
Tulsa, Oklahma 74103-3832
(918) 596-5314 FAX: (918) 596-5402
E-mail: carlos.chappelle@oscn.net

Charles G. Hill, Special Court Judge
Oklahoma County Courthouse
321 Park Avenue - Room 512
Oklahoma City, Oklahoma 73102
(405) 278-1185 Law Library FAX: (405) 278-1852

David Lewis, Special Court Judge
Comanche County Courthouse
300 S.W. 5th Street
Lawton, Oklahoma 73501
(580) 581-4575 FAX: (580) 581-1339

Ozella Willis, Judge
Worker's Compensation Court
5308 North Stonewall Drive
Oklahoma City, Oklahoma 73111
(405) 522-8600 FAX: (405) 522-8049

Charles L. Owens, Judge (Retired)
District Court - 7th Judicial District
Oklahoma County Courthouse - Room 811
321 Park Avenue
Oklahoma City, Oklahoma 73102

OREGON: (3)

FEDERAL

Ancer L. Haggerty, Judge
U. S. District Court for the District of Oregon
1307 Mark O. Hatfield U. S. Courthouse
1000 Southwest Third Avenue
Portland, Oregon 97204-2902
(503) 326-8320 FAX: (503) 326-3683

STATE

Clifford L. Freeman, Judge
Multnomah County Circuit Court
1021 S.W. 4th Avenue
Portland, Oregon 97204
(503) 248-3227 FAX: (503) 276-0949

Roosevelt Robinson, Judge
Multnomah County Circuit Court
Multnomah County Courthouse
1021 S.W. 4th Avenue
Portland, Oregon 97204-1123
(503) 248-3731 FAX: (503) 248-3698

PENNSYLVANIA: (69)

FEDERAL

Theodore A. McKee, Judge
U. S. Court of Appeals for the Third Circuit
20614 U. S. Courthouse
601 Market Street
Philadelphia, Pennsylvania 19106
(215) 597-9601 FAX: (215) 597-0104

James T. Giles, Chief Judge
U. S. District Court
for the Eastern District of Pennsylvania
9614 U. S. Courthouse
Independence Mall West
601 Market Street
Philadelphia, Pennsylvania 19106-1771
(215) 597-0692 FAX: (215) 580-2147

Herbert J. Hutton, Judge
U. S. District Court
for the Eastern District of Pennsylvania
8613 U. S. Courthouse
Independence Mall West
601 Market Street
Philadelphia, Pennsylvania 19106-1764
(215) 597-5646 FAX: (215) 580-2162

J. Curtis Joyner, Judge
U. S. District Court
for the Eastern District of Pennsylvania
20613 U. S. Courthouse
Independence Mall West
601 Market Street
Philadelphia, Pennsylvania 19106
(215) 597-1537 FAX: (215) 580-2312

Gary L. Lancaster, Judge
U. S. District Court
for the Western District of Pennsylvania
911 U. S. Post Office & Courthouse
700 Grant Street
Pittsburgh, Pennsylvania 15219
(412) 208-7400 FAX: (412) 208-7407

Petrese B. Tucker, Judge
U. S. District Court
for the Eastern District of Pennsylvania
601 Market Street - Suite 3810
Philadelphia, Pennsylvania 19106
(267) 299-7610 FAX: (267) 299-5072.

Clifford Scott Green, Senior Judge
U. S. District Court
for the Eastern District of Pennsylvania
15613 U. S. Courthouse
601 Market Street
Philadelphia, Pennsylvania 19106-1781
(215) 597-9149 FAX: (215) 580-2135

Paul A. Simmons, Judge (Retired)
U. S. District Court
for the Western District of Pennsylvania
700 Meade Street
Monongahela, Pennsylvania 15063
(412) 258-5079

Carol Sandra Moore Wells, Magistrate Judge
U. S. District Court
for the Eastern District of Pennsylvania
3730 U.S. Courthouse
Independence Mall West
601 Market Street
Philadelphia, Pennsylvania 19106
(215) 597-7833 FAX: (215) 580-2157

William F. Hall, Jr., Magistrate Judge (Retired)
U. S. District Court
for the Eastern District of Pennsylvania
1515 Market Street, 9th Floor
Philadelphia, Pennsylvania 19102
(215) 851-8413 FAX: (215) 851-8383

U. S. Administrative Law Judges

David C. Harty, Acting Assistant Regional Chief Administrative Law Judge
Office of Hearings and Appeals
Social Security Administration
300 Spring Garden Street - 4th Floor
Post Office Box 13496
Philadelphia, Pennsylvania 19101
(215) 597-4100 or 597-1200 FAX: (215) 597-4183

Lonnie L. Crawford
Chief Administrative Judge
Merit Systems Protection Board
Room 501, U. S. Customhouse
2nd & Chestnut Streets
Philadelphia, Pennsylvania 19106
(215) 597-4446 FAX: (215) 597-3456

Sandra Squire, Administrative Judge
U. S. Merit Systems Protection Board
Room 501, U. S. Customhouse
2nd & Chestnut Streets
Philadelphia, Pennsylvania 19106
(215) 597- 4446 FAX: (215) 597-3456

Wilhelmina D. Stevenson, Administrative Judge
U. S. Merit Systems Protection Board
Room 501, U. S. Customhouse
2nd & Chestnut Streets
Philadelphia, Pennsylvania 19106
(215) 597-4446 FAX: (215) 597-3456

STATE

Robert N.C. Nix, Jr., Chief Justice (Retired)
Supreme Court of Pennsylvania
The Widener Building, Suite 500
One South Penn Square
Philadelphia, Pennsylvania 19107
(215) 560-3071

Justin M. Johnson, Judge
Superior Court
2701 Grant Building – 330 Grant Street,
Pittsburgh, Pennsylvania 15219
(412) 565-3604 FAX: (412) 565-7943

Jacqueline F. Allen, Judge
Court of Common Pleas
Suite 1222, Criminal Justice Center
1301 Filbert Street
Philadelphia, Pennsylvania 19107
(215) 686-7083 FAX: (215) 683-7085
E-mail: Jacqueline.Allen@courts.Phila.gov

Willis W. Berry, Jr., Judge
Court of Common Pleas
Suite 1409, Criminal Justice Center
1301 Filbert Street
Philadelphia, Pennsylvania 19107
(215) 683-7124 FAX: (215) 683-7126
E-mail: Willis.Berry@courts.Phila.gov

Gwendolyn N. Bright, Judge
Court of Common Pleas
Family Court Division, Juvenile Branch
Suite 1208, Criminal Justice Center
1301 Filbert Street
Philadelphia, Pennsylvania 19107
(215) 683-7041 FAX: (215) 683-7043
E-mail: Gwendolyn.Bright@courts.Phila.gov

Genece Brinkley, Judge
Court of Common Pleas
Suite 1219, Criminal Justice Center
1301 Filbert Street
Philadelphia, Pennsylvania 19107
(215) 683-7074 FAX: (215) 683-7076
E-mail: Genece.Brinkley@courts.Phila.gov

Joan A. Brown, Judge
Court of Common Pleas
Suite 1215, Criminal Justice Center
1301 Filbert Street
Philadelphia, Pennsylvania 19107
(215) 683-7062 FAX: (215) 683-7064
E-mail: Joan.Brown@courts.Phila.gov.

Sandy L. V. Byrd, Judge
Court of Common Pleas
Room 540, City Hall
Philadelphia, Pennsylvania 19107
(215) 686-7338 FAX: (215) 686-7375

Tama Myers Clark, Judge
Court of Common Pleas
First Judicial District of Pennsylvania
Room 342, City Hall
Philadelphia, Pennsylvania 19107
(212) 686-7322 FAX: (215) 686-7499
E-mail: tama.clark@courts.phila.gov

Cheryl Allen Craig, Judge
Allegheny County
Court of Common Pleas, Juvenile Section
3333 Forbes Avenue
Pittsburgh, Pennsylvania 15213
(412) 578-8261 FAX: (412) 621-4749

Horace A. Davenport, Sr., Judge
Court of Common Pleas
Montgomery County Courthouse
Post Office Box 311
Norristown, Pennsylvania 19404
(610) 278-3181 FAX: (610) 278-1214

Legrome D. Davis, Judge
Court of Common Pleas
Suite 1201, Criminal Justice Center
1301 Filbert Street
Philadelphia, Pennsylvania 19107
(215) 683-7020 FAX: (215) 683-7022
E-mail: Legrome.Davis@courts.Phila.gov.

Glynnis Hill, Judge
Court of Common Pleas
Family Court Division, Juvenile Branch
Room 329, 1801 Vine Street
Philadelphia, Pennsylvania 19103
(215) 686-4210 FAX: (215) 686-4254

Renee Cardwell Hughes, Judge
Court of Common Pleas
Suite 1406, Criminal Justice Center
Philadelphia, Pennsylvania 19107
(215) 683-7115 FAX: (215) 683-7117
E-mail: Renee.Hughes@courts.Phila.gov

George E. James, Judge
Court of Common Pleas
Beaver County Courthouse
Third Street
Beaver, Pennsylvania 15009
(724) 728-5700 Ext. 311 FAX: (724) 728-8708

Livingstone Johnson, Judge
Court of Common Pleas
5th Judicial District
705 City County Building
Pittsburgh, Pennsylvania 15219
(412) 350-1380 FAX: (412) 350-6998

C. Darnell Jones, Judge
Court of Common Pleas
Suite 1207, Criminal Justice Center
1301 Filbert Street
Philadelphia, Pennsylvania 19107
(215) 683-7038 FAX: (215) 683-7040
E-mail: Darnell.Jones@courts.Phila.gov.

Kathryn S. Lewis, Administrative Judge
Court of Common Pleas
Orphans' Court Division
Room 342, City Hall
Philadelphia, Pennsylvania 19107
(215) 686-9532 FAX: (202) (217) 686-7499
E-mail: Kathryn.Lewis@courts.Phila.gov.

Frederica Massiah-Jackson, Judge
Court of Common Pleas
Room 506, City Hall
Philadelphia, Pennsylvania 19107
(215) 686-2523 FAX: (215) 686-2865

Rayford A. Means, Judge
Court of Common Pleas
Suite 1204, Criminal Justice Center
1301 Filbert Street
Philadelphia, Pennsylvania 19107
(215) 683-7029 FAX: (215) 683-7031
E-mail: Rayford.Means@courts..Phila.gov.

Ronald B. Merriweather, Judge
Court of Common Pleas
Suite 1308, Criminal Justice Center
1301 Filbert Street
Philadelphia, Pennsylvania 19107
(215) 683-7220 FAX: (215) 683-7222
Ronald.Merriweather@courts.Phila.gov.

Lillian Harris Ransom, Judge
Court of Common Please of Philadelphia County
Family Court Division, Juvenile Branch
Room 347, 1801 Vine Street
Philadelphia, Pennsylvania 19103
(215) 686-4058 FAX: (215) 686-4220

Abram Frank Reynolds, Judge
Court of Common Pleas of Philadelphia County
Family Court Division, Juvenile Branch
Room 159, 1801 Vine Street
Philadelphia, Pennsylvania 19103
(215) 686-8387 FAX: (215) 686-4231

Rosalyn K. Robinson, Judge
Court of Common Pleas of Philadelphia County
Family Court Division
Suite 404, 27 South 12th Street
Philadelphia, Pennsylvania 19107
(215) 686-4030 FAX: (215) 686-9302

Peter F. Rogers, Judge
Court of Common Pleas
Suite 1408, Criminal Justice Center
1301 Filbert Street
Philadelphia, Pennsylvania 19107
(215) 683-7121 FAX: (215) 683-7123

Karen Shreeves, Judge
Court of Common Pleas
Suite 542, City Hall
Philadelphia, Pennsylvania 19107
(215) 686-7510 FAX: (215) 686-7375

Sheila Woods Skipper, Judge
Court of Common Pleas
Suite 1216, Criminal Justice Center
1301 Filbert Street
Philadelphia, Pennsylvania 19107
(215) 683-7065 FAX: (215) 683-7067

Gregory E. Smith, Judge
Court of Common Pleas
Suite 1407, Criminal Justice Center
1301 Filbert Street
Philadelphia, Pennsylvania 19107
(215) 683-7118 or 683-7119 FAX: (215) 683-7120
E-mail: Gregory.Smith@courts.Phila.gov

John M. Younge, Judge
Court of Common Pleas
Suite 1405, Criminal Justice Center
1301 Filbert Street
Philadelphia, Pennsylvania 19107
(215) 683-7112 FAX: (215) 683-7114
E-mail: John.Younge@courts.Phila.gov.

James A. Lineberger, Senior Judge
Court of Common Pleas
Suite 1203, Criminal Justice Center
1301 Filbert Street
Philadelphia, Pennsylvania 19107
(215) 683-7026 FAX: (215) 683-7028

Clarence C. Morrison, Senior Judge
Court of Common Pleas of Dauphin County
Dauphin County Courthouse
Front and Market Streets
Harrisburg, Pennsylvania 17101
(717) 255-2783 FAX: (717) 255-2805

Lynnwood Blount, Judge (Retired)
Court of Common Pleas
2444 North 56th Street
Philadelphia, Pennsylvania 19107

John L. Braxton, Judge (Retired)
Court of Common Pleas
410 St. John Newman Way
Philadelphia, Pennsylvania 19123
(215) 923-7227 FAX: (215) 923-1185

Curtis Carson, Judge (Retired)
Court of Common Pleas
547 Pelham Road
Philadelphia, Pennsylvania 19119
(215) 848-3139

Paul A. Dandridge, Judge (Retired)
Court of Common Pleas
Philadelphia Health Management
206 South Broad Street, 20th Floor
Philadelphia, Pennsylvania 19102
(215) 985-6887 FAX: (215) 985-2555

Levan Gordon, Judge (Retired)
Court of Common Pleas
906 E. Slocum Street
Philadelphia, Pennsylvania 19150
(215) 276-8899 FAX: (215) 276-8899

Ricardo Jackson, Judge (Retired)
Court of Common Pleas
Department of Labor
Curtis Center
7th & Walnut Street, Suite 637
170 S. Independence Mall
Philadelphia, Pennsylvania 19106-3305
(215) 861-5027 FAX: (215) 861-5029

Lawrence Prattis, Judge (Retired)
Court of Common Pleas
5209 Woodbine Avenue
Philadelphia, Pennsylvania 19131
(215) 877-1046

Doris Smith, Judge
Commonwealth Court
Widener Building, Suite 920
Philadelphia, Pennsylvania 19107
(215) 560-3694 FAX: (215) 560-3038

Linda F. Anderson, Judge
Municipal Court
Room 242, City Hall
Philadelphia, Pennsylvania 19107
(215) 686-7369 or 686-7783 FAX: (215) 686-7487
E-mail: Linda.Anderson@courts.Phila.gov.

Gwendolyn Conway, Judge
Municipal Court
Room 640, City Hall
Philadelphia, Pennsylvania 19107
(215) 686-4175 FAX: (215) 686-9539
E-mail: Gwendolyn.Conway@courts.Phila.gov

James DeLeon, Judge
Municipal Court
Suite 1311, Criminal Justice Center
Philadelphia, Pennsylvania 19107
(215) 683-7222 FAX: (215) 683-7231

Lydia Y. Kirkland, Judge
Municipal Court
Suite 1306, Criminal Justice Center
1301 Filbert Street
Philadelphia, Pennsylvania 19107
(215) 683-7215 FAX: (215) 683-7126
E-mail: Lydia.Kirkland@courts.Phila.gov.

Jimmie Moore, Judge
Municipal Court
Suite 1320, Criminal Justice Center
Philadelphia, Pennsylvania 19107
(215) 683-7256 FAX: (215) 683-7258

Craig M. Washington, Judge
Municipal Court
Room 642, City Hall
Philadelphia, Pennsylvania 19107
(215) 686-7370 FAX: (215) 686-9539
E-mail: Craig.Washington@courts.Phila.gov.

William Adams, Judge
Philadelphia Traffic Court
800 Spring Garden Street
Philadelphia, Pennsylvania 19123
(215) 686-1735 FAX: (215) 686-1655

Thomasine Tynes, Judge
Philadelphia Traffic Court
800 Spring Garden Street
Philadelphia, Pennsylvania 19123
(215) 686-1621 FAX: (215) 686-1622 *51

Edward S. Cox, Judge (Retired)
Philadelphia Traffic Court
2258 North 52nd Street
Philadelphia, Pennsylvania 19131

Charles Cuffeld, Judge (Retired)
Philadelphia Traffic Court
513 Glen Echo Road
Philadelphia, Pennsylvania 19119
(215) 248-5553

Juanita E. Holden, Master
27 South 12th Street
3rd Floor
Philadelphia, Pennsylvania 19107
(215) 686-8865 FAX: (215) 686-8868

Elizabeth Jackson, Master
355 C. Master Unit
34 South 11th Street
Philadelphia, Pennsylvania 19107
(215) 686-8865 FAX: (215) 686-8868

Administrative Law Judges

Cynthia Williams Fordham
Administrative Law Judge
Public Utility Commission
1302 State Office Building
Broad & Spring Garden Street
Philadelphia, Pennsylvania 19130
(215) 560-2105 FAX: (215) 560-3133

Aida Louise Harris, Administrative Law Judge
Pennsylvania Bureau of Workers' Compensation
2901 Grant Avenue
Philadelphia, Pennsylvania 19114
(215) 560-2125 FAX: (215) 560-2539

Charles E. Rainey, Jr., Administrative Law Judge
Public Utilities Commission
1302 Philadelphia State Office Building
1400 West Spring Garden Street
Philadelphia, Pennsylvania 19130
(215) 560-2105 FAX: (215) 560-3133

Tania F. Wright, Judge
Pennsylvania Liquor Control Board
Meeting House Business Center
140 West Germantown Pike
Suite 100
Plymouth Meeting, Pennsylvania 19462
(610) 832-1744 FAX: (610) 832-1747

PUERTO RICO: (0)

RHODE ISLAND: (2)

Edward C. Clifton, Associate Justice
Superior Court
250 Benefit Street
Providence, Rhode Island 02903
(401) 222-3250 FAX: (401) 222-2794

O. Rogeriee Thompson, Associate Justice
Superior Court
250 Benefit Street
Providence, Rhode Island 02903
(401) 222-3250? FAX: (401) 222-2794

SOUTH CAROLINA: (25)

FEDERAL

Margaret B. Seymour, Judge
U. S. District Court
for the District of South Carolina
Post Office Box 1985
201 Magnolia Street
Spartanburg, South Carolina 29304
(864) 582-2167 FAX: (864) 582-3736

Matthew J. Perry, Jr., Senior Judge
U. S. District Court
for the District of South Carolina
Strom Thurmond Federal Courthouse
1845 Assembly Street
Columbia, South Carolina 29201-2431
(803) 765-5408 FAX: (803) 253-3692

STATE

Supreme Court

Ernest A. Finney, Jr., Chief Justice (Retired)
Supreme Court of South Carolina
Post Office Drawer 1309
Sumter, South Carolina 29151-1309
(803) 436-2203 FAX: (803) 773-3113

Court of Appeals

Jasper Marshall Cureton, Associate Justice
South Carolina Court of Appeals
Post Office Box 11629
Columbia, South Carolina 29211-1629
(803) 734-1914 FAX: (803) 734-1853

Circuit Courts

Donald W. Beatty, Judge
Circuit Court
7th Judicial Circuit
Spartanburg County Courthouse
Post Office Box 3543
Spartanburg, South Carolina 29304
(864) 596-3450 FAX: (864) 596-2202

Allison R. Lee, Judge
Circuit Court
Post Office Box 192
Columbia, South Carolina 29202-0192
(803) 748-4668 FAX: (803) 748-4742

Daniel R. Martin, Sr., Judge
Circuit Court
9th Judicial Circuit
2144 Melbourne Avenue, Suite 220
North Charleston, South Carolina 29405
(843) 740-5740 FAX: (843) 740-5882

L. Casey Manning, Judge
Circuit Court
5th Judicial Circuit
Richland Judicial Center
Post Office Box 192
Columbia, South Carolina 29202-0192
(803) 929-6270 FAX: (803) 929-6273

Clifton Newman, Judge
Circuit Court
125 West Main Street
Kingstree, South Carolina 29556
(843) 354-9321 FAX: (843) 355-9301

Family Court Judges

Reuben L. Gray, Judge
Family Court
3rd Judicial Circuit
Post Office Box 2636
Sumter, South Carolina 29151-2636
(803) 436-2373 FAX: (803) 436-2397
E-mail: Rgraysc@scjd.state.sc.us

Deadra L. Jefferson, Judge
Family Court
9th Judicial Circuit
Post Office Box 934
2 Courthouse Square
Charleston, South Carolina 29402-0934
(843) 958-4406 FAX: (843) 958-4437
E-mail: Djeffersonsc@scjd.state.sc.us

Robert N. Jenkins, Sr., Judge
Family Court, 13th Judicial Circuit
301 University Ridge
Post Office Box 757
Greenville, South Carolina 29602-0757
(864) 467-5854 FAX: (864) 467-5845
E-mail: RJenkinsc@scjd.state.sc.us

Master-in-Equity

Joseph M. Strickland, Judge
Master-in-Equity
Richland County Court Judicial Center
1701 Main Street - Suite 212
Post Office Box 192
Columbia, South Carolina 29202-0192
(803) 748-4811 FAX: (803) 748-4824

Probate Court

Harry C. Brown, Judge
Jasper County Probate Court
Post Office Box 1739
Ridgeland, South Carolina 29936-1739
(803) 726-8758 or 726-5299

Vivian Ross-Bennett, Judge
Orangeburg County Probate Court
Post Office Drawer 29116-9000
Orangeburg, South Carolina 29116
(803) 533-8280 FAX: (803) 533-6279

Margaret K. Thompson, Judge
Orangeburg County Probate Court
429 Jamison Avenue
Orangeburg, South Carolina 29116
(803) 533-6280 FAX: (803) 534-3848

Tamara C. Curry, Associate Probate Judge
2144 Melbourne Avenue
North Charleston, South Carolina 29405
(843) 740-5700 FAX: (843) 740-5887

Jacqueline Davis-Belton
Associate Probate Judge
Post Office Box 192
Columbia, South Carolina 29202
(803) 748-4712 FAX: (803) 748-4814

Municipal Court

Merl F. Code, Judge
Municipal Court
Greenville County
1300-D East Washington Street
Greenville, South Carolina 29607-1858
(864) 271-4973 FAX: (864) 242-2921

Lincoln C. Jenkins, III, Judge
Municipal Court
Post Office Box 644
Columbia, South Carolina 29202-0644
(803) 733-8422 or 256-0288 FAX: (803) 401-8821

Arthur C. McFarland, Judge
Municipal Court – Charleston County
205 King Street, Suite 409
Charleston, South Carolina 29401
(843) 722-3376 FAX: (843) 763-3900

Jennifer Peters-Wilson
Chief Municipal Court Judge
Myrtle Beach Municipal Court
1101 Oak Street
Myrtle Beach, South Carolina 295778
(843) 918-1357 FAX: (843) 918-1446

Joseph Thomas, Judge
Municipal Court – Lee County
Route # 2, Box 64
Lynchburg, South Carolina 29080
(803) 437-7154 or 484-6463

Samuel Pea, Judge
Summary Court
Richland County
4919 Rhett Street
Columbia, South Carolina 29203-4522
(803) 754-2250 FAX: (803) 786-6065

Administrative Law Judges

John D. Geathers
Administrative Law Judge Seat No. 4
Edgar A. Brown Building, Suite 224
1205 Pendleton Street
Columbia, South Carolina 29201
(803) 734-0550 FAX: (803) 734-6400

SOUTH DAKOTA: (0)

TENNESSEE: (34)

FEDERAL

Curtis Lynn Collier, Judge
U. S. District Court
for the Eastern District of Tennessee
Post Office Box 831
900 Georgia Avenue, Room 104
Chattanooga, Tennessee 37401-0831
(423) 752-5287 FAX: (423) 752-5246

Bernice Bouie Donald, Judge
U. S. District Court
for the Western District of Tennessee
1111 Clifford Davis Federal Building
167 North Main Street
Memphis, Tennessee 38103-2303
(901) 495-1299 FAX: (901) 495-1303

William Joseph Haynes, Jr., Judge
U. S. District Court
for the Middle District of Tennessee
649 U. S. Courthouse
801 Broadway
Nashville, Tennessee 37203
(615) 736-7217 FAX: (615) 736-5285

Odell Horton, Sr., Judge
U. S. District Court
for the Western District of Tennessee
Clifford Davis Federal Building
167 North Main Street
Memphis, Tennessee 38103-2328
(901) 544-4268

Administrative Law Judge

Audrey M. Scott
Supervisory Administrative Judge
U. S. Equal Employment
Opportunity Commission
Memphis District Office
1407 Union Avenue, Suite 621
Memphis, Tennessee 38104
(901) 544-0070 FAX: (901) 544-0111

STATE

Adolpho A. Birch, Jr., Associate Justice
Tennessee Supreme Court
304 Supreme Court Building
401 7th Avenue North
Nashville, Tennessee 37219-1407
(615) 741-6750 FAX: (615) 741-5809 or 253-3804

Walter L. Evans, Chancellor
Chancery Court – 30th Judicial District, Part I
140 Adams Avenue, Room 308
Memphis Tennessee 38103-2018
(901) 545-4000 FAX: (901) 545-3309

Irvin H. Kilcrease, Jr., Chancellor
Chancery Court – 20th Judicial District, Part I
401 Metro Courthouse
Nashville, Tennessee 37201
(615) 862-5700 FAX: (615) 862-5341

Floyd Peete, Jr., Chancellor
Chancery Court – 30th Judicial District, Part II
140 Adams Avenue, Room 308
Memphis, Tennessee 38103-2018
(901) 545-4000 FAX: (901) 545-3309

D'Army Bailey, Judge
Circuit Court
30th Judicial District – Division VIII
140 Adams Avenue, Room 212
Memphis, Tennessee 38103-2018
(901) 545-4022 FAX: (901) 545-5659

George H. Brown, Jr., Judge
Circuit Court
30th Judicial District – Division VI
140 Adams Avenue - Room 212
Memphis, Tennessee 38103-2018
(901) 545-4022 FAX: (901) 545-5659

Rita L. Stotts, Judge
Circuit Court
30th Judicial District – Division IV
140 Adams Avenue
Memphis, Tennessee 38103
(901) 545-4022 FAX: (901) 545-5659

Arthur T. Bennett, Judge
Criminal Court
30th Judicial District – Division VII
519 Shelby County Justice Center
201 Poplar Avenue
Memphis, Tennessee 38103-1947
(901) 545-5858 FAX: (901) 545-3557

Carolyn Wade Blackett, Judge
Criminal Court
30th Judicial District – Division IV
519 Shelby County Justice Center
201 Poplar Avenue
Memphis, Tennessee 38103-1947
(901) 545-5858 FAX: (901) 545-3557

W. Otis Higgs, Jr., Judge
Criminal Court
30th Judicial District –Division II
519 Shelby County Justice Center
201 Poplar Avenue
Memphis, Tennessee 38103
(901) 545-5850 FAX: (901) 545-3557

J. C. McLin, Judge
Criminal Court
30th Judicial District – Division IX
519 Shelby County Justice Center
201 Poplar Avenue
Memphis, Tennessee 38103-1947
(901) 545-3773 FAX: (901) 545-3557

Mischelle Alexander-Best, Judge
General Sessions Court
30th Judicial District, Division 11
Shelby County Justice Center
201 Poplar Avenue, Suite LL-56
Memphis, Tennessee 38103
(901) 545-5195 FAX: (901) 545-3766

Joyce C. Broffit, Judge
General Sessions Court
30th Judicial District, Division 9
Shelby County Justice Center
201 Poplar Avenue, Suite LL-56
Memphis, Tennessee 38103-1947
(901) 545-5190 FAX: (901) 545-3766

John A. Donald, Judge
General Sessions Court
30th Judicial District, Division 3
Shelby County Courthouse
140 Adams Avenue, Room 110
Memphis, Tennessee 38103
(901) 545-4050 FAX: (901) 545-5062

C. Anthony Johnson, Judge
General Sessions Court,
30th Judicial District, Division 10
Shelby County Justice Center
201 Poplar Avenue, Suite LL-56
Memphis, Tennessee 38103
(901) 545-5194 FAX: (901) 545-3766

Loyce Lambert, Judge
General Sessions Court
30th Judicial District, Division 15
201 Poplar Avenue
Memphis, Tennessee 38103
(901) 545-5190 FAX: (901) 545-3766

Russell B. Sugarmon, Jr., Judge
General Sessions Court
30th Judicial District, Division 4
104 Adams Avenue, Room 110
Memphis, Tennessee 38103
(901) 545-4050 FAX: (901) 545-5062

Betty J. Thomas, Judge
General Sessions Court
30th Judicial District, Division 5
Shelby County Courthouse
140 Adams Avenue, Room 110
Memphis, Tennessee 38103
(901) 545-4090 FAX: (901) 545-5062

Lonnie B. Thompson, Judge
General Sessions Court
30th Judicial District, Division 6
Shelby County Courthouse
140 Adams Avenue, Room 110
Memphis, Tennessee 38103
(901) 545-4087 FAX: (901) 545-5062

Jayne R. Chandler, Judge
City Court
30th Judicial District, Division 3
201 Poplar Avenue, LL-06
Memphis, Tennessee 38103
(901) 545-5443 FAX: (901) 545-3666

Ernestine Hunt-Dorse, Judge
City Court
30th Judicial District, Division 1
201 Poplar Avenue, Room LL-06
Memphis, Tennessee 38103
(901) 545-5441 FAX: (901) 545-3666

Tarik B. Sugarmon, Judge
City Court
30th Judicial District, Division 2
201 Poplar Avenue, LL-06
Memphis, Tennessee 38103
(901) 545-5441 FAX: (901) 545-3666

Walter F. Williams, Judge
City Court
11th Judicial District, Division 1
Hamilton County Courts Building
600 Market Street
Chattanooga, Tennessee 37402
(423) 757-5148 FAX: (423) 757-4965

Felicia Marie Hogan, Referee
Juvenile Court
30th Judicial District
616 Adams Avenue
Memphis, Tennessee 38105
(901) 405-8607 FAX: (901) 575-8853

Andrei Ellen Lee, Referee
Juvenile Court
30th Judicial District
100 Woodland Street
Nashville, Tennessee 37213
(615) 862-8000 FAX: (615) 862-7143

Carlton Lewis, Referee
Juvenile Court
30th Judicial District
100 Woodland Street
Nashville, Tennessee 37213
(615) 862-8000 FAX: (615) 862-7143

Administrative Law Judges

Melvin J. Malone, Director
(Administrative Law Judge)
Tennessee Regulatory Authority
460 James Robertson Parkway
Nashville, Tennessee 37243-0505
(615) 741-3668 FAX: (615) 741-5015

Berry Springfield, Administrative Law Judge
Tennessee Secretary of State's Office
1700 James K. Polk Building
505 Deadrick Street
Nashville, Tennessee 37243-0307
(615) 741-4469 FAX: (615) 741-4472

Mattielyn Williams, Administrative Law Judge
Tennessee Secretary of State's Office
1700 James K. Polk Building
505 Deadrick Street
Nashville, Tennessee 37243-0307
(615) 741-4469 FAX: (615) 741-4472

TEXAS: (93)

FEDERAL

Vanessa Diane Gilmore, Judge
U. S. District Court
for the Southern District of Texas
9513 Bob Casey U. S. Courthouse
515 Rusk Avenue
Houston, Texas 77002
(713) 250-5931 FAX: (713) 250-5477

Kenneth M. Hoyt, Judge
U. S. District Court
for the Southern District of Texas
11144 Bob Casey U. S. Courthouse
515 Rusk Avenue
Houston, Texas 77002
(713) 250-5613 FAX: (713) 250-5368

Sam A. Lindsay, Judge
U. S. District Court
for the Northern District of Texas
1100 Commerce Street
Room 13b31
Dallas, Texas 75243
(214) 753-2365 FAX: (214) 753-2372

Calvin Botley, Magistrate Judge
U. S. District Court
for the Southern District of Texas
7720 Bob Casey U. S. Courthouse
515 Rusk Avenue
Houston, Texas 77002
(713) 250-5757 FAX: (713) 250-5055

Administrative Law Judges

Harold G. Adams, Administrative Law Judge
Office of Hearings and Appeals
Social Security Administration
12270 Merit Drive, Suite 800
Dallas, Texas 75251
(972) 341-5123 FAX: (972) 341-5125

Clarease E. Mitchell Rankin
U. S. Immigration Judge
2320 LaBranch Street, Room 2235
Houston, Texas 77004
(713) 750-3870 FAX: (713) 718-3879

Dietrich Sims, U. S. Immigration Judge
100 Commerce Street, Suite 4B41
Dallas, Texas 75242
(214) 767-3504 FAX: (214) 767-6410

Ulysses Sidney Cornelius, Jr.
Administrative Judge
U. S. Merit Systems Protection Board
100 Commerce Street, Room 6F20
Dallas, Texas 75242
(214) 767-0555 FAX: (214) 767-0102

Donna M. Edwards, Administrative Judge
U. S. Equal Employment Opportunity
Commission
207 South Houston Street
Dallas, Texas 75202
(214) 655-3341 FAX: (214) 655-3443

Sharon Jackson, Chief Administrative Judge
U. S. Merit Systems Protection Board
100 Commerce Street, Suite 6f20
Dallas, Texas 75242
(214) 767-0555 FAX: (214) 767-0102

Dwight A. Lewis, Chief Administrative Judge
U. S. Equal Employment
Opportunity Commission
Dallas District Office
207 South Houston Street
Dallas, Texas 75202
(214) 655-3343 FAX: (214) 655-3443

Cora P. Williams, Administrative Judge
U. S. Equal Employment
Opportunity Commission
Dallas District Office
207 South Houston Street
Dallas, Texas 75202
(214) 655-3342 FAX: (214) 655-3443

STATE

Appellate Courts

Morris L. Overstreet, Justice (Retired)
Texas Court of Criminal Appeals
Capitol Station
Post Office Box 12308
Austin, Texas 78711
(512) 463-1560 FAX: (512) 469-0950

Carolyn I. Wright, Justice
Fifth Court of Appeal
George L. Allen, Sr. Courts Building
600 Commerce Street
Dallas, Texas 75202-4658
(214) 712-3410 FAX: (214) 745-1083

State District Courts

Levi J. Benton, Judge
215th Judicial District Court
301 Fannin, Room 607
Houston, Texas 77002
(713) 755-6382 FAX: (713) 223-4840

Wilford Flowers, Judge
147th Judicial District Court
Travis County Courthouse
Post Office Box 1748
Austin, Texas 78767
(512) 473-9311 FAX: (512) 473-9140

Donald Joseph Floyd, Judge
172nd Judicial District Court
Jefferson County Courthouse
1001 Pearl Street
Post Office Box 3707
Beaumont, Texas 77704-3707
(409) 835-8485 FAX: (409) 784-5829

Brenda Garrett Green, Judge
256th Judicial District Court
George L. Allen, Sr. Courts Building
600 Commerce Street
Dallas, Texas 75202-4606
(214) 653-6449 FAX: (214) 653-6267

Nanette Hasette, Judge
28th Judicial District Court
901 Leopard Street, Room 803
Corpus Christi, Texas 78401
(361) 888-0506 FAX: (361) 888-0634

Belinda Hill, Judge
230th Judicial District Court
1302 Preston, 2nd Floor
Houston, Texas 77002
(713) 755-6782 FAX: (713) 755-8903

Faith Johnson, Judge
363rd Judicial District Court
Criminal Courts Building
133 North Industrial Boulevard, L.B. #36
Dallas, Texas 75207-4313
(214) 653-5890 FAX: (214) 653-5777

Carmen Y. Kelsey, Judge
289th Judicial District Court
600 Mission Road
San Antonio, Texas 78210-3851
(210) 531-1180 or 531-1185 FAX: (210) 531-1174

Laura J. Livingston, Judge
261st Judicial District Court
Travis County Courthouse
Post Office Box 1748
Austin, Texas 78767
(512) 473-9309 FAX: (512) 473-9332

Cheryl Lee Shannon, Judge
305th Judicial District Court
George L. Allen, Sr. Courts Building
2600 Lone Star Drive
Dallas, Texas 75212-6307
(214) 698-4924 FAX: (214) 698-5553

Dale J. Wainwright, Judge
334th Judicial District Court
301 Fannin, Room 212
Houston, Texas 77002
(713) 755-7793 FAX: (713) 755-4744

Criminal District Courts

John C. Creuzot, Judge
Criminal District Court No. 4
Frank Crowley Courts Building
133 North Industrial Boulevard
Dallas, Texas 75207
(214) 653-5930 FAX: (214) 712-5015

Wayne Salvant, Judge
Criminal District Court No. 2
Justice Center
401 West Belknap
Fort Worth, Texas 76196-0214
(817) 884-1347 FAX: (817) 884-1542

Juvenile/Family District Court

Veronica Morgan-Price, Judge
District Court
Juvenile/Family Division
3540 West Dallas
Houston, Texas 77019
(713) 521-4100 FAX: (713) 521-7326

District Court Magistrates

Andrew Wyatt Carruthers
Criminal Law Magistrate of Bexar County
300 Dolorosa Street, Suite 1054
San Antonio, Texas 78205
(210) 220-2900 FAX: (210) 220-2790

Terry McVay, Dallas County Magistrate Judge
133 North Industrial Boulevard
Dallas, Texas 75207
(214) 653-5792 FAX: (214) 653-5699

District Court Masters

George Collins, Presiding Court Master
IV-D Family Court No. 1
600 Commerce Street, 4th Floor
Dallas, Texas 75202
(214) 653-7683

Gracie Lewis, Juvenile Court Master
305th District Court
2600 Lone Star Drive, 3rd Floor
Dallas, Texas 75212
(214) 698-4924 FAX: (214) 698-5533

Delbra Wilson, Presiding Court Master
IV-D Family Court
100 Weatherford
Fort Worth, Texas 76196
(817) 884-3299 FAX: (817) 336-5914

State County Courts

Keith A. Anderson, Judge
County Criminal Court # 9
Frank Crowley Criminal Courts Building
133 North Industrial Boulevard
Dallas, Texas 75207-4313
(214) 653-5687 FAX: (214) 653-5777

John Paul Davis, Judge
County Court-at-Law No. 3
Jefferson County Courthouse
1001 Pearl Street
Beaumont, Texas 77701
(409) 835-8698 FAX: (409) 839-2326

Michael R. Fields, Judge
County Criminal Court #14
301 San Jacinto, 7th Floor
Houston, Texas 77002
(713) 755-5683 FAX: (713) 368-9281

Brenda Picola Kennedy, Judge
County Court-at-Law No. 7
Travis County Courthouse
Post Office Box 1748
Austin, Texas 78767-1748
(512) 473-9679 FAX: (512) 708-4683

Joel Bernard Bennett, Judge
Travis County
Drug Diversion Court
Travis County Courthouse
1000 Guadalupe Street
Austin, Texas 78701
(512) 476-8595

Judges of Justices of the Peace Courts

Thurman Bill Bartie, Judge
Justice of the Peace Court, Jefferson County
Precinct 8, Place 1
525 Lakeshore Drive
Port Arthur, Texas 77640
(409) 983-8330 FAX: (409) 983-8303

Quincy Beavers, Jr., Judge
Justice of the Peace Court
Smith County – Precinct 1
106 East Elm
Tyler, Texas 75702
(903) 535-0560

Betty Brock Bell, Judge
Justice of the Peace Court
Harris County – Precinct 7, Place 1
5737 Cullen Boulevard
Houston, Texas 77021
(713) 747-3776 FAX: (713) 747-3768

Paul A. Brown, Judge
Justice of the Peace Cour
Jefferson County – Precinct 6, Place 1
5030 Highway 69 South, #300
Beaumont, Texas 77705
(409) 726-2578 FAX: (409) 726-2589

Sadie F. Clay, Judge
Justice of the Peace Court, Harrison County
County Courthouse
1402 Field Street
Marshall, Texas 75670
(903) 935-4866 FAX: (903) 935-4866

Joel C. Clouser, Sr., Judge
Justice of the Peace Court
Fort Bend County - Precinct 2
Post Office Box 428
Missouri City, Texas 77459
(281) 403-8080 FAX: (281) 403-8089

Alexander Green, Judge
Justice of the Peace Court, Harris County
Precinct 7, Place 2
5300 Griggs Road, 2nd Floor
Houston, Texas 77021
(713) 643-1512 FAX: (713) 741-7103

Thomas G. Jones, Judge
Justice of the Peace Court, Dallas County
Precinct 7, Place 1
7201 South Polk Street
Dallas, Texas 75232
(972) 228-0280 FAX: (972) 228-2737

Albert W. McKnight, Judge
Justice of the Peace Court, Bexar County
Precinct 4, Place 1
4462 East Houston, Suite 200
San Antonio, Texas 78220
(210) 333-9373 FAX: (210) 337-1614

Charles R. Rose, Judge
Justice of the Peace Court, Dallas County
Precinct 8, Place 1
414 South R. L. Thornton Freeway
Dallas, Texas 75203-2435
(214) 860-4300 FAX: (214) 860-4411

Richard Eley Scott, Judge
Justice of the Peace Court, Travis County
Precinct 1, Place 1
1811 Springdale Road, Suite 110
Austin, Texas 78721
(512) 929-0593 FAX: (512) 929-3047

Cleophas Steele, Jr., Judge
Justice of the Peace Court, Dallas County
Precinct 8, Place 2
414 South R. L. Thornton Freeway
Dallas, Texas 75203-2435
(214) 948-0841 FAX: (214) 860-4411

Sidney Thompson, Judge
Justice of the Peace Court, Tarrant County
Precinct 8, Place 1
3212 Miller Avenue
Fort Worth, Texas 76119
(817) 531-5625 FAX: (817) 531-5666

James C. Williams, Judge
Justice of the Peace Court
Kaufman County - Precinct 3
408 East College Street
Terrell, Texas 75160
(972) 498-8759

Municipal Courts

Howard O. Banks, Judge
Dallas Municipal Court
2014 Main Street, Suite 210
Dallas, Texas 75201
(214) 670-5573 FAX: (214) 670-4457

W. E. B. Blackmon, Judge
Houston Municipal Court No. 4
1400 Lubbock, Basement
Houston, Texas 77002
(713) 755-5464 FAX: (713) 247-8747

Prince Cartwright, Jr., Judge
Kendleton Municipal Court
Post Office Box 809
Kendleton, Texas 77451
(979) 532-8240

Rhoda P. Cato, Judge
Houston Municipal Court No. 5
1400 Lubbock, Basement
Houston, Texas 77002
(713) 247-5464 or 247-5757 FAX: (713) 247-8747

Debra Champagne, Judge
Houston Municipal Court No. 7
1400 Lubbock Street, Room 214
Houston, Texas 77002
(713) 247-5464 or 247-5799 FAX: (713) 247-8747

Clarence Eugene Culberson, Jr.
Presiding Judge
Smithville Municipal Court
3317 Main Street
Post Office Box 449
Smithville, Texas 78957-0449
(512) 237-3282 FAX: (512) 237-4549

Herbert L. Hawkins, Jr., Judge
Bay City Municipal Court
1824 Sixth Street
Bay City, Texas 77414
(979) 245-0035 FAX: (979)323-1649

Vonciel Jones Hill, Associate Judge
Dallas Municipal Court
2014 Main Street, Suite 210
Dallas, Texas 75201
(214) 670-5573 FAX: (214) 670-6947

Theodore Johns, Sr., Judge
Beaumont Municipal Court
Post Office Box 3827
Beaumont, Texas 77704-3827
(979) 880-3885

Frankie B. Ledbetter, Presiding Judge
Prairie View Muncipal Court
300 A Highway 290
Post Office Box 817
Prairie View, Texas 77446
(936) 857-5327 FAX: (936) 857-5611

C. Victor Lander, Judge
Dallas Municipal Court
2014 Main Street, Suite 210
Dallas, Texas 75201
(214) 670-5573 FAX: (214) 670-6947

Beverly J. Landers, Judge
Austin Municipal Court
700 East Seventh Street
Austin, Texas 78768-2135
(512) 433-4841 FAX: (512) 433-4837

Evelyn P. McKee, Judge
Austin Municipal Court
700 East Seventh Street
Post Office Box 2135
Austin, Texas 78768-2135
(512) 433-4841 FAX: (512) 433-4837

Kermit C. Morrison, Jr., Judge
Post Arthur Municipal Court
645 Fourth Street
Port Arthur, Texas 77641-1089
(409) 983-8686 FAX (409) 983-8758

Sharon Newman-Stanfield, Judge
Forth Worth Municipal Court
1000 Throckmorton
Fort Worth, Texas 76102-6382
(817) 871-6715

Victor Ortiz, Judge
Dallas Municipal Court
2014 Main Street, Suite 210
Dallas, Texas 75201
(214) 670-5573 FAX: (214) 670-6947

Daniel Jay Simms
Presiding Judge and Magistrate
Municipal Court No. 17
1400 Lubbock Street - Suite 214
Houston, Texas 77002
(713) 247-5759 FAX: (713) 247-8747

Reedy M. Spigner, Presiding Judge
Princeton Municipal Court
306 North Front
Post Office Box 970
Princeton, Texas 75407-0970
(972) 881-0581

Seth Stein, Presiding Judge
Henderson Municipal Court
502 West Main
Henderson, Texas 75652
(903) 657-5061

Elaine M. Timberlake, Judge
Houston Municipal Court No. 12
1400 Lubbock Street, Room 214
Houston, Texas 77002
(713) 247-5758 FAX: (713) 247-8747

Homer Walls, Judge
San Antonio Municipal Court
401 South Frio
San Antonio, Texas 78207
(210) 299-8967 FAX: (210) 299-4259

Cheryl D. Williams, Presiding Judge
Dallas Municipal Court
2014 Main Street, Suite 210
Dallas, Texas 75201
(214) 670-5573 FAX: (214) 670-6947

Fad Wilson, Jr., Associate Presiding Judge
Houston Municipal Court No. 2
1400 Lubbock Street, Room 214
Houston, Texas 77002
(713) 247-8745 or 247-5464 FAX: (713) 247-8747

Associate Municipal Judges

Jerry G. Bradford, Associate Judge
Dallas Municipal Court
2014 Main Street, Suite 210
Dallas, Texas 75201
(214) 670-5573 FAX: (214) 670-6947

Grant Coleman, Associate Judge
City of Houston Municipal Courts
1400 Lubbock Street, Room 214
Houston, Texas 77002
(713) 247-5464 FAX: (713) 247-8747

Elizabeth I. Davis, Presiding Judge
Balch Springs Municipal Court
3117 Hickory Tree Road
Balch Springs, Texas 75180
(972) 557-6056
Associate Judge Dallas Municipal Court
2014 Main Street, Suite 210
Dallas, Texas 75201
(214) 670-5573 FAX: (214) 670-6947

Victoria Dawson, Associate Judge
Houston Municipal Courts
1400 Lubbock Street, Room 214
Houston, Texas 77002
(713) 247-5464 FAX: (713) 247-8747

Nikita V. Harmon, Associate Judge
Houston Municipal Court
1400 Lubbock Street
Houston, Texas 77002
(713) 247-5464 FAX: (713) 247-8747

Christopher Hodge, Associate Judge
Houston Municipal Court
1400 Lubbock Street, Room 214
Houston, Texas 77002
(713) 755-8745 FAX: (713) 247-8747

Lydia D. Johnson, Associate Judge
Houston Municipal Court
1400 Lubbock Street
Houston, Texas 77002
(713) 247-5464 FAX: (713) 247-8747

Phyllis Lister, Associate Judge
Dallas Municipal Court
2014 Main Street, Suite 210
Dallas, Texas 75201
(214) 670-5573 FAX: (214) 670-6947

Oswald Scott, Jr., Associate Judge
Houston Municipal Court
1400 Lubbock Street
Houston, Texas 77002
(713) 247-5464 FAX: (713) 247-8747

Yvonne Qlyamah Taylor, Associate Judge
Houston Municipal Court
1400 Lubbock Street
Houston, Texas 77002
(713) 247-5464 FAX: (713) 247-8747

Francella E. Totty, Associate Judge
Houston Municipal Court
1400 Lubbock Street
Houston, Texas 77002
(713) 247-5464 FAX: (713) 247-8747

April Walker, Associate Judge
Houston Municipal Court
1400 Lubbock Street
Houston, Texas 77002
(713) 247-5464 FAX: (713) 247-8747

Retired Judges

Harriet M. Murphy, Judge (Retired)
Austin Municipal Court
6635 Greensboro Drive
Austin, Texas 78723
(512) 928-2045 FAX: (512) 928-0773

Harrison Gregg, Associate Judge (Retired)
Harris County District Court
Harris County Attorney's Office
1001 Preston Street
Houston, Texas 77002
(713) 755-5101

State Administrative Law Judges

Brenda Coleman, Administrative Law Judge
State Office of Administrative Hearings
6330 Forest Park Road, Suite 150-A
Dallas, Texas 75235
(214) 956-8616 FAX: (214) 956-8611

Veronica Dorsey, Administrative Law Judge
State Office of Administrative Hearings
North Freeway Business Plaza
2020 N. Loop West, Suite 111
Houston, Texas 77018
(713) 957-6010 FAX: (713) 812-1001

Samuel T. Jackson
Presiding Administrative Law Judge
Texas Attorney General Office
Post Office Box 12017 - Mail Code 039-3
Austin, Texas 78711-2017
(512) 460-6000 FAX: (512) 460-6024

Sheila Bailey Taylor
Chief Administrative Law Judge
State Office of Administrative Hearing
300 West 15th Street, Suite 502
Austin, Texas 78701
(512) 475-4993 FAX: (512) 463-7791

UTAH: (2)

Tyrone E. Medley, Judge
Third Judicial District Court
Scott M. Matheson Courthouse
450 South State Street - # W46
Salt Lake City, Utah 84114
(801) 238-7503 FAX: (801) 238-7542

Shauna Graves-Robertson, Judge
Salt Lake County - Justice Court
2001 South State Street
Salt Lake City, Utah 84190
(801) 468-3419 FAX: (801) 468-3419

VERMONT: (0)

VIRGIN ISLANDS: (11)

FEDERAL

Raymond L. Finch, Chief Judge
U. S. District Court
for the District of Virgin Islands
373 Almeric L. Christian Federal Building
3013 Estate Golden Rock,Christiansted
St. Croix, Virgin Islands 00820-4355
(340) 773-5021 FAX: (340) 773-2113
E-mail: judgefinch@vid.uscourts.gov

Territorial Court:

Alphonso G. Andrews, Jr., Associate Judge
Territorial Court of the Virgin Islands
RFD #2 - Post Office Box 9000, Kingshill
St. Croix, Virgin Islands 00851
(340) 778-9750 FAX: (340) 778-4044 or 778-4218

Maria M. Cabret, Presiding Judge
Territorial Court of the Virgin Islands
RFD #2 - Post Office. Box 9000, Kingshill
St. Croix, Virgin Islands 00851
(340) 778-9750 FAX: (340) 778-4044 or 778-4218
E-mail: mmcabret@court.gov.vi

Soraya Diase, Associate Judge
Territorial Court of the Virgin Islands
Post Office Box 70
St. Thomas, Virgin Islands 00801
(340) 774-6680 FAX: (340) 776-9889

Brenda Hollar, Associate Judge
Territorial Court of the Virgin Islands
Post Office Box 70
St. Thomas, Virgin Islands 00801
(340) 778-6680 FAX: (340) 776-9889

Ishmael A. Meyers, Associate Judge
Territorial Court of the Virgin Islands
Post Office Box 70
St. Thomas, Virgin Islands 00801
(340) 774-6680 FAX: (340) 776-9889

Edgar D. Ross, Associate Judge
Territorial Court of the Virgin Islands
RFD #2 Post Office Box 9000, Kingshill
St. Croix, Virgin Islands 00851
(340) 778-9750 FAX: (340) 778-4044 or 778-4218
E-mail: marshall@court.gov.vi

Ive A. Swan, Associate Judge
Territorial Court of the Virgin Islands
Post Office Box 70
St. Thomas, Virgin Islands 00801
(340) 774-6680 FAX: (340) 776-9889

Patricia D. Steele, Family Judge
Territorial Court of the Virgin Islands
RFD # 2 - Post Office Box 9000, Kingshill
St. Croix, Virgin Islands 00821
(340) 778-9750 FAX: (340) 778-4044 or 778-4218
E-mail:socrates@court.gov.vi

Verne A. Hodge, Senior Judge
Territorial Court of the Virgin Islands
Post Office Box 70
St. Thomas, Virgin Islands 00801
(340) 774-6680 FAX: (340) 776-9889
E-mail: chiefbank@court.gov.vi

Eileen R. Petersen, Senior Judge
Territorial Court of the Virgin Islands
Post Office Box 2183, Kingshill
St. Croix, Virgin Islands 00851
(340) 773-3616 FAX: (340) 773-3136
E-mail: epetersen@viaccess.net

VIRGINIA: (56)

FEDERAL

Roger Gregory, Judge
U. S. Court of Appeals For the Fourth Circuit
Lewis F. Powell, Jr. U. S. Courthouse
1000 East Main Street
Richmond, Virginia 23219
(804) 916-2700

Raymond Alvin Jackson, Judge
U. S. District Court
for the Eastern District of Virginia
307 Walter E. Hoffman Courthouse
600 Granby Street
Norfolk, Virginia 23510-1915
(757) 441-3173 FAX: (757) 441-3174

Gerald Bruce Lee, Judge
U. S. District Court
for the Eastern District of Virginia
Albert V. Bryan U.S. Courthouse
401 Courthouse Square
Alexandria, Virginia 22314
(703) 299-2117 FAX: (703) 299-3339
(Clerk's Office 703-299-2100)

James R. Spencer, Judge
U. S. District Court
for the Eastern District of Virginia
305 Lewis F. Powell, Jr. U. S. Courthouse
1000 East Main Street
Richmond, Virginia 22319-3525
(804) 916-2250 FAX: (804) 916-2259

Administrative Judges

Allan F. Ellmore, Administrative Judge
Armed Services Board of Contract Appeals
5109 Leesburg Pike, Suite 703
Falls Church, Virginia 22401
(703) 681-8522 FAX: (703) 681-8535

Gail M. Frazier, Administrative Judge
Board of Land Appeals
U. S. Department of the Interior
4015 Wilson Boulevard
Arlington, Virginia 22203
(703) 235-3750 FAX: (703) 235-8349
E-mail: gail_frazier@ios.doi.gov

Richard Shackleford, Administrative Judge
Armed Services Board of Contract Appeals
5109 Leesburg Pike, Suite 703
Falls Church, Virginia 22041
(703) 681-8513 FAX: (703) 681-8535

STATE

Supreme Court

Leroy R. Hassell, Sr., Justice
Virginia Supreme Court
P.O. Box 1315
100 North Ninth Street
Richmond, Virginia 23218-1315
(804) 786-6404 FAX: (804) 371-8530

Appellate Court

James W. Benton, Jr., Judge
Virginia Court of Appeals
101 North Eighth Street
Richmond, Virginia 23219-2305
(804) 786-6176 FAX: (804) 786-6738
E-mail: benton@courts.state.va.us

Circuit Court Judges

Verbena Askew, Judge
Circuit Court
7th Judicial Circuit
2500 Washington Avenue
Newport News, Virginia 23607
(757) 926-8561 FAX: (757) 926-8531

Junius P. Fulton, III, Judge
Circuit Court
4th Judicial Circuit
100 St. Paul Boulevard
Norfolk, Virginia 23510
(757) 664-4591 FAX: (757) 664-4581
E-mail: jfulton@courts.state.va.us

Samuel Bernard Goodwyn, Judge
Circuit Court – 1st Judicial Circuit
Chesapeake Circuit Court
307 Albemarle Drive, Suite 400A
Chesapeake, Virginia 23322
(757) 382-3000, 382-3050 or 382-3051
FAX: (757) 382-3090

Gary A. Hicks, Judge
Circuit Court – 14th Judicial Circuit
Henrico Circuit Court
Post Office Box 27032
Parham & Hungary Springs Road
Richmond, Virginia 23261-7032
(804) 501-4705 FAX: (804) 501-5505

Melvin R. Hughes, Jr., Judge
Circuit Court
13th Judicial Circuit
John Marshall Courts Building
400 North Ninth Street
Richmond, Virginia 23219
(804) 646-6505 FAX: (804) 646-6562

Jerome James, Chief Judge
Circuit Court – 4th Judicial Circuit
100 St. Paul Boulevard
Norfolk, Virginia 23510
(757) 664-4591 FAX: (757) 664-4581
E-mail: jjames@courts.state.va.us

Randall G. Johnson, Judge
Circuit Court – 13th Judicial Circuit
John Marshall Courts Building
400 North Ninth Street
Richmond, Virginia 23225
(804) 646-6505 FAX: (804) 646-6562

Johnny E. Morrison, Judge
Circuit Court – 3rd Judicial Circuit
Post Office Drawer 1217
Portsmouth, Virginia 23705
(757) 393-8671 FAX: (757) 499-4826

William T. Newman, Jr., Judge
Circuit Court – 17th Judicial Circuit
1425 North Courthouse Road
Arlington, Virginia 22201
(703) 228-7000 FAX: (703) 228-7128

Cleo E. Powell, Judge
Chesterfield Circuit Court
12th Judicial Circuit
Post Office Box 57
Chesterfield, Virginia 23832
(804) 748-1333 FAX: (804) 751-4173
powell@co.chesterfield.va.us

John W. Scott, Jr., Judge
Circuit Court
15th Judicial Circuit
1300 Courthouse Road
Post Office Box 69
Stafford, Virginia 22555
(540) 658-8750 FAX: (540) 372-1174

Margaret P. Spencer, Judge
Circuit Court
13th Judicial Circuit
John Marshall Courts Building
400 North Ninth Street
Richmond, Virginia 23219
(804) 646-6505 FAX: (804) 646-6562
E-mail: spencer@ci.richmond.va.us

Wilford Taylor, Jr., Judge
Circuit Court
8th Judicial Circuit
Post Office Box 40
Courthouse Building
101 Kings Way Mall
Hampton, Virginia 23669
(757 727-6105 FAX: (757) 728-3505

Marcus Williams, Judge
Circuit Court
19th Judicial Circuit
4410 Chain Bridge Road
Fairfax, Virginia 22030
(703) 246-4690 FAX: (703) 385-4432

General District Courts

D. Eugene Cheek, Sr., Judge
General District Court
13th Judicial District
501 North Ninth Street
Richmond, Virginia 23219
(804) 646-6681 FAX: (804) 646-6684

Joel C. Cunningham, Judge
General District Court
10th Judicial District Court
Halifax General District Court
Post Office Box 458
Courthouse, Main Street
Halifax, Virginia 24558
(804) 476-3385 FAX: (804) 476-3387

Archie Elliott, Jr., Judge
General District Court
3rd Judicial District
Post Office Box 129
Portsmouth, Virginia 23705
(757) 393-8506 FAX: (757) 393-8010

George W. Harris, Jr., Judge
General District Court
23rd Judicial District
Roanoke County Court
305 E. Main Street
Salem, Virginia 24153
(540) 387-6168 FAX: (540) 387-6066

Gwendolyn Jones Jackson, Chief Judge
General District Court
4th Judicial District
811 East City Hall Avenue
Norfolk, Virginia 23510
(757) 664-4913 FAX: (757) 664-4901

Birdie H. Jamison, Judge
General District Court – 13th Judicial District
John Marshall Courts Building
400 North Ninth Street, Room 209
Richmond, Virginia 23219
(804) 646-6431 FAX: (804) 646-6659

Bonnie L. Jones, Judge
General District Court – 8th Judicial District
Hampton General District Court
236 North King Street
Post Office Box 70
Hampton, Virginia 23669-0070
(757) 727-6724 FAX: (757) 727-6035

Katherine H. Jones, Judge
General District Court – 4th Judicial District
Norfolk General District Court
811 East City Hall Avenue
Norfolk, Virginia 23510-2772
(757) 664-4915 FAX: (757) 644-4901

Gammiel Poindexter, Judge
General District Court – 6th Judicial District
Post Office Box 1335
Surry, Virginia 22883
(804) 246-5511, Ext. 3266 FAX: (804) 246-6604

David F. Pugh, Judge
General District Court – 7th Judicial District
2500 Washington Avenue
Newport News, Virginia 23607
(757) 926-3520 FAX: (757) 926-8496

Joi Jeter Taylor, Judge
General District Court – 13th Judiciial District
Richmond General District Court - Civil Division
John Marshall Courts Building - 2nd Floor
400 North 9th Street
Richmond, Virginia 23219-1508
(804) 646-6461 FAX: (804) 646-8758
E-mail: jeffnjoi@earthlink.net

Substitute Judges - Can Sit in all Courts within the Judges' District

James Banks, Substitute Judge
13th Judicial District
McGuire Woods
901 E. Cary Street
Richmond, Virginia 23219
(804) 775-1699 FAX: (804) 698-2124
E-mail: jbanks@mcguire woods. com

Arnold Henderson, Substitute Judge
13th Judicial District
116 E. Franklin Street, Suite 102
Richmond, Virginia 23219
(804) 644-9600 FAX: (804) 644-9603

Curtis M. Hairston. Jr., Substitute Judge
13th Judicial District
2 James Center
Richmond, Virginia 23219
(804) 783-6482 FAX: (804) 783-6507

Renée Hicks, Substitute Judge
13th Judicial District
1417 Brook Road
Richmond, Virginia 23220
(804) 643-6641 FAX: (804) 643-6642

Leonard W. Lambert, Substitute Judge
13th Judicial District
321 North 23rd Street
Richmond, Vigina 23223
(804) 648-3325 FAX: (804) 648-3336
E-mail: lambertlaw@erols.com

Robert A. Williams, Substitute Judge
21st Judicial District
45 Jones Street
Martinsville, Virginia 24112
(703) 638-2491 FAX: (703) 638-8171

Juvenile and Domestic Relations Court

Rufus A. Banks, Jr., Judge
Chesapeake Juvenile and
Domestic Relations Court
1st Judicial District
301 Albemarle Drive
Chesapeake, Virginia 23320
(757) 382-8100 FAX: (757) 382-8152

Janice Brice, Judge
Prince William Juvenile and Domestic
Relations Court
31st Judicial District
9311 Lee Avenue
Manasses, Virginia 23110
(703) 792-6160 FAX: (703) 792-6858

Gayl Branum Carr, Judge
Fairfax County Juvenile and Domestic
Relations District Court
4000 Chain Bridge Road
Fairfax, Virginia 22030
(703) 246-3074 FAX: (703) 352-8934

Nolan B. Dawkins, Judge
Alexandria Juvenile and
Domestic Relations District Court
520 King Street, 1st Floor
Alexandria, Virginia 22314-3160
(703) 838-4141 FAX: (703) 838-4092

Aundria D. Foster, Judge
Newport News Juvenile and Domestic
Relations District Court
7th Judicial District
230 25th Street
Newport News, Virginia 23607
(757) 926-3630 FAX: (757) 926-3598

William O. Hawkins, Judge
Norfolk Juvenile and
Domestic Relations District Court
4th Judicial District
800 East City Hall Avenue
Norfolk, Virginia 23510
(757) 664-4390 FAX: (757) 683-2219

James E. Hume, Judge
Petersburg Juvenile and
Domestic Relations District Court
11th Judicial District
27 East Tabb Street
Petersburg, Virginia 23813
(804) 733-2372 FAX: (804) 733-2385

Woodrow Lewis, Jr., Judge
Virginia Beach Juvenile and Domestic
Relations District Court
2nd Judicial District
Judicial Complex - Municipal Center
Virginia Beach, Virginia 23456-9017
(757) 427-4391 or 563-1012 FAX: (757) 426-5683

B. Bryan Milbourne, Judge
Accomack Juvenile and Domestic Relations
District Court
2A Judicial District
23312 Courthouse Avenue
Post Office Box 299
Accomack, Virginia 23301
(757) 787-0920

Eileen A. Olds, Chief Judge
Chesapeake Juvenile and Domestic Relations
District Court
1st Judicial District
Post Office Box 16404
301 Albemarle Drive
Chesapeake, Virginia 23328-6404
(757) 382-8100 FAX: (757) 382-8152

Angela E. Roberts, Judge
Richmond Juvenile and
Domestic Relations Court
13th Judicial District
Oliver Hill Courts Building
1600 North 17th Street, Suite C181
Richmond, Virginia 23219-1214
(804) 646-2918 FAX: (804) 646-3398

Alfreda Talton-Harris, Judge
Franklin Juvenile and
Domestic Relations Court
5th Judicial District
900 Armory Drive
Franklin, Virginia 23851
(757) 562-8559 FAX: (757) 562-8561

Richard D. Taylor, Chief Judge
Richmond Juvenile and
Domestic Relations Court
13th Judicial District
Oliver Hill Courts Building
1600 North 17th Street
Richmond, Virginia 23219
(804) 646-2918 FAX: (804) 646-3398
E-mail: taylrrd@ci.richmond.va.us

Esther L. Wiggins, Judge
Arlington County Juvenile and Domestic
Relations Court – 17th Judicial District
Post Office Box 925
Arlington, Virginia 22216
(703) 228-4500 FAX: (703) 228-3741

Dale M. Wiley, Judge
Danville Juvenile and
Domestic Relations Court
22nd Judicial District
401 Patton Street
Danville Courthouse
Post Office Box 3300
Danville, Virginia 24543
(804) 799-5173 or 799-5174 FAX: (804) 799-5025

Alotha C. Willis, Judge
Portsmouth Juvenile and
Domestic Relations Court
3rd Judicial District
605 Crawford Street
Portsmouth, Virginia 23705-1073
(757) 393-8851 FAX: (757) 393-5166

WASHINGTON: (22)

FEDERAL

Jerome Farris, Senior Judge
U. S. Court of Appeals for the Ninth Circuit
1030 U. S. Courthouse
1010 Fifth Avenue
Seattle, Washington 98104-1130
(206) 553-2672

Franklin D. Burgess, Judge
U. S. District Court
for the Western District of Washington
3124 U. S. Courthouse
1717 Pacific Avenue
Tacoma, Washington 98402-3226
(253) 593-6307 FAX: (253) Call on phone first

Jack E. Tanner, Senior Judge
U. S. District Court
for the Western District of Washington
3144 U. S. Courthouse
1717 Pacific Avenue
Tacoma, Washington 98402-3226
(253) 593-6542 FAX: (253) (253) 593-6444

Monica J. Benton, U. S. Magistrate Judge
U. S. District Court for the
Western District of Washington
304 U. S. Courthouse
1010 Fifth Avenue
Seattle, Washington 98104-1130
(206) 553-4463 FAX: (206) 553-1397
E-mail: monica_benton@wa.wd.uscourts.gov

Administrative Law Judges

Ruperta A. Alexis
Chief Administrative Law Judge
Office of Hearings and Appeals
Social Security Administration
2201 Sixth Avenue, Suite 500
Seattle, Washington 98121-2312
(206) 615-3700 FAX: (615) 3731

Arthur E. Joyner, Administrative Law Judge
Office of Hearings and Appeals
Social Security Administration
2201 Sixth Avenue, Suite #500
Seattle, Washington 98121-2312
(206) 615-3700, Ext. 8339 FAX: (206) 615-3731

STATE

Charles Z. Smith, Justice
Washington State Supreme Court
P.O. Box 40929
Olympia, Washington 98504-0929
(360) 357-2053 FAX: (360) 357-2103

Ronald E. Cox, Court of Appeals
Division 1
600 University Street
Seattle, Washington 98101-4170
(206) 464-7654 FAX: (206) 389-2614

Patricia Hall Clark, Judge
King County Superior Court
516 Third Avenue, Room E-854
Seattle, Washington 98104-2381
(206) 296-9190 FAX: (206) 296-0986

Donald D. Haley, Judge
King County Superior Court
516 Third Avenue, Room MS C-2
Seattle, Washington 98104-2381
(206) 296-9165 FAX: (206) 296-0986
E-mail: Donald.Haley@MetroKC.Gov

Philip G. Hubbard, Judge
King County Superior Court
516 Third Avenue, Room MS C-2
Seattle, Washington 98104-2381
(206) 296-9175 FAX: (206) 296-0986

Norma Smith Huggins, Judge
King County Superior Court
516 Third Avenue, Room MS C-2
Seattle, Washington 98104-2381
(206) 296-9096 FAX: (206) 296-0986

Richard A. Jones, Judge
King County Superior Court
516 Third Avenue, Room MS C-2
Seattle, Washington 98104-2381
(206) 296-9260 FAX: (206) 296-0986

LeRoy McCullough, Judge
King County Superior Court
516 Third Avenue, MS C-2
Seattle, Washington 98104-2381
(206) 296-9245 FAX: (206) 296-0986

Michael S. Spearman, Judge
King County Superior Court
516 Third Avenue, Room C-203
Seattle, Washington 98104-2381
(206) 296-9211 FAX: (206) 296-0986

Charles V. Johnson, Judge (Retired)
King County Superior Court
516 Third Avenue, MS C-2
Seattle, Washington 98104-2381
(206) 296-9310 (Sits Pro Tem periodically)

Herbert M. Stephens, Judge (Retired)
King County Superior Court
517 Third Avenue
Seattle, Washington 98104-2381
(Sits Pro Tem periodically)

J. Wesley Saint Clair, Judge
King County District Court – Northeast Division
15920 NE 85th
Redmond, Washington 98073-0425
(206) 296-3667 FAX: (206) 296-0592

Fred Bonner, Judge
Seattle Municipal Court
610 Third Avenue, Room 1100
Seattle, Washington 98104-1852
(206) 684-8709 FAX: (206) 233-0056

Judith Montgomery Hightower, Judge
Seattle Municipal Court
610 Third Avenue, Room 1100
Seattle, Washington 98104-1818
(206) 684-8709 FAX (206) 233-0056

George W. Holifield, Judge
Seattle Municipal Court
610 Third Avenue, Room 1100
Seattle, Washington 98104-1852
(206) 684-8709 FAX: (206) 833-0051

Bonnie Canada-Thurston, Commissioner
King County Superior Court – Juvenile Division
516 Third Avenue
Seattle, Washington 98104-2381
(206) 296-9335 FAX: (206) 296-0986

West Virginia: (7)

Supreme Court

Franklin D. Cleckley, Justice (Retired)
Supreme Court of Appeals
Supreme Court Courthouse
Charleston, West Virginia 25305
(304) 558-2601

Circuit Court

Irene C. Berger
Kanawha County Judicial Annex
111 Court Street
Charleston, West Virginia 25301
(304) 357-0361 FAX: (304) 357-0310

Herman G. Canady, Jr.
Kanawha County Judicial Annex
111 Court Street
Charleston, West Virginia 25301
(304) 357-0366 FAX: (304) 357-0310

Booker T. Stephens, Chief Judge
Eighth Judicial Circuit
McDowell County Circuit Court
Post Office Box 310
Welch, West Virginia 24801-8531
(304) 436-8531 FAX: (304) 436-3340

Darlene Ratliff, Family Law Master
Region 5
Kanawha County Courthouse
409 Virginia Street, East Room 262
Charleston, West Virginia 25301
(304) 558-0554 FAX: (304) 558-4237

Nancy Starks, Magistrate
Kanawha County Magistrate Court
111 Court Street
P.O. Box 3318
Charleston, West Virginia 25333
(304) 357-0402 FAX: (304) 357-0205

Administrative Law Judge

Sarah N. Hall, Administrative Law Judge
Bureau of Employment Programs
Workers Compensation Office of Judges
127 Grant Street
Beckley, West Virginia 25801
(304) 256-6730 FAX: (304) 256-6737

Wisconsin: (16)

Federal

Charles N. Clevert, Judge
U. S. District Court for the Eastern District of Wisconsin
162 U. S. Courthouse and Federal Building
517 East Wisconsin Avenue
Milwaukee, Wisconsin 53202
(414) 297-1585 FAX: (414) 297-1548

State

Circuit Court Judges

Carl Ashley, Judge
Circuit Court
Milwaukee County Circuit Court – Branch 33
901 North 9th Street
Milwaukee, Wisconsin 53233-1425
(414) 278-4472 FAX: (414) 223-1264
E-mail:carl.ashley@milwaukee.courts.state.wi.us

Martin Joseph Donald, Judge
Milwaukee County Circuit Court, Branch 02
821 West State Street
Milwaukee, Wisconsin 53233-1427
(414) 278-4775 FAX: (414) 223-1262

Paul B. Higginbotham, Judge
Dane County Circuit Court, Branch 17
210 Martin Luther King Jr. Boulevard - Room 323
Madison, Wisconsin 53709-0001
(608) 266-4937 FAX: (608) 267-4151

Stanley A. Miller, Judge
Milwaukee County Circuit Court, Branch 21
Milwaukee County Courthouse
901 North 9th Street
Milwaukee, Wisconsin 53233-1425
(414) 278-4564 FAX: (414) 223-1264

Marshall B. Murray, Judge
Milwaukee County Circuit Court, Branch 43
Children's Court Center
10201 Watertown Plank Road
Wauwatosa, Wisconsin 53226-3532
(414) 257-7121 FAX: (414) 454-4074 or 223-1264

Maxine Aldridge White, Judge
Milwaukee County Circuit Court
Milwaukee County Courthouse
901 North 9th Street
Milwaukee, Wisconsin 53233-1425
(414) 278-4482 FAX: (414) 223-1938
E-mail:maxine.white@milwaukee.courts.state.wi.us

Municipal Court

Louis Butler, Presiding Judge
Milwaukee Municipal Court
951 North 7th Street
Milwaukee, Wisconsin 53233
(414) 286-9759 FAX: (414) 286-3615

Judicial Officers

Lindsey D. Draper, Judicial Court Commissioner
Children's Court Center
10201 West Watertown Plank Road
Wauwatosa, Wisconsin 53226-3532
(414) 257-7740 or 257-6527 FAX: (414) 454-4074

Valarie A. Hill, Judicial Court Commissioner
Children's Court Center
10201 Watertown Plank Road
Wauwatosa, Wisconsin 53226-3532
(414) 257-6967 FAX: (414) 454-4074

Frederick C. Rosa, Family Court Commissioner
901 North 9th Street - Room 707
Milwaukee, Wisconsin 53233-1425
(414) 278-4401 or 278-5169
FAX: (414) 223-1262 or 223-1884

Andrew Reneau, Family Court Commissioner
Retired (Reserve)
Chief Judge Office
901 North 9th Street
Milwaukee, Wisconsin 53233-1425
(414) 278-4417 FAX: (414) 223-1264

Administrative Law Judges

John Grandberry, Administrative Law Judge
Wisconsin Department of Work
Force Development – Equal Rights Division
819 North 6th Street, Room 255
Milwaukee, Wisconsin 53203
(414) 227-4385 FAX: (414) 227-4084

Sherman Mitchell, Administrative Law Judge
Wisconsin Department of Work
Force Development
Worker's Compensation Division
819 North 6th Street, Room 330
Milwaukee, Wisconsin 53203
(414) 227-4382 FAX: (414) 227-4012.

Emma Parker, Administrative Law Judge
Wisconsin Department of Work
Force Development
Unemployment Compensation Division
819 North 6th Street, Room 382
Milwaukee, Wisconsin 53203
(414) 227-4511 FAX: (414) 227-4264

William Phillips, Jr.,
Administrative Law Judge
Wisconsin Department of Work
Force Development
Worker's Compensation Division
819 North 6th Street, Room 330
Milwaukee, Wisconsin 53203
(414) 227-4381 or (414) 227-4382
FAX: (414) 227-4012

WYOMING: (0)

U.S. ARMED FORCES: (2)

U. S. ARMY

Kenneth D. Pangburn (Colonel)
Chief Circuit Judge
Second Judicial Circuit
U.S. Army Trial Judicary
ATTN: AFZP-TJ
Fort Stewart, Georgia 31314
(912) 767-3003

U. S. NAVY-MARINE CORPS

Alvin W. Keller (Colonel USMC)
Navy-Marine Corps Trial Judiciary
Piedmont Judicial Circuit
67 Virginia Dare Drive, Suite 145
Camp Lejeune, North Carolina 28547
(910) 451-3503 or 451-3179
FAX: (910) 451-5444 (DSN) 751

Section II

ASIAN/PACIFIC JUDGES OF THE UNITED STATES

Prepared by
The Honorable Authur L. Burnett, Sr. and the Honorable Marilyn Dolan Go

ALABAMA: (0)

ALASKA: (1)

Sen K. Tan, Judge
Superior Court
Third Judicial District
825 West Fourth Avenue, Room 416
Anchorage, Alaska 99501-2004
(907) 264-0408 FAX: (907) 264-0720

ARIZONA: (5)

STATE

James E. Don, Presiding Judge
Pinal County Superior Court
Post Office Box 828
Florence, Arizona 85232-0828
(520) 868-6332 FAX:(520) 868-6500 or 868-4741

Brian K. Ishikawa, Judge
Maricopa County Superior Court
222 East Javeline Avenue
Mesa, Arizona 85210
(602) 506-5225 FAX: (602) 506-2029

Kenneth Lee, Presiding Civil Judge
Pima County Superior Court – Division 3
110 West Congress Street
Tucson, Arizona 85701-1331
(520) 740-8531 FAX: (520) 740-5254 or 622-0269

Roxanne K. Song Ong, Judge
Phoenix Municipal Court
400 North Seventh Street, Division 15
Phoenix, Arizona 85006-3386
(602) 261-8247 FAX: (602) 534-4779

Harry Gin, Judge (Retired)
Pima County Superior Court – Division 14
110 West Congress
Tucson, Arizona 85701
(602) 740-8941 FAX: (602) 622-0269

ARKANSAS: (0)

CALIFORNIA: (113)

FEDERAL

A. Wallace Tashima, Judge
U. S. Court of Appeals for the Ninth Circuit
Richard H. Chambers Court of Appeals Building
122 South Grand Avenue
Pasadena, California 91105-1652
(626) 229-7374 FAX: (626) 229-7387

Anthony W. Ishii, Judge
U. S. District Court
for the Eastern District of California
1130 O Street
Fresno, California 93721
(559) 498-7341 FAX: (559) 498-7367

George H. King, Judge
U. S. District Court
Central District of California
312 North Spring Street, Room 660
Los Angeles, California 90012
(213) 894-6907 FAX: (213) 894-2059

Ronald S. W. Lew, Judge
U. S. District Court
Central District of California
312 North Spring Street
Los Angeles, California 90012
(213) 894-2682 FAX: (213) 894-6860
E-mail: Ronald_Lew@cacd.uscourts.gov

Robert M. Takasugi, Senior Judge
U. S. District Court Central District of California
312 North Spring Street
Los Angeles, California 90012
(213) 894-5858 FAX: (213) 894-2059

Arthur Nakazato, Magistrate Judge
U. S. District Court Central District of California
411 West Fourth Street
Santa Ana, California 92701-4516
(714) 338-4714 or 338-4756 FAX: (714) 338-4719
E-mail: Arthur_Nakazato@cacd.uscourts.gov

Administrative Law Judges

Gary J. Lee, Chief Administrative Law Judge
Office of Hearings & Appeals
Social Security Administration
301 Howard Street - 3rd Floor
San Francisco, California 94105
(415) 744-3080 FAX: (415) 744-2548

Albert Tom, Administrative Law Judge
Office of Hearings & Appeals
Social Security Administration
750 "B" Street, Suite 1100
San Diego, California 92101
(619) 557-5081 FAX: (619) 557-7633

Thomas Y. K. Fong, U. S. Immigration Judge
300 North Los Angeles Street, Room 2001
Los Angeles, California 90012
(213) 894-2811 FAX: (213) 894-5196

Tue Phan Quang, U. S. Immigration Judge
550 Kearny Street, Suite 800
San Francisco, California 94108
(415) 705-4415 FAX: (415) 705-4418

Mimi S. Yam, U. S. Immigration Judge
550 Kearny Street, Suite 800
San Francisco, California 94108
(Mailing address: Post Office Box 2326
San Francisco, California 94126-2326)
(415) 705-4415 FAX: (415) 705-4418

Michael J. Yamaguchi, U. S. Immigration Judge
550 Kearny Street, Suite 800
San Francisco, California 94108
(Mailing address: Post Office Box 2326
San Francisco, California 94126-2326)
(415) 705-4415 FAX: (415) 705-4418

Jennifer Gee, Administrative Judge
U. S. Merit Systems Protection Board
250 Montgomery Street, Suite 400
San Francisco, California 94105
(415) 705-2935 FAX: (415) 705-2945

Portia K. Igarashi, Administrative Judge
U. S. Merit Systems Protection Board
250 Montgomery Street, Suite 400
San Francisco, California 94105
(415) 705-2935 FAX: (415) 705-2945

State

Supreme Court

Ming W. Chin, Associate Justice
California Supreme Court
350 McAllister Street
San Francisco, California 94102-3600
(415) 865-7050 FAX: (415) 865-7183

Joyce L. Kennard, Associate Justice
California Supreme Court
350 McAllister Street
San Francisco, California 94102-3600
(415) 865-7100 FAX: (415) 865-7183

Courts of Appeal

Nathan D. Mihara, Associate Justice
Court of Appeal – Sixth Appellate District
333 West Santa Clara Street, Suite 1060
San Jose, California 95113
(408) 277-1004 FAX: (408) 277-1996

Katherine Doi Todd, Associate Justice
Court of Appeal, Second Appellate District
Division Two
300 South Spring Street, Floor 2, North Tower
Los Angeles, California 90013
(213) 897-8774FAX: (213) 897-9005

Morio Fukuto, Associate Justice (Retired)
Court of Appeal – Second Appellate District
Division Two
300 South Spring Street, 3rd Floor
Los Angeles, California 90013

Harry W. Low, Associate Justice (Retired)
Court of Appeal, First District
104 Turquoise Way
San Francisco, California 94131
(415) 774-2603 FAX: (415) 982-5287

Elwood Lui, Justice (Retired)
Court of Appeals
Jones Day Reavis & Pogue
555 West Fifth Street, Suite 4600
Los Angeles, California 90039-1025
(213) 243-2435 FAX: (213) 243-2359

State Trial Judges

Kathleen Akao, Judge
Superior Court
State of California, County of Santa Cruz
Juvenile Court
Main Courthouse - 701 Ocean Street
Santa Cruz, California 95060-4086
(831) 454-2380 FAX: (831) 454-3297

Thang Nguyen Barrett, Judge
Superior Court
State of California, County of Santa Clara
San Jose Facility
200 West Hedding Street
San Jose, California 95110
(408) 299-2266 FAX: (408) 920-0229

Tani G. Cantil-Sakauye, Judge
Superior Court, State of California
County of Sacramento
Lorenzo Patino Hall of Justice
720 Ninth Street
Sacramento, California 95814-1310
(916) 874-6893 FAX: (916) 874-5620

James H. Chang, Judge
Superior Court
State of California, County of Santa Clara
190 West Hedding Street
San Jose, California 95110-1706
(408) 299-8973 FAX: (408) 295-5074

Patricia Yim Cowett, Judge
Superior Court
State of California, County of San Diego
East County Regional Center
250 East Main Street
El Cajon, California 92020
(619) 441-4500 FAX: (619) 441-6610

David I. Doi, Judge
Superior Court
State of California, County of Los Angeles
Civil Courts Building
110 North Grand Avenue
Los Angeles, California 90012-3014
(213) 974-6239 FAX: (213) 621-2701

Keith H. Fudenna, Judge
Superior Court
State of California, County of Alameda
Fremont Hall of Justice
39439 Paseo Padre Parkway
Fremont, California 94538
(510) 795-2329 FAX: (510) 795-2354

Fred J. Fujioka, Judge
Superior Court
State of California, County of Los Angeles
Central District - Criminal Courts Building
210 West Temple Street
Los Angeles, California 90012
(213) 974-9680

Roy Hashimoto, Judge
Superior Court
State of California, County of Alameda
Hayward Hall of Justice
24405 Amador Street
Hayward, California 94544-1369
(510) 670-5972 FAX: (510) 670-5687

Robert J. Higa, Judge
Superior Court
State of California, County of Los Angeles
12720 Norwalk Boulevard
Norwalk, California 90650
(562) 807-7331 FAX: (562) 863-8757 or 863-6702

Joni T. Hiramoto, Judge
Superior Court
State of California, County of Contra Costa
100 37th Street
Richmond, California 94805-2136
(510) 374-3383 FAX: (510) 374-1634

Ernest M. Hiroshige, Judge
Superior Court
State of California, County of Los Angeles
Civil Courts Building
111 North Hill Street
Los Angeles, California 90012-3117
(213) 974-5681 FAX: (213) 617-7176

Rose Hom, Judge
Superior Court
State of California, County of Los Angeles
South Central District - Compton Court
200 West Compton Boulevard
Compton, California 90220
(310) 603-7727 FAX: (310) 639-8724

Garry T. Ichikawa, Judge
Superior Court
State of California, County of Solano
Hall of Justice
600 Union Avenue
Fairfield, California 94533
(707) 435-2483 FAX: (707) 421-7828

Lance A. Ito, Judge
Superior Court
State of California, County of Los Angeles
Criminal Courts
210 West Temple Street
Los Angeles, California 90012-3210
(213) 974-5723 FAX: (213) 680-8867

Gale E. Kaneshiro, Judge
Superior Court
State of California, County of San Diego
220 West Broadway
San Diego, California 92101-3409
Mailing Address: Post Office Box 122724
San Diego, California 92112-2724
(619) 531-3896 FAX: (619) 687-2155

Ken M. Kawaichi, Judge
Superior Court
State of California, County of Alameda
County Administration Building
1221 Oak Street
Oakland, California 94612-4293
(510) 272-6165 or 272-6119 FAX: (510) 272-6072

Ben T. Kayashima, Judge
Superior Court
State of California, County of San Bernardino
Rancho Cucamonga Court
8030 North Haven Avenue
Rancho Cucamonga, California 91730
(909) 945-4177 or 945-4147
FAX: (909) 948-4636 or 945-4154

Abraham Aponte Khan, Judge
Superior Court
State of California, County of Los Angeles
Criminal Courts Building
210 West Temple Street
Los Angeles, California 90012-3210
(213) 974-6023 FAX: (213) 680-8867

Charles C. Kobayashi, Judge
Superior Court
State of California, County of Sacramento
William R. Ridgeway Family Relations Court
3341 Power Inn Road
Sacramento, California 95826
(916) 875-2529 FAX: (916) 874-5347

Ruth Ann Kwan, Judge
Superior Court
State of California, County of Los Angeles
Eastlake Juvenile Court
1601 Eastlake Avenue
Los Angeles, California 90033
(323) 226-8916 FAX: (323) 221-2223

Owen Lee Kwong, Judge
Superior Court
State of California, County of Los Angeles
Civil Courts Courthouse
111 North Hill Street, Department 49
Los Angeles, California 90012-3117
(213) 974-5671 FAX: (213) 617-7176

Arthur M. Lew, Judge
Superior Court
State of California, County of Los Angeles
South Central District - Compton Court
200 West Compton Boulevard
Compton, California 90220-3194
(310) 603-7731 FAX: (510) 639-8724

Lillian Y. Lim, Judge
Superior Court
State of California, County of San Diego
500 Third Avenue
Chula Vista, California 91910
(619) 691-4433 FAX: (619) 691-4438

Lenard D. Louie, Judge
Superior Court
State of California, County of San Francisco
Hall of Justice
850 Bryant Street
San Francisco, California 94103-4667
(415) 553-1399 FAX: (415) 553-1661

Kazuharu Makino, Judge
Superior Court
State of California, County of Orange
Central Justice Center
700 Civic Center Drive West
Post Office Box 1994
Santa Ana, California 92702-1994
(714) 834-3792 FAX: (714) 953-9032

Jon M. Mayeda, Judge
Superior Court
State of California, County of Los Angeles
110 North Hill Street, Department 72
Los Angeles, California 90012-3117
(213) 974-6237 FAX: (213) 621-2701

Cheryl Chun Meegan, Judge
Superior Court
State of California, County of Sacramento
Main Courthouse - 720 Ninth Street
Sacramento, California 95814-1398
(916) 874-5245 or 440-5476 FAX: (916) 440-5620

Vernon K. Nakahara, Judge
Superior Court
State of California, County of Alameda
1225 Fallon Street
Oakland, California 94612-4293
(510) 272-6086 or 272-6090 FAX: (510) 272-6072

Eric M. Nakata, Judge
Superior Court
State of California, County of San Bernardino
Victorville District
14455 Civic Drive
Victorville, California 92392
(760) 243-8917 FAX: (760) 243-8794 or 243-8790

Ngo Trong Nguyen, Judge
Superior Court
State of California, Orange County
West Justice Center
8141 13th Street
Westminster, California 92683-4593
(714) 896-7152 FAX: (714) 896-7219

Cary H. Nishimoto, Judge
Superior Court
State of California, County of Los Angeles
Southwest District - Torrance Court
825 Maple Avenue
Torrance, California 90503-5096
(310) 222-8866 FAX: (310) 782-7326

Sam Ohta, Judge
Superior Court
State of California, County of Los Angeles
Criminal Courts Building
210 West Temple, Department 40
Los Angeles, California 90012-3210
(213) 974-6031 FAX: (213) 680-7804 or 680-8867

Dan Thomas Oki, Judge
Superior Court
State of California, County of Los Angeles
East District
400 Civic Center Plaza
Pomona, California 91766
(909) 620-3050 FAX: (909) 620-6547 or 622-2305

Tomson T. Ong, Judge
Superior Court
State of California, County of Los Angeles
South District - Long Beach
415 West Ocean Avenue
Long Beach, California 90802-4591
(562) 491-6243 FAX: (562) 435-5469

Ronald E. Quidachay, Judge
Superior Court
State of California, County of San Francisco
400 McAllister Street
San Francisco, California 94102
(415) 551-3723 FAX: (415) 551-5721

Mel Red Recana, Judge
Superior Court
State of California, County of Los Angeles
Civil Courts Courthouse
111 North Hill Street
Los Angeles, California 90012-3117
(213) 974-6217 or 974-6209 FAX: (213) 626-4854

Cesar C. Sarmiento, Judge
Superior Court
State of California, County of Los Angeles
Civil Courts Building
111 North Hill Street
Los Angeles, California 90012-3117
(213) 974-5683 FAX: (213) 617-7176

B. Tam Nomoto Schumann, Judge
Superior Court, State of California
County of Orange
700 Civic Center Drive West
Post Office Box 1994
Santa Ana, California 92702-1994
(714) 834-3886 or 834-3273 FAX: (714) 953-9032

Ramona G. See, Judge
Superior Court
State of California, County of Los Angeles
Criminal Courts Building
210 West Temple Street
Los Angeles, California 90012-3210
(213) 974-9680 FAX: (213) 626-4854

Lillian Kwok Sing, Judge
Superior Court
State of California, County of San Francisco
Hall of Justice
850 Bryant Street
San Francisco, California 94103
(415) 553-1175 FAX: (415) 553-1661

Kenneth K. So, Judge
Superior Court
State of California, County of San Diego
220 West Broadway
San Diego, California 92101-3877
(619) 531-4005 FAX: (619) 615-6968

Steven C. Suzukawa, Judge
Superior Court
State of California, County of Los Angeles
West District - Airport Court
11701 South La Cienega Boulevard
Los Angeles, California 90045
(310) 727-6114 FAX: (310) 727-0501

Julie Tang, Judge
Superior Court
State of California, County of San Francisco
Hall of Justice
850 Bryant Street
San Francisco, California 94103
(415) 553-9415 FAX: (415) 553-1661

Fumiko Hachiya Wasserman, Judge
Superior Court, State of California
County of Los Angeles, Civil Courts Courthouse
111 North Hill Street
Los Angeles, California 90012
(213) 974-8806FAX: (213) 621-2701

Cerena Wong, Judge
Superior Court
State of California, County of Sonoma
600 Administration Drive, Room 209J
Santa Rosa, California 95403-2818
(707) 565-2641 FAX: (707) 565-6146

George H. Wu, Judge
Superior Court
State of California, County of Los Angeles
Criminal Courts Building
210 West Temple Street
Los Angeles, California 90012
(213) 974-5745 FAX: (213) 680-8867 or 680-7804

Debra Wong Yang, Judge
Superior Court
State of California, County of Los Angeles
West Los Angeles Court
1633 Purdue Avenue
Los Angeles, California 90025-3117
(310) 312-6593 FAX: (310) 312-2902

Hiroshi Fujisaki, Judge (Retired)
Superior Court
State of California, County of Los Angeles
1725 Main Street
Santa Monica, California 90401-3299

Edward Y. Kakita, Judge (Retired)
Superior Court
State of California, County of Los Angeles
111 North Hill Street
Los Angeles, California 90012-3117
(213) 974-5621

Frank Kim, Judge (Retired)
Superior Court
State of California, County of San Joaquin
222 East Weber Avenue
Stockton, California 05202

Harjook Paik, Judge (Retired)
Superior Court
State of California, County of Monterey
Post Office Box 1819
Salinas, California 93906
(408) 755-5060

Mamoru Sakuma, Judge (Retired)
Superior Court
State of California, County of Sacramento
Kong, Yun & Sugano
2430 J Street
Sacramento, California 95816
(916) 441-6255 FAX: (916) 448-8435

Taketsugu Takei, Judge (Retired)
Superior Court
State of California, County of Santa Clara
191 North First Street
San Jose, California 95112
(408) 299-3405

Madge S. Watai, Judge (Retired)
Superior Court
State of California, County of Los Angeles
1149 South Hill Street
Los Angeles, California 90015
(213) 765-1400

Delbert Wong, Judge (Retired)
Superior Court
State of California, County of Los Angeles
2416 West Silverlake Drive
Los Angeles, California 90039-3170
(213) 666-6616

James S. Yip, Judge (Retired)
Superior Court
State of California, County of Los Angeles
110 North Grand Avenue
Los Angeles, California 90012

George Yoneshiro, Judge (Retired)
Superior Court
State of California, County of Placer
Post Office Box 237
Applegate, California 95703
(916) 889-7072

Richard Hanki, Judge (Retired)
Municipal Court
Los Cerritos Judicial District
10025 Flower Street
Bellflower, California 90706
(562) 804-8041 FAX: (562) 920-8040

Irene Takahashi, Judge (Retired)
Municipal Court
Oakland Judicial District
Kincaid, Gianunzio, Caudle & Hubert
200 Webster Street, Suite 200
Oakland, California 94607
(510) 465-5212

Mikio Uchiyama, Judge (Retired)
Municipal Court
Fowler-Caruthers Judicial District
16 South Sixth Street
Fowler, California 93625
(209) 834-3215

Court Commissioners

Alberta C. Chew, Commissioner
Superior Court
State of California, County of Solano
Hall of Justice
530 Union Avenue
Fairfield, California 94533
(707) 421-7450 FAX: (707) 421-7828

John H. Ing, Commissioner
Superior Court
State of California County of Los Angeles
South District - Long Beach
415 West Ocean Boulevard
Long Beach, California 90802-4591
(562) 491-6596 FAX: (562) 435-5469

Patricia M. Ito, Commissioner
Superior Court
State of California, County of Los Angeles
San Fernando Court
900 Third Street
San Fernando, California 91340
(818) 898-2449 FAX: (818) 838-2586

James F. Iwasko, Commissioner
Superior Court
State of California, County of Santa Barbara
Anacapa Division
1100 Anacapa Street
Santa Barbara, California 93101
Mailing Address: Post Office Box 21107
Santa Barbara, California 93121-1107
(805) 568-2886 FAX:(805) 568-2899

Newton Jue Lam, Commissioner
Superior Court
State of California, County of San Francisco
Hall of Justice
850 Bryant Street
San Francisco, California
(415) 553-9384 FAX: (415) 553-1661

Laura Magsunaga, Commissioner
Superior Court
State of California, County of Siskiyou
Family Law Branch
510 Main Street
Yreka, California 96097
(530) 842-0181 FAX: (530) 842-0191

Eugene Moriguchi, Commissioner
Superior Court
State of California, County of Sacramento
Carol Miller Justice Center
301 Bicentennial Circle
Sacramento, California 95826-2881
(916) 875-7270 FAX: (916) 875-7755

Patricia H. Wong, Commissioner
Superior Court
State of California, County of Sacramento
Carol Miller Justice Center
301 Bicentennial Circle
Sacramento, California 95826-2881
(916) 875-7799 FAX: (916) 874-5347 or 874-5620

Margie Gunthhardt Woods, Commissioner
Superior Court
State of California, County of San Diego
Central Division - Kearney Mesa Branch
8950 Clairemont Mesa Boulevard
San Diego, California 92123
(858) 571-4236 FAX: (858) 694-3609

Court Referees

Hideo Chino, Referee
Superior Court
State of California, County of San Diego
South County Regional Center
Juvenile Branch
500 Third Avenue
Chula Vista, California 91910
(619) 691-4414 FAX: (619) 691-4438 or 691-4584

Administrative Law Judges

Margaret Banez, Administrative Law Judge
Administrative Adjudications Division
California Department of Social Services
355 West Grand Avenue, Suite 4
Escondido, California 92025-2649
(619) 735-5070 FAX: (619) 735-5084

Betty Buccat, Administrative Law Judge
Administrative Adjudications Division
California Department of Social Services
1515 Clay Street, Room 1203
Oakland, California 94612
(510) 662-4000 FAX: (510) 622-3929

Peter Hemingway, Administrative Law Judge
Administrative Adjudications Division
California Department of Social Services
1515 Clay Street, Room 1203
Oakland, California 94612
(510) 662-4007 FAX: (510) 622-3929

Jeffrey Kolling, Administrative Law Judge
Unemployment Insurance Appeals Board
Post Office Box 7038
433 Fair Oaks Avenue, #200
Pasadena, California 91109-7038
(626) 304-7962 FAX: (626) 304-7981

Jonathan Lew, Administrative Law Judge
Office of Administrative Hearings
1515 Clay Street, Suite 206
Oakland, California 94612
(510) 622-2722 FAX: (510) 622-3929

Kee Choo Ling, Administrative Law Judge
Unemployment Insurance Appeals Board
Post Office Box 7038
Pasedena, California 91109-7038
(626) 304-7962 FAX: (626) 304-7981

Jessie Louie, Administrative Law Judge
Workers Compensation Appeals Board
300 Oceangate, 2nd Floor
Long Beach, California 90802
(562) 590-5018 or 590-5019
FAX: Call on phone first

Lawrence Low, Administrative Law Judge
Workers Compensation Appeals Board
2701 Ocean Park Boulevard, Suite 220
Santa Monica, California 90405
(310) 452-9114 FAX: (310) 499-6304

John K. C. Mah, Administrative Law Judge
Worker's Compensation Appeals Board
6150 Van Nuys Boulevard, Suite 110
Long Beach, California 91491
(818) 901-5306 FAX: (818) 901-5578

Jasmine Mukai, Administrative Law Judge
Unemployment Insurance Appeals Board
Post Office Box 7038
Pasedena, California 911109-7038
(626) 304-7962 FAX: (626) 304-7981

Vincent H. Nafarrete, Administrative Law Judge
Office of Administrative Hearings
314 West First Street
Los Angeles, California 90012-4542
(213) 576-7200 FAX: (213) 576-7244

Robert Y. Nakagawa, Administrative Law Judge
Workers Compensation Appeals Board
320 West 4th Street, 9th Floor
Los Angeles, California 90012
(213) 576-7335 FAX: (213) 576-7386

Eleanor Nisperos, Administrative Law Judge
Unemployment Insurance Appeals Board
1515 Clay Street, Room 902
Oakland, California 94612-1413
(510) 622-3900 FAX: (510) 622-3929

Herbert Nobriga, Administrative Law Judge
Administrative Adjudications Division
California Department of Social Services
107 South Broadway, Room 6005
Los Angeles, California 90012-4569
(213) 897-3983 FAX: (213) 897-3204

Ken Nomura, Administrative Law Judge
Administrative Adjudications Division
California Department of Social Services
744 P Street, M.S. 19 44
Sacramento, California 95814
(916) 387-4787 FAX: (916) 387-4803

Priscilla Gin Orida, Administrative Law Judge
Unemployment Insurance Appeals Board
3517 Camino del Rio South, Suite 310
San Diego, California 92108-4027
(619) 521-3300 FAX: (619) 521-3334

Judith Ota, Administrative Law Judge
Unemployment Insurance Appeals Board
Post Office Box 7038
Pasadena, California 91109-7038
(626) 304-7962 FAX: (626) 304-7981

Lilian S. Shek, Administrative Law Judge
Unemployment Insurance Appeals Board
2400 Venture Oaks Way, #300
Sacramento, California 95833-4224
(916) 263-6706 FAX: (916) 263-6765

Casimiro U. Tolentino, Assistant Presiding Administrative Law Judge
California Department of Social Service
State Hearings Division
811 Wilshire Boulevard, Suite 1118
Los Angeles, California 90017
(213) 833-2200 FAX: (213) 833-2230
E-mail: cutol@aol.com or ctolentino@dss.ca.gov

Bryan M. Yagi, Administrative Law Judge
Unemployment Insurance Appeals Board
160 West Santa Clara Street, #300
San Jose, California 95113-1700
(408) 277-1561 FAX: (408) 277-1217

Michael L. Yee, Administrative Law Judge
Unemployment Insurance Appeals Board
3517 Camino del Rio South, Suite 310
San Diego, California 92108-4027
(619) 521-3300 FAX: (619) 521-3334

COLORADO: (4)

FEDERAL

Michael J. Watanabe, Magistrate Judge
U. S. District Court for the District of Colorado
1929 Stout Street
Denver, Colorado 80294
(303) 844-5922 FAX: (303) 844-2403
E-mail: michael_j_watanabe@cod.uscourts.gov

Administrative Law Judge

Wayne N. Araki, Administrative Law Judge
Office of Hearings & Appeals
Social Security Administration
1244 Speer Boulevard, Suite 752
Denver, Colorado 80204-3584
(303) 844-5800 FAX: (303) 844-5817
E.Mail: wayne.n.araki@ssa.gov

Ronald W. Taoka, Administrative Judge
U. S. Equal Employment Opportunity Commission
303 East 17th Avenue, #510
Denver, Colorado 80203
(303) 866-1300 FAX: (303) 866-1085
E-mail: ronald.taoka@eeoc.gov

STATE

Melvin Okomoto, Judge
Denver County Courts
City & County Building
1427 Bannock Street
Denver, Colorado 80253
(303) 640-5102FAX: (303) 640-3410
E-mail: mokamoto@ci.denver.co.us

CONNECTICUT: (0)

DELAWARE: (0)

DISTRICT OF COLUMBIA: (2)

FEDERAL

Chung K. Pak, Administrative Patent Judge
U. S. Board of Patent Appeals and Interferences
U. S. Patent and Trademark Office
Washington, D.C. 20231
(703) 308-9797 FAX: (703) 308-7952

Stephen T. Shih, Administrative Judge
U. S. Equal Employment Opportunity Commission
1400 L Street, N.W., Suite 200
Washington, D.C. 20005
(202) 275-6693 or 275-7377 FAX: (202) 275-6834

FLORIDA: (0)

GEORGIA: (3)

STATE

Alvin T. Wong, Judge
State Court of DeKalb County
608 DeKalb County Courthouse
Decatur, Georgia 30030
(404) 371-2591 FAX: (404) 678-3820
E-mail: atwong@co.dekalb.ga.us

Chong Kim, Magistrate Judge Pro Hac Vice
Fulton County Magistrate Court
185 Central Avenue, S.W.
Atlanta, Georgia 30303
(404) 730-4245

Chung H. Lee, Magistrate
Magistrate Court of Gwinnett County
75 Langley Drive
Lawrenceville, Georgia 30045-1250
(770) 822-8081

GUAM: (8)

FEDERAL

John S. Unpingco, Chief Judge
U. S. District Court
Pacific News Building, Sixth Floor
238 Archbishop F.C. Flores Street
Agana, Guam 96910
(671) 472-7292 FAX: (671) 472-7345

Territorial Court Judges

Alberto Lamorena III, Presiding Judge
Superior Court of Guam
120 West O'Brien Drive
Agana, Guam 96910
(671) 475-3410 FAX: (671) 477-1852

Benjamin J. F. Cruz, Judge
Superior Court of Guam
120 West O'Brien Drive
Agana, Guam 96910
(671) 475-3110 FAX: (671) 477-3184

Joaquin V. E. Manibusan, Jr., Judge
Superior Court of Guam
120 West O'Brien Drive
Agana, Guam 96910
(671) 475-3130 FAX: (671) 477-3184

Katherine A. Maraman, Judge
Superior Court of Guam
120 West O'Brien Drive
Agana, Guam 96910
(671) 475-3410 FAX: (671) 477-3184

Peter C. Siguenza, Judge
Superior Court of Guam
120 West O'Brien Drive
Agana, Guam 96910
(671) 475-3220/3510 FAX: (671) 477-3184

Frances Tydingco-Gatewood, Judge
Superior Court of Guam
120 West O'Brien Drive
Agana, Guam 96910
(671) 475-3323 FAX: (671) 477-3184

Janet Healy Weeks, Judge
Superior Court of Guam
120 West O'Brien Drive
Agana, Guam 96910
(671) 475-3150 FAX: (671) 477-3184

HAWAII (98)

FEDERAL

Herbert Y. C. Choy, Senior Judge
U. S. Court of Appeals for the Ninth Circuit
C-305 Prince Kuhio Federal Building
300 Ala Moana Boulevard
Honolulu, Hawaii 96850-0305
(808) 541-1801 FAX: (808) 541-3667

Susan Oki Mollway, Judge
U. S. District Court for the District of Hawaii
C-409 Prince Kuhio Federal Building
300 Ala Moana Boulevard
Honolulu, Hawaii 96850
(808) 541-1720 FAX: (808) 541-1724

Kevin S.C. Chang, Magistrate Judge
U. S. District Court for the District of Hawaii
300 Ala Moana Boulevard
Honolulu, Hawaii 96850-0353
(808) 541-1308 FAX: (808) 541-3519

Leslie E. Kobayashi, Magistrate Judge
U. S. District Court for the District of Hawaii
300 Ala Moana Boulevard
Honolulu, Hawaii 96850-0353
(808) 541-1331 FAX: (808) 541-1386

Francis I. Yamashita, Magistrate Judge
U. S. District Court for the District of Hawaii
C-209 Prince Kuhio Federal Building
300 Ala Moana Boulevard
Honolulu, Hawaii 96850-0209
(808) 541-1308 FAX: (808) 541-3519
(Term to Expire in early 2001)

Jon J. Chin, Bankruptcy Judge (Retired) (Recalled)
First Hawaiian Tower, Suite 2501
1132 Bishop Street
Honolulu, Hawaii 96813-2830
(808) 522-8111

Lawrence N. C. Ing, Magistrate Judge (Retired)
U. S. District Court for the District of Hawaii
Wailuku, Hawaii 96793
(808) 242-4555

Sylvester V. Quitiquit, Magistrate Judge (Retired)
U. S. District Court for the District of Hawaii
U. S. Courthouse
Kailua, Hawaii 96740

Bert S. Tokairin, Magistrate Judge (Retired)
U. S. District Court for the District of Hawaii
300 Ala Moana Boulevard
Honolulu, Hawaii 96850
(808) 541-1306

Administrative Law Judges

Henry M. Tai, Chief Administrative Law Judge
Office of Hearings & Appeals
Social Security Administration
Kuhio Federal Building
300 Ala Moana Boulevard, Room 3209
Honolulu, Hawaii 96850
(808) 541-2915 FAX: (808) 541-3536

STATE

Supreme Court

Simeon R. Acoba, Jr., Associate Justice
Supreme Court of Hawaii, Ali'lolani Hale
417 South King Street
Honolulu, Hawaii 96804
(808) 539-4725 FAX: (808) 539-4703

Ronald T. Y. Moon, Chief Justice
Supreme Court of Hawaii, Ali'lolani Hale
417 South King Street, 2d Floor
Honolulu, Hawaii 96804-2902
(808) 539-4700 FAX: (808) 539-4703

Paula A. Nakayama, Associate Justice
Supreme Court of Hawaii, Ali'lolani Hale
417 South King Street
Honolulu, Hawaii 96804
(808) 539-4720 FAX: (808) 539-4703

Mario R. Ramil, Associate Justice
Supreme Court of Hawaii, Ali'lolani Hale
417 South King Street
Honolulu, Hawaii 96804
(808) 539-4716 FAX: (808) 539-4703

William S. Richardson, Chief Justice (Retired)
Supreme Court of Hawaii
Kamehameha Schools/Bishop Estate
Post Office Box 3466
Honolulu, Hawaii 96801-3466
(808) 541-5367

Court of Appeals

John S. W. Lim, Judge
Court of Appeals
Kapuaiwa Building, 2nd Floor
426 Queen Street
Honolulu, Hawaii 96813
(Post Office Box 2560
Honolulu, Hawaii 96804-2560)
(808) 539-4059 FAX: (808) 539-4778

Corinne K. A. Watanabe, Judge
Court of Appeals
Kapuaiwa Building, 2nd Floor
426 Queen Street
Honolulu, Hawaii 96813
(Post Office Box 2560
Honolulu, Hawaii 96804-2560)
(808) 539-4752 FAX: (808) 539-4778

Trial Court Judges

Karen S. S. Ahn, Judge First Circuit Court
1111 Alakea Street
Honolulu, Hawaii 96813
(808) 539-4066 FAX: (808) 538-5107

Riki May Amano, Judge
Third Circuit Court
75 Aupuni Street
Hilo, Hawaii 96720-4253
(808) 961-7454 FAX: (808) 961-7416

Artemio C. Baxa, Judge
Second Circuit Court – Courtroom 1
2145 Main Street
Wailuku, Maui, Hawaii 96793-1679
(808) 244-2955 FAX: (808) 244-2732

Karen N. Blondin, Judge
First Circuit Court – Ka'ahumanu Hale
777 Punchbowl Street
Honolulu, Hawaii 96813
(808) 539-4116 FAX: (808) 548-8153 or 538-5107

Derrick H. M. Chan, Judge
First Circuit Court
1111 Alakea Street
Honolulu, Hawaii 96813
(808) 538-5193 FAX: (808) 539-4218

Gary W. B. Chang, Judge
First Circuit Court
777 Punchbowl Street
Honolulu, Hawaii 96813-5093
(808) 539-4084 FAX: (808) 538-5107

Kevin S. C. Chang, Judge
First Circuit Court
1111 Alakea Street
Honolulu, Hawaii 96813-5093
(808) 539-4006 FAX: (808) 538-5107

Dexter D. Del Rosario, Judge
First Circuit Court
777 Punchbowl Street
Honolulu, Hawaii 96813
(808) 5394078 FAX: (808) 548-8153 or 538-5107

Reynaldo D. Graulty, Judge
First Circuit Court
777 Punchbowl Street
Honolulu, Hawaii 96813
(808) 539-4109 FAX: (808) 538-5107

Eden Elizabeth Hifo, Judge
First Circuit Court – Ka'ahumanu Hale
777 Punchbowl Street
Honolulu, Hawaii 96813-5093
(808) 539-4025 FAX: (808) 538-5107

Colleen K. Hirai, Judge
First Circuit Court
777 Punchbowl Street
Honolulu, Hawaii 96813
(808) 539-4640 FAX: (808) 548-8153 or 538-5107

Ronald Ibarra, Judge
Circuit Court of the Third Circuit, Kona Division
79-7595A Haukapila Street
Post Office Box 1970
Kealakekua, Hawaii 96750-1970
(808) 322-8755 FAX: (808) 322-8730

Gerald H. Kibe, Judge
Circuit Court of the First Circuit
Kaulkeaouli Hale
1111 Alakea Street, 11th Floor
Honolulu, Hawaii 96813-2897
(808) 538-5004 FAX: (808) 538-5232

Dan T. Kochi, Judge
First Circuit Court
Ka'ahumanu Hale
777 Punchbowl Street
Honolulu, Hawaii 96813-5093
(808) 539-4600 FAX: (808) 538-5107 or 548-8153

George M. Masuoka, Judge
Fifth Circuit Court
3059 Umi Street, Room 101
Lihue, Hawaii 96766-1809
(808) 246-3322 FAX: (808) 246-3310

Sabrina S. McKenna, Judge
First Circuit Court
1111 Alakea Street
Honolulu, Hawaii 96813-2921
(808) 539-4220 FAX: (808) 538-5107 or 538-5232

Marie Nakanishi Milks, Judge
First Circuit Court
777 Punchbowl Street
Honolulu, Hawaii 96813
(808) 539-4100 FAX: (808) 539-4322

Boyd P. Mossman, Judge
Circuit Court of the Second Circuit
2145 Main Street
Wailuku, Hawaii 96793
(808) 244-2860 FAX: (808) 244-2932

Greg K. Nakamura, Judge
Third Circuit Court
75 Aupuni Street
Hilo, Hawaii 96720-4253
(Post Office Box 1007
Hilo, Hawaii 96721-1007)
(808) 961-7464 FAX: (808) 961-7416

Gail C. Nakatani, Judge
First Circuit Court
Ka'ahumanu Hale
777 Punchbowl Street
Honolulu, Hawaii 96813-5093
(808) 539-4019 FAX: (808) 539-4108

Clifford L. Nakea, Judge
Fifth Circuit Court
3059 Umi Street
Lihue, Hawaii 96766-1809
(808) 246-3300 FAX: 246-3310

Karl Sakamoto, Judge
First Circuit Court
1111 Alakea Street
Honolulu, Hawaii 96813
(808) 538-5130 FAX: (808) 538-5107

Wilfred K. Watanabe, Judge
First Circuit Court
777 Punchbowl Street
Honolulu, Hawaii 96813
(808) 539-4060
FAX: (808) 538-5107 or 548-8153

Frances Q. F. Wong, Judge
First Circuit Court
Ka'ahumanu Hale
777 Punchbowl Street
Honolulu, Hawaii 96813-5093
(808) 539-4440 FAX: (808) 548-8153

George M. Masuoka, Senior Judge
Administrative Judge
Circuit Court of the Fifth Circuit
3059 Umi Street, Room 101
Lihue, Hawaii 96766
(808) 246-3322 FAX: (808) 246-3310

Ernest H. Kubota, Judge (Retired)
Circuit Court of the Third Circuit
75 Aupuni Street
Hilo, Hawaii 96720

Melvin K. Soong, Judge (Retired)
Circuit Court of the First Circuit
Family Court
777 Punchbowl Street
Honolulu, Hawaii 06813

District Courts

Jeffrey Choi, Administrative Judge
District Court of the Third Circuit
75 Aupuni Street, Room 205
Hilo, Hawaii 96720
(Post Office Box 4879
Hilo, Hawaii 96720-4879)
(808) 961-7494 FAX: (808) 961-7416 or 961-7447

Joseph P. Florendo, Jr., Judge
District Court
Third Judicial Circuit-Kona Division
Post Office Box P
Kealakekua, Hawaii 96750
(808) 322-8710
FAX: (808) 322-8700 or 961-7447

David Fong, Judge
District Court of the First Circuit
Kaulkeaouli Hale
1111 Alakea Street, 11th Floor
Honolulu, Hawaii 96813-2897
(808) 538-5008 FAX: (808) 538-5232

Colette Garibaldi, Judge
District Court of the First Circuit
Kaulkeaouli Hale
1111 Alakea Street, 11th Floor
Honolulu, Hawaii 96813-2897
(808) 538-5009 FAX: (808) 538-5232

Leslie Ann Hayashi, Judge
District Court of the First Circuit
Kaulkeaouli Hale
1111 Alakea Street
Honolulu, Hawaii 96813
(808) 538-5003 FAX: (808) 538-5232

Douglas H. Ige, Judge
District Court of the Second Circuit
Wailuku Division
2145 Main Street
Wailuku, Hawaii 96793-1679
(808) 244-2714 FAX: (808) 244-2849

George Kimura, Administrative Judge
District Court of the First Circuit
Kaulkeaouli Hale
1111 Alakea Street, 11th Floor
Honolulu, Hawaii 96813-2897
(808) 538-5000 FAX: (808) 538-5232

Rhonda Lai Loo, Judge
District Court of the Second Circuit
Wailuku Division
2145 Main Street
Wailuku, Hawaii 96793-1679
(808) 244-2723 FAX: (808) 244-2849

David Lo, Judge
District Court of the First Circuit
Kaulkeaouli Hale
1111 Alakea Street, 11th Floor
Honolulu, Hawaii 96813-2897
(808) 538-5010 FAX: (808) 538-5232

Calvin K. Murashige, Judge
District Court of the Fifth Circuit
3059 Umi Street
Lihue, Hawaii 96766-1809
(808) 246-3390 FAX: (808) 246-3353

Russel S. Nagata, Judge
District Court of the First Circuit
Kaulkeaouli Hale
1111 Alakea Street, 11th Floor
Honolulu, Hawaii 96813-2897
(808) 538-5007 FAX: (808) 538-5232

Clifford L. Nakea, Judge
District Court, Fifth Circuit
3059 Umi Street
Lihue, Hawaii 96766
(808) 246-3348 FAX: (808) 246-3310

Rhonda Nishimura, Judge
District Court of the First Circuit
Kaulkeaouli Hale
1111 Alakea Street, 11th Floor
Honolulu, Hawaii 96813-2897
(808) 538-5319 FAX: (808) 538-5111 or 538-5232

Yoshio Shigezawa, Administrative Judge
District Court of the Second Circuit
Wailuku Division
2145 Main Street
Wailuku, Hawaii 96793-1679
(808) 244-2730 FAX: (808) 242-5834

Tenney Z. Tongg, Judge
District Court of the First Circuit
Kaulkeaouli Hale
1111 Alakea Street, 11th Floor
Honolulu, Hawaii 96813-2897
(808) 538-5011 FAX: (808) 538-5232

Fa'auuga To'oto'o, Judge
District Court of the First Circuit
Kaulkeaouli Hale
1111 Alakea Street, 11th Floor
Honolulu, Hawaii 96813-2897
(808) 538-5021 FAX: (808) 538-5232

William S. Chillingworth, Judge (Retired)
District Court of the Third Circuit
75 Aupuni Street
Hilo, Hawaii 96720
(808) 961-7484 FAX: (808) 935-3852

Hiroshi Oshiro, Judge (Retired)
District Court of the First Circuit
1111 Alakea Street
Honolulu, Hawaii 96813
(808) 538-5008 FAX: (808) 548-6093

Edwin Y. Sasaki, Judge (Retired)
District Court of the First Circuit
1111 Alakea Street
Honolulu, Hawaii 96813
(808) 538-5009 FAX: (808) 548-6093

Frederick J. Titcomb, Judge (Retired)
District Court of the First Circuit
1111 Alakea Street
Honolulu, Hawaii 96813
(808) 548-2523 FAX: (808) 548-6093

District Family Court Judges

Aley K. Auna, Jr., District Family Judge
Family Court of the Third Circuit
75 Aupuni Street
Hilo, Hawaii 96720-4253
(808) 961-7430 FAX: (808) 961-7447

Darryl Y. C. Choy, District Family Judge
Family Court of the First Circuit
Ka'ahumanu Hale
777 Punchbowl Street
Honolulu, Hawaii 96813-5093
(808) 539-4435 FAX: (808) 539-4504

Linda K. C. Luke, District Family Judge
Family Court of the First Circuit
Ka'ahumanu Hale
777 Punchbowl Street
Honolulu, Hawaii 96813-5093
(Post Office Box 3498
Honolulu, Hawaii 96811-3498)
(808) 539-4432 FAX: (808) 539-4504

Allene R. Suemori, District Family Judge
Family Court of the First Circuit
Ka'ahumanu Hale
777 Punchbowl Street
Honolulu, Hawaii 96813-5093
(Post Office Box 3498
Honolulu, Hawaii 96811-3498)
(808) 539-4439 FAX: (808) 539-4504

Bode Uale, District Family Judge
Family Court of the First Circuit
Ka'ahumanu Hale
777 Punchbowl Street
Honolulu, Hawaii 96813-5093
(Post Office Box 3498
Honolulu, Hawaii 96811-3498)
(808) 539-4438 FAX: (808) 539-4504

Diana Warrington, District Family Judge
Family Court of the First Circuit
Ka'ahumanu Hale
777 Punchbowl Street
Honolulu, Hawaii 96813-5093
(Post Office Box 3498
Honolulu, Hawaii 96811-3498)
(808) 539-4434 FAX: (808) 539-4504

Terence T. Yoshioka, District Family Judge
Family Court of the Third Circuit
75 Aupuni Street
Hilo, Hawaii 96720-4253
(808) 961-7430 FAX: (808) 961-7447

Per Diem District Court Judges

James R. Aliona, Jr., Per Diem Judge
District Court of the First Circuit
1111 Alakea Street
Honolulu, Hawaii 96813-2897

Karen Napua Brown, Per Diem Judge
District Court of the Third Circuit
75 Aupuni Street
Hilo, Hawaii 96720-4253

Gale L. F. Ching, Per Diem Judge
District Court of the First Circuit
1111 Alakea Street
Honolulu, Hawaii 96813-2897

Paula Devens-Matayoshi, Per Diem Judge
District Court of the First Circuit
1111 Alakea Street
Honolulu, Hawaii 96813-2897

Phillip Doi, Per Diem Judge
District Court of the First Circuit
1111 Alakea Street
Honolulu, Hawaii 96813-2897

Peter C. K. Fong, Per Diem Judge
District Court of the First Circuit
1111 Alakea Street
Honolulu, Hawaii 96813-2897

Walton D. Y. Hong, Per Diem Judge
District Court of the Fifth Circuit
3059 Umi Street
Lihue, Hawaii 96766-1809

Joseph Kobayshi, Per Diem Judge
District Court of the Fifth Circuit
3059 Umi Street
Lihue, Hawaii 96766-1809

Christine E. Kuriyama, Per Diem Judge
District Court of the First Circuit
1111 Alakea Street
Honolulu, Hawaii 96813-2897

Lenore K. J. H. Lee, Per Diem Judge
District Court of the First Circuit
1111 Alakea Street
Honolulu, Hawaii 96813-2897

Lono J. Lee, Per Diem Judge
District Court of the First Circuit
1111 Alakea Street
Honolulu, Hawaii 96813-2897

Wilson M. N. Loo, Per Diem Judge
District Court of the First Circuit
1111 Alakea Street
Honolulu, Hawaii 96813-2897

Michael A. Marr, Per Diem Judge
District Court of the First Circuit
1111 Alakea Street
Honolulu, Hawaii 96813-2897

Gerald S. Matsunaga, Per Diem Judge
District Court of the Fifth Circuit
3059 Umi Street
Lihue, Hawaii 96766-1809

Paul T. Murakami, Per Diem Judge
District Court of the First Circuit
1111 Alakea Street
Honolulu, Hawaii 96813-2897

Shawn Maile Nakoa, Per Diem Judge
District Court of the Third Circuit
75 Aupuni Street
Hilo, Hawaii 96720-4253

Clarence A. Pacarro, Per Diem Judge
District Court of the First Circuit
1111 Alakea Street
Honolulu, Hawaii 96813-2897

Matthew S. K. Pyun, Jr., Per Diem Judge
District Court of the Third Circuit
75 Aupuni Street
Hilo, Hawaii 96720-4253

Douglas J. Sameshima, Per Diem Judge
District Court of the Second Circuit
2145 Main Street
Wailukiu, Hawaii 96793-1679

Yvonne R. Shinmura, Per Diem Judge
District Court of the First Circuit
1111 Alakea Street
Honolulu, Hawaii 96813-2897

Barbara Takase, Per Diem Judge
District Court of the Third Circuit
75 Aupuni Street
Hilo, Hawaii 96720-4879

Timothy David Woo, Jr., Per Diem Judge
District Court of the First Circuit
1111 Alakea Street
Honolulu, Hawaii 96813-2897

Vernon Y. T. Woo, Per Diem Judge
District Court of the First Circuit
1111 Alakea Street
Honolulu, Hawaii 96813-2897

George S. Yuda, Per Diem Judge
District Court of the Third Circuit
75 Aupuni Street
Hilo, Hawaii 96720-4253

Administrative Law Judges

Russell Tadao Higa, Board Member
Labor Relations Board
550 Halekauwila Street, Second Floor
Honolulu, Hawaii 96813
(808) 586-8610 FAX: (808) 586-8613

Rodney Allan Maile, Hearing Officer
Office of Administrative Hearings
250 South Kings Street, Penthouse
Honolulu, Hawaii 96813
(808) 586-2828 FAX: (808) 586-2827

Sheryl Lee A. Nagata, Hearing Officer
Office of Administrative Hearings
Department of Commerce & Consumer Affairs
250 South King Street, Penthouse
Honolulu, Hawaii 96813
(808) 586-2828 FAX: (808) 586-2755

IDAHO: (0)

ILLINOIS: (6)

FEDERAL

Administrative Law Judges

James R. Fujimoto, U. S. Immigration Judge
55 East Monroe Street, Suite 1900
Chicago, Illinois 60603-5701
(312) 353-7312 or 353-7313 FAX: Call on phone first

Damien A. Lee, Administrative Judge
U. S. Equal Employment Opportunity Commission
500 West Madison Street, Suite 2800
Chicago, Illinois 60661
(630) 682-7305 FAX: (680) 682-6810

STATE

Kenneth Moy, Judge
Circuit Court of DuPage County
505 North County Farm Road
Wheaton, Illinois 60187
(630) 682-7305 FAX: (630) 682-6810

Sandra R. Otaka, Judge
Circuit Court of Cook County – Traffic Court
321 North LaSalle Street, Room 120
Chicago, Illinois 60610
(312) 822-3530

Holly Fujita Clemons, Associate Judge
Circuit Court of Champaign County
101 East Main Street, Courtroom F
Urbana, Illinois 61801
(217) 384-3705 FAX: (217) 384-8424

Lynne Kawamoto, Associate Judge
Circuit Court of Cook County - Juvenile Court
1100 South Hamilton Street
Chicago, Illinois 60612
(312) 433-6990 FAX: (312) 433-6591 or 433-7900

INDIANA: (1)

STATE

G. Michael Witte, Judge
Dearborn Superior Court
215 West High Street
Lawrenceburg, Indiana 47025-1999
(812) 537-8874 FAX: (812) 532-2032

IOWA: (1)

Anuradha Vaitheswaran, Judge
Court of Appeals – State Capitol
Des Moines, Iowa 50319
(515) 281-5221 FAX: (515) 281-6467

KANSAS: (0)

KENTUCKY: (0)

LOUISIANA: (0)

MAINE: (0)

MARYLAND: (2)

FEDERAL

Jag Jit Singh, Administrative Law Judge
Office of Hearings & Appeals
Social Security Administration
The Rotunda, Rotunda Room 415
West 40th Street
Baltimore Maryland 21211
(410) 962-3361 FAX: (410) 889-5968

STATE

David M. Valderrama, Judge (Retired)
Maryland Orphan's Court
Maryland House of Delegates
205 Lowe House Office Building
Annapolis, Maryland 21401-1991
(410) 841-3012 FAX: (410) 889-5968

MASSACHUSETTS: (2)

STATE

Richard J. Chin, Justice
Superior Court
New Courthouse, 11th Floor
Boston, Massachusetts 02108-1783
(617) 725-8130 FAX: (617) 725-8137

Fernande R. V. Duffly, Judge
Probate and Family Court
Middlesex Probate and Family Court
208 Cambridge Street
East Cambridge, Massachusetts 02141
(617) 494-4548 FAX: (617) 225-0781

MICHIGAN: (0)

Minnesota: (2)

State

Tony N. Leung, Judge
District Court
4th Judicial District
Hennepin County Government Center
300 South Sixth Street
Minneapolis, Minnesota 55487
(612) 348-3802 FAX: (612) 348-2131

Wesley C. Iijima, Referee
Juvenile Court, 4th Judicial District
Hennepin County Government Center
Minneapolis, Minnesota 55487
(612) 348-3781 FAX: (612) 348-2067

Mississippi: (0)

Missouri: (0)

Montana: (0)

Nebraska: (1)

Federal

Cheryl M. Rini, Administrative Law Judge
Office of Hearings and Appeals
Social Security Administration
9239 West Center Road, Suite 102
Omaha, Nebraska 68124
(402) 391-7118 Ext. 3018 FAX: (402) 398-1557
E-mail: CherylRini@ssa.gov

Nevada: (0)

New Hampshire: (0)

New Jersey: (4)

Federal

Nicole Yae Kyoung Kim
United States Immigration Judge
970 Broad Street, Room 1135
Newark, New Jersey 07102
(973) 645-3524 FAX: (973) Call on phone first

State

Randolph M. Subryan, Judge
Superior Court of New Jersey
Passaic County Court House
County Administration Building - Room 952
77 Hamilton Street
Paterson, New Jersey 07505-2017
(973) 247-8420 FAX: (973) 247-8417
E-mail: Judge_R_Subryan@judiciary.state.nj.us

Patricia Medina Talbert, Judge
Superior Court of New Jersey
New Courts Building - Room 1018
50 West Market Street
Newark, New Jersey 07102
E-mail: Judge_P_Talbert@judiciary.state.nj.us

Suk Young Kim, Judge
Municipal Court
Borough of Little Ferry
215 - 217 Liberty Street
Little Ferry, New Jersey 07643
(201) 440-2111 FAX (212) 835-6001
FAX in New York Law Office

New Mexico: (1)

Vicky A. Hudson, Judge
Municipal Court
Post Office Box 610
Angel Fire, New Mexico 87110
(505) 377-3800 FAX: (505) 377-5915

NEW YORK: (15)

FEDERAL

Denny Chin, Judge
U. S. District Court
for the Southern District of New York
500 Pearl Street, Room 1020
New York, New York 10007
(212) 637-0200 FAX: (212) 637-6262
E-mail: denny_chin@nysd.uscourts.gov

Marilyn Dolan Go, Magistrate Judge
U. S. District Court
for the Eastern District of New York
U. S. Courthouse
225 Cadman Plaza East
Brooklyn, New York 11201
(718) 330-7736 FAX: (718) 330-7634
E-mail: marilyn_go@nyed.uscourts.gov

Administrative Law Judges

Christopher P. Lee, Administrative Law Judge
Office of Hearings and Appeals
Social Security Administration
75 South Broadway - Suite 202
White Plains, New York 10601
(914) 761-7190 FAX: (914) 682-7006

George T. Chew, U. S. Immigration Judge
Executive Office of Immigration Review
26 Federal Plaza, Room 1237
New York, New York 10278
(212) 264-2173 FAX: Call on phone first

Sandy Hom, U. S. Immigration Judge
Executive Office of Immigration Review
26 Federal Plaza, Room 1237
New York, New York 10278
(212) 264-5958 FAX: Call on phone first

Kenneth W. Chu, Chief Administrative Judge
U. S. Equal Employment Opportunity
Commission
7 World Trade Center, 18th Floor
New York, New York 10048-1102
(212) 748-8466 FAX: (212) 748-8465

STATE

Appellate Court

Peter Tom, Justice
Appellate Division
1st Department
New York Supreme Court
27 Madison Avenue
New York, New York 10010
(212) 340-0403 FAX: (212) 340-0571

Trial Judges

Randall T. Eng, Judge
New York Supreme Court Queens County
125-01 Queens Boulevard
Kew Gardens, New York 11415
(718) 520-2846 FAX: (718) 520-2236

Douglas S. Wong, Acting Supreme Court Judge
New York Supreme Court, Queens County
125-01 Queens Boulevard
Kew Gardens, New York 11415
(718) 520-2221, 520-1764 or 520-3855
FAX: Call on phone first

Dorothy Chin Brandt, Judge
Civil Court of the City of New York
125-01 Queens Boulevard
Kew Gardens, New York 11415
(718) 520-3616 FAX: (718) 520-3992

Oymin Chin, Judge
Civil Court of the City of New York, Housing Part
141 Livingston Street
Brooklyn, New York 11201
(718) 643-6060 FAX: Call on phone first

Daniel Chun, Judge
Criminal Court of the City of New York
120 Schermerhorn Street
Brooklyn, New York 11201
(718) 643-3227 FAX: Call on phone first

Doris Ling-Cohan, Judge
Civil Court of the City of New York
111 Centre Street
New York, New York 10013
(212) 374-8464 FAX: (212) 401-9175

Laurie Lau, Judge
Civil Court of the City of New York
Housing Part
111 Centre Street
New York, New York 10013
(212) 374-4517 or 374-8428
FAX: (212) 374-8416 or 401-9187

Elizabeth Tao, Judge
Civil Court of the City of New York
Housing Part
1118 Grand Concourse Boulevard
Bronx, New York 10456
(718) 466-3025 FAX: (718) 466-3006

NORTH CAROLINA: (0)

NORTH DAKOTA: (0)

NORTH MARIANA ISLANDS: (7)

Supreme Court

Alexandro C. Castro, Associate Justice
Supreme Court
Post Office Box 502165
Saipan, Northern Mariana Islands 96950
(670) 236-9700 FAX: (670) 236-9702

Miguel S. Demapan, Chief Justice
Supreme Court
Post Office Box 502165
Saipan, Northern Mariana Islands 96950
(670) 236-9700 FAX: (670) 236-9702

John A. Manglona, Associate Justice
Supreme Court
Post Office Box 502165
Saipan, Northern Mariana Islands 96950
(670) 236-9700 FAX: (670) 236-9702

Trial Court Judges

Timothy H. Bellas, Associate Judge
Superior Court
Post Office Box 500307
Saipan, Northern Mariana Islands 96950
(670) 236-9740 FAX: (670) 236-9742

Juan T. Lizama, Associate Judge
Superior Court
Post Office Box 500307
Saipan, Northern Mariana Islands 96950
(670) 236-9740 FAX: (670) 236-9742

Edward Manibusan, Presiding Judge
Superior Court
Post Office Box 500307
Saipan, Northern Mariana Islands 96950
(670) 236-9740 FAX: (670) 236-9741

Virginia Sablan-Onerheim, Associate Judge
Superior Court
Post Office Box 500307
Saipan, Northern Mariana Islands 96950
(670) 236-9740 FAX: (670) 236-9742

OHIO: (1)

Thomas L. Wang, Administrative Law Judge
Board of Tax Appeals
30 East Broad Street, 24th Floor
Columbus, Ohio 43215
(614) 466-6700 FAX: (614) 644-5196
E-mail: tommy1ok@excite.com

OKLAHOMA: (0)

OREGON: (1)

STATE

Michael S. Loy, Judge Circuit Court
Multnomah County Courthouse
1021 S.W. 4th Avenue
Portland, Oregon 97204
(503) 248-3813 FAX: (503) 276-0973

PENNSYLVANIA: (2)

STATE

Ida Chen, Judge
Court of Common Pleas
27 South 12th Street, Suite 400
Philadelphia, Pennsylvania 19107
(215) 686-2545 FAX: (215) 686-9302

William M. Marutani, Judge (Retired)
Court of Common Pleas
310 Woodridge Lane
Media, Pennsylvania 19063
(215) 566-1905 FAX: (215) 566-0155

PUERTO RICO: (0)

RHODE ISLAND: (0)

SOUTH CAROLINA: (0)

SOUTH DAKOTA: (0)

TENNESSEE: (0)

TEXAS: (14)

STATE

State District Court Judges

Michael K. Sinha, Presiding Judge
360th District Court – Tarrant County
Ft. Worth, Texas 76114
(817) 884-2721 FAX: Call on phone first

Peter A. Sakai, Associate Judge
290th District Court
100 Dolorosa - Room 205
San Antonio, Texas 78205
(210) 335-2768 or 228-3841 FAX: (210) 335-2286

Municipal Court Judges

Linh Van Chau, Presiding Judge
Palacios Municipal Court
Post Office Box 845
Palacios, Texas 77465
(361) 972-3305 or 972-3325 FAX: (361) 972-6555

Riddhi Pankaj Desai, Judge
Houston Municipal Court
1400 Lubbock Street, Room 214
Houston, Texas 77002
(713) 247-5464 FAX: (713) 247-8747

Sam M. Eng, Judge
Houston Municipal Court
1400 Lubbock Street, Room 214
Houston, Texas 77002
(713) 247-5464 or 460-3868 FAX: (713) 247-8747

Herbert Gee, Judge
Houston Municipal Court
1400 Lubbock, Basement
Houston, Texas 77002
(713) 247-5464 FAX: (713) 247-8747

Kathy Bao-Khann Han, Judge
Houston Municipal Court
8300 Mykawa
Houston, Texas 77002
(713) 247-5464 or (713) 731-5155
FAX: (713) 247-8747 or (713) 731-5159

Antonia Ingversen, Judge
Houston Municipal Court
1400 Lubbock, Basement
Houston, Texas 77002
(713) 247-5464 FAX: (713) 247-8747

Michael K. Sinha*, Presiding Judge
Sansom Park Muncipal Court
Tarrant County
5500 Buchanan Street
Ft. Worth, Texas 76114
(817) 626-3793 FAX: (817) 884-3594

Vikram Deivanayagam, Associate Judge
Woodway Municipal Court
920 Estates Drive
Woodway, Texas 76712
(254) 772-4489 FAX: (254) 772-9219

Wendy N. Duong, Associate Judge
Houston Municipal Court
700 Louisiana Street, Suite 1600
Houston, Texas 77002
(713) 546-5267 FAX: (713) 224-9511

**Asterisk indicates that the person serves in more than one judicial position.*

Min Un Lee, Associate Judge
Houston Municipal Court
1400 Lubbock
Houston, Texas 77002
(713) 247-5464 FAX: (713) 247-8747

Timothy K. Seo, Associate Judge
Houston Municipal Court
1400 Lubbock, Room 214
Houston, Texas 77027
(713) 247-5464 or 623-0600
FAX: (713) 247-8747 or 623-0697

Ted Wu, Associate Judge
Houston Municipal Court
1400 Lubbock Street, Room 214
Houston, Texas 77002
(713) 247-5464 FAX: (713) 247-8747

UTAH: (5)

STATE

Glenn K. Iwasaki, Judge
Third Judicial District Court
Salt Lake County - Salt Lake City District Court
450 South State Street
Salt Lake City, Utah 84114
(801) 238-7505 FAX: (801) 238-7542

Howard H. Maetani, Judge
Fourth Judicial District Court
Utah County-American Fork District Court
98 North Center Street
American Fork, Utah 84003
(801) 756-9654 FAX: (801) 463-0153

Michael W. Kwan,
City of Taylorsville
Municipal Justice Court
5486 South 1900 West, Suite A
Taylorsville, Utah 84118
(801) 963-0268 FAX: (801) 963-0576

James Sawaya, Senior Judge
Third Judicial District Court
230 South 500 East, Suite 300
Salt Lake City, Utah 84102
(801) 535-5111 FAX: (801) 535-5957

Raymond S. Uno, Senior Judge
Third Judicial District Court
1135 Second Avenue
Salt Lake City, Utah 84103

VERMONT: (1)

Robert M. Pu, Judge
Probate Court
District of Marlboro
West River Road
Post Office Box 523
Brattleboro, Vermont 05302
(802) 257-2898 FAX: (802) 254-6746

VIRGIN ISLANDS: (0)

VIRGINIA: (1)

Somsanith Khamuongsa, Magistrate
Fairfax General District Court
4110 Chain Bridge Road
Fairfax, Virginia 22030
(703) 246-2178

WASHINGTON: (22)

FEDERAL

Anna Ho, U. S. Immigration Judge
Key Tower Building
1000 Second Avenue, Suite 2500
Seattle, Washington 98104
(206) 553-5953 FAX: Call on phone first

Douglas W. Luna, Administrative Judge
U. S. Equal Employment
Opportunity Commission
2815 Second Avenue, Suite 800
Seattle, Washington 98121
(206) 553-2441 FAX: (206) 553-1308

STATE

Appellate Judges

Kenneth H. Kato, Judge
Washington State Court of Appeals, Division III
500 North Cedar Street
Spokane, Washington 99201-1987
(509) 456-4032 FAX: (253) 456-4288

Art Wang, Judge
Washington State Court of Appeals Division II
949 Market Street, Suite 500
MB TB-06
Tacoma, Washington 98402-3694
(253) 593-5447FAX: (253) 593-2060

State Trial Court Judges

Ellen Kalama Clark, Judge
Spokane County Superior Court
1116 West Broadway Avenue
Spokane, Washington 99260-0350
(509) 477-6006 FAX: (509) 447-5714

Richard M. Ishikawa, Judge
King County Superior Court
King County Courthouse, Dept. 11
516 Third Avenue
Seattle, Washington 98104-2381
(206) 296-9285 FAX: (206) 205-2585

Linda Lau, Judge
King County Superior Court
King County Courthouse
516 Third Avenue
Seattle, Washington 98104-2381
(206) 296-9242 FAX: (206) 296-0986

Dean Scott Lum, Judge
King County Superior Court
C-203 King County Courthouse
516 Third Avenue
Seattle, Washington 98104-2381
(206) 296-9295 FAX: (206) 296-0986

Mary Yu, Judge
King County Superior Court
King County Courthouse
516 Third Avenue
Seattle, Washington 98104-2381
(206) 296-9275 FAX: (206) 296-0986
Courts of Limited Jurisdiction Judges:

Mark C. Chow, Judge
King County District Court
King County Courthouse, E341
516 Third Avenue
Seattle, Washington 98104-2381
(206) 296-3620 FAX: (206) 296-0910

Eileen A. Kato, Judge
King County District Court
King County Courthouse
516 Third Avenue
Seattle, Washington 98104-2381
(206) 296-3615 FAX: (206) 296-0910
E-mail: eileen.kato@metrokc.gov

Alicia Nakata, Judge
Chelan County District Court
350 Orondo
Post Office Box 2182
Wenatchee, Washington 98807-2182
(509) 664-4292 FAX: (509) 664-5456

Mariane C. Spearman, Judge
King County District Court
King County Courthouse
516 Third Avenue
Seattle, Washington 98104-2381
(206) 296-3630 FAX: (509) 296-0910

Les Ching, Judge
Ranier Municipal Court
102 Rochester Street
Post Office Box 258
Ranier, Washington 98576-0151
(360) 446-2744 FAX: (360) 446-2720

C. Kimi Kondo, Judge
Seattle Municipal Court
424 Public Safety Building
Seattle, Washington 98104
(206) 684-8709 FAX: (206) 684-0056

Ron A. Mamiya, Judge
Seattle Municipal Court
424 Public Safety Building
Seattle, Washington 98104
(206) 684-8709 FAX: (206) 684-0056

Commissioners and Magistrates:

Robert W. Inouye, Commissioner
Yakima County Superior Court
128 North 2nd Street
Yakima, Washington 98901-2639
(509) 574-2710 FAX: (509) 574-2701

C. Bradley Chinn, Commissioner
Spokane County District Court
1100 West Mallon Avenue
Spokane, Washington 99260-0150
(509) 477-3661 FAX: (509) 459-6445

Francis DeVilla, Magistrate
Seattle Municipal Court
610 Third Avenue
Seattle, Washington 98104-1852
(206) 684-5607 FAX: (206) 615-0766

Park Eng, Commissioner
Tukwila Municipal Court
6200 Southcenter Boulevard
Tukwila, Washington 98188-2544
(206) 433-1840 FAX: (206) 433-7160

Administrative Law Judges

Chris Blas, Administrative Law Judge
32 North Third Street, Suite 320
Yakima, Washington 98901
(509) 575-2147 FAX: (509) 454-7281

Randolph F. Bolong, Administrative Law Judge
921 Lakeridge Way, Suite C
Olympia, Washington 98504
(360) 753-7328 FAX: (360) 586-6562

West Virginia: (0)

Wisconsin: (0)

Wyoming : (0)

U. S. Armed Forces: (1)

Navy-Marine Corps Trial Judges

Ronald Leo (Captain)
U.S. Navy-Marine Corps
Court of Criminal Appeals
716 Sicand Street
Washington, Navy Yard
Washington, D.C. 20374

Section III

HISPANIC JUDGES OF THE U. S.

Initially prepared by
The Honorable Athur L. Burnett, Sr. with the assistance of Justice Joseph Baca of New Mexico

ALABAMA: (1)

FEDERAL

Administrative Law Judge

Ricardo M. Ryan, Administrative Law Judge
Office of Hearings and Appeals
Social Security Administration
3605 Springhill Business Park
Mobile, Alabama 36608
(334) 441-5441 FAX: (334) 441-5993

ALASKA: (1)

René J. Gonzalez, Judge
Superior Court
Third Judicial District
825 West Fourth Avenue, Room 638
Anchorage, Alaska 99501-2083
(907) 264-0425 FAX: (907) 264-0518

ARIZONA: (63)

FEDERAL

Frank R. Zapata, Judge
U. S. District Court for the District of Arizona
405 West Congress Street
Tucson, Arizona 85701-4530
(520) 205-4530 FAX: (520) 205-4209

Alfredo C. Marquez, Senior Judge
U. S. District Court for the District of Arizona
405 West Congress Street
Tucson, Arizona 85701
(520) 205-4500 FAX: (520) 505-4209

STATE

Appellate Judges

Philip G. Espinosa, Judge
Arizona Court of Appeals, Division 2
Arizona State Office Complex
400 West Congress
Tucson, Arizona 85701-1374
(520) 628-6948 or 628-6955 FAX: (520) 628-6959

M. Jan Flórez, Judge
Arizona Court of Appeals, Division 2
State Office Building
400 West Congress
Tucson, Arizona 85701-1374
(520) 628-6949 FAX: (520) 628-6959

Superior Court Judges

Mark F. Aceto, Judge
Superior Court in Maricopa County
222 E. Javelina Avenue, 4-B
Mesa, Arizona 85210
(602) 506-5261 FAX: (602) 506-2029

Edward B. Acuna, Judge
Superior Court in Pima County
110 West Congress, 9th Floor
Tucson, Arizona 85701
(520) 740-3620 FAX: (520) 740-3664

Louis A. Araneta, Judge
Superior Court in Maricopa County
201 West Jefferson, 9-D
Phoenix, Arizona 85003-2205
(602) 506-1179 FAX: (602) 506-7867

Silvia R. Arellano, Judge
Superior Court in Maricopa County
Juvenile Court Center
1810 South Lewis Street, # 1080
Mesa, Arizona 85010
(602) 506-3649 FAX: (602) 506-4132

Anna Maria Baca, Judge
Superior Court in Maricopa County
201 West Jefferson Street, 6-A
Phoenix, Arizona 85003
(602) 506-1810 FAX: (602) 506-7867

Paul Banales, Judge Pro Tempore
Superior Court in Pima County
110 West Congress, 9th Floor
Tucson, Arizona 85701
(520) 740-3620 FAX: (520) 740-8193

James E. Chavez, Judge
Superior Court in Mohave County
Presiding Juvenile Court Judge
401 East Spring Street
Post Office Box 7000
Kingman, Arizona 86402-7000
(520) 753-0785 FAX: (520) 718-5506

Gilberto V. Figueroa, Judge
Superior Court in Pinal County
Post Office Box 1583
Florence, Arizona 85232
(520) 868-6290 FAX: (520) 868-6500

J. Richard Gama, Judge
Superior Court in Maricopa County
201 West Jefferson, 5-C
Phoenix, Arizona 85003
(602) 506-1245 FAX: (602) 506-7867

Jose M. Lerma, Judge
Superior Court in Santa Cruz County
Presiding Juvenile Court Judge
Post Office Box 1929
Nogales, Arizona 85628
(520) 761-7806 FAX: (520) 761-7934

Roberto C. Montiel, Presiding Judge
Superior Court in Santa Cruz County
Post Office Box 1929
Nogales, Arizona 85628
(520) 761-7806 FAX: (520) 761-7934

Barbara Rodriguez Mundell, Judge
Superior Court in Maricopa County
201 West Jefferson, 4-C
Phoenix, Arizona 85003
(602) 506-6130 FAX: (602) 506-7867

Barbara A. Rodriguez, Judge
Maricopa County Superior Court
201 West Jefferson
Phoenix, Arizona 85003
(602) 506-6130 FAX: (602) 506-7867

Lina S. Rodriguez, Judge
Superior Court in Pima County
Presiding Arbitration Judge
110 West Congress, 9th Floor
Tucson, Arizona 85701
(520) 740-8241 FAX: (520) 740-3790

David M. Talamante, Judge
Superior Court in Maricopa County
222 East Javelina Avenue, 4-D
Mesa, Arizona 85210
(602) 506-6251 FAX: (602) 506-7867

Bernardo P. Velasco, Judge
Superior Court in Pima County
110 West Congress, 9th Floor
Tucson, Arizona 85701
(520) 740-8441 FAX: (520) 740-8140

Gilbert Veliz, Jr., Judge
Superior Court in Pima County
110 West Congress, 9th Floor
Tucson, Arizona 85701
(520) 740-4200 FAX: (520) 740-8313

Maria del Mar Verdin, Judge
Superior Court in Maricopa County
222 East Javelina Avenue, 2-E
Mesa, Arizona 85210
(602) 506-2603 FAX: (602) 506-7867

Stephen C. Villarreal, Judge
Superior Court in Pima County
110 West Congress, 9th Floor
Tucson, Arizona 85701
(520) 740-8045 FAX: (520) 740-8313
Superior Court Commissioners

Hector E. Campoy, Commissioner
Superior Court in Pima County
110 West Congress, 9th Floor
Tucson, Arizona 85701
(520) 740-4215 FAX: (520) 740-3082
E-mail: campoy@sc.co.pima.az.us

Harriett Chavez, Commissioner
Superior Court in Maricopa County
201 West Jefferson, 12-C
Phoenix, Arizona 85003
(602) 506-4208 FAX: (602) 506-7867
E-mail: hchavez@smtpgw.maricopa.gov

Municipal Courts

Linda Aguilar, Magistrate Judge
Graham County Municipal Court
Post Office Box 426
Pima, Arizona 85543
(520) 485-2611 FAX: (520) 485-9230

David Arrow, Magistrate, Judge Pro Tempore
Phoenix Municipal Court
300 West Washington
Phoenix, Arizona 85003-2103
(602) 534-3864 FAX: (602) 534-3552

Margarita Solano Bernal, Magistrate
Municipal Court
103 East Alameda Street
Post Office Box 27210
Tucson, Arizona 85726-7210
(520) 791-3260 FAX: (520) 791-4667

Robert L. Castillo, Magistrate
Municipal Court
103 East Alameda Street
Post Office Box 27210
Tucson, Arizona 85726-7210
(520) 791-3260 FAX: (520) 791-5454

Francisca J. Cota, Magistrate
Phoenix Municipal Court
300 West Washington
Phoenix, Arizona 85003-2103
(602) 261-8613 FAX: (602) 534-4779

Louis F. Dominguez, Magistrate
Phoenix Municipal Court
300 West Washington
Phoenix, Arizona 85003-2103
(602) 261-8162 FAX: (602) 495-7363

Hector Figueroa, Chief Magistrate
South Tucson Municipal Court
Post Office Box 7307
South Tucson, Arizona 85725-7307
(520) 917-1569 FAX: (520) 628-9619

Manuel D. Figueroa, Magistrate
Somerton Municipal Court
Post Office Box 458
Somerton, Arizona 85350
(520) 627-8152 FAX: (520) 627-1076

Richard A. Garcia, Magistrate
Phoenix Municipal Court
300 West Washington
Phoenix, Arizona 85003-2103
(602) 261-6994 FAX: (602) 534-4779

David O. Lagunas, Presiding Magistrate
Municipal Court
206 Griffin Avenue
Winkelman, Arizona 85292
(520) 356-7854 FAX: (520) 356-7709

Michael Morales, Magistrate
Chandler Municipal Court
255 East Buffalo Street
Chandler, Arizona 85225-5519
(602) 786-7872 FAX: (602) 786-2613

Rosendo Morales, Jr., Magistrate
San Luis Municipal Court
23222 First Street
Post Office Box 1170
San Luis, Arizona 85349-0429
(520) 627-2020, Ext. 18 FAX: (520) 627-2335

Victor M. Ortiz, Magistrate
Mesa Municipal Court
245 West Second Street
Mesa, Arizona 85201-6599
(480) 644-3408 FAX: (408) 644-2927

Diana T. Quezada, Presiding Judge, Magistrate
Tolleson Municipal Court
9555 West Van Buren Street
Tolleson, Arizona 85353
(623) 936-7111 FAX: (623) 936-7117

Laura Reckart, Magistrate, Judge Pro Tempore
Phoenix Municipal Court
300 West Washington
Phoenix, Arizona 85003-2103
(602) 534-3864 FAX: (602) 534-3552

Antonio F. Riojas, Jr., Magistrate
Tucson Municipal Court
103 East Alameda Street
Post Office Box 27210
Tucson, Arizona 85726-7210
(520) 791-3260 FAX: (520) 791-5474

Jose Matias Tafoya, Magistrate
Phoenix Municipal Court
300 West Washington
Phoenix, Arizona 85003-2103
(602) 262-7434 FAX: (602) 495-7383

Gilda M. Terrazas, Magistrate
Municipal Court
Post Office Box 27210
Tucson, Arizona 85726-7210
(520) 791-3260 FAX: (520) 791-4667

County Justice Courts

Raquel Abel, Justice of the Peace, Pro Tempore
Tucson Justice Court
115 North Church Avenue
Tucson, Arizona 85701
(520) 740-3535 FAX: (520) 798-1842

Rachel T. Carrillo, Justice of the Peace
West Phoenix Justice Court
527 West McDowell Road
Phoenix, Arizona 85003
(602) 256-0292 FAX: (602) 256-7959

José Luis Castillo, Jr., Justice of the Peace
Presiding Judge
Tucson Justice Court
115 North Church Avenue
Tucson, Arizona 85701
(520) 740-3505 FAX: (520) 798-1842

Christina Correllejo, Justice of the Peace
Pro Tempore
Greenlee County Justice Court
Post Office Box 517
Clifton, Arizona 85533
(520) 865-4312 FAX: (520) 865-4417

Carmen Dolny, Justice of the Peace
Associate Presiding Judge
Tucson Justice Court
115 North Church Avenue
Tucson, Arizona 85701
(520) 798-3502 FAX: (520) 798-1842

Andrew Gastelum, Justice of the Peace
Maryvale Justice Court
4622 West Indian School Road, # D10
Phoenix, Arizona 85031-2970
(623) 245-0432 FAX: (623) 245-1216

Martin Green, Justice of the Peace
Pro Tempore
Tucson Justice Court
115 North Church Avenue
Tucson, Arizona 85701
(520) 798-3505 FAX: (520) 798-1842

Joe Guzman, Justice of the Peace
9550 West Van Buren, Suite 6
Tolleson, Arizona 85353
(602) 936-1449 FAX: (602) 936-4859

Luis V. Guzman, Justice of the Peace
Tolleson Justice Court
9550 West Van Buren, Suite #6
Tollerson, Arizona 85353-2827
(602) 506-8380 FAX: (623) 936-4859

David Juarez, Justice of the Peace
Pro Tempore
Tucson Justice Court
115 North Church Avenue
Tucson, Arizona 85701
(520) 798-3505 FAX: (520) 798-1842

Marie A. Lorona, Justice of the Peace
Eloy Justice Court
Post Office Box 586
Eloy, Arizona 85231
(520) 466-9221 FAX: (520) 466-4473

Manuel Manuz, Presiding Justice of the Peace
for Clifton and Morenci, Arizona
Greenlee County Justice Court
Post Office Box 517
Clifton, Arizona 85533
(520) 865-4312 FAX: (520) 865-4417

David C. Morales, Justice of the Peace
Bisbee Justice Court
207 North Judd Drive
Bisbee, Arizona 85603
(520) 432-9540 FAX: (520) 432-9594

Mark Ryan Moran, Presiding City Magistrate
Flagstaff Justice Court
15 North Beaver
Flagstaff, Arizona 86001
(520) 774-1401, Ext. 113 FAX: (520) 556-1284

Tomas M. Rodriguez, Justice of the Peace
for Maricopa and Stanfeld
Arizona Pinal County Justice Court
Post Office Box 201
Maricopa, Arizona 85239
(520) 568-2451 FAX: (520) 568-2924

Joe A. Ruiz, Justice of the Peace
for Mammoth and San Manuel
Arizona Pinal County Justice Court
Post Office Box 777
Mammoth, Arizona 85618
(520) 487-2262 FAX: (520) 487-2585

James J. Sedillo, Presiding Justice of the Peace
100 East Birch Avenue
Flagstaff, Arizona 86001
(520) 779-6806 FAX: (520) 779-6744

Nellie A. Soto, Justice of the Peace
Pro Tempore
Justice Court Services
111 West Monroe, Suite 820
Phoenix, Arizona 85003-1336
(602) 506-1337 FAX: (602) 506-8582

Gracie Villarreal, Justice of the Peace
Pro Tempore
Justice Court Services
111 West Monroe, Suite 820
Phoenix, Arizona 85003-1836
(602) 506-1337 FAX: (602) 506-8582

Joseph A. "Fred" Lizarraga, Judge
Town Court
155 North Tegner, Suite B
Wickenburg, Arizona 85390
(520) 684-5451, Ext. 509 FAX: (602) 306-1580

ARKANSAS: (0)

CALIFORNIA: (215)

FEDERAL

Ferdinand F. Fernandez, Circuit Judge
U. S. Court of Appeals for the Ninth Circuit
Richard H. Chambers Court of Appeals Building
125 South Grand Avenue
Pasadena, California 91105-1621
(626) 229-7121 FAX: (626) 229-7142

Richard A. Paez, Circuit Judge
U. S. Court of Appeals for the Ninth Circuit
125 South Grand Avenue
Pasadena, California 91105-1621.
(626) 229-7180 FAX: (626) 229-7459

Arthur L. Alarcon, Sr., Circuit Judge
U. S. Court of Appeals for the Ninth Circuit
U. S. Courthouse
312 North Spring Street, Suite 160
Los Angeles, California 90012
(213) 894-2693 FAX: (213) 894-2996

Lourdes G. Baird, Judge
U. S. District Court
for the Central District of California
Edward R. Roybal Federal Building
and Courthouse
255 East Temple Street, Chambers 770
Los Angeles, California 90012
(213) 894-1478 FAX: (213) 894-4392

Irma E. Gonzales, Judge
U. S. District Court
for the Southern District of California
Edward J. Schwartz U. S. Courthouse
880 Front Street
San Diego, California 92101-8900
(619) 557-7107 FAX: (619) 702-9928

Carlos Moreno, Judge
U. S. District Court
for the Central District of California
312 North Spring Street
Los Angeles, California 90012
(213) 894-3067 FAX: (213) 894-8860

Manuel L. Real, Judge
U. S. District Court
for the Central District of California
U. S. Courthouse
312 North Spring Street
Los Angeles, California 90012
(213) 894-5267 FAX: (213) 894-3389

Edward J. Garcia, Sr. Judge
U. S. District Court
for the Eastern District of California
501 "I" Street
Sacramento, California 95814
(916) 930-4225

Edward A. Infante, Chief Magistrate Judge
U. S. District Court
for the Northern District of California
2112 U. S. Courthouse
280 South First Street
San Jose, California 95113-3008
(408) 535-5340 FAX: (408) 535-5569

Ernest M. Robles, Bankruptcy Judge
U. S. District Court
for the Central District of California
Edward R. Roybal Federal Building
and Courthouse - 15th Floor
255 East Temple Street
Los Angeles, California 90012-3300
(213) 894-1522 FAX: (213) 894-1536

Administrative Law Judges

Antonio Acevedo-Torres
Administrative Law Judge
Office of Hearings and Appeals
Social Security Administration
2031 Howe Avenue, Suite 200
Sacramento, California 95825
(916) 566-7200 FAX: (916) 925-5014

Joel Martinez, Administrative Law Judge
Office of Hearings and Appeals
Social Security Administration
Grosvenor Plaza
150 South Los Robles Avenue, Suite 500
Pasadena, California 91101
(626) 793-1121 FAX: (626) 793-3080

Plauche Villere, Jr., Administrative Law Judge
Office of Hearings and Appeals
Social Security Administration
2031 Howe Avenue, Suite 200
Sacramento, California 95825
(916) 566-7200 FAX: (916) 925-5014

Isabel Bronzina, U. S. Immigration Judge
606 South Olive Street – Suite 1500
Los Angeles, California 90014
(213) 894-2811 FAX: (213) 894-5196

Zsa Zsa De Paolo, U. S. Immigration Judge
Otay Mesa Border Station
2500 Paseo Inernational
San Diego, California 92173
(619) 661-3119 FAX: (619) 557-6405

Lawrence N. DiConstanzo
U. S. Immigration Judge
550 Kearney Street, Suite 800
San Francisco, California 94108
(Mailing address: Post Office Box 2326
San Francisco, California 94126-2326)
(415) 705-4415 FAX: (415) 705-4418

Ignacio Fernandez-Valdes
U. S. Immigration Judge
401 West A Street, Suite 800
San Diego, California 92101-7904
(619) 557-6052 FAX: (619) 557-6405

Alberto E. Gonzalez, U. S. Immigration Judge
550 Kearney Street, Suite 800
San Francisco, California 94108
(Mailing Address: Post Office Box 2326
San Francisco, California 94126-2326)
(415) 705-4415 FAX: (415) 705-4418

Henry P. Ipema, U. S. Immigration Judge
606 South Olive Street, Suite 1500
Los Angeles, California 90014
(213) 894-2811 FAX: (213) 894-5196

Rose Callantes Peters, U. S. Immigration Judge
INS San Pedro Service Processing Center
2001 Seaside Avenue, Room 136
San Pedro, California 90731
(310) 241-2424 FAX: Call on phone first

Joseph M. Ragusa, U. S. Immigration Judge
401 West A Street, Suite 800
San Diego, California 92101
(619) 557-6052 FAX: (619) 557-6405

Laura L. Ramirez, U. S. Immigration Judge
550 Kearny Street, Suite 800
San Francisco, California 94108
(Mailing Address: Post Office Box 2326
San Francisco, California 94126-2326)
(415) 705-4415 FAX: Call on phone first

Michael K. Suarez, U. S. Immigration Judge
Mira Loma Facility
45100 North 60th Street, West
Lancaster, California 93536
(661) 942-8633 FAX: Call on phone first

STATE

Supreme Court

John Arguelles, Justice (Retired)
California Supreme Court
Gibson, Dunn and Crutcher
Jamboree Center
4 Park Plaza
Irvine, California 92614-8557
(249) 451-3976

Cruz Reynoso, Justice (Retired)
California Supreme Court
Kaye, Scholer, Fierman, Hays and Handlen
1999 Avenue of the Stars, Suite 1600
Los Angeles, California 90067—6022
(310) 788-1000

Courts of Appeal

Consuelo Maria Callahan, Associate Justice
Court of Appeal
Third Appellate District
914 Capitol Mall
Sacramento, California 95814-8189
(916) 654-0209 FAX: (916) 653-5043

Ramona Godoy-Perez, Associate Justice
Court of Appeal
Second Appellate District, Division Five
300 South Spring Street
Floor 2 - North Tower
Los Angeles, California 90013-1213
(213) 830-7333 FAX: (213) 897-7813

Gilbert Nares, Associate Justice
Court of Appeal
Fourth Appellate District Division One
750 B Street, Suite 300
San Diego, California 92101-8189
(619) 645-2761 FAX: (619) 645-2939

Reuben A. Ortega, Associate Justice
Court of Appeal
Second Appellate District, Division One
300 South Spring Street
Floor 2 - North Tower
Los Angeles, California 90013-1213
(213) 830-7533 FAX: (213) 897-7813

Manuel A. Ramirez, Presiding Justice
Court of Appeal – Fourth Appellate District
Division Two
3389 Twelfth Street
Riverside, California 92501
(909) 248-0200 or 0302 FAX:(909) 248-0235

Trial Court

Gregory W. Alarcon, Judge
Superior Court
State of California, County of Los Angeles
210 West Temple Street
Los Angeles, California 90012-3210
(213) 974-5855 FAX: (213) 680-8867

Paul H. Alvarado, Judge
Superior Court
State of California, County of San Francisco
Civic Center Courthouse
400 McAllister Street - Room 305
San Francisco, California 94102 - 4514
(415) 551-3732 FAX: (415) 551-5721

Robert Ambrose, Judge
Superor Court
State of California, County of Santa Clara
161 North First Street
San Jose, California 95113-1090
(408) 229-2268 FAX: (408) 298-0562

Conrad Richard Aragon, Judge
Superior Court
State of California, County of Los Angeles
East Los Angeles Court
214 South Fetterly Avenue
Los Angeles, California 90022-1644
(213) 780-2007 FAX: (213) 780-3538

Rafael A. Arreola, Judge
Superior Court
State of California, County of San Diego
Central Division
220 West Broadway
San Diego, California 92101-3409
(Mailing Address: Post Office Box 122724
San Diego, California 92112-2724)
(619) 531-3825 FAX: (619) 615-6968

Elvira S. Austin, Judge
Superior Court
State of California, County of Los Angeles
415 West Ocean Avenue
Long Beach, California 90802
(562) 491-6240 FAX: (562) 435-5469

Henry T. Barela, Judge
Superior Court
State of California, County of Los Angeles
214 South Fetterly Avenue
Los Angeles, California 90022-1644
(213) 780-2015 FAX: (213) 780-3538

Antonio Barreto, Jr., Judge
Superior Court
State of California, County of Los Angeles
Culver City Court
4130 Overland Avenue
Post Office Box 2785
Culver City, California 90230-3788
(310) 202-3152 or 202-3153 FAX: (310) 559-7016

Carlos Bea, Judge
Superior Court
State of California, County of San Francisco
Civic Center Courthouse
400 McAllister Street
San Francisco, California 92102
(415) 551-3788 FAX: (415) 551-5721

Roger T. Benitez, Judge
Superior Court
State of California, County of Imperial
939 West Main Street County Courthouse
El Centro, California 92243-2842
(760) 339-4709 FAX: (760) 352-3184

Paul R. Bernal, Judge
Superior Court
State of California, County of Santa Clara
San Jose Facility
200 West Hedding Street
San Jose, California 95110-1717
(408) 299-2599 FAX: (408) 920-0229

Francisco P. Briseno, Judge
Superior Court
State of California, County of Orange
Post Office Box 1994
Santa Ana, California 92702-1994
(714) 834-4596 FAX: (714) 834-6171

Carlos A. Cabrera, Judge
Superior Court
State of California, County of Fresno
Fowler Division
127 East Merced Street
Post Office Box 400
Fowler, California 93625-2438
(559) 834-5141or 834-3215 FAX: (559) 864-3160
Sanger Division
619 N Street
Sanger, California 93657-2484
(559) 875-7158

Delores Carr, Judge
Superior Court
State of California, County of Santa Clara
200 West Hedding Street
San Jose, California 95119
(408) 299-2267 FAX: (408) 920-0229

Cecilia Patricia Castellanos, Judge
Superior Court,
State of California, County of Alameda
Wiley W. Manuel Courthouse
661 Washington Street
Oakland, California 94607-3986
(510) 268-7606 or 268-7647 FAX: (510) 268-7695

Federico Castro, Judge
Superior Court
State of California, County of San Diego
Post Office Box 122724
San Diego, California 92112-2724
(619) 531-3844 or 531-3434 FAX: (619) 615-6968

Roy B. Cazares, Judge
Superior Court
State of California, County of San Diego
South County Regional Center
500 Third Avenue
Chula Vista, California 92110-2724
(619) 691-4632 FAX: (619) 691-4438

Victor E. Chave, Presiding Judge
Superior Court
State of California, County of Los Angeles
111 North Hill Street
Los Angeles, California 90012
(213) 974-5600 FAX: (213) 680-1263

Victoria M. Chavez, Judge
Superior Court
State of California, County of Los Angeles
11701 South La Cienega Boulevard
Los Angeles, California 90045-6260
(310) 727-6106 FAX: (310) 727-0501

Matias R. Contreras, Judge
Superior Court
State of California, County of Imperial
939 West Main Street County Courthouse
El Centro, California 92243-2842
(760) 339-4362 FAX: (760) 352-3184

Jaime R. Corral, Judge
Superior Court
State of California, County of Los Angeles
Alhambra Court
150 West Commonwealth
Alahambra, California 91801
(626) 308-5172 FAX: (626) 281-5754

Geary D. Cortes, Judge
Superior Court
State of California, County of San Diego
Juvenile Court
2851 Meadow Lark Drive
San Diego, California 92123
(858) 694-4411 FAX: (858) 694-4773

Raymond Ayala Cota, Judge
Superior Court
State of California, County of Imperial
939 West Main County Courthouse
El Centro, California 92243-2842
(760) 339-4257 FAX: (760) 352-3184

Marta S. Diaz, Judge
Superior Court
State of California, County of San Mateo
Hall of Justice - 400 County Center
Redwood City, California 94063-1655
(650) 363-4807 FAX: (650) 363-4698

Rudolph A. Diaz, Judge
Superior Court
State of California, County of Los Angeles
Eastlake Juvenile Court - Room J
1601 Eastlake Avenue
Los Angeles, California 90033-1094
(323) 226-8911 FAX: (323) 221-2223.

Steven Dylina, Judge
Superior Court
State of California, County of San Mateo
Hall of Justice - 400 County Center
Redwood City, California 94063-1655
(650) 363-4817 FAX: (650) 363-4698

Leopoldo Edward Dorado, Judge
Superior Court
State of California, County of Alameda
Hayward Hall of Justice
24405 Amador Street
Hayward, California 94544-1369
(510) 670-5629 FAX: (510) 670-5687

Peter Paul Espinoza, Judge
Superior Court
State of California, County of Los Angeles
7500 East Imperial Highway
Downey, California 90242-3378
(562) 803-7027 FAX: (562) 803-6392

Ruffo Espinoza, Jr., Judge
Superior Court
State of California, County of Los Angeles
210 West Temple Street
Los Angeles, California 90012-3210
(213) 974-5765 FAX: (213) 680-7804

Teresa Estrada-Mullaney, Judge
Superior Court
State of California, County of San Luis Obispo
County Government Center
1035 Palm Street
San Luis Obispo, California 93408-2510
(805) 781-5473 FAX: (805) 781-1071

Alfonso Fernandez, Judge
Superior Court
State of California, County of Santa Clara
Hall of Justice
190 West Hedding Street
San Jose, California 95110-1706
(408) 299-2383 FAX: (408) 280-6057 or 295-5074

Francisco F. Firmat, Judge
Superior Court
State of California, County of Orange
700 Civic Center Drive West
Post Office Box 1994
Santa Ana, California 92702-1994
(714) 834-5005 FAX: (714) 834-5555

Rogelio R. Flores, Judge
Superior Court
State of California, County of Santa Barbara
Miller Division
312-M East Cook Street
Santa Maria, California 93454-5165
(805) 346-7596 FAX: (805) 346-7591 or 346-7553

David A. Garcia, Judge
Superior Court, State of California
County of San Francisco
Civic Center Courthouse
400 McAllister Street
San Francisco, California 94102-4514
(415) 551-3721 FAX: (415) 551-5721

Michael T. Garcia, Judge
Superior Court
State of California, County of Sacramento
720 Ninth Street
Sacramento, California 95814-1311
(916) 874-5684 FAX: (916) 874-5620

George Genesta, Judge
Superior Court
State of California, County of Los Angeles
214 South Fetterly Avenue
Los Angeles, California 90022-1644
(323) 780-2011 FAX: (323) 780-3538

Nazario "Tito" Gonzales, Judge
Superior Court
State of California, County of Santa Clara
190 West Hedding Street
San Jose, California 95110-1706
(408) 299-2331 FAX: (408) 295-5074
E-mail: ngonzales@mail.mct.CO.SantaClara.CA.US

Auturo F. Gutierrez, Judge
Superior Court
State of California, County of Ventura
Hall of Justice - 800 South Victoria Avenue
Ventura, California 93009-0001
Mailing Address: Post Office Box 6489
Ventura, California 93006-6489
(805) 654-2960 FAX: (805) 654-5110

Phillip S. Gutierrez, Judge
Superior Court
State of California, County of Los Angeles
Whittier Court
7339 South Painter Avenue
Whittier, California 90602-1891
(562) 907-3143 FAX: (562) 696-9285

George C. Hernandez, Jr., Judge
Superior Court,
State of California, County of Alameda
Gale-Schenone Hall of Justice
5672 Stoneridge Drive
Pleasanton, California 94588-8501
(925) 551-6886 FAX: (925) 734-9568

Daniel S. Lopez, Judge
Superior Court
State of California, County of Los Angeles
1427 West Covina Parkway
West Covina, California 91790-2799
(626) 813-3318 FAX: (626) 338-7364

Ana Maria Luna, Judge
Superior Court
State of California, County of Los Angeles
111 North Hill Street - Department No. 9
Los Angeles, California 90012-3117
(213) 974-5598 FAX: (213) 680-1043

Albert H. Maldonado, Judge
Superior Court
State of California, County of Monterey
Salinas Division
240 Church Street
Post Office Box 1051
Salinas, California 93902-1051
(831) 755-5050 FAX: (831) 755-5483

John L. Martinez, Presiding Judge
Superior Court
State of California, County of Los Angeles
Alhambra Court
150 West Commonwealth Avenue
Alhambra, California 91801-3794
(626) 308-5505 FAX: (626) 570-4667 or 281-5754

Robert M. Martinez, Judge
Superior Court
State of California, County of Los Angeles
400 Civic Center Plaza
Pomona, California 91766-3229
(909) 620-3084 or 620-3086 FAX: (909) 620-6547

Victor L. Miceli, Judge
Superior Court
State of California, County of Riverside
Civil Department
4050 Main Street
Riverside, California 92501-3703
(909) 955-1462 or 955-1735 FAX: (909) 955-1751

Marilyn B. Miles, Judge
Superior Court
State of California, County of Humboldt
Humboldt County Courthouse
825 Fifth Street
Eureka, California 95501-1153
(707) 269-1294 FAX: (707) 445-7041

Raymond D. Mireles, Judge
Superior Court
State of California, County of Los Angeles
300 East Walnut Street
Pasadena, California 91101-1566
(626) 356-5673 FAX: (626) 796-5706

Aurelio Munoz, Judge
Superior Court
State of California, County of Los Angeles
Central District - Civil Courts Courthouse
111 North Hill Street
Los Angeles, California 90012-3117
(213) 974-5667 FAX: (213) 625-8536

Frances Munoz, Judge
Superior Court
State of California, County of Orange
Harbor Justice Center
4601 Jamboree Road
Newport Beach, California 92660-2595
(949) 476-4707 FAX: (949) 476-4752

Gregory Munoz, Judge
Superior Court
State of California, County of Orange
Post Office Box 1994
Santa Ana, California 92702-1994
(714) 834-3347 or 834-3139 FAX: (714) 834-5555

Rene Navarro, Judge
Superior Court
State of California, County of Santa Clara
Terraine Street Facility
115 Terraine Street
San Jose, California 95110-2449
(408) 299-2817 FAX: (408) 920-0229

Ralph Nunez, Judge
Superior Court
State of California, County of Fresno
1100 Van Ness Street
Fresno, California 93721-2059
(559) 488-3037 FAX: (559) 488-3263

Frank J. Ochoa, Jr., Judge
Superior Court
State of California, County of Santa Barbara
1100 Anacapa Street
Santa Barbara, California 93101-2099
Post Office Box 21107
Santa Barbara, California 93121-1107
(805) 568-3160 FAX: (805) 568-2899

James S. Otero, Judge
Superior Court
State of California, County of Los Angeles
111 North Hill Street, Division 83
Los Angeles, California 90012-3117
(213) 974-5707 FAX: (213) 625-8536

Yvette M. Palanzuelos, Judge
Superior Court
State of California, County of Los Angeles
Los Angeles Superior Court - Rio Hondo
11234 Valley Boulevard
El Monte, California 91731-3288
(626) 575-4143 or 575-4124 FAX: (626) 444-9029

David D. Perez, Judge
Superior Court
State of California, County of Los Angeles
Santa Monica Court
1725 Main Street
Santa Monica, California 90401-3299
(310) 260-3729 FAX: (310) 394-4847

Daniel Solis Pratt, Judge
Superior Court
State of California, County of Los Angeles
12720 Norwalk Boulevard
Norwalk, California 90650-3188
(562) 807-7244 FAX: (562) 863-8757

Daniel P. Ramirez, Judge
Superior Court
State of California, County of Los Angeles
Huntington Park Court
6548 Miles Avenue
Post Office Box 609
Huntington Park, California 90255-0609
(323) 586-6371 FAX: (323) 589-6769

Victor E. Ramirez, Judge
Superior Court
State of California, County of San Diego
Vista Regional Center
325 South Melrose Drive
Vista, California 92083
(760) 806-6309 FAX: (760) 806-6319

Richard E. Rico, Judge
Superior Court
State of California, County of Los Angeles
214 South Fetterly Avenue
Los Angeles, California 90022-3117
(323) 780-2009 FAX: (323) 780-3538

Maria P. Rivera, Judge
Superior Court
State of California, County of Contra Costa
725 Court Street - Department 7
Post Office Box 911
Martinez, California 94553-1233
(925) 646-4007 FAX: (925) 646-1312

Jesse I. Rodriguez, Judge
Superior Court
State of California, County of Los Angeles
7500 East Imperial Highway
Downey, California 90242-3378
(562) 803-7012 FAX: (562) 803-6392

Jésus Rodriguez, Supervising Judge
Superior Court, State of California
County of San Diego – South County Division
500 Third Avenue, Department 16
Chula Vista, California 92110
(619) 691-4784 FAX: (619) 691-4584

Luis Antonio Rodriguez, Judge
Superior Court,
State of California, County of Orange
Lamoreaux Justice Center
341 The City Drive
Post Office Box 14169
Fullerton, California 92863-1569
(714) 935-7227 FAX: (714) 935-6465

Richard R. Romero, Judge
Superior Court
State of California, County of Los Angeles
South District - Long Beach
415 West Ocean Boulevard
Long Beach, California 90802-4591
(562) 491-6134 FAX: (562) 435-5469

Gilbert Ruiz, Judge
Superior Court
State of California, County of Los Angeles
Rio Hondo Court
11234 East Valley Boulevard
El Monte, California 91731-3288
(626) 575-4147 FAX: (626) 575-4111

Raul A. Sahagun, Judge
Superior Court
State of California, County of Los Angeles
Whittier Court - 7339 South Painter Avenue
Whittier, California 90602-1891
(562) 907-3142 or 907-3127 FAX: (562) 696-9285

John Steven Salazar, Judge
Superior Court
State of California, County of Santa Cruz
Main Courthouse - 701 Ocean Street
Santa Cruz, California 95060
(831) 454-3800 or 454-3802 FAX: (831) 454-3297

Alex Saldamando, Judge
Superior Court
State of California, County of San Francisco
Civic Center Courthouse
400 McAllister Street - Room 318
San Francisco, California 94102-4512
(415) 551-3738 FAX: (415) 551-5721

Yvonne T. Sanchez, Judge
Superior Court
State of California, County of Los Angeles
Whittier Court
7339 South Painter Avenue
Whittier, California 90602-1891
(562) 907-3145 FAX: (562) 696-9285

Teresa Sanchez-Gordon, Judge
Superior Court
State of California, County of Los Angeles
150 West Commonwealth Avenue
Alhambra, California 91801-3722
(626) 308-5163 FAX: (626) 281-5754

Jose Sandoval, Judge
Superior Court
State of California, County of Los Angeles
18501 South Figueroa Street
Gardenia, California 90248
(310) 768-1178 FAX: (310) 516-7967

Robert Sandoval, Judge
Superior Court
State of California, County of Los Angeles
Glendale Courthouse
600 East Broadway
Glendale, California 91206
(818) 500-3540 or 500-3525

Phillip L. Soto, Judge
Superior Court
State of California, County of Los Angeles
South Gate Court
8640 California Avenue
South Gate, California 90280-3074
(323) 563-4006 FAX: (323) 569-4840

Ricardo A. Torres, Judge
Superior Court
State of California, County of Los Angeles
Central Civil West
600 South Commonwealth Avenue
Los Angeles, California 90005-4001
(213) 974-5687 or 974-8893
FAX: (213) 625-8536 or 381-7951

Juan Ulloa, Judge
Superior Court
State of California, County of Imperial
Calexico Court Department
415 East 4th Street
Calexico, California 92231-2887
(760) 357-3726 FAX: (760) 357-6571

Carlos A. Uranga, Judge
Superior Court
State of California, County of Los Angeles
150 West Commonwealth Avenue
Alhambra, California 91801-3794
(626) 308-5511 FAX: (626) 570-4667 or 281-5754

Luis R. Vargas, Judge
Superior Court
State of California, County of San Diego
South County Regional Center
500 Third Avenue
Chula Vista, California 91910
(619) 691-4770 FAX: (619) 691-4584

David C. Velasquez, Judge
Superior Court
State of California, County of Orange
700 Civic Center Drive West
Post Office Box 1994
Orange, California 92613-1569
(714) 834-4710 FAX: (714) 834-5555

Jose Angel Velasquez, Judge
Superior Court
State of California, County of Monterey
Salinas Division - 240 Church Street
Post Office Box 1051
Salinas, California 93901-2683
(831) 755-5050 FAX: (831) 759-9857 or 755-5483

Luis M. Villareal, Judge
Superior Court
State of California, County of Solano
Hall of Justice - 600 Union Avenue
Post Office Box 2463
Fairfield, California 94533-0246
(707) 421-7410 FAX: (707) 421-7439

Carlos G. Ynostroza, Judge
Superior Court
State of California, County of Alameda
Wiley W. Manuel Courthouse
661 Washington Street
Oakland, California 94607-3986
(510) 268-7606 or 268-7656 FAX: (510) 268-7695

Barbara A. Zuniga, Judge
Superior Court
State of California, County of Contra Costa
A. F. Bray Building
1020 Ward Street
Martinez, California 94553-1233
(925) 646-4002 FAX: (925) 646-1312

Retired Superior Court Trial Judges

Robert T. Baca, Judge (Retired)
Superior Court
State of California, County of Kern
1415 Truxtun Avenue
Bakersfield, California 93301-5216
(661) 868-4934

Arthur Baldonado, Judge (Retired)
Superior Court
State of California, County of Los Angeles
111 North Hill Street
Los Angeles, California 90012
(213) 974-5615 FAX: (213) 625-8536

Luis Cardenas, Judge (Retired)
Superior Court
State of California, County of Orange
JAMS/Endispute
500 North State College Boulevard
Orange, Califronia 92668
(714) 939-1300 FAX: (714) 939-1787

Raymond Cardenas, Judge (Retired)
Superior Court
State of California, County of Los Angeles
1262 El Hito Circle
Pacific Palisades, California 90272
(310) 230-0346 FAX: (310) 230-0396

William J. Fernandez, Judge (Retired)
Superior Court
State of California, County of Santa Clara
Post Office Box 718
Menlo Park, California 94026
(415) 321-5022 or (408) 292-6021

Richard Ibanez, Judge (Retired)
Superior Court
State of California, Los Angeles County
600 South Commonwealth Street
Los Angeles, California 90005-4001
(213) 351-8739 FAX: (213) 381-7951

Leopoldo G. Sanchez, Judge (Retired)
Superior Court
State of California, County of Los Angeles
5428 East Beverly Boulevard, Suite 5
Los Angeles, California 90022
(213) 728-8076

State Bar Court

Carlos E. Velarde, Judge
State Bar Court
1149 South Hill Street – Courtroom E
Los Angeles, California 90015
(213) 765-1400 FAX: (213) 765-1568

Municipal Court Retired Judges

Charles E. Aguilar, Judge (Retired)
Municipal Court, Stanislaus County
1100 "I" Street
Modesto, California 95353
(209) 525-6509

Reynaldo Chaparro, Judge (Retired)
Municipal Court, Downey Judicial District
1316 South Gembrook Avenue
Hacienda Heights, California 91745-2516
(818) 968-4371

Armando O. Rodriguez, Judge (Retired)
Municipal Court, Fresno County
1100 Van Ness Street
Fresno, California 93724
(209) 299-4964

Gilbert Rudy Ruiz, Judge (Retired)
Municipal Court, East Los Angeles
Judicial District
214 South Fetterly Avenue
Los Angeles, California 90022
(213) 780-2011 FAX: (213) 780-3538

Superior Court Commissioners

Abby Abinanti, Commissioner
Superior Court
State of California, County of San Francisco
Juvenile Dependency
United Family Law Court
400 McAllister Street - Room 406
San Francisco, California 94102-4514
(415) 551-3750 FAX: (415) 551-4002

Patrick M. Alderete, Commissioner
Superior Court
State of California, County of Kern
1215 Truxtun Avenue
Bakersfield, California 93301-4698
(661) 868-2608 FAX: (661) 861-2207 or 868-2620

Ralph Amado, Commissioner
Superior Court
State of California, County of Los Angeles
San Pedro Court
505 South Centre Street
San Pedro, California 90731-3332
(310) 519 6014

Maria Arroyo-Tobin, Commissioner
Superior Court
State of California, County of San Diego, San Diego Juvenile Court
Post Office Box 122724
San Diego, California 92112-2724
(619) 694-4227 FAX: (619) 694-4773

Steven Belasco, Commissioner
Superior Court
State of California, County of Santa Barbara
Miller Division
312-M East Cook Street
Santa Barbara, California
(805) 346-7596 FAX: (805) 346-7553 or 346-7553

Carla Bonilla, Commissioner
Superior Court
State of California, County of Sonoma
Juvenile Court
Hall of Justice - Room 107-J
600 Administration Drive
Santa Rosa, California 95403-2818
(707) 537-6307

Daniel F. Calabro, Commissioner
Superior Court
State of California, County of Los Angeles
Glendale Court
600 East Broadway
Glendale, California 91206-4395
(818) 500-3525 FAX: (818) 548-0486

Norma Castellanos-Perez
Family Support Commissioner
Superior Court
State of California, County of Tulare
County Civic Center
Visalia, California 93291-1228
(559) 730-2570 FAX: (559) 737-4290 or 730-2676

Nancy A. Cisneros, Commissioner
Superior Court
State of California, County of Fresno
1100 Van Ness
Fresno, California 93724-0002
(559) 488-3060 FAX: (559) 488-3263

Manuel J. Covarrubias, Commissioner
Superior Court
State of California, County of Ventura
Hall of Justice - 800 South Victoria Avenue
Ventura, California 93009-0001
(Mailing Address: Post Office Box 6489
Ventura, California 93006-6484)
(805) 654-2995 FAX: (805) 654-5110

Edward DeCaro, Commissioner
Superior Court
State of California, County of Santa Barbara
Figeroa Division
118 East Figueroa Street
Santa Barbara, California 93101-2168
(805) 568-2766 FAX: (805) 568-2847

Ruben De La Torre, Commissioner
Superior Court
State of California, County of Ventura
Hall of Justice
800 South Victoria Avenue
Ventura, California 93009-0001
(Mailing Address: Post Office Box 6489
Ventura, California 93006-6489)
(805) 654-2960 FAX: (805) 654-5110

Carol Muehling Frausto, Commissioner
Superior Court
State of California, County of San Diego
South County Division
500 Third Avenue
Chula Vista, California 91910
(619) 619-4763 FAX: (619) 691-4584

Albert Garcia, Commissioner
Superior Court
State of California, County of Los Angeles
Children's Court
201 Centre Plaza Drive #3
Monterey Park, California 91754-2158
(323) 526-6416 FAX: (323) 881-3794 or 526-6688

Arthur A. Garcia, Commissioner
Superior Court
State of California, County of Santa Barbara
Juvenile Court
812-B East Cook Street
Santa Maria, California 93454-5369
(805) 934-6353 FAX: (805) 934-6355

Patricia Garcia, Commissioner
Superior Court
State of California, County of San Diego
Central Division
220 West Broadway
San Diego, California 92101-3409
(Mailing Address: Post Box 122724
San Diego, California 92112-2724)
(619) 531-3024 FAX: (619) 531-4428

Ernest A. Lopez, Commissioner
Superior Court
State of California, County of Los Angeles
Inglewood Court
1 Regent Street
Inglewood, California 90301-1295
(310) 419-5105 FAX: (310) 673-5931

Gilbert Lopez, Commissioner
Superior Court
State of California, County of Los Angeles
Huntington Park Court
6548 Miles Avenue
Post Office Box 609
Huntington Park, California 90255-0609
(323) 586-6377 FAX: (323) 589-6769

Hugo J. Loza, Commissioner
Superior Court
State of California, County of Tulare
Juvenile Court Commissioner
County Civic Center - Room 303
Visalia, California 93291
(559) 713-3157 FAX: (559) 730-2676

Katherine Lucero, Commissioner
Superior Court
State of California, County of Santa Clara
Terraine Street Facility
115 Terraine Street
San Jose, California 95110-2449
(408) 299-4390 FAX: (408) 998-8174

Antonio Luna, Commissioner
Superior Court
State of California, County of Los Angeles
214 South Fetterly Avenue
Los Angeles, California 90022-1644
(323) 780-2001 FAX: (323) 780-3538

Marilyn Martinez-Kading, Commissioner
Superior Court
State of California, County of Los Angeles
Children's Court
201 Centre Plaza Drive #3
Monterey Park, California 91754-2158
(323) 526 6414 FAX: (323) 526-6688 or 881-3794

Armando V. Moreno, Commissioner
Superior Court
State of California, County of Los Angeles
Juvenile Court
400 Civic Center Plaza
Ponoma, California 91766-3201
(909) 620-3088 FAX: (909) 620-3051

Donald A. Plantanida, Commissioner
Superior Court
State of California, County of Del Norte
Pittsburg Court
45 Civic Avenue
Post Office Box 431
Pittsburg, California 94565-0431
(925) 427-8151

James Odriozola, Commissioner
Superior Court
State of California, County of Orange
Lamoreaux Justice Center
341 The City Drive
Orange, California 92868
(Mailing Address: Post Office Box 14169
Orange, California 92863-1569)
(714) 935-7465 FAX: (714) 935-7638

Daniel Martin Ornelas, Commissioner
Superior Court
State of California, County of San Diego
East County Regional Center
250 East Main Street
El Cajon, California 92020
(760) 940-4378 FAX: (760) 940-4812

Robert Padia, Commissioner
Superior Court
State of California, County of Riverside
Hall of Justice
4100 Main Street
Riverside, California 92501-3626
(909) 955-4097 or 955-1603 FAX: (909) 955-4056

Preciliano P. Recendez, Commissioner
Superior Court
State of California, County of Los Angeles
Los Padrinos Juvenile Center
7281 East Quill Drive
Downey, California 90242
(562) 940-8846 FAX: (562) 803-6392

Jose A. Rodriguez, Commissioner
Superior Court
State of California, County of Los Angeles
Rio Hondo Court
11234 East Valley Boulevard
El Monte, California 91731-3288
(626) 575-4144 FAX: (626) 575-4111 or 444-9029

Gregory H. Saldivar, Commissioner
Superior Court
State of California, County of Santa Clara
Los Gatos Facility - 14205 Capri Drive
Los Gatos, California 95032
(408) 370-1404 FAX: (408) 379-1438

Steven P. Sanora, Commissioner
Superior Court
State of California, County of Los Angeles
11234 East Valley Boulevard
El Monte, California 91731-3288
(626) 575-4134 FAX: (626) 444-9029

Salvador Sarmiento, Commissioner
Superior Court, State of California
County of Orange – Lamoreaux Justice Center
341 The City Drive
Orange, California 92868
(Mailing Address: Post Office Box 14169
Orange, California 92863-1569)
(714) 935-7869 FAX: (7:4) 935-6465

Collette N. Serio, Commissioner
Superior Court
State of California, County of Los Angeles
Pasadena Court
300 East Walnut Street
Pasadena, California 91101-1566
(626) 356-5665 FAX: (818) 568-3903

Phillip A. Silva, Commissioner
Superior Court
State of California, County of Fresno
1100 Van Ness
Fresno, California 93724-0002
(559) 488-3392 FAX: (559) 448-5349

David Sotelo, Commissioner
Superior Court
State of California, County of Los Angeles
East Los Angeles Court
214 South Fetterly Avenue
Los Angeles, California 90022-1644
(323) 780-2005 FAX: (323) 780-3538

William R. Torres, Commissioner
Superior Court
State of California, County of Los Angeles
Torrance Court
825 Maple Avenue
Torrance, California 90503-5096
(310) 222-6826 FAX: (310) 328-7535

Louie L. Vega, Commissioner
Superior Court
State of California, County of Kern
1215 Truxtun Avenue
Bakersfield, California 93301-4698
(661) 868-2608 FAX: (661) 861-2207 or 868-2620

Referees

Maria T. Arroyo-Prokop, Referee
Superior Court
State of California, County of San Diego
Juvenile Court
2851 Meadow Lark Drive
San Diego, California 92123
(858) 694-4224 FAX: (858) 694-4773

Guillermina G. Byrne, Referee
Superior Court
State of California, County of Los Angeles
Children's Court
201 Centre Plaza Drive #3
Monterey Park, California 91754-2158
(323) 526-6407 FAX: (323) 881-3794

Steff Padilla, Referee
Superior Court
State of California, County of Los Angeles
Juvenile Court
200 West Compton Boulevard - Room 902
Compton, California 90220
(323) 526-6655 FAX: (323) 526-6670

Frank Soliz, Referee
Superior Court
State of California, County of Los Angeles
Pasadena Branch
300 East Walnut Street
Pasadena, California 91101
(626) 356-5507 FAX: (626) 397-9175

Administrative Law Judges and Administrative Judges

Martin E. Aguilar, Administrative Law Judge
Unemployment Insurance Appeals Board
2400 Venture Oaks Way, Suite 100
Sacramento, California 95833
(916) 263-6706 FAX: 263-6765

Octavio Aguilar, Administrative Law Judge
Unemployment Insurance Appeals Board
3517 Camino del Rio South, Suite 100
San Diego, California 92108
(619) 237-7596 FAX: (619) 521-3334

Jack Alanis, Administrative Law Judge
Department of Social Services
State Hearings Division
811 Wilshire Boulevard, Room 1118
Los Angeles, California 90017
(213) 833-2000 FAX: (213) 833-223-3204
E-mail: jalanis@dss.ca.gov

Juan J. Arcellana
Chief Administrative Law Judge
Unemployment Insurance Appeals Board
2400 Venture Oaks Way, Suite 150
Sacramento, California 95833
(916) 263-6722 or 454-3889
FAX: (916) 263-6764 or 263-6765

Richard C. Armendariz
Administrative Law Judge
Unemployment Insurance Appeals Board
6 Centerpointe Drive, Fourth Floor
La Palma, California 90623
(714) 652-5560 FAX: (714) 562-5592

Miguel AuClair-Valdez
Administrative Law Judge
Unemployment Insurance Appeals Board
160 West Santa Clara Street, Suite 800
San Jose, California 95113-1700
(408) 277-1561 FAX: (408) 277-1217

George S. Avila, Administrative Law Judge
Unemployment Insurance Appeals Board
2400 Venture Oaks Way, Suite 100
Sacramento, California 95833
(916) 263-6706 FAX: (916) 263-6765

Jose Banuelos, Administrative Law Judge
Department of Social Services
State Hearings Division
2550 Mariposa Mall # 3088
Fresno, California 93721
(559) 445-5775 FAX: (559) 449-5779
E-mail: jbanuelo@dss.ca.gov

Peter Apodaca Barbosa
Administrative Law Judge
Unemployment Insurance Appeals Board
2400 Venture Oaks Way, Suite 100
Sacramento, California 95833
(916) 263-6706 FAX: (916) 263-6765

Esther L. Beltran, Administrative Law Judge
Unemployment Insurance Appeals Board
2550 Mariposa Street, Suite 4067
Fresno, California 93721
(559) 445-5363 FAX: (559) 248-2546

Jorge Carrillo, Administrative Law Judge
Unemployment Insurance Appeals Board
2400 Venture Oaks Way, Suite 100
Sacramento, California 95833
(916) 263-6706 FAX: (916) 263-6765

John R. Castello
Chief Administrative Law Judge
Department of Social Services
State Hearings Division
744 P Street, MS 17-50
Sacramento, California 95814
(916) 657-3550 FAX: (916) 651-6258
E-mail: jcastell@dss.ca.gov

Emma Alicia Castillo
Administrative Law Judge
Unemployment Insurance Appeals Board
2400 Venture Oaks Way, Suite 100
Sacramento, California 95833
(916) 263-6820 FAX: (916) 263-6837

Federico G. Chavez, Administrative Law Judge
Unemployment Insurance Appeals Board
2400 Venture Oaks Way, Suite 100
Sacramento, California 95833
(916) 263-6707 FAX: (916) 263-6765

Joel G. Contreras, Chief Administrative Law Judge, Appellate Operations
Unemployment Insurance Appeals Board
2400 Venture Oaks Way, Suite 100
Sacramento, California 95833
(916) 263-6706 FAX: (916) 263-6765

Ignacio S. Cota, Administrative Law Judge
Unemployment Insurance Appeals Board
433 North Fair Oaks Avenue, Suite 200
Pasadena, California 91109-7038
(626) 304-7962 FAX: (626) 304-7981

Cassie De Silvestore, Administrative Law Judge
Unemployment Insurance Appeals Board
9800 La Cienega Boulevard, Suite 901
Inglewood, California 90301
(310) 337-4302 FAX: (310) 337-4395

Rufino Diaz, Administrative Law Judge
Department of Social Services
State Hearings Division
355 West Grand Avenue, Suite 4
Escondido, California 92025-2649
(760) 735-5070 FAX: (760) 735-5084
E-mail: rufino.diaz@dss.ca.gov

Rodolfo Echeverria, Administrative Law Judge
Alcohol Beverage Control Agency
107 South Broadway
Los Angeles, California 90012
(916) 263-7963 FAX: (916) 263-7975

Albert Escobedo, Administrative Law Judge
Unemployment Insurance Appeals Board
300 South Spring Street, Room 1502
Los Angeles, California 90013
(213) 897-5267 FAX: (213) 897-5282

Carmen S. Flores, Administrative Law Judge
Unemployment Insurance Appeals Board
185 Berry Street, Suite 200, Lobby 5
San Francisco, California 94107
(415) 357-3801 FAX: (415) 357-3830

Humberto Flores, Administrative Law Judge
Office of Administrative Hearings
320 West First Street #630
Los Angeles, California 90012
(213) 897-4542 or 576-7200 FAX: (213) 897-4548

Joseph Garcia, Administrative Law Judge
Unemployment Insurance Appeals Board
2400 Venture Oaks Way, Suite 100
Sacramento, California 95833
(916) 263-6706 FAX: (916) 263-6765

Anthony Gurrola, Administrative Law Judge
Department of Social Services
State Hearings Division
355 West Grand Avenue, Suite 4
Escondido, California 92025-2649
(760) 735-5070 FAX: (760) 735-5084
E-mail: anthony.gurrola@dss.ca.gov

Susana Halfon, Administrative Law Judge
Unemployment Insurance Appeals Board
2400 Venture Oaks Way, Suite 100
Sacramento, California 95833
(916) 263-6706 FAX: (916) 263-6765

Alfred Haro, Administrative Law Judge
Unemployment Insurance Appeals Board
1515 Clay Street
Oakland, California 94612
(510) 286-0695 FAX: (510) 622-3929

Robert L. Hernandez, Administrative Law Judge
Unemployment Insurance Appeals Board
2550 Mariposa Street, Suite 4067
Fresno, California 93721
(209) 445-5363 FAX: (209) 248-2546

Richard J. Lopez, Administrative Law Judge
Office of Administrative Hearings
320 West Fourth Street, #630
Los Angeles, California 90013
(213) 576-7200 FAX: (213) 897-4548

Alfredo Magallanes, Administrative Law Judge
Unemployment Insurance Appeals Board
300 South Spring Street, Room 1502
Los Angeles, California 90013
(213) 897-5267 FAX: (213) 897-5282

Miguel D. Martin, Administrative Law Judge
Unemployment Insurance Appeals Board
4604 Venuta West Court
Elk Grove, California 95758
(916) 263-6706 FAX: (916) 263-6765

Richard G. Martinez, Administrative Law Judge
Unemployment Insurance Appeals Board
3517 Camino del Rio South, Suite 100
San Diego, California 92108
(619) 237-7596 FAX: (619) 521-3334

Ronald Mendoza, Administrative Law Judge
Department of Social Services
State Hearings Division
811 Wilshire Boulevard, Room 1118
Los Angeles, California 90017
(213) 897-4441 FAX: (213) 897-3204
E-mail: rmendoza@dss.ca.gov

Joseph D. Montoya, Administrative Law Judge
Office of Administrative Hearings
320 West First Street, #630
Los Angeles, California 90013
(213) 620-4650 or 576-7200 FAX: (213) 897-4548

Ricardo Florian Munoz
Chief Administrative Law Judge
Unemployment Insurance Appeals Board
300 South Spring Street, Room 1502
Los Angeles, California 90013
(213) 897-5267 FAX: (213) 897-5282

Charles D. Nabarrete, Administrative Law Judge
Unemployment Insurance Appeals Board
300 South Spring Street, Room 1502
Los Angeles, California 90013
(213) 897-5267 FAX: (213) 897-5282

Rene Quintanilla, Administrative Law Judge
Department of Social Services
Disability Hearing Bureau
State Hearings Division
8745 Folsom Boulevard, Suite 220
Sacramento, California 95826
(916) 229-4174 FAX: (916) 229-4194

Samuel D. Reyes, Administrative Law Judge
Office of Administrative Hearings
314 West First Street
Los Angeles, California 90012
(213) 897-4542 or 576-7200 FAX: (213) 897-4548

Richard J. Reyna, Administrative Law Judge
Workers Compensation Appeal Board
107 South Broadway, Room 407
Los Angeles, California 90012
(213) 897-1551

Georgina Torres Rizk
Administrative Law Judge
Unemployment Insurance Appeals Board
300 South Spring Street, Room 1502
Los Angeles, California 90013
(213) 897-5267 FAX: (213) 897-5282

Margarita Vela Rosenthal
Administrative Law Judge
Unemployment Insurance Appeals Board
1515 Clay Street, Suite 902
Oakland, California 94612-1413
(510) 622-3900 FAX: (510) 622-3929

Juliette Sarmiento, Administrative Law Judge
Unemployment Insurance Appeals Board
3517 Camino Del Rio South
San Diego, California 92108
(619) 622-3900 FAX: (619) 521-3334

Louis Sotello, Administrative Law Judge
Unemployment Insurance Appeals Board
2400 Venture Oaks Way, Suite 100
Sacramento, California 95883
(916) 263-6706 FAX: (916) 263-6765

Victor Tan, Administrative Law Judge
Unemployment Insurance Appeals Board
1515 Clay Street, Suite 902
Oakland, California 94612-1413
(510) 622-3900 FAX: (510) 622-3929

Melvin Trujillo, Administrative Law Judge
Department of Social Services
State Hearings Division
8745 Folsom Boulevard, Suite 220
Sacramento, California 95826
(916) 229-4187 FAX: (916) 229-3483

Zaida F. Vierra-Hackett
Administrative Law Judge
Unemployment Insurance Appeals Board
160 West Santa Clara Street, Suite 800
San Jose, California 95113-1700
(408) 277-1561 FAX: (408) 277-1217

Martha Villanea, Administrative Law Judge
Unemployment Insurance Appeals Board
9800 La Cienega Boulevard, Suite 901
Inglewood, California 90301
(310) 337-4302 FAX: (310) 337-4395

Mary Lou Villar, Administrative Law Judge
Unemployment Insurance Appeals Board
300 South Spring Street, Room 1502
Los Angeles, California 90013
(213) 897-5267 FAX: (213) 897-5282

Rafael E. Vivero, Administrative Law Judge
Workers Compensation Appeals Board
107 South Broadway
Los Angeles, California 90012-4419
(213) 897-1551

COLORADO: (32)

FEDERAL

Carlos F. Lucero, Judge
U. S. Court of Appeals for the Tenth Circuit
420 Byron White U. S. Courthouse
1823 Stout Street
Denver, Colorado 80257
(303) 844-2200 FAX: (303) 844-2201

Donald E. Cordova, Judge
U. S. Bankruptcy Court
U. S. Custom House
721 19th Street
Denver, Colorado 80202-2508
(303) 844-2525 FAX: Call on phone first

Administrative Law Judges

David J. Cordova, Immigation Judge
Byron G. Rogers Federal building
1961 Stout Street, Room 1403
Denver, Colorado 80294
(303) 844-5815 FAX: Call on phone first

STATE

Supreme Court

Alex J. Martinez, Justice
Colorado Supreme Court
Colorado State Judicial Building
2 East Fourteenth Avenue
Denver, Colorado 80203-2116
(303) 837-3761 FAX: (303) 864-4531
E-mail: alex.martinez@judicial.state.co.us

Luis D. Rovira, Chief Justice (Retired)
4810 East 6th Avenue
Denver, Colorado 80220
(303) 322-6943

Court of Appeals

Jose D. L. Marquez, Judge
Colorado Court of Appeals – Room 350
2 East 14th Avenue
Denver, Colorado 80203
(303) 837-3786 FAX: (303) 837-3702
E-mail: jose.marquez@judicial.state.co.us

Henry E. Nieto, Judge
Colorado Court of Appeals
2 East 14th Avenue
Denver, Colorado 80203
(303) 837-3711 FAX: (303) 837-3702
E-mail: henry.nieto@judicial.state.co.us

District Court Trial Judges

Theresa M. Cisneros, Judge
El Paso County District Court
Fourth Judicial District
20 East Vermijo
Colorado Springs, Colorado 80903
(719) 448-7528 FAX: (719) 329-7046
E-mail:theresa.cisneros@judicial.state.co.us

Charles Dennis Maes, Chief Judge
Pueblo County District Court
Tenth Judicial District
320 West 10th Street
Pueblo, Colorado 81003
(719) 583-7011 FAX: (719) 583-7126
E-mail: dennis.maes@judicial.state.co.us

Jesse C. Manzanares, Chief Judge
Las Animas County District Court
Third Judicial District
200 East First Street, Suite 304
Trinidad, Colorado 81082
(719) 846-3316 FAX: (719) 846-9367
E-mail: jesse.manzanares@judicial.state.co.us

Lawrence A. Manzanares, Judge
Denver District Court
1437 Bannock Street
Denver, Colorado 80202
(303) 640-2366 FAX: (720) 865-8485
E-mail: lawrence.manzanares@judicial.state.co.us

Frank Martinez, Judge
Denver District Court
2nd Judicial District
1437 Bannock Street
Denver, Colorado 80202
(303) 640-2981 FAX: (303) 640-2089
E-mail: frank.martinez@judicial.state.co.us

Gilbert A. Martinez, Chief Judge
El Paso County District Court
4th Judicial District
20 East Vermijo
Colorado Springs, Colorado 80903
(719) 448-7536 FAX: (719) 329-7046
E-mail: gilbert.martinez@judicial.state.co.us

Michael Martinez, Judge
Denver District Court
1437 Bannock Street, Room 256
Denver, Colorado 80202
(720) 865-8304 FAX: (720) 865-8485
Michael.martinez@judicial.state.co.us

Victor Reyes, Judge
Pueblo County District Court
320 West 10th Street
Pueblo, Colorado 81003
(719) 583-7001 FAX: (719) 583-7184
E-mail: victor.reyes@judicial.state.co.us

Gloria Rivera, Judge
Denver District Court
2nd Judicial District
1437 Bannock Street
Denver, Colorado 80202
(303) 640-2208 FAX: (720) 865-8485
E-mail: gloria.rivera@judicial.state.co.us

John Jess Vigil, Judge
Adams County District Court
17th Judicial District
1931 East Bridge Street
Brighton, Colorado 80601
(303) 654-3270 FAX: (303) 654-3216
E-mail: john.vigil@judicial.state.co.us

David E. Ramirez, Judge, Sr. Judge
1437 Bannock Street, Room 159
Denver, Colorado 80202
(303) 640-2868 FAX: (303) 740-3410

County Trial Judges

David Archuleta, Judge
Boulder County Court
Boulder Justice Center
Post Office Box 4249
Boulder, Colorado 80306-4249
(303) 441-3735 FAX: (303) 441-4824
E-mail: david.archuleta@judicial.state.co.us

Judy Lynn Archuleta, Judge
Jefferson County Court
100 Jefferson County Parkway
Golden, Colorado 80401
(303) 271-6220 FAX: (303) 271-6272
E-mail: judy.archuleta@judicial.state.co.us

Ed Casias, Judge
Summit County
Post Office Box 185
501 North Park Avenue
Breckenridge, Colorado 80424
(970) 453-2272 FAX: (970) 453-1134
E-mail: ed.casias@judicial.state.co.us

Martin Gonzales, Judge
Alamosa County Court
702 Fourth Street
Alamosa, Colorado 81101
(970) 589-6213 FAX: (970) 589-4998
E-mail: martin.gonzales@judicial.state.co.us

Gilbert A. Guitierrez, Judge
Weld County Court
Weld County Courthouse
Post Office Box C
901 Ninth Avenue
Greeley, Colorado 80632
(970) 351-4609 FAX: (970) 356-4000
E-mail: gilbert.guitierrez@judicial.state.co.us

Sylvia A. Manzanares, Judge
El Paso County Court
20 East Vermijo Street, Suite 323
Colorado Springs, Colorado 80903
(719) 448-7628 FAX: (719) 329-7046
E-mail: sylvia.manzanares@judicial.state.co.us

Aleene Ortiz-White, Judge
Denver County Court
City and County Building
1437 Bannock Street
Denver, Colorado 80202
(303) 640-3074 FAX: (303) 640-1065
E-mail: aleene.ortiz-white@ci.denver.co.us

Ernest J. Ruybalid, Judge
Pueblo County Court
Pueblo County Judicial Building
320 West Tenth Street
Pueblo, Colorado 81003
(719) 583-7044 FAX: (719) 583-7184
E-mail: ernest.ruybalid@judicial.state.co.us

Michael H. Trujillo, Judge
Rio Grande County Court
Drawer W, 6th and Cherry
Del Norte, Colorado 81132
(719) 657-3394 FAX: (719) 657-2636
E-mail: michael.trujillo@judicial.state.co.us

Sharon M. Gallegos, Judge
Aurora Municipal Court
15401 East Alameda Drive
Aurora, Colorado 80112
(303) 341-8900 FAX: (303) 739-6532

Magistrates

John Barajas, Magistrate
Adams County District Court
1100 Judicial Center Drive
Brighton, Colorado 80601
(303) 654-3726 FAX: (303) 654-3216

Evelyn Hernandez-Sullivan, Magistrate
El Paso County District Court
20 East Vermijo
Colorado Springs, Colorado 80903
(719) 448-7567 FAX: (719) 329-7046

Janet L. Rodriguez, Magistrate
County Court
Larimer County Courthouse
200 West Oak
Ft. Collins, Colorado 80522
(970) 498-7566 FAX: (970) 498-6110

Administrative Law Judges

Edward R. Martinez
Administrative Law Judge
Office of Administrative Hearings
1120 Lincoln Street #1400
Denver, Colorado 81503
(970) 248-7340 FAX: (970) 248-7342

CONNECTICUT: (6)

FEDERAL

José A. Cabranes, Judge
U. S. Court of Appeals
for the Second Circuit U. S. Courthouse
141 Church Street
New Haven, Connecticut 96510
(203) 867-8782 New York FAX: (212) 857-2331

STATE

Carmen Elisa Espinosa, Judge
Superior Court
20 Franklin Square
New Britain, Connecticut 06051
(860) 515-5303 FAX: (860) 515-5051
E-mail: Carmen.Espinosa@jud.state.ct.us

Carmen Lopez, Judge
Superior Court
300 Grand Street
Waterbury, Connecticut 06702
(203) 596-4033 FAX: (203) 596-4488
E-mail: Carmen.Lopez@jud.state.ct.us
also 784 Fairfield Avenue
Bridgeport, Connecticut 06604
(203) 579-6544 FAX: (203) 382-8430

Antonio Robaina, Judge
Superior Court
1 Court Street
Middletown, Connecticut 06457
(860) 343-6570 FAX: (860) 343-6589
E-mail: Antonio.Robaina@jud.state.ct.us
also 920 Broad Street
Hartford, Connecticut 06106
(860) 556-8290 FAX: (860) 566-1658

Eddie Rodriguez, Jr., Judge
Superior Court
1061 Main Street
Bridgeport, Connecticut 06604
(203) 579-6540 FAX: (203) 382-8406 or 579-6928
E-mail: Eddie.Rodriguez@jud.state.ct.us

Jorge Simon, Judge
Superior Court
410 Center Street
Manchester, Connecticut 06040
(860) 646-5874 FAX: (860) 645-7540
E-mail: Jorge.Simon@jud.state.ct.us

DELAWARE: (0)

DISTRICT OF COLUMBIA: (12)

FEDERAL

Ricardo M. Urbina, Judge
U. S. District Court
for the District of Columbia
333 Constitution Avenue, N.W., Room 4311
Washington, D.C. 20011
(202) 273-0576 FAX: (202) 273-0328

Juan F. Vasquez, Judge
U. S. Tax Court
400 Second Street, N.W., Room 406
Washington, D.C. 20217
(202) 606-8986 FAX: Call on phone first

Administrative Law Judges

Jose Anglada, Sr. Administrative Law Judge
Department of Health and Human Services
Departmental Appeals Board
Civil Remedies Division
Room 637-D, HHH Building
500 Independence Avenue, N.W.
Washington, D.C. 20202
(202) 260-0677 FAX: (202) 205-0278

Alfonso J. Montano, Administrative Law Judge
Department of Health and Human Services
Departmental Appeals Board
Civil Remedies Division
Room 637-D, HHH Building
200 Independence Avenue, S.W.
Washington, D.C. 20201
(202) 260-0677 FAX: (202) 205-0278

Gladys O. Collazo, Administrative Judge
U. S. Equal Employment
Opportunity Commission
1400 L Street, N.W., Suite 200
Washington, D.C. 20000
(202) 275-2377 FAX: (202) 275-0076

Jeannette Walters-Marquez
Administrative Judge
U. S. Equal Employment
Opportunity Commission
1400 L. Street, N.W., Suite 200
Washington, D.C. 20005
(202) 275-7377 FAX: (202) 275-6834

STATE

Appellate Court

Vanessa Ruiz, Judge
Court of Appeals
of the District of Columbia
500 Indiana Avenue, N.W.
Washington, D.C. 20001
(202) 879-2761 FAX: (202) 626-8840

Trial Court Judges

Rafael Diaz, Judge
Superior Court
of the District of Columbia
500 Indiana Avenue, N.W.
Chambers JM 430
Washington, D.C. 20001
(202) 879-1125 FAX: (202) 879-0170

Jose M. López, Judge
Superior Court
of the District of Columbia
500 Indiana Avenue, N.W.
Chambers 3410
Washington, D.C. 20001
(202) 879-7877 FAX: (202) 879-0144

Hiram Puig-Logo, Judge
Superior Court
of the District of Columbia
500 Indiana Avenue, N.W.
Chambers 1020
Washington, D.C. 20001
(202) 879-8370 FAX: (202) 879-8374

Court Hearing Commissioner

Aida L. Melendez, Hearing Commissioner
Superior Court
of the District of Columbia
500 Indiana Avenue, N.W., Room # 4450
Washington, D.C. 20001
(202) 879-1552 FAX: (202) 393-6738
E-mail: melenda@dcsc.gov

Administrative Law Judges

Blanca E. Torres, Administrative Judge
District of Columbia Office of Employee Appeals
717 14th Street, N.W., 3rd Floor
Washington, D.C. 20005
(202) 727-0004 FAX: (202) 727-5631

FLORIDA: (63)

FEDERAL

Rosemary Barkett, Circuit Judge
U. S. Court of Appeals for the Eleventh Circuit
Federal Justice Building
99 N.E. Fourth Street, Suite 1223
Miami, Florida 33132
(305) 536-7335 FAX: (305) 536-7382

Adalberto Jose Jordan, Judge
U. S. District Court
for the Southern District of Florida
301 North Miami Avenue, 8th Floor
Miami, Florida 33128
(305) 523-5560 FAX: Call on phone first

Federico A. Moreno, Judge
U. S. District Court
for the Southern District of Florida
99 N.E. 4th Street, Suite 1061
Miami, Florida 33132
(305) 523-5110 FAX: Call on phone first

Jose A. Gonzalez, Jr., Sr. Judge
U. S. District Court
for the Southern District of Florida
299 East Broward Boulevard, Room 205-D
Fort Lauderdale, Florida 33101
(954) 769-5560 FAX: (954) 356-7987

Administrative Law Judges

Jose Anglada, Administrative Law Judge
Office of Hearings and Appeals
Social Security Administration
Times Building, Suite #200
100 North Ashley Drive
Tampa, Florida 33602
(813) 228-2581 FAX: (813) 228-2603

Edward Bayouth-Babilonia
Administrative Law Judge
Office of Hearings and Appeals
Social Security Administration
3733 University Boulevard, West - Suite 210
Jacksonville, Florida 32217-2100
(904) 232-2248 FAX: (904) 232-3961

Blanca B. de la Torre, Administrative Law Judge
Office of Hearings and Appeals
Social Security Administration
51 S.W. First Avenue, Suite 1600
Miami, Florida 33130-9651
(305) 536-5761 FAX: (305) 536- 4788

Ruben O. Figueroa, Administrative Law Judge
Office of Hearings and Appeals
Social Security Administration
Glenridge Building
3505 Lake Lynda Drive, Suite 300
Orlando, Florida 32817
(407) 380-2345 FAX: (407) 380-3658

Appolo Garcia, Administrative Law Judge
Office of Hearings and Appeals
Social Security Administration
Glenridge Building
3505 Lake Lynda Drive, Suite 300
Orlando, Florida 32817
(407) 308-2345 FAX: (407) 308-3658

Dolores S. McNerney, Administrative Law Judge
Office of Hearings and Appeals
Social Security Administration
3733 University Boulevard, West - Suite 210
Jacksonville, Florida 32217-2100
(904) 232-2248 FAX: (904) 232-3961

Jose G. Rolon Rivera, Administrative Law Judge
Office of Hearings and Appeals
Social Security Administration
51 S.W. First Avenue - Suite 1600
Miami, Florida 33130-9651
(305) 536-5761 FAX: (305) 536-4788

Ruben Rivera, Jr., Administrative Law Judge
Office of Hearings and Appeals
Social Security Administration
New River Center, Suite 1550
200 East Las Olas Boulevard
Fort Lauderdale, Florida 33301
(954) 356-7385 FAX: (954) 356-7901

Marcos A. Rodriguez, Administrative Law Judge
Office of Hearings and Appeals
Social Security Administration
New River Center, Suite 1550
200 East Las Olas Boulevard
Fort Lauderdale, Florida 33301
(954) 356-7385 FAX: (954) 356-7901

Charles D. Romo, Administrative Law Judge
Office of Hearings and Appeals
Social Security Administration
3733 University Boulevard, West - Suite 210
Jacksonville, Florida 32217-2100
(904) 232-2248 FAX: (904) 232-3961

Albert Tutera, Administrative Law Judge
Office of Hearings and Appeals
Social Security Administration
Glenridge Building - Suite 300
3505 Lake Lynda Drive
Orlando, Florida 32817
(407) 380-2345 FAX: (407) 380-3658

U. S. Immigration Judges

Teofilo Chapa, U. S. Immigration Judge
155 South Miami Avenue, Room 800
Miami, Florida 33130
(305) 530-6455 Ext. 179 FAX: (305) 530-7001

Denise A. Marks Lane, U. S. Immigration Judge
155 South Miami Avenue, 8th Floor
Miami, Florida 33130
(305) 530-6455 Ext. 208 FAX: (305) 530-7001

Pedro A. Miranda, U. S. Immigration Judge
155 South Miami Avenue, Room 800
Miami, Florida 33130
(305) 530-6455 Ext. 206 FAX: (305) 530-7001

Roberto Moreno, U. S. Immigration Judge
5449 South Semoran Boulevard, Suite 200
Orlando, Florida 32803
(407) 648-6565 FAX: (407) 648-6911

Rafael B. Ortiz-Segura, U. S. Immigration Judge
5449 South Semoran Boulevard, Suite 200
Orlando, Florida 32803
(407) 648-6565 FAX: (407) 648-6911

Anthony J. Randall, U. S. Immigration Judge
135 South Miami Avenue, 8th Floor
Miami, Florida 33130
(305) 530-6455 Ext. 214 FAX: (305) 530-7001

Elisa M. Sukkar, U. S. Immigration Judge
135 South Miami Avenue, Room 800
Miami, Florida 33130
(305) 530-6455 Ext. 174 FAX: (305) 530-7001

Lilliana Torreh-Bayouth
U. S. Immigration Judge
155 South Miami Avenue, 8th Floor
Miami, Florida 33130
(305) 530-6455 Ext. 215 FAX: (305) 530-7001

STATE

Appellate Judges

Mario P. Goderich, Judge
Third District Court of Appeals
2001 Southwest 117th Avenue
Miami, Florida 33175-1716
(305) 229-3200 FAX: (305) 229-3206

Juan Ramirez, Judge
Third District Court of Appeals
2001 Southwest 117th Avenue
Miami, Florida 33175-1716
(305) 229-3200 FAX: (305) 229-3206

E. J. Salcines, Judge
Second District Court of Appeals
801 East Twiggs Street, Suite 600
Tampa, Florida 33602
(813) 272-3430 FAX: (813) 229-6534

Rodolfo Sorondo, Jr., Judge
Third District Court of Appeals
2001 Southwest 117th Avenue
Miami, Florida 33175-1716
(305) 229-3200 FAX: (305) 229-3206

Circuit Court Judges

F. Dennis Alvarez, Chief Judge
Circuit Court
Thirteenth Judicial Circuit
419 Pierce Street, Room 214"F"
Tampa, Florida 33602
(813) 272-6022 FAX: (813) 272-5522

Ronald V. Alvarez, Judge
Circuit Court
Fifteenth Judicial Circuit
Palm Beach County Courthouse
205 North Dixie Highway
West Palm Beach, Florida 33401
(561) 274-1415 FAX: Call on phone first

Rex Barbas, Judge
Circuit Court
Thirteenth Judicial Circuit
800 East Kennedy Boulevard, Room 122
Tampa, Florida 33602-3549
(813) 272-5450 FAX: (813) 276-2329

Gisela Cardonne, Judge
Circuit Court
Eleventh Judicial Circuit
1500 Dade County Courthouse
73 West Flagler Street
Miami, Florida 33130
(305) 375-5429 FAX: (305) 375-4211

Manuel A. Crespo, Judge
Circuit Court
Eleventh Judicial Circuit
Richard E. Gerstein Justice Building, Room 625
1351 Northwest 12th Street
Miami, Florida 33125
(305) 548-5536 FAX: (305) 548-5555

Pedro P. Echarte, Jr., Judge
Circuit Court
Eleventh Judicial Circuit
Room 602, R.E.G. Building
1351 Northwest 12th Street
Miami, Florida 33125
(305) 548-5403 FAX: (305) 548-5555

Jack Espinosa, Jr., Judge
Circuit Court
Thirteenth Judicial Circuit
419 Pierce Street, Room 214A
Tampa, Florida 33602-3549
(813) 301-7288 FAX: (813) 276-8015

Margarita G. Esquiroz, Judge
Circuit Court
Eleventh Judicial Circuit
Dade County Courthouse, Room 505
73 West Flagler Street
Miami, Florida 33130
(305) 375-5484 FAX: (305) 375-4211

Alex E. Ferrer, Judge
Circuit Court
Eleventh Judicial Circuit
Richard Gerstein Justice Building, Room 410
1351 N.W. 12th Street
Miami, Florida 33125
(305) 547-7125 FAX: (305) 547-3206

William Fuente, Judge
Circuit Court
Thirteenth Judicial Circuit
800 E. Kennedy Boulevard, Room 124
Tampa, Florida 33602-3549
(813) 272-6851 FAX: (813) 276-2339

Ana Isabel Gardiner, Judge
Circuit Court
Seventeenth Judicial Circuit
201 S.E. Sixth Street, Room 4910
Fort Lauderdale, Florida 33301
(954) 831-6767 FAX: (954) 831-6707

Maria M. Korvick, Judge
Circuit Court
Eleventh Judicial Circuit
73 West Flagler Street, Room 310
Miami, Florida 33130
(305) 375-5386 FAX: (305) 375-4211

Jorge Labarga, Judge
Circuit Court
Fifteenth Judicial Circuit
Palm Beach County Courthouse
205 North Dixie Highway
West Palm Beach, Florida 33401
(561) 355-3964 FAX: (561) Call on phone first

Peter R. Lopez, Judge
Circuit Court
Eleventh Judicial Circuit
Dade County Courthouse
Richard E. Gerstein Justice Building, Room 229
1351 Northwest 12th Street
Miami, Florida 33125
(305) 547-5072 FAX: (305) 548-5555

Manuel Mendendez, Jr., Judge
Circuit Court
Thirteenth Judicial Circuit
375 Hillsborough County Courthouse
419 Pierce Street
Tampa, Florida 33602-3549
(813) 272-6990 FAX: (813) 276-2329

Vivian C. Maye, Judge
Circuit Court
13th Judicial Circuit
332B Hillsborough County Courthouse
419 Pierce Street
Tampa, Florida 3602-3549
(813) 272-5496 FAX: (813) 276-2232

Robert M. Pineiro, Judge
Circuit Court
Eleventh Judicial Circuit
Richard E. Gerstein Justice Building, Room 603
1351 Northwest 12th Street
Miami, Florida 33125
(305) 548-5405 FAX: (305) 548-5555

Frank Quesada, Judge
Circuit Court
Sixth Judicial Circuit
Pinellas County Criminal Justice Center
14250 49th Street North
Clearwater, Florida 33762
(727) 582-7408 FAX: Call on phone first

Jose M. Rodriguez, Judge
Circuit Court
Eleventh Judicial Circuit
County Court of Dade County
Richard E. Gerstein Justice Building
1351 N.W. 12th Street
Miami, Florida 33125
(305) 547-7888 FAX: (305) 548-5555

Jose R. Rodriguez, Judge
Circuit Court
Ninth Judicial Circuit
Juvenile Justice Center
2000 East Michigan Avenue
Orlando, Florida 32806
(407) 836-7590 FAX: (407) 836-7599

Rosa I. Rodriguez, Judge
Circuit Court
Eleventh Judicial Circuit
Juvenile Justice Center, Room 208
3300 Northwest 27th Avenue
Miami, Florida 33142
(305) 638-6873 FAX: (305) 349-6178

County Court Judges

Cecilia M. Altonaga, County Judge
Dade County – Eleventh Judicial Circuit
Dade County Courthouse, Room 60
73 West Flagler Street
Miami, Florida 33130
(305) 548-5476 FAX: (305) 548-5553

Roberto Antonio Arias, County Judge
Duval County – Fourth Judicial Circuit
332 Duval County Courthouse
330 East Bay Street
Jacksonville, Florida 32202
(904) 630-2580 FAX: (904) 630-2579

Mercedes Armas Bach, County Judge
Dade County – Eleventh Judicial Circuit
1351 N.W. 12th Street
Room 102
Miami, Florida 33125
(305) 548-5400 FAX: (305) 548-5332

Robert F. Diaz, County Judge
Broward County
Seventeenth Judicial Circuit
423 Broward County Courthouse
201 Southeast 6th Street
Fort Lauderdale, Florida 33301
(954) 831-7783 FAX: (954) 831-5572

James V. Dominguez, County Judge
Hillsborough County
Thirteenth Judicial Circuit
253 Annex Tower
801 East Twiggs Street
Tampa, Florida 33602-3549
(813) 272-5228 FAX: (813) 272-6635

Frank A. Gomez, County Judge
Hillsborough County
Thirteenth Judicial Circuit
801 East Twiggs Street, Room 202
Tampa, Florida 33602-3549
(813) 272-5778 FAX: (813) 276-2325

Rolando Gonzalez, County Judge
Hillsborough County
Thirteenth Judicial Circuit
Hillsborough County Courthouse
Tampa, Florida 33602
(813) 276-8100 FAX: (813) 276-2437

Robert W. Lee, County Judge
Broward County – Seventeenth Judicial Circuit
201 S.E. Sixth Street
421 Broward County Courthouse
Fort Lauderdale, Florida 33301
(954) 831-5509 FAX: Call on phone first

Manual A. Lopez, County Judge
Hillsborough County
Thirteenth Judicial Circuit
801 East Twiggs Street, Room 225
Tampa, Florida 33602-3549
(813) 276-2781 FAX: (813) 272-6635

Elvin L. Martinez, County Judge
Hillsborough County
Thirteenth Judicial Circuit
801 East Twiggs Street, Room 232
Tampa, Florida 33602-3549
(813) 272-6853 FAX: (813) 272-6635

Wilfredo Martinez, County Judge
Orange County — Ninth Judicial Circuit
425 North Orange Avenue
Orlando, Florida 32801
(407) 836-0521 FAX: (407) 836-0492

Raul C. Palomino, Jr., County Judge
Hillsborough County
Thirteenth Judicial Circuit
800 East Kennedy Boulevard, Room 203B
Plant City, Florida 33566
(813) 272-5122 FAX: (813) 276-2329

Maria Cristina Pereyra-Shuminer
County Judge
Dade County
Eleventh Judicial Circuit
Richard E. Gerstein Justice Building, Room 616
1351 Northwest 12th Street - 9th Floor
Miami, Florida 33125
(305) 252-5848 FAX: (305) Call on phone first

Nancy Perez, County Judge
Palm Beach County — Fifteenth Judicial Circuit
Palm Beach County Courthouse
205 North Dixie Highway
West Palm Beach, Florida 33401
(561) 355-2534 FAX: Call on phone first

Bertila Soto, County Judge
Dade County
Eleventh Judicial Circuit
Richard E. Gerstein Building, Room 519
1351 Northwest 12th Street
Miami, Florida 33125
(305) 547-7069 FAX: Call on phone first

GEORGIA: (4)

FEDERAL

Administrative Law Judges

Charles E. Auslander, Jr.
Administrative Law Judge
Office of Hearings and Appeals
Social Security Administration
3105 Clairmont Road
Atlanta, Georgia 30329
(404) 325-3256 FAX: (404) 325-7856

Carlos Cuevas, U. S. Immigration Judge
55 East Monroe Street, Suite #1900
Chicago, Illinois 60603-5701
(312) 353-7313 FAX: Call on phone first

Ramon Gomez, Administrative Judge
U. S. Merit Systems Protection Board
401 West Peachtree Street, N.W. — Suite #1050
Atlanta, Georgia 30309
(404) 730-2751 FAX: (404) 730-2767
E-mail: ramon.gomez@mspb.gov

STATE

Roland Castellanos, Judge
State Court of Cobb County — Division II
12 E. Park Square
Marietta, Georgia 30090
(770) 528-1700 FAX: (770) 528-1788

GUAM: (0)

HAWAII: (0)

IDAHO: (1)

STATE

Sergio A. Guiterrez, Judge
District Court of Idaho — Third Judicial District
Canyon County Courthouse
1115 Albany Street
Caldwell, Idaho 83605
(208) 454-7370 FAX: (208) 454-7525
E-mail: jdgsag@micron.net

ILLINOIS: (21)

FEDERAL

Ruben Castillo, Judge
U. S. District Court
for the Northern District of Illinois
Everett McKinley Dirksen
U. S. Courthouse
219 South Dearborn Street
Chicago, Illinois 60604
(312) 435-5878 FAX: (312) 435-7578

Ronald A. Guzman, Judge
U. S. District Court
for the Northern District of Illinois
Everett McKinley Dirksen
U. S. Courthouse
219 South Dearborn Street
Chicago, Illinois 60604
(312) 435-5363 FAX: Call on phone first

Manuel Barbosa, Judge
U. S. Bankruptcy Court
Federal Building
211 South Court Street
Rockford, Illinois 61101
(815) 987-4366 FAX: (815) 987-4313

Administrative Law Judge

Carlos Cuevas, U. S. Immigration Judge
55 East Monroe Street, Suite 1900
Chicago, Illinois
(312) 353-7312 or 353-7313 FAX: Call on phone first

State

Court of Appeals

David Cerda, Judge
Appellate Court of Illinois
Richard J. Daley Center, Suite N-1406
160 North LaSalle Street
Chicago, Illinois 60602
(312) 793-4484 FAX: (312) 793-2598

Circuit Court Trial Judges

Robert Lopez Cepero, Judge
Circuit Court of Cook County
1303 Richard J. Daley Center
160 North LaSalle Street
Chicago, Illinois 60602
(312) 443-7959 FAX: (312) 443-4211

David Delgado, Judge
Circuit Court of Cook County
2810 Richard J. Daley Center
160 North LaSalle Street
Chicago, Illinois 60602
(312) 603-3914 FAX: (312) 603-6453

Raymond A. Figueroa, Judge
Circuit Court of Cook County
3002 Richard J. Daley Center
Chicago, Illinois 60605
(312) 603-6667 FAX: (312) 603-6453

Rodolfo Garcia, Judge
Circuit Court of Cook County
2600 South California Avenue
Courtroom 204
Chicago, Illinois 60608
(773) 869-7422 FAX: (773) 869-3093

Edmund Ponce de Leon, Judge
Circuit Court of Cook County
1902 Richard J. Daley Center
160 North LaSalle Avenue
Chicago, Illinois 60602
(312) 603-3008 FAX: (312) 603-6453

Leida J. Santiago, Judge
Circuit Court of Cook County
3008 Richard J. Daley Center
160 North LaSalle Street
Chicago, Illinois 60604
(312) 603-7503 FAX: (312) 603-6453

Associate Judges

Richard A. Aguirre, Associate Judge
20th Judicial District
St. Clair County Building
No. 10 Public Square
Belleville, Illinois 62220
(618) 277-7325 FAX: (618) 277-1398

Consuelo E. Bedoya, Associate Judge
Circuit Court of Cook County
5600 Old Orchard Road, Room 23
Skokie, Illinois 60077
(847) 470-7200 FAX: (847) 470-5133

Grace Guerra Dickler, Associate Judge
Circuit Court of Cook County
5600 Old Orchard Road, Room 24
Skokie, Illinois 60077
(847) 470-7200 FAX: (847) 470-7235

Daniel R. Miranda, Associate Judge
Circuit Court of Cook County
1500 Maybrook Drive, Room 140
Maywood, Illinois 60153
(708) 865-6060 FAX: (708) 865-4952

Ralph Reyna, Associate Judge
Circuit Court of Cook County – Criminal Court
2650 South California Street, Room 504
Chicago, Illinois 60608
(773) 869-3201 FAX: (773) 869-3093

Administrative Law Judges

Gilberto M. Galicia, Administrative Law Judge
Illinois Industrial Commission
100 Randolph Street, Suite 8-200
Chicago, Illinois 60601
(312) 814-6630 FAX: (312) 814-6523

George Irizarry, Administrative Law Judge
Illinois Department of Employment Security
30 Dupage Court
Elgin, Illinois 60120
(847) 888-7891 FAX: (847) 931-2799
E-mail: irizarryusa@netscape.com

Joseph Prieto, Administrative Law Judge
Illinois Industrial Commission
100 West Randolph Street, Suite 8-200
Chicago, Illinois 60601
(312) 814-6500 FAX: (312) 814-6523

Bertha Requena, Administrative Judge
(Hearing Officer)
32 West Randolph Street, 14th Floor
Chicago, Illinois 60601
(312) 609-3795 FAX: Call First

Cynthia Ruiz, Administrative Law Judge
Illinois Department of Employment Security
401 South State Street
Chicago, Illinois 60605
(773) 467-0545 FAX: (773) 467-0827

INDIANA: (7)

FEDERAL

Rudy Lozano, Judge
U. S. District Court
for the Northern District of Indiana
205 Federal Building
507 State Street
Hammond, Indiana 46320
(219) 937-5292 FAX: (219) 937-5200

Administrative Law Judges

Manuel J. Cardé, Administrative Law Judge
Office of Hearings and Appeals
Social Security Administration
Market Square Center
151 North Delaware Street - Suite 300
Indianapolis, Indiana 46204
(317) 226-5802 or 226-5803 FAX: (317) 226-5827

Robert Droker, Administrative Law Judge
Office of Hearings and Appeals
Social Security Administration
Market Square Center
151 North Delaware Street - Suite 300
Indianapolis, Indiana 46204
(317) 226-5802 or 226-5803 FAX: (317) 226-5827

Albert J. Velazquez, Administrative Law Judge
Office of Hearings and Apeals
Social Security Administration
Market Square Center
151 North Delaware Street - Suite 300
Indianapolis, Indiana 46204
(317) 226-5802 or 226-5803 FAX: (317) 226-5827

STATE

Lorenzo Arredondo, Judge
Lake Circuit Court
31st Judicial Circuit
Government Center
2293 North Main Street
Crown Point, Indiana 46307
(219) 755-3488 FAX: (219) 755-3484

Jesse Villalpando, Judge
Lake Superior Court
County Division Four
232 Russell Street
Hammond, Indiana 46320
(219) 933-2808 FAX: (219) 933-2828

Itsia Rivera, Probate Commissioner
Lake Superior Court
3711 Main Street
East Chicago, Indiana 46312
(219) 392-2486 FAX: (219) 392-0047

IOWA: (0)

KANSAS: (2)

FEDERAL

Carlos Murguia, Judge
U. S. District Court
for the District of Kansas
Robert J. Dole U. S. Courthouse
500 State Avenue
Kansas City, Kansas 66101-2437
(913) 551-5817 FAX: (913) 551-5831

STATE

Joseph Bribiesca, Judge
District Court of Kansas
18th Judicial District, Division 22
Sedgwick County Courthouse
525 North Main Street
Wichita, Kansas 67203-3790
(316) 383-7601 FAX: (316) 383-7560

KENTUCKY: (0)

LOUISIANA: (3)

FEDERAL

Administrative Law Judges

Juan C. Marrero, Administrative Law Judge
Office of Hearings and Appeals
Social Security Administration
First Bank Center
One Galleria Boulevard, Suite 2000
Metarie, Louisiana 70001
(504) 589-4556 FAX: (504) 589-4669

Lee J. Romero, Administrative Law Judge
Office of Administrative Law Judges
U. S. Department of Labor
111 Veterans Memorial Boulevard, Suite 530
Metarie, Louisiana 70005
(504) 589-6201 FAX: (504) 588-6268

Elving L. Torres, Administrative Law Judge
Office of Hearings and Appeals
Social Security Administration
1515 Poydras Street, Suite 1600
New Orleans, Louisiana 70112
(504) 589-2418 FAX: (504) 589-4585

MAINE: (1)

Manuel Rodriguez
Chief Administrative Law Judge
Office of Hearings and Appeals
Social Security Administration
One Portland Square - Suite 600
Portland, Maine 04101-4092
(207) 780-3271 FAX: (207) 780-3705

MARYLAND: (2)

STATE

Audrey J.S. Carrion, Associate Judge
Circuit Court for Baltimore City
329 Courthouse East
111 North Calvert Street
Baltimore, Maryland 21202
(410) 396-5130 FAX: (410) 545-7329
E-mail: AudreyCarrion@compuserve.com

Marielsa A. Bernard, Judge
District Court of Maryland
27 Courthouse Square
Rockville, Maryland 20850
(301) 279-1468 FAX: (301) 279-1551

MASSACHUSETTS: (7)

STATE

Isaac Borenstein, Associate Justice
Superior Court
1417 John W. McCormack Post Office
and Courthouse
90 Devonshire Street
Boston, Massachusetts 02109
(617) 788-8130 FAX: (617) 788-8137

Charles M. Grabau, Associate Justice
Middlesex Superior Court
1417 John W. McCormack Post Office
and Courthouse
90 Devonshire Street
Boston, Massachusetts 02109
(617) 788-8130 FAX: (617) 788-8137
E-mail: cgrabau@socialaw.com
Grabau_c@jud.state.ma.us

Maria I. Lopez, Associate Justice
Superior Court
1417 John W. McCormack Post Office
and Courthouse
90 Devonshire Street
Boston, Massachusetts 02109
(617) 788-8130 FAX: 788-7137
E-mail: lopez_m@jud.state.ma.us

Diane Maldonado, Associate Justice
District Court – Chelsea Division
121 Broadway
Chelsea, Massachusetts 02150
(617) 660-9200 FAX: (617) 660-9213
E-mail: maldonado_d@jud.state.ma.us

Luis G. Perez, Associate Justice
Juvenile Court
Worcester County Division
1 Highland Street, Suite #5
Worcester, Massachusetts 01068
(508) 754-8337 FAX: (508) 754-9048
E-mail: perez_l@jud.state.ma.us

Kenneth Cote, Jr., First Justice
District Court
Palmer Division
235 Sykes Street
Palmer, Massachusetts 01069
(413) 283-8916 FAX: (413) 283-6775
E-mail: cote_k@jud.state.ma.us

Jose Sanchez, Justice
Juvenile Court
Essex County Division
10 Railroad Street
Lawrence, Massachusetts 01841
(978) 725-4900 FAX: (978) 725-3878

MICHIGAN: (4)

FEDERAL

Henry D. Perez, Jr., Administrative Law Judge
Office of Hearings and Appeals
Social Security Administration
Crown Pointe, Room 430
25900 Greenfield Road
Oak Park, Michigan 48237
(248) 968-0800 FAX: (248) 968-0205

STATE

Dorothy Comstock Riley, Justice
Supreme Court
500 Woodward Avenue
Detroit, Michigan 48226
(313) 256-9127 FAX: (313) 256-9796

Richard J. Garcia, Judge
Circuit Court
30th Judicial Circuit
333 South Capitol, Suite C
Lansing, Michigan 48901
(517) 483-6500 FAX: (517) 483-6501

Isidore B. Torres, Judge
Circuit Court
3rd Judicial Circuit
1441 St. Antoine Street, Room 510
Detroit, Michigan 48226
(313) 224-2447 FAX: (313) 224-6070

MINNESOTA: (4)

STATE

Isabel Gomez, Judge
District Court
4th Judicial District Court
Hennepin County Government Center C-13
Minneapolis, Minnesota 55487-0421
(612) 348-8284 FAX: (612) 348-2131
E-mail: isabel.gomez@co.hennepin.mn.us

Salvador M. Rosas, Judge
District Court
2nd Judicial District Court
870 County Courthouse
St. Paul, Minnesota 55102
(651) 266-8157 FAX: (651) 767-8948
E-mail: Salvador.Rosas@Courts.State.MN.US

George W. Perez, Judge
Minnesota Tax Court
Judicial Center
25 Constitution Avenue
Saint Paul, Minnesota 55155
(651) 296-1549 FAX: (651) 297-8737
E-mail: George.Perez@Taxcourt.State.MN.US

Manuel J. Cervantes, Referee
2nd Judicial District
City Hall, Room 1640
50 West Kellogg Boulevard
Saint Paul, Minnesota 55102
(651) 266-2895 FAX: (651) 266-2810
E-mail: Manuel.Cervantes@Courts.State.MN.US

MISSISSIPPI: (0)

MISSOURI: (5)

FEDERAL

Fernando J. Gaitan, Jr., Judge
U. S. District Court for
the Western District of Missouri
7552 Charles Evans Whittaker U. S. Courthouse
400 East Ninth Street
Kansas City, Missouri 64106
(816) 512-5630 FAX: (816) 512-5643

STATE

Justine Elisa Del Muro, Judge
Circuit Court
16th Judicial Circuit, Division 4
415 East 12th Street
Kansas City, Missouri 64106
(816) 881-3604 FAX: (816) 881-3233

Marco A. Roldan, Judge
Circuit Court
16th Judicial Circuit, Division 16
308 West Kansas
Independence, Missouri 64050
(816) 881-4416 FAX: (816) 881-8693

Victor M. Rocha, Judge
Kansas City Municipal Court – Division 207
1101 Locust Street
Kansas City, Missouri 64106
(816) 513-2700 FAX: (816) 340-4911

Administrative Law Judge

Salvador L. Alstorre, Sr., Appeals Referee
Division of Employment Security
505 Washington Avenue
St. Louis, Missouri 63101
(314) 340-4830 FAX: (314) 340-4911

MONTANA: (1)

Pedro R. Hernandez, Justice of the Peace
Yellowstone County Courthouse
P.O. Box 35032
Billings, Montana 59107-5032
(406) 256-2898 FAX: (406) 256-2898

NEBRASKA: (1)

Joseph S. Ramirez, Judge
Nebraska Workers' Compensation Court
Hall of Justice - #173
1701 Farnum Street
Omaha, Nebraska 68183-0001
(402) 595-3901 FAX: (402) 595-1299
E-mail: jramirez@wcc.state.ne.us

NEVADA: (4)

Valorie J. Vega, Judge
Eighth Judicial District Court
200 South Third Street
Las Vegas, Nevada 89155-2362
(702) 455-4645 FAX: (702) 382-0006
E-mail: DEPT02EA@co.clark.nv.us

Fernando Guzman, Juvenile Hearing Master
Juvenile Court
3401 East Bonanzo Road
Las Vegas, Nevada 89101
(702) 455-5301 FAX: (702) 455-5551

Fidel Salcedo, Justice of the Peace
Washoe County Courthouse
75 Court Street
Reno, Nevada 89510
(775) 325-6505 FAX: (775) 325-6510

Victor Trujillo, Justice of the Peace
Mineral County Courthouse
First and A Streets
Hawthorne, Nevada 89415
(702) 945-3859 FAX: (702) 945-0700

NEW HAMPSHIRE: (0)

NEW JERSEY: (35)

FEDERAL

Julio M. Fuentes, Judge
U. S. Court of Appeals for the Third Circuit
5032 Martin Luther King, Jr. Federal Building
and U. S. Courthouse
50 Walnut Street
Newark, New Jersey 07102
(973) 645-3831 FAX: (973) 645-5032 or 645-3681

Joseph H. Rodríguez, Sr., Sr. Judge
U. S. District Court for the District of New Jersey
Mitchell H. Cohen U.S. Courthouse - Room 6060
John F. Gerry Plaza - Post Office Box 886
Camden, New Jersey 08101-0886
(856) 757-5002 FAX: (856) 757-5077

Esmeralda C. Cabrera, U. S. Immigration Judge
U. S. Immigration Court - Elizabeth Office
625 Evans Street - Room 148A
Elizabeth, New Jersey 07201
(973) 693-4113 FAX: (973) 693-4121

Alberto J. Riefkohl, U. S. Immigration Judge
U. S. Immigration Court - Newark Office
970 Broad Street - Room 1135
Newark, New Jersey 07102
(973) 645-3524 FAX: Call on phone first

Mirlande Tadal, U. S. Immigration Judge
625 Evans Street, Room 148A
Elizabeth, New Jersey 07201
(973) 693-4114 FAX: (973) 693-4121

STATE

Appellate

Ariel A. Rodríguez, Judge
Superior Court of New Jersey
Appellate Division
Justice W. J. Brennan Courthouse
583 Newark Avenue, Third Floor
Jersey City, New Jersey 07306
(201) 659-6869 FAX: (201) 659-0480
E-mail: judge_a_rodriquez@judiciary.state.nj.us

Trial Judges

Roberto Alcazar, Judge
Superior Court of New Jersey – Union County
Courthouse Tower Building Basement
2 Broad Street
Elizabeth, New Jersey 07207
(908) 659-3419 FAX: (908) 282-4829
E-mail: judge_r_alcazar@judiciary.state.nj.us

Carmen J. Alvarez, Judge
Superior Court of New Jersey
Cape May Courthouse
9 North Main Street
Cape May, New Jersey 08210
(609) 463-6588 FAX: (609) 463-6458
E-mail: judge_c_alvarez@judiciary.state.nj.us

Estela M. De La Cruz, Judge
Superior Court of New Jersey
Bergen County Courthouse
Justice Center - Room 328
10 Main Street
Hackensack, New Jersey 07601
(201) 646-3374 FAX: (201) 646-6783
E-mail: Estela_De_La_Cruz@judiciary.state.nj.jus

Héctor E. De Soto, Judge
Superior Court of New Jersey
Essex County New Courts Building
50 West Market Street - Room 1216
Newark, New Jersey 07102
(973) 693-5849 FAX: (973) 424-2446 or 693-5753
E-mail: judge_h_desoto@judiciary.state.nj.us

Gerald C. Escala, Judge
Superior Court of New Jersey – General Equity Division
Bergen County Courthouse - Room 504
10 Main Street
Hackensack, New Jersey 07601
(201) 646-3148 FAX: (201) 752-4414
E-mail: Gerald_Escala@judiciary.state.nj.us

José L. Fuèntes, Judge
Superior Court of New Jersey – Hudson County
Justice W. J. Brennan Courthouse
595 Newark Avenue
Jersey City, New Jersey 07306-2301
(201) 795-6650 or 795-6392 FAX: (201) 795-6174
E-mail: Jose_Fuentes@judiciary.state.nj.us

Nestor F. Guzmán, Judge
Superior Court of New Jersey
Passaic County Courthouse
New Administration Building - Room 954
401 Grand Street
Paterson, New Jersey 07505-2017
(973) 247-8441 FAX (973) 247-8444
E-mail: judge_n_guzman@judiciary.state.nj.us

José L. Linares, Judge
Superior Court of New Jersey
Hall of Records - Room 328
465 Dr. Martin Luther King Boulevard
Newark, New Jersey 07102
(973) 693-6490 FAX: (973) 693-693-6540
E-mail: Judge_J_Linares@judiciary.state.nj.us

Severiano Lisboa, III, Judge
Superior Court of New Jersey
Hudson County Courthouse
Administration Building - Room 814
595 Newark Avenue
Jersey City, New Jersey 07206-2392
(201) 795-6627 FAX: (201) 795-6376
E-mail: judge_s_lisboa@judiciary.state.nj.us

Mathias E. Rodríguez, Judge
Superior Court of New Jersey
Middlesex County Courthouse
1 John F. Kennedy Square - Room 307
New Brunswick, New Jersey 08903-0964
(732) 981-3111 FAX: (732) 981-3279
E-mail: judge_m_rodriguez@judiciary.state.nj.us

Peter J. Vázquez, Judge
Superior Court of New Jersey
Essex County Courthouse
New Courts Building - Room 808
50 West Market Street
Newark, New Jersey 07102
(973) 693-6453 FAX: (973) 424-2465
E-mail: judge_p_vazquez@judiciary.state.nj.us

Héctor R. Velázquez, Judge
Superior Court of New Jersey, Hudson County
Administration Building, Room 808
595 Newark Avenue
Jersey City, New Jersey 07306-2392
(201) 795-6645 FAX: (201) 795-6603
E-mail: judge_h_velazquez@judiciary.state.nj.us

José M. Cameroon, Judge
Perth Amboy Municipal Court
56 Lafayette Street
Perth Amboy, New Jersey 08861
(732) 442-6011 or 442-2001 FAX: (732) 442-2571

Joseph Cerame, Judge
Central Municipal Court – Bergen County
Bergen County Courthouse
10 Main Street - Room 123
Hackensack, New Jersey 07601-7691
(201) 646-3486

Carmen M. Garcia, Judge
Trenton Municipal Court
225 North Clinton Avenue
Post Office Box 1360
Trenton, New Jersey 08607-1360
(609) 989-3721 FAX: (609) 989-4247

Armando C. Hernández, Judge
West New York Municipal Court
Municipal Building
428 60th Street
West New York, New Jersey 07093
(201) 295-5118 or 295-5188 FAX: (201) 868-6074

Antonio Inacio, Judge
Municipal Court of Clark Township
315 Westfield Avenue
Clark, New Jersey 07066-1797
(732) 381-5395 FAX: (732) 381-9630

Gladys Mendoza-Garbin, Judge
Paterson Municipal Court
111 Broadway
Paterson, New Jersey 07505
(973) 881-6878 FAX: (973) 684-4149
E-mail: GarbinEsq@aol.com

Teòfilo Montañez-Santiago, Judge
Camden Municipal Court - City Hall
Post Office Box 95120
Camden, New Jersey 08101
(609) 757-7100 FAX: (609) 567-0062

Diana E. Montes-Infante, Judge
Newark Municipal Court
Brennan/Marshall Court Complex
31 Green Street
Newark, New Jersey 07102
(973) 733-8905 FAX: (973) 733-8553

Román A. Montes, Judge
Elizabeth Municipal Court
One Police Plaza
Elizabeth, N.J. 07208-1503
(908) 527-6550 FAX: (908) 558-1503

Richard T. Nieto, Judge
Jersey City Municipal Court
Central Judicial Processing Court
595 Newark Avenue - Room G-5
Jersey City, New Jersey 07306
(201) 795-6717 FAX: (201) 547-4984
E-mail: Richn53@bellatlantic.net

Héctor M. Rodríguez, Judge
Municipal Court of Jersey City
769 Montgomery Street
Jersey City, New Jersey 07306
(201) 292-8063 FAX: (201) 547-4984

Augustin Sánchez, Judge
Union City Municipal Court
City Hall
3715 Palisade Avenue
Union City, New Jersey 07087
(201) 348-5763 FAX: (201) 348-4927

Ramona Santiago, Judge
Municipal Court City of Newark
31 Green Street
Newark, New Jersey 07102
(973) 733-8905 FAX: (973) 733-8533

Michael A. Toto, Judge
Municipal Court of Jamesburg
131 Perrineville Road
Jamesburg, New Jersey 08831
(732) 521-0614 FAX: (732) 238-6171
and Judge MunicipalCourt of East Brunswick
1 Jean Walling Civic Center
Post Office Box 1081
East Brunswick, new Jersey 08816-1081
(732) 390-6915

Amilkar Velez-Lopez, Judge
Newark Municipal Court
31 Green Street
Newark, New Jersey 07102
(973) 773-8905 FAX: Call on phone first

Administrative Law Judges

Arcides Cruz
Workers' Compensation Law Judge
Division of Workers' Compensation
506 Jersey Avenue
New Brunswick, New Jersey 08901-3502
(732) 937-6333 FAX: (732) 828-0698

Nilda C. Hernández
Workers' Compensation Law Judge
Division of Workers' Compensation
438 Summit Avenue, CN 381
Jersey City, New Jersey 07306-0603
(201) 217-7205 FAX: (201) 217-7210

NEW MEXICO: (108)

FEDERAL

Martha Vazquez, Judge
U. S. District Court for New Mexico
Post Office Box 2710
Santa Fe, New Mexico 87504
(505) 988-6330 FAX: (505) 988-6332

Santiago E. Campos, Sr., Judge
U. S. District Court for New Mexico
South Federal Place
Post Office Box 2244
Santa Fe, New Mexico 87504
(505) 988-6341 FAX: (505) 988-6340

Joe H. Galvan, Magistrate Judge
U. S. District Court for New Mexico
Federal Building
200 East Griggs
Las Cruces, New Mexico 88001
(505) 527-6918 FAX: (505) 527-6919

Lorenzo F. Garcia, Magistrate Judge
U. S. District Court for New Mexico
333 Lomas, N.W., Suite 680
Albuquerque, New Mexico 87102
(505) 348-2320 FAX: (505) 348-2324

STATE

Supreme Court

Joseph F. Baca, Justice
Supreme Court of New Mexico
237 Don Gaspar, Room 248
Post Office Box 848
Santa Fe, New Mexico 87504-0848
(505) 827-4892 FAX: (505) 827-4837

Petra Jimenez-Maes, Justice
Supreme Court of New Mexico
237 Don Gaspar, Room 229
Post Office Box 848
Santa Fe, New Mexico 87504-0848
(505) 827-4883 FAX: (505) 827-4837

Patricio M. Serna, Justice
Supreme Court of New Mexico
237 Don Gaspar, Room 235
Post Office Box 848
Santa Fe, New Mexico 87504-0848
(505) 827-4887 FAX: (505) 827-4837

Dan Sosa, Jr., Chief Justice (Retired)
Supreme Court of New Mexico
305 Mesa Vista
Santa Fe, New Mexico 87501

Court of Appeals

A. Joseph Alarid, Judge
New Mexico Court of Appeals
1117 Stanford, N.E.
Albuquerque, New Mexico 87131
(505) 841-4612 FAX: (505) 841-4614

Christina Armijo, Judge
New Mexico Court of Appeals
237 Don Gaspar
Post Office Box 2008
Santa Fe, New Mexico 88504-2008
(505) 827-4912 FAX: (505) 827-4946

Michael D. Bustamante, Judge
New Mexico Court of Appeals
1117 Stanford, N.E.
Albuquerque, New Mexico 87131
(505) 841-4650 FAX: (505) 841-4614

Benny E. Flores, Judge (Retired)
New Mexico Court of Appeals
932 Gallinas Street # 12
Las Vegas, New Mexico 87701
(505) 454-0038 FAX: (505) 454-8478

Trial Courts

Theresa Baca, Judge
Second Judicial District - Division X
Post Office Box 488
County Courthouse
415 Tijeras Street, N.W.
Albuquerque, New Mexico 87103
(505) 841-7512 FAX: (505) 841-7446

Ted Baca, Judge
Second Judicial District – Division V
Post Office Box 488
County Courthouse
Albuquerque, New Mexico 87103
(505) 841-7522 FAX: (505) 841-7446

Neil C. Candelaria, Judge
Second Judicial District – Division VI
Post Office Box 488
County Courthouse
Albuquerque, New Mexico 87103
(505) 841-7486 FAX: (505) 841-7446

Grace B. Duran, Judge
Third Judicial District – Division VI
201 West Picacho, Suite A
District Court
Las Cruces, New Mexico 88005
(505) 523-8292 FAX: (505) 523-8290

Art Encinias, Judge
First Judicial District – Division V
Post Office Box 2268
Santa Fe, New Mexico 87504-2268
(505) 827-5059 FAX: (505) 827-5055

Lourdes A. Martinez, Judge
Third Judicial District
Dona Ana County District Court – Division III
201 West Picacho, Suite A
Las Cruces, New Mexico 88005
(505) 523-8220 FAX: (505) 523-8290

Michael E. Martinez, Judge
Second Judicial District – Division I
Post Office Box 488
County Courthouse
415 Tijeras Street, N.W.
Albuquerque, New Mexico 87103
(505) 841-7602 FAX: (505) 841-7446

Eugenio S. Mathis, Judge
Fourth Judicial District – Division I
Post Office Box 1540
Las Vegas, New Mexico 87701-5402
(505) 425-7131 FAX: (505) 425-6307

Geraldine E. Rivera, Judge
Second Judicial District – Division XXIII
Post Office Box 488
County Courthouse
Albuquerque, New Mexico 87103
(505) 841-7311 FAX: (505) 841-7446

Robert E. Robles, Judge
Third Judicial District
201 W. Picacho, Suite A
District Court
Las Cruces, New Mexico 88005
(505) 523-8225 FAX: (505) 523-8290

Daniel A. Sanchez, Judge
First Judicial District – Division VII
Post Office Box 2268
Santa Fe, New Mexico 87504
(505) 827-5056 FAX: (505) 827-5055

Ross C. Sanchez, Judge
Second Judicial District – Division VIII
Post Office Box 488
County Courthouse
Albuquerque, New Mexico 87103
(505) 841-7476 FAX: (505) 841-7446

Sam B. Sanchez, Judge
Eighth Judicial District
Post Office Box 160
Raton, New Mexico 87740
(505) 445-5585 FAX: (505) 455-2626

William A. Sanchez, Judge
Thirteenth Judicial District
Post Office Box 1089
Los Lunas, New Mexico 87031
(505) 865-4010 FAX: (505) 866-5819

Michael E. Vigil, Chief Judge
First Judicial District – Division IV
Post Office Box 2268
Santa Fe, New Mexico 87504-2268
(505) 827-5053 FAX: (505) 827-5055

Barbara J. Vigil, Judge
First Judicial District – Division I
Post Office Box 2268
Santa Fe, New Mexico 87504-2268
(505) 827-4196 FAX: (505) 827-5055

Carol J. Vigil, Judge
First Judicial District – Division III
Post Office Box 2268
Santa Fe, New Mexico 87504-2268
(505) 827-5083 FAX: (505) 827-5055

Rozier E. Sanchez, Judge (Retired)
Second Judicial District
7612 Palo Duro, N.E.
Albuquerque, New Mexico 871210

County Metropolitan Courts

Eliseo L. Alcon, Judge
Metropolitan Court
Post Office Box 130
Grants, New Mexico 87020
(505) 285-4605 FAX: (505) 285-6485

Marie A. Baca, Judge
Metropolitan Court
Post Office Box 133
401 Roma, N.W.
Albuquerque, New Mexico 87103-0133
(505) 841-8220 FAX: (505) 841-8192 or 222-4812

Eugene M. De Los Santos, Judge
Metropolitan Court
200 East 4th Street
Roswell, New Mexico 88201
(505) 624-6088 FAX: (505) 624-6092

Frank W. Gentry, Judge
Metropolitan Court
Post Office Box 133
111 Lomas Blvd., N.W.
Albuquerque, New Mexico 87103-0133
(505) 841-8297 FAX: (505) 841-8192 or 222-4810

Theresa Ann Gomez, Judge
Metropolitan Court
Post Office Box 133
401 Roma, N.W.
Albuquerque, New Mexico 87103-0133
(505) 841-8196 FAX: (505) 841-8192 or 222-4814

J. Michael Kavanaugh, Chief Judge
Metropolitan Court
Post Office Box 133
401 Roma, N.W.
Albuquerque, New Mexico 87103-0133
(505) 841-8193 FAX: (505) 841-8192 or 222-4813

Anna G. Martinez, Judge
Metropolitan Court
111 Lomas Blvd., N.W.
Albuquerque, New Mexico 87103-0133
(505) 841-8291 FAX: (505) 222-4815

Richard C. Martinez, Judge
Metropolitan Court
410 Paseo de Onate
Espanola, New Mexico 87532
(505) 753-2532 FAX: (505) 753-4802

Tony F. Martinez, Judge
Metropolitan Court
410 Paseo de Onate
Espanola, New Mexico 87532
(505) 753-2532 FAX: (505) 753-4802

Rudy C. Montoya, Judge
Metropolitan Court
Post Office Box 131
Mora, New Mexico 87732
(505) 387-2937 FAX: (505) 387-9081

Ygnacio B. Morales, Judge
Metropolitan Court
Post Office Box 125
Bayard, New Mexico 88023
(505) 537-3042 FAX: (505) 537-7365

Jim Naranjo, Judge
County Metropolitan Court
404 Park Avenue
Socorro, New Mexico 87801
(505) 835-2500 FAX: (505) 838-0428

Michael Romero, Judge
Metropolitan Court
603 Parker Avenue
Santa Rosa, New Mexico 88435
(505) 472-3237 FAX: (505) 472-3592

Denise Barela Shepherd, Judge
Metropolitan Court
111 Lomas Blvd., N.W.
Albuquerque, New Mexico 87103-0133
(505) 841-8263 FAX: (505) 222-4801

Archie A. Valdez, Judge
Metropolitan Court
Post Office Box 68
Raton, New Mexico 87740
(505) 445-2220 FAX: (505) 445-8966

Municipal Courts

Barbara R. Aidaz, Judge
City of Aztec Municipal Court
201 West Chaco
Aztec, New Mexico 87410
(505) 334-7640 FAX: (505) 334-7639

Manuel C. Chavez, Judge
Municipal Court
525 Becker Avenue
Belen, New Mexico 87002
(505) 864-7543 FAX: (505) 864-0361

Richard G. Chavez, Judge
Municipal Court
114 Civic Plaza Drive
Taos, New Mexico 87571
(505) 737-2602 FAX: (505) 737-2604

Joe L. Dominguez, Judge
Tucumcari Municipal Court
Post Office Box 1186
225 East Center
Tucumcari, New Mexico 88401
(505) 461-6375 FAX: (505) 461-0439

Dorothy Enoinlas, Judge
Moriarty Municipal Court
Post Office Drawer 115
Moriarty, New Mexico 87035
(505) 832-6354 FAX: (505) 832-6919

Tim Flores, Judge
Tularose Municipal Court
705 St. Francis Drive
Tularose, New Mexico 88352
(505) 585-2901 FAX: (505) 585-2965

Frances Gallegos, Judge
Santa Fe Municipal Court
Post Office Box 909
2511 Camino Entrade
Santa Fe, New Mexico 87504
(505) 473-5070 FAX: (505) 438-5159

Hector Grijalda, Judge
Village of Santa Clara
Municipal Court
Post Office Box 316
105 North Bayard Street
Santa Clara, New Mexico 88026-0316
(505) 537-6417 FAX: (505) 537-2452

Rudy Jasquez, Judge
Silver city Municipal Court
215 North Bullard
Silver City, New Mexico 88062
(505) 388-4504 FAX: (505) 388-0465

Richard Luna, Judge
Los Lunes Municipal Court
Post Office Box 1388
660 West Main Street
Los Lunas, New Mexico 87031-0153
(505) 865-5656 FAX: (505) 865-7256

Charles Maestas, Judge
City of Espanola Municipal Court
406 Paseo de Onate
Espanola, New Mexico 87532
(505) 747-6033 FAX: (505) 747-6049

Joe Eddie Martinez, Judge
City of Santa Rosa Municipal Court
Post Office Box 429
141 South 5th Street
Santa Rosa, New Mexico 88435-0429
(505) 472-4232 FAX: (505) 472-2543

Nancy K. Martinez, Judge
Mountainair Municipal Court
Post Office Box 115
Mountainair, New Mexico 87036
(505) 847-2595 FAX: (505) 847-2413

Theresa Martinez, Judge
San Jon Municipal Court
Post Office Box 37
San Jon, New Mexico 88434-0037
(505) 576-2922 FAX: (505) 576-2722

Samuel L. Ortiz, Judge
Municipal Court
1 Central Avenue
Post Office Box 788
Bayard, New Mexico 88023
(505) 537-5438 FAX: (505) 537-2511

Corrine Padilla, Judge
Grants Municipal Court
Post Office Box 879
620 West Santa Fe Avenue
Grants, New Mexico 87020
(505) 287-3927 FAX: (505) 287-7502

Linda G. Padilla, Judge
City of Gallup Municipal Court
Post Office Drawer 430
451 State Road 584
Gallup, New Mexico 87305
(505) 863-4469 FAX: (505) 863-1308

Ofelio Padilla, Judge
Town of Springer Municipal Court
Post Office Box 488
806 Colbert Avenue
Springer, New Mexico 87747-0452
(505) 483-2682 FAX: (505) 483-2910

Mary Jo Pina, Judge
Village of Chama Municipal Court
Post Office Box 794
Chama, New Mexico 87520
(505) 756-2184 FAX: (505) 756-2412

Hector Pineda, Judge
City of Roswell Municipal Court
Post Office Box 2124
Roswell, New Mexico 88202-2124
(505) 624-6725 FAX: (505) 624-6763

Michael G. Rael, Judge
Village of Questa Municipal Court
Post Office Box 1162
Questa, New Mexico 87556
(505) 586-1313 FAX: (505) 586-0699

David J. Ramos, Judge
Town of Hurley Municipal Court
Post Office Box 65
Hurley, New Mexico 88043
(505) 537-3220 FAX: (505) 537-2797

Michael G. Real, Judge
Questa Municipal Court
Post Office Box 1182
Questa, New Mexico 87556
(505) 586-1313 FAX: (505) 586-0699

Martin Resendiz, Judge
City of Sunland Park Municipal Court
Post Office Box 1150
Sunland Park, New Mexico 88063-1150
(505) 589-0709 FAX: (505) 589-1222

Angie Romero, Judge
Wagon Mound Municipal Court
Post Office Box 87
Wagon Mound, New Mexico 87752
(505) 666-2408 FAX: (505) 666-9071

Oliver Romero, Judge
Bernalillo Municipal Court
Post Office Box 683
829 Camino del Pueblo
Bernallillo, New Mexico 87004
(505) 867-3311 FAX: (505) 867-0481

Esperanza B. Tarango, Judge
City of Lordsburg Municipal Court
206 South Main Street
Lordsburg, New Mexico 88045
(505) 542-3124 FAX: (505) 542-8064

Angie Trujillo, Judge
Village of San Ysidro Municipal Court
Post Office Box 175
Highway 4 - #372
San Ysidro, New Mexico 87053
(505) 834-7701 FAX: (505) 834-7591

Eddie Trujillo, Judge
City of Los Vegas Municipal Court
Post Office Box 1471
Las Vegas, New Mexico 87701-1471
(505) 425-9403 FAX: (505) 454-6943

Mabel Varela, Judge
Village of Pecos Municipal Court
Post Office Drawer 337
Pecos, New Mexico 87552
(505) 757-2297 FAX: (505) 757-2833

Probate Judges

José "Billy" Caseus, Judge
Guadalupe County Probate Court
420 Parker Avenue #1
Santa Rosa, New Mexico 88435
(505) 584-2614 FAX: (505) 472-3735

Susie Gallegos, Judge
Cibola County Probate Court
Post Office Box 190
515 West Highway Street
Grants, New Mexico 87020
(505) 287-9431 FAX: (505) 285-5434

Olivia Garcia, Judge
Dona Ana County Probate Court
180 West Amador Avenue
Las Cruces, New Mexico 88005
(505) 647-7419 FAX: (505) 526-3922

Lorenzo V. Martinez, Judge
Rio Arriba County Probate Court
Rio Arribe County Courthouse
Post Office Box 158
Tierra Amarilla, New Mexico 87575
(505) 588-7724 FAX: (505) 753-1258

Sally Perea, Judge
Valencia County Probate Court
Post Office Box 939
Los Lunas, New Mexico 87031-0939
(505) 866-2098 FAX: (505) 866-2023

Della Perez, Judge
Luna County Probate Court
Post Office Box 1838
Deming, New Mexico 88031
(505) 546-0491 FAX: (505) 546-4708

Melanie Rivera, Judge
San Miguel County Probate Court
San Miguel County Courthouse
500 West National Avenue
Las Vegas, New Mexico 87701
(505) 425-9331 FAX: (505) 425-7019

Daniel Romero, Judge
Socorro County Probate Court
Post Office Box 1
Socorro, New Mexico 87801-0001
(505) 835-0589 FAX: (505) 835-1043

Joann Salcido, Judge
Grants County Probate Court
Post Office Box 898
Silver City, New Mexico 88062-0898
(505) 538-5240 FAX: (505) 538-8926

Janice Sanchez, Judge
Sierra County Probate Court
311 Date Street
T or C, New Mexico 87801
(505) 894-4416 FAX: (505) 894-2516

Lupe Torrez, Judge
Mora County Probate Court
Post Office Box 36
Mora, New Mexico 87732
(505) 387-5702 FAX: (505) 387-9022

Beatrice R. Vigil, Judge
Taos County Probate Court
105 Albright Street, Suite D
Taos, New Mexico 87551
(505) 758-8266 FAX: (505) 751-3391
Magistrates Courts

Eliseo L. Alcon, Judge
Cibola County Magistrate Court
Post Office Box 130
Grants, New Mexico 87020-0130
(505) 285-4605 FAX: (505) 285-6485

Margaret A. Cassidy-Baca, Judge
Sandoval County Magistrate Court
Post Office Box 818
Bernalillo, New Mexico 87004-0818
(505) 867-5202 FAX: (505) 867-0970

Susana Chaparro, Judge
Dona Ana Magistrate Court
151 North Church Street
Las Cruces, New Mexico 88001
(505) 524-2814 FAX: (505) 525-2951

William Dimas, Judge
Santa Fe County Magistrate Court
2052 Galisteo Street
Santa Fe, New Mexico 87505
(505) 984-9914 FAX: (505) 986-5866

F. Kenneth Eichwald, Judge
Sandoval County Magistrate Court
Post Office Box 1497
Cuba, New Mexico 87013
(505) 289-3519 FAX: (505) 289-3013

Oscar C. Fritze, Judge
Dona Ana Magistrate Court
151 North Church Street
Las Cruces, New Mexico 88001
(505) 524-2814 FAX: (505) 525-2951

Betty J. Gonzales, Judge
Taos County Magistrate Court
Post Office Box 1121
Taos, New Mexico 87571
(505) 758-4030 FAX: (505) 758-0983

Leo Gonzales, Judge
San Miguel County Magistrate Court
1927 7th Street
Las Vegas, New Mexico 87701
(505) 425-5204 FAX: (505) 425-0422

Ermenio E. Martinez, Judge
Taos County
Post Office Box 1121
Taos, New Mexico 87571
(505) 758-4030 FAX: (505) 758-0983

Richard C. Martinez, Judge
Rio Arriba County Magistrate Court
410 Paseo De Onate
Espanola, New Mexico 87532
(505) 753-2532 FAX: (505) 753-4802

Tony F. Martinez, Judge
Rio Arriba County Magistrate Court
410 Paseo De Onate
Espanola, New Mexico 87532
(505) 753-2532 FAX: (505) 753-4802

Rudy C. Montoya, Judge
Mora County Magistrate Court
Post Office Box 131
Mora, New Mexico 87732-0131
(505) 387-2937 FAX: (505) 387-9081

Y. B. Morales, Judge
Grant County Magistrate Court
Post Office Box 125
Bayard, New Mexico 88023-0125
(505) 537-3042 FAX: (505) 537-7365

Jim Naranjo, Judge
Socorro County Magistrate Court
404 Park Street
Socorro, New Mexico 87801
(505) 835-2500 FAX: (505) 838-0428

Richard M. Padilla, Judge
Santa Fe County Magistrate Court
2052 Galisteo Street
Santa Fe, New Mexico 87505
(505) 984-9914 FAX: (505) 986-5866

Toribio L. Perea, Judge
Valencia County Magistrate Court
121 Don Diego Street
Los Lunas, New Mexico 87031
(505) 865-4637 FAX: (505) 865-0639

Michael Romero, Judge
Guadalupe County Magistrate Court
603 Parker Avenue
Santa Rosa, New Mexico 88435
(505) 472-3237 FAX: (505) 472-3592

Philip J. Romero, Judge
San Miguel Magistrate Court
1927 7th Street
Las Vegas, New Mexico 87701
(505) 425-5204 FAX: (505) 425-0422

John W. Sanchez, Judge
Valencia County Magistrate Court
121 Don Diego
Los Lunas, New Mexico 87031
(505) 865-4637 FAX: (505) 865-0639

Archie A. Valdez, Judge
Colfax County Magistrate Court – Division 1
Post Office Box 68
Raton, New Mexico 87740-0068
(505) 445-2220 FAX: (505) 445-8966

Administrative Law Judges

Gregory D. Griego
Workers' Compensation Judge
Post Office Box 27198
Albuquerque, New Mexico 87106
(505) 841-6023 or 1-800-255-7965
FAX: (505) 841-6009

NEW YORK: (64)

FEDERAL

Sonia Sotomayor, Judge
U. S. Court of Appeals for the Second Circuit
500 Pearl Street
New York, New York 10007-1312
(212) 805-0250 or 805-0251 FAX: (212) 857-2729
E-mail: sonia_sotomayor@ca2.uscourts.gov

Victor Marrero, Judge
U. S. District Court
for the Southern District of New York
U. S. Courthouse
500 Pearl Street
New York, New York 10007
(212) 805-6374 FAX: (212) 805-6382

Arlene Rosario Lindsay, U. S. Magistrate Judge
U. S. District Court
for the Eastern District of New York
U. S. Courthouse
300 Rabro Drive
Hauppauge, New York 11788
(516) 582-1114 FAX: Call on phone first

Arthur J. Gonzalez, Judge
U. S. Bankruptcy Court for the Southern
District of New York
One Bowling Green, Room 517
New York, New York 10004-1408
(212) 668-2894 FAX: (212) 668-3189
E-mail: arthur_gonzalez@nysd.uscourts.gov

Administrative Law Judges

Manuel Cofresi, Administrative Law Judge
Office of Hearings and Appeals
Social Security Administration
59-07 175th Place - lst Floor
Fresh Meadows, New York 11365
(718) 357-7934 or 357-8805
FAX: (718) 357-9591 or (718) 590-1673

Louis V. Zamora
Chief Administrative Law Judge
Office of Hearings and Appeals
Social Security Administration
226 East 161st Street
2nd Floor, Suite 4
Bronx, New York 10451
(718) 537-4958 FAX: (718) 590-1673

Paul DeFonzo, U. S. Immigration Judge
26 Federal Plaza, 12th Floor, Room 1237
New York, New York 10278
(212) 264-5958 FAX: Call on phone first

Grabriel Videla, U. S. Immigration Judge
26 Federal Plaza
New York, New York 10278
(212) 264-5959 FAX: (212) Call on phone first

STATE

Appellate Courts

Carmen Beauchamp Ciparick, Judge
Court of Appeals for the State of New York
122 East 42nd Street
New York, New York 10017
(212) 661-2144 or (518) 455-7725
FAX: (212) 661-9380 or (518) 463-8782

John Carro, Judge (Retired)
Supreme Court
Appellate Division
Carro, Velez, Carro and Mitchell
245 Fifth Avenue, 26th Floor
New York City, New York 10010
(212) 213-5003 FAX: (212) 213-5004

Supreme Court of New York

Betsy Barros, Justice
Supreme Court of the State of New York
360 Adams Street
Brooklyn, New York 11201-3712
(718) 643-3780 FAX: (718) 643-3549
E-mail: bbarros@courts.state.ny.us

Ariel E. Belen, Justice
Supreme Court of the State of New York
360 Adams Street
Brooklyn, New York 11201
(718) 643-5485 FAX: (718) 643-2095
E-mail: abelen@courts.state.ny.us

Nicholas Figueroa, Justice
Supreme Court of the State of New York
100 Centre Street
New York, New York 10013-4386
(212) 374-5719 FAX: (212) 748-5089
E-mail: nfigueroa@courts.state.ny.us

Luis Antonio Gonzalez, Justice
Supreme Court of the State of New York
851 Grand Concourse
Bronx, New York 10451-2978
(718) 590-3786 FAX: (718) 590-8899
E-mail: lgonzalez@courts.state.ny.us

Yvonne Gonzalez, Justice
Supreme Court of the State of New York
851 Grand Concourse
Bronx, New York 10451-2978
(718) 590-6358 FAX: (718) 590-7296
E-mail: ygonzalez@courts.state.ny.us

Charles Edward Ramos, Justice
Supreme Court of the State of New York
60 Centre Street
New York, New York 10007-1474
(212) 374-8216 FAX: (212) 374-3326
E-mail: cramos@courts.state.ny.us

Jaime A. Rios, Justice
Supreme Court of the State of New York
125-01 Queens Boulevard
Jamaica, New York 11415-3791
(718) 520-6652 FAX: (718) 520-2494
E-mail: jrios@courts.state.ny.us

Francois A. Rivera, Justice
Supreme Court of the State of New York
360 Adams Street
Brooklyn, New York 11201-3712
(718) 643-5195 FAX: (718) 643-3549
E-mail: frivera@courts.state.ny.us

Reinaldo E. Rivera, Justice
Supreme Court of the State of New York
360 Adams Street
Brooklyn, New York 11201-3712
(718) 643-8183 FAX: (718) 643-3549
E-mail: rrivera@courts.state.ny.us

Norma Ruiz, Justice
Supreme Court of the State of New York
851 Grand Concourse
Bronx, New York 10451
(718) 590-3837 FAX: (718) 590-1467
E-mail: nruiz@courts.state.ny.us

Lucindo Suarez, Justice
Supreme Court of the State of New York
Acting Justice, Appellate Term, 1st Department
60 Centre Street
New York, New York 10007-1474
(212) 374-8373 FAX: (212) 374-8159
E-mail: lsuarez@courts.state.ny.us

Edwin Torres, Justice
Supreme Court of the State of New York
100 Centre Street
New York, New York 10013-4386
(212) 374-4966 FAX: (718) 748-5089
E-mail: etorres@courts.state.ny.us

Laura Visitacion-Lewis, Justice
Supreme Court of the State of New York
111 Centre Street
New York, New York 10013-4386
(212) 374-8003 FAX: (212) 374-1145
E-mail: lvlewis@courts.state.ny.us

Civil Court of the City of New York

Rolando T. Acosta, Judge
Civil Court
111 Centre Street
New York, New York 10013-4389
(212) 374-8491 FAX: (212) 374-0402
E-mail: racosta@courts.state.ny.us

Gilbert Badillo, Judge
Civil Court Housing Part
89-17 Sutphin Boulevard
Jamaica, New York 11435
(718) 262-7350 or 262-7351
FAX: (718) 262-7291 or 262-7107
E-mail: gbadillo@courts.state.ny.us

Maryann Briganiti-Hughes, Judge
Civil Court
851 Grand Concourse
Bronx, New York 10451-2978
(718) 590-3606 FAX: (718) 590-7292
E-mail: mbrigant@courts.state.ny.us

Lizbeth Gonzalez, Judge
Civil Court Housing Part
1118 Grand Concourse
Bronx, New York 10456
(718) 466-3055 FAX: (718) 466-3006
E-mail: lgonzale@courts.state.ny.us

Raymond Guzman, Judge
Civil Court
Acting Judge Criminal Court
111 Centre Street
New York, New York 10013
(212) 374-2067 FAX: (212) 374-2579
E-mail: jrguzman@courts.state.ny.us

Wilma Guzman, Judge
Civil Court
141 Livingston Street
Brooklyn, New York 11201
(718) 643-3318 FAX: (718) 643-3733
E-mail: wguzman@courts.state.ny.us

Dawn Marie Jiminez, Judge
Civil Court - Housing Part
141 Livingston Street
Brooklyn, New York 11201
(718) 643-1228 FAX: (718) 643-3733
E-mail: djiminez@courts.state.ny.us

Margarita Lopez-Torres, Judge
Civil Court Acting Judge Criminal Court
141 Livingston Street
Brooklyn, New York 11201
(718) 643-8318 or 643-7430 FAX (718) 643-3733
E-mail: mlopez@courts.state.ny.us

Sallie Manzanet, Judge
Civil Court
851 Grand Concourse
Bronx, New York 10451
(718) 590-3606 FAX: (718) 590-3606
E-mail: smanzane@courts.state.ny.us

Ruben Andres Martino, Judge
Civil Court Housing Part
1118 Grand Concourse
Bronx, New York 10456
(718) 466-3030 or 466-3150 FAX: (718) 466-3006
E-mail: rmartino@courts.state.ny.us

Jose A. Padilla, Jr., Judge
Civil Court
Acting Justice, Supreme Court
111 Centre Street
New York, New York 10013-4389
(212) 374-8072 FAX: (212) 374-0402
E-mail: jpadilla@courts.state.ny.us

Eduardo Padro, Judge
Civil Court Acting Judge
Criminal Court
215 East 161st Street
Bronx, New York 10451-3592
(718) 590-2937 FAX: (212) 590-7297
E-mail: epadro@courts.state.ny.us
E-mail: epocquinyc@aol.com

Richard Rivera, Supervising Judge
Civil Court
141 Livingston Street
Brooklyn, New York 11201
(718) 643-2860 FAX: (718) 643-3537
E-mail: rrivera@courts.state.ny.us

Jose Rodriguez, Judge
Civil Court - Housing Part
141 Livingston Street
Brooklyn, New York 11201
(718) 643-8086 or 643-8339
FAX: (718) 643-3733 or (212) 401-9206
E-mail: jrodrigu@courts.state.ny.us

Julia J. Rodriguez, Judge
Civil Court - Housing Part
111 Centre Street
New York, New York 10013-4389
(212) 374-2241 FAX: (212) 374-0402

Nelson S. Roman, Judge
City Court - Housing Part
1118 Grand Concourse
Bronx, New York 10456
(718) 466-3170 FAX: (718) 466-3006
E-mail: nroman@courts.state.ny.us

Faviola A. Soto, Judge
Civil Court
111 Centre Street
New York, New York 10013-4389
(212) 374-8005 FAX: (212) 374-0402
E-mail: fsoto@courts.state.ny.us

Analisa Torres, Judge
Civil Court
111 Centre Street
New York, New York 10013
(212) 374-8071 or 374-8479
FAX: (212) 374-2579 or (212) 374-0402
E-mail: atorres@courts.state.ny.us

Robert E. Torres, Judge
Civil Court
Acting Judge Criminal Court
215 East 161st Street
Bronx, New York 10451
(718) 537-5161 FAX: (718) 590-7297
E-mail: rtorres@courts.state.ny.us

Criminal Court of the City of New York

Efrain Alvarado, Judge Criminal Court
Acting Justice, Supreme Court of the State of New York
851 Grand Concourse
Bronx, New York 10451-2978
(718) 590-5263 FAX: (718) 590-8899
E-mail: ealvarado@courts.state.ny.us

Peter J. Benitez, Judge Criminal Court
Acting Justice, Supreme Court of the State of New York
851 Grand Concourse
Bronx, New York 10451-2978
(718) 590-6272 FAX: (718) 590-8899
E-mail: pbenitez@courts.state.ny.us

Fernando M. Camacho, Judge Criminal Court
120 Schermerhorn Street
Brooklyn, New York 11201
(718) 643-3798 FAX: (718) 643-7733
E-mail: fcamacho@courts.state.ny.us

Gregory Carro, Judge Criminal Court
100 Centre Street
New York, New York 10013-4386
(212) 748-5372 FAX: (212) 374-2579
E-mail: gcarro@courts.state.ny.us

Suzanne J. Melendez, Judge Criminal Court
125-01 Queens Boulevard
Kew Gardens, New York 11415
(718) 520-2617 FAX: (718) 520-4712
E-mail: smelende@courts.state.ny.us

Patricia M. Nunez, Judge Criminal Court
100 Centre Street
New York, New York 10013
(212) 374-3599 FAX: (212) 374-3579
E-mail: pnunez@courts.state.ny.us

Robert A. Sackett, Judge
Criminal Court
215 East 161st Street
Bronx, New York 10451
(718) 590-2933 FAX: (718) 590-7297
E-mail: rsacke@courts.sttae.ny.us
E-mail: :rasjudge@aol.com

Family Court of New York

Alma Cordova, Judge
Family Court of the State of New York
900 Sheridan Avenue
Bronx, New York 10451-3308
(718) 590-3384 FAX: (718) 590-7305
E-mail: acordova@courts.state.ny.us

Cira A. Martinez, Supervising Judge
Family Court of the State of New York
900 Sheridan Avenue
Bronx, New York 10451
(718) 590-3389 FAX: (718) 590-7305
E-mail: cmartinez@courts.state.ny.us

Myrna Martinez-Perez, Judge
Family Court of the State of New York
900 Sheridan Avenue
Bronx, New York 10451-3308
(718) 590-3382 FAX: (718) 590-7305
E-mail: mmartinp@courts.state.ny.us

Gloria Sosa-Lintner, Judge
Family Court of the State of New York
60 Lafayette Street
New York, New York 10013-4096
(212) 374-3612 FAX: (212) 374-2623
E-mail: gsosalin@courts.state.ny.us

Court of Claims

Dora L. Irizarry, Judge
Court of Claims of the State of New York
111 Centre Street
New York, New York 10013-4389
(212) 347-8067 FAX: (212) 748-5058
E-mail: dirizarry@courts.state.ny.us

Charles J. Tejada, Judge
Court of Claims of the State of New York
Acting Justice, Supreme Court of the State of New York
100 Centre Street
New York, New York 10013-4386
(212) 374-4741 FAX: (212) 748-5089
E-mail: ctejada@courts.state.ny.us

Cesar H. Quinones, Judge (Retired)
Court of Claims of the State of New York
360 Adams Street
Brooklyn, New York 11201

City Courts

Laura Estela Cardona, Judge
City Court
511 South State Street
Public Safety Building
Syracuse, New York 13202-2126
(315) 477-2765 or 477-2785 FAX: (315) 477-2601

Melchor E. Castro, Judge
City Court
One Hall of Justice
Rochester, New York 14614
(716) 428-2437 FAX: (716) 428-2740
E-mail: mcastro@courts.state.ny.us

Raul Figueroa, Judge
City Court
50 Delaware Avenue
Buffalo, New York 14202
(716) 847-8267 FAX: (716) 856-4670
E-mail: rfigueroa@courts.state.ny.us

County District Court

Sonia M. Veras, Judge
District Court, Suffolk County
400 Carlton Avenue
Central Islip, New York 11722
(631) 853-5370 E-mail: sveras@courts.state.ny.us

Village Courts

William Sanchez, Village Justice
Village Court
68 Violet Place
Rhinebeck, New York 12572
(914) 876-3920

Jose E. Suarez, Village Justice
Village Court
54 Wilshire Drive
Chestnut Ridge, New York 10977-7030
(914) 425-0026

Administrative Law Judges

Rosemarie Maldonado
Chief Administrative Law Judge
New York City Commission on Human Rights
40 Rector Street
New York, New York 10006
(212) 306-7500 FAX: (212) 306-7648

Norma Ramirez, Administrative Law Judge
New York City Environmental Control Board
1250 Broadway
New York, New York 10010
(212) 971-3600 FAX: (212) 967-6563

NORTH CAROLINA: (0)

NORTH DAKOTA : (0)

OHIO: (5)

FEDERAL

Administrative Law Judge

Melvin A. Padilla, Administrative Law Judge
Office of Hearings and Appeals
Social Security Administration
Suite 800, Fifth Third Center
110 North Main Street
Dayton, Ohio 45402
(937) 225-7233 FAX: (937) 225-7701

STATE:

Joseph A. Flores, Judge
Lucas County Court of Common Pleas
Juvenile Division
429 Michigan Street
Toledo, Ohio 43624
(419) 249-6777 FAX: (419) 249-6898
E-mail: LucCty.jvct@aol.com

José A. Villanueva, Judge
Cuyahoga County Court of Common Pleas
Justice Center # 21 C
1200 Ontario Street
Cleveland, Ohio 44113
(216) 443-8737 FAX: (216) 348-4034
E-mail: cpjav@www.cuyahoga.oh.us

Gustalo Nuñez, Judge
Lorain Municipal Court
100 West Erie Avenue
Lorain, Ohio 44052
(440) 244-2143 FAX: (440) 244-3458
E-mail: Judge_nuñez@ci.lorain.oh.us

Administrative Law Judge

Lawrence J. LaSalle, Administrative Law Judge
Board of Tax Appeals
30 East Broad Street
Columbus, Ohio 43215
(614) 466-6700 FAX: (614) 644-5196
E-mail: LawrenceL@copper.net

OKLAHOMA: (0)

OREGON: (4)

STATE

Paul J. De Muniz, Judge
Oregon Court of Appeals
Justice Building - Third Floor
1162 Court Street, N.E.
Salem, Oregon 97310
(503) 986-5672 or 986-5658 FAX: (503) 986-5865

Marco A. Hernandez, Judge
District Court
Washington County Courthouse
145 N.E. Second Avenue
Hillsboro, Oregon 97124
(503) 681-3851 FAX: (503) 846-2951

Joseph V. Ochoa, Judge
District Court, Third Judicial District
Marion County Courthouse
Post Office Box 12869
Salem, Oregon 97309-0869
(503) 373-4361 FAX: (503) 589-3224

Joseph F. Ceniceros, Judge (Retired)
Circuit Court
Multomah County Courthouse
1021 S.W. Fourth Avenue
Portland, Oregon 97204

PENNSYLVANIA: (7)

FEDERAL

Eduardo C. Robreno, Judge
U. S. District Court for the Eastern
District of Pennsylvania
3810 U. S. Courthouse
601 Market Street, Room 7614
Philadelphia, Pennsylvania 19106-1745
(215) 597-4073 FAX: (267) 299-7428

Administrative Law Judges

George Alemón, Administrative Law Judge
National Labor Relations Board
Division of Judges
1115 Huntington Pike
Huntington Valley, Pennsylvania 19006
(215) 914-1213 FAX: (215) 947-5429

Javier A. Arrastia, Administrative Law Judge
Office of Hearings and Appeals
Social Security Administration
1601 Market Street, 9th Floor
Philadelphia, Pennsylvania 19103
(215) 656-3990 FAX: (215) 656-6965
E-mail: Javier.Arrastia@ssa.gov

Alma S. De Leon, Administrative Law Judge
Office of Hearings and Appeals
Social Security Administration
601 Grant Street, Suite #500
Pittsburgh, Pennsylvania 15219-4400
(412) 644-6615 Ext. 3011 FAX: (412) 281-1396
E-mail: mangal@bellatlantic.net
E-mail: Alma.S.Deleon@ssa.gov

STATE

Nitza I. Quinones Alejandro, Judge
Court of Common Pleas
First Judicial District
Criminal Justice Center, Suite # 1418
1301 Filbert Street
Philadelphia, Pennsylvania 19107
(215) 683-7151 FAX: (215) 683-7153

Juan R. Sanchez, Judge
Chester County Court of Common Pleas
Courthouse, Two N. High Street
Post Office Box 2748
West Chester, Pennsylvania 19380
(610) 344-6184 FAX: (610) 344-5422 or 344-6127

M. Teresa Sarmina, Judge
Philadelphia Court of Common Pleas
285 City Hall
Philadelphia, Pennsylvania 19107
(215) 686-7920 FAX: (215) 686-7488

PUERTO RICO: (390)

FEDERAL

Juan R. Torruella, Chief Judge
U. S. Court of Appeals for the First Circuit
U. S. Courthouse - 4th Floor
300 Recinto Sur Street
San Juan, Puerto Rico 00901
(787) 977-6146 or 977-6147 FAX: (787) 729-6660

Salvador E. Casellas, Judge
U. S. District Court for Puerto Rico
CH-111 Clemente Ruiz Nazario, U. S. Courthouse
150 Carlos Chardón Avenue
San Juan, Puerto Rico 00918-1761
(787) 772-3150 or 772-3151 FAX: (787) 766-5763

Carmen Consuelo Cerezo, Judge
U. S. District Court for Puerto Rico
CH-131 Clemente Ruiz Nazario
U. S. Courthouse
150 Carlos Chardón Avenue
San Juan, Ruerto Rico 00918-1764
(787) 772-3110 or 772-3111
FAX: (787) 766-5737 or 766-5763

Daniel R. Dominguez, Judge
U. S. District Court for Puerto Rico
CH-129 Clemente Ruiz Nazario
U. S. Courthouse
150 Carlos Chardón Avenue
San Juan, Puerto Rico 00918-1766
(787) 772-3160 or 772-3161 FAX: (787) 766-5604

José Antonio Fusté, Judge
U. S. District Court for Puerto Rico
CH-133 Clemente Ruiz Nazario
U. S. Courthouse
150 Carlos Chardón Avenue
San Juan, Puerto Rico 00918-1761
(787) 772-3120 or 772-3121 FAX: (787) 766-5443

Jay A. Garcia-Gregory, Judge
U. S. District Court for Puerto Rico
CH-151 Clemente Ruiz Nazario
U. S. Courthouse
150 Carlos Chardón Avenue
San Juan, Puerto Rico 00918-1765
(787) 772-3170 or 772-3171 FAX: (787) 772-3209

Héctor M. Laffitte, Chief Judge
U. S. District Court for Puerto Rico
CH-142 Clemente Ruiz Nazario U. S. Courthouse
150 Carlos Chardón Avenue
San Juan, Puerto Rico 00918-1757
(787) 772-3130 or 772-3131
FAX: (787) 766-5778 or 772-5778

Juan M. Pérez-Giménez, Judge
U. S. District Court for Puerto Rico
CH-125 Clemente Ruiz Nazario
U. S. Courthouse
150 Carlos Chardón Avenue
San Juan, Puerto Rico 00918-1765
(787) 772-3140 or 772-3141 FAX: (787) 766-6474

Raymond L. Acosta, Sr. Judge
U. S. District Court for Puerto Rico
U. S. Courthouse and
Post Office Building, Suite 348
300 Recinto Sur Street
San Juan, Puerto Rico 00901
(787) 977-6070 FAX: (787) 977-6075

Gilberto Gierbonlini-Ortiz, Sr. Judge
U. S. District Court for Puerto Rico
U. S. Courthouse and
Post Office Building, Suite 342
300 Recinto Sur Street
San Juan, Puerto Rico 00901
(787) 766-6060 FAX: (787) 977-6065

Jaime Pieras, Jr., Sr. Judge
U. S. District Court for Puerto Rico
U. S. Courthouse and
Post Office Building, Suite 353
300 Recinto Sur Street
San Juan, Puerto Rico 00901
(787) 977-6050 FAX: (787) 977-6055

Justo Arenas, Magistrate Judge
U. S. District Court for Puerto Rico
Room 198 - Federico Degetau Federal Building
150 Carlos Chardón Avenue
San Juan, Puerto Rico 00918-1760
(787) 772-3190 or 772-3191
FAX: (787) 281-4958 or 766-4958

Jesús Antonio Castellanos, Magistrate Judge
U. S. District Court for Puerto Rico
Room 182 - Federico Degetau Federal Building
150 Carlos Chardón Avenue
San Juan, Puerto Rico 00918-1759
(787) 772-3185 or 772-3186 FAX: (787) 766-5676

Aida M. Delgado Colón, Magistrate Judge
U. S. District Court for Puerto Rico
Room 181 - Federico Degetau Federal Building
150 Carlos Chardón Avenue
San Juan, Puerto Rico 00918-1756
(787) 772-3195 or 772-3196 FAX: (787) 766-5676

Gerardo A. Carlo-Altieri, Chief Judge
U. S. Bankruptcy Court for Puerto Rico
U. S. Courthouse and Post Office Building
300 Recinto Sur Street
San Juan, Puerto Rico 00901
(787) 977-6040 FAX: (787) 977-6045

Sara E. De Jesús, Judge
U. S. Bankruptcy Court for Puerto Rico
U. S. Courthouse and Post Office Building
300 Recinto Sur Street
San Juan, Puerto Rico 00901
(787) 977-6020 FAX: (787) 977-6025

Enrique S. Lamoutte-Inclan, Judge
U. S. Bankruptcy Court for Puerto Rico
U. S. Courthouse and Post Office Building
300 Recinto Sur Street
San Juan, Puerto Rico 00901
(787) 977-6030 FAX: (787) 977-6035

Administrative Law Judges

Luis J. D. Anglade, Administrative Law Judge
Office of Hearings and Appeals
Social Security Administration
Union Plaza Building
416 Ponce de Leon Avenue, Room 501
San Juan, Puerto Rico 00918-3418
(787) 766-5502 FAX: (787) 766-6415

Jose R. Gautier, Administrative Law Judge
Office of Hearings and Appeals
Social Security Administration – Executive Hall
441 Calle Ferrocarril, Suite 281
Ponce, Puerto Rico 00731-5617
(787) 841-3176 FAX: (787) 841-3180

Rafael Lugo-Vilanova
Chief Administrative Law Judge
Office of Hearings and Appeals
Social Security Administration
Executive Hall
441 Calle Ferrocarril, Suite 281
Ponce, Puerto Rico 00731-5617
(787) 841-3176 FAX: (787) 841-3180

Gregui J. Mercado, Administrative Law Judge
Office of Hearings and Appeals
Social Security Administration
416 Ponce de Leon Avenue - 5th Floor
San Juan, Puerto Rico 00918-3418
(787) 498-5502 FAX: (787) 766-6415

Miguel A. Montalvo
Chief Administrative Law Judge
Office of Hearings and Appeals
Social Security Administration
Medical Emporium Building
351 Avenue Hostos, Suite 301
Mayaguez, Puerto Rico 00680-1507
(787) 831-3300 FAX: (787) 831-3452

Quintin Morales-Ramirez
Administrative Law Judge
Office of Hearings and Appeals
Social Security Administration
Executive Hall
441 Calle Ferrocarril, Suite 281
Ponce, Puerto Rico 00731-5617
(787) 841-3176 FAX: (787) 841-3180

Ramon E. Quinones, Administrative Law Judge
Office of Hearings and Appeals
Social Security Administration
416 Ponce de Leon Avenue - 5th Floor
San Juan, Puerto Rico 00918-3418
(787) 766-5502 FAX: (787) 766-6415

Marta A. Ramirez de Vera
Administrative Law Judge
Office of Hearings and Appeals
Social Security Administration
416 Ponce de Leon Avenue - 5th Floor
San Juan, Puerto Rico 00918-3418
(787) 766-5502 FAX: (787) 766-6415

Ana R. Rodriguez, Administrative Law Judge
Office of Hearings and Appeals
Social Security Administration
416 Ponce de Leon Avenue - 5th Floor
San Juan, Puerto Rico 00918-3418
(787) 766-5502 FAX: (787) 766-6415

Jose J. Santiago, Administrative Law Judge
Office of Hearings and Appeals
Social Security Administration
Union Plaza Building
416 Ponce de Leon Avenue, Room 501
San Juan, Puerto Rico 00918-3418
(787) 766-5502 FAX: (787) 766-6415

Nestor E. Vega Soto, Administrative Law Judge
Office of Hearings and Appeals
Social Security Administration
Medical Emporium Building
351 Avenue Hostos, Suite 301
Mayaguez, Puerto Rico 00680-1507
(787) 831-3300 FAX: (787) 831-3452

Irma Lopez-Defillo, U. S. Immigration Judge
GSA 651 Federal Drive, Suite 111-14
Guaynabo (San Juan), Puerto Rico 00965
(787) 749-4386 FAX: Call on phone first

Supreme Court

José Antonio Andréu-Garcia, Chief Justice
Supreme Court of Puerto Rico
Post Office Box 9022392
San Juan, Puerto Rico 00902-2392
(787) 724-3535 FAX: (787) 725-4910
E-mail: andreujp@tld.net

Baltasar Corrada del Rio, Justice
Supreme Court of Puerto Rico
Post Office Box 9022392
Jan Juan, Puerto Rico 00902-2392
(787) 723-0294 FAX: (787) 725-4910

Jaime B. Fuster Berlingeri, Justice
Supreme Court of Puerto Rico
Post Office Box 9022392
San Juan, Puerto Rico 00902-2392
(787) 723-0858 or 723-0856 FAX: (787) 725-4910

Federico Hernández Denton, Justice
Supreme Court of Puerto Rico
Post Office Box 9022392
San Juan, Puerto Rico 00902-2392
(787) 723-0648 FAX: (787) 725-4910

Miriam Naveira de Rodón, Justice
Supreme Court of Puerto Rico
Post Office Box 9022392
San Juan, Puerto Rico 00902-2392
(787) 721-6625 FAX: (787) 725-4910

Francisco Rebollo López, Justice
Supreme Court of Puerto Rico
Post Office Box 9022392
San Juan, Puerto Rico 00902-2392
(787) 723-0343 FAX: (787) 725-4910

Efrain E. Rivera Perez, Justice
Supreme Court of Puerto Rico
Post Office Box 9022392
San Juan, Puerto Rico 00902-2392
(787) 723-0752 FAX: (787) 725-4910

Appellate Court

Lady Alfonso de Cumpiano, Appellate Judge
San Juan Judicial Center
Post Office Box 191067
San Juan, Puerto Rico 00919-1067
(878) 281-4303 FAX: (787) 250-7791

Nestor S. Aponte Hernández, Appellate Judge
San Juan Judicial Center
Post Office Box 191067
San Juan, Puerto Rico 00919-1067
(787) 281-4320 FAX: (787) 250-7791

José M. Aponte Jiménez, Appellate Judge
San Juan Judicial Center
Post Office Box 191067
San Juan, Puerto Rico 00919-1067
(787) 281-4322 FAX: (787) 250-7791

Guillermo Arbona Lago, Appellate Judge
San Juan Judicial Center
Post Office Box 191067
San Juan, Puerto Rico 00919-1067
(787) 281-4305 FAX: (787) 250-7791

Germán J. Brau Ramírez, Appellate Judge
San Juan Judicial Center
Post Office Box 191067
San Juan, Puerto Rico 00919-1067
(787) 281-4302 FAX: (787) 250-7791

Ismael Colón Birriel, Appellate Judge
San Juan Judicial Center
Post Office Box 191067
San Juan, Puerto Rico 00919-1067
(787) 281-4316 FAX: (787) 250-7791

Charles A. Cordero Peña, Appellate Judge
San Juan Judicial Center
Post Office Box 191067
San Juan, Puerto Rico 00919-1067
(787) 281-4318 FAX: (787) 250-7791

Roberto L. Córdova Arone, Appellate Judge
San Juan Judicial Center
Post Office Box 191067
San Juan, Puerto Rico 00919-1067
(787) 281-4306 FAX: (787) 250-7791

Nydia M. Cotto Vives, Appellate Judge
San Juan Judicial Center
Post Office Box 191067
San Juan, Puerto Rico 00919-1067
(787) 281-4317 FAX: (787) 250-7791

Jorge L. Escribano Medina, Appellate Judge
San Juan Judicial Center
Post Office Box 191067
San Juan, Puerto Rico 00919-1067
(787) 281-4323 FAX: (787) 250-7791

Ivonne Feliciano Acevedo, Appellate Judge
San Juan Judicial Center
Post Office Box 191067
San Juan, Puerto Rico 00919-1067
(787) 281-4304 FAX: (787) 250-7791

Líana Fiol Matta, Presiding Appellate Judge
San Juan Judicial Center
Post Office Box 191067
San Juan, Puerto Rico 00919-1067
(787) 281-4355 FAX: (787) 250-7791

Gilberto Gierbolini Rodríguez, Appellate Judge
San Juan Judicial Center
Post Office Box 191067
San Juan, Puerto Rico 00919-1067
(787) 281-4325 FAX: (787) 250-7791

Roberto González Rivera, Appellate Judge
San Juan Judicial Center
Post Office Box 191067
San Juan, Puerto Rico 00919-1067
(787) 281-4320 FAX: (787) 250-7791

Angel González Román, Appellate Judge
San Juan Judicial Center
Post Office Box 191067
San Juan, Puerto Rico 00919-1067
(787) 281-4353 FAX: (787) 250-7791

Zaida Hernández Torres, Appellate Judge
San Juan Judicial Center
Post Office Box 191067
San Juan, Puerto Rico 00919-1067
(787) 281-4310 FAX: (787) 250-7791

Joceyln López Vilanova, Appellate Judge
San Juan Judicial Center
Post Office Box 191067
San Juan, Puerto Rico 00919-1067
(787) 281-4354 FAX: (787) 250-7791

Rafael L. Martinez Torres, Appellate Judge
San Juan Judicial Center
Post Office Box 191067
San Juan, Puerto Rico 00919-1067
(787) 281-4326 FAX: (787) 250-7791

José L. Miranda de Hostos, Appellate Judge
San Juan Judicial Center
Post Office Box 191067
San Juan, Puerto Rico 00919-1067
(787) 281-4324 FAX: (787) 250-7791

Ramón Negrón Soto, Appellate Judge
San Juan Judicial Center
Post Office Box 191067
San Juan, Puerto Rico 00919-1067
(787) 281-4300 FAX: (787) 250-7791

Antonio J. Negroni Cintrón, Appellate Judge
San Juan Judicial Center
Post Office Box 191067
San Juan, Puerto Rico 00919-1067
(787) 281-4307 FAX: (787) 250-7791

Rafael Ortiz Carrión, Appellate Judge
San Juan Judicial Center
Post Office Box 191067
San Juan, Puerto Rico 00919-1067
(787) 281-4311 FAX: (787) 250-7791

Mildred G. Pabón Charneco, Appellate Judge
San Juan Judicial Center
Post Office Box 191067
San Juan, Puerto Rico 00919-1067
(787) 281-4321 FAX: (787) 250-7791

Carmen A. Pesante Martínez, Appellate Judge
San Juan Judicial Center
Post Office Box 191067
San Juan, Puerto Rico 00919-1067
(787) 281-4301 FAX: (787) 250-7791

Jeannette Ramos Buonomo, Appellate Judge
San Juan Judicial Center
Post Office Box 191067
San Juan, Puerto Rico 00919-1067
(787) 281-4357 FAX: (787) 250-7791

Dolores Rodríguez de Oronoz, Appellate Judge
San Juan Judicial Center
Post Office Box 191067
San Juan, Puerto Rico 00919-1067
(787) 281-4356 FAX: (787) 250-7791

Frank Rodríguez García, Appellate Judge
San Juan Judicial Center
Post Office Box 191067
San Juan, Puerto Rico 00919-1067
(787) 281-4313 FAX: (787) 250-7791

Carlos M. Rodríguez Muñiz, Appellate Judge
San Juan Judicial Center
Post Office Box 191067
San Juan, Puerto Rico 00919-1067
(787) 281-4312 FAX: (787) 250-7791

Andrés E. Salas Soler, Appellate Judge
San Juan Judicial Center
Post Office Box 191067
San Juan, Puerto Rico 00919-1067
(787) 281-4314 FAX: (787) 250-7791

Hiram Sánchez Martínez, Appellate Judge
San Juan Judicial Center
Post Office Box 191067
San Juan, Puerto Rico 00919-1067
(787) 281-4352 FAX: (787) 250-7791

Jorge Segarra Olivero, Appellate Judge
San Juan Judicial Center
Post Office Box 191067
San Juan, Puerto Rico 00919-1067
(787) 281-4319 FAX: (787) 250-7791

Carlos Soler Aquino, Appellate Judge
San Juan Judicial Center
Post Office Box 191067
San Juan, Puerto Rico 00919-1067
(787) 281-4317 FAX: (787) 250-7791

Héctor Urgell-Cuebas, Appellate Judge
San Juan Judicial Center
Post Office Box 191067
San Juan, Puerto Rico 00919-1067
(787) 281-4309 FAX: (787) 250-7791

Superior Court

Manuel Acevedo Hernández, Judge
Superior Court de Aguadilla
Post office Box 1010
Aguadilla, Puerto Rico 00605-1010
(787) 819-4046

Wilfredo Alicia Lopéz, Judge
Superior Court de San Juan
Post Office Box 190887
San Juan, Puerto Rico 00919-0887
(787) 641-6180 FAX: (787) 641-6102

Angel M. Almodóvar Correa, Judge
Superior Court de San Juan
Post Office Box 190887
San Juan, Puerto Rico 00919-0887
(787) 641-6194 FAX: (787) 641-6102

César J. Almodóvar Marchany, Judge
Superior Court de Ponce
Post Office Box 331791
Ponce, Puerto Rico 00733-1791
(787) 841-3660

Carlos A. Alvarado Arroyo, Chief Judge
Superior Court de Mayagüez
Post Office Box 1210
Mayagüez, Puerto Rico 00681-1210
(787) 832-3165

Luis Amorós Alvarez, Judge
Superior Court de Humacao
Post Office Box 885
Humacao, Puerto Rico 00792-0885
(787) 850-5062

Eva Araya Ramírez, Judge
Superior Court de Carolina
Post Office Box 267
Carolina, Puerto Rico 00986-0267
(787) 725-7990

Iván Ayala Cádiz, Judge
Superior Court de Ponce
Post Office Box 331791
Ponce, Puerto Rico 00733-1791
(787) 841-4560

Kalil Baco Viera, Judge
Superior Court de Bayamón
Post Office Box 600619
Bayamón, Puerto Rico 00960-0619
(787) 785-6950

Etienne Badillò Anazagasty, Judge
Superior Court de Carolina
Post Office Box 267
Carolina, Puerto Rico 00986-0267
(787) 752-7321

Francisco Báez Nazario, Judge
Superior Court de Arecibo
Post Office Box 6005
Arecibo, Puerto Rico 00613-6005
(787) 878-7536

José A. Bagué Ramos, Judge
Superior Court de Arecibo
Post Office Box 860
Manati, Puerto Rico 00674-0860
(787) 854-2715

Zadette Bajandas Vélez, Judge
Superior Court de San Juan
Post Office Box 190887
San Juan, Puerto Rico 00919-0887
(787) 641-6190 FAX: (787) 641-6102

Jaime Banuchi Hernández, Judge
Superior Court de Arecibo
Post Office Box 6005
Arecibo, Puerto Rico 00613-6005
(787) 878-8580

Julio Berríos Jiménez, Judge
Superior Court de Bayamón
Post Office Box 600619
Bayamón, Puerto Rico 00960-0619
(787) 785-3320

Ileana M. Bonet Fernández, Judge
Superior Court de Bayamón
Post Office Box 600619
Bayamón, Puerto Rico 0960-0619
(787) 785-7617

Manuel Bravo Gatell, Judge
Superior Court de Bayamón
Post Office Box 600619
Bayamón, Puerto Rico 00960-0619
(787) 785-7617

Ramón A. Buitrago Iglesias, Judge
Superior Court de Caguas
Post office Box 491
Caguas, Puerto Rico 00726
(787) 743-2181 FAX: (787) 743-3500

Carlos A. Cabán Garcia, Judge
Superior Court de San Juan
Post Office Box 190887
San Juan, Puerto Rico 00919-0887
(787) 641-6163 FAX: (787) 641-6102

Heidi Scherrer Caillet-Bois, Judge
Superior Court de Bayamón
Post Office Box 600619
Bayamón, Puerto Rico 00960-0619
(787) 785 7617

Marcos T. Calderón Vásquez, Judge
Superior Court de Arecibo
Post Office Box 6005
Arecibo, Puerto Rico 00613-6005
(787) 878-5517

Georgina Candal Segurola, Judge
Superior Court de Bayamón
Post Office Box 600619
Bayamón, Puerto Rico 00960-0619
(787) 785-7539

Carlos E. Carrasquillo Soto, Judge
Superior Court de San Juan
Post Office Box 190887
San Juan, Puerto Rico 00919-0887
(787) 641-6156

Luis G. Cerra Carreira, Judge
Superior Court de Caguas
Post Office Box 491
Caguas, Puerto Rico 00726
(787) 633-0131 FAX: (787) 743-3500

Blanca Collazo Colón, Judge
Superior Court de San Juan
Post Office Box 190887
San Juan, Puerto Rico 00919-0887
(787) 641-6175 FAX: (787) 641-6102

Bernardo Colón Barbosa, Judge
Superior Court de Guayama
Post Office Box 300
Guayama, Puerto Rico 00785-0300
(787) 864-1580

Carlos F. Colón Santini, Judge
Superior Court de Caguas
Post Office Box 491
Caguas, Puerto Rico 00726
(787) 743-4505 FAX: (787) 743-3500

Bruno Cortés Trigo, Judge
Superior Court de Caguas
Post Office Box 491
Caguas, Puerto Rico 00726
(787) 746-4346

Juan Corujo Collazo, Judge
Superior Court de San Juan
Post Office Box 190887
San Juan, Puerto Rico 00919-0887
(787) 641-6195 FAX: (787) 641-6102

José A. Cruz Noel, Judge
Superior Court de Mayagüez
Post Office Box 1210
Mayagüez, Puerto Rico 00681-1210
(787) 833-3280

Elmer Cuerda Acevedo, Judge
Superior Court de Mayagüez
Post Office Box 1210
Mayagüez, Puerto Rico 00681-1210
(787) 833-3280

Ismael Colón Pérez, Judge
Superior Court de Fajardo
Post Office Box 70009
Fajardo, Puerto Rico 00738-7009
(787) 863-2204

Héctor J. Conty Pérez, Judge
Superior Court de Aguadilla
Post Office Box 1010
Aguadillo, Puerto Rico 00605-1010
(787) 819-3640

Georgina Dávila Altieri, Judge
Superior Court de Bayamón
Post Office Box 600619
Bayamón. Puerto Rico 00960-0619
(787) 787-1678

Manuel De Jesús Cubán Soto, Judge
Superior Court de San Juan
Post Office Box 190887
San Juan, Puerto Rico 00919-0877
(787) 641-6192 FAX: (787) 641-6102

Victor D. De Jesús Cubano, Judge
Superior Court de Utuado
Post Office Box 2555
Utuado, Puerto Rico 00641-2555
(787) 894-6560

Reinaldo de León Martínez, Chief Judge
Superior Court de Humacao
Post Office Box 885
Humacao, Puerto Rico 00792-0885
(787) 852-0150

Sonia L. Del Toro Padin, Judge
Superior Court de Guayama
Post Office Box 300
Guayama, Puerto Rico 00785-0300
(787) 864-6566

Juan J. Delgado Delgado, Judge
Superior Court de Ponce
Post Office Box 331791
Ponce, Puerto Rico 00733-1791
(787) 841-4025

Angel L. Díaz del Valle, Judge
Superior Court de Bayamón
Post Office Box 600619
Bayamón, Puerto Rico 00960-0619
(787) 648-3740

Manuel Díaz Morales, Judge
Superior Court de Ponce
Post Office Box 331791
Ponce, Puerto Rico 00733-1791
(787) 841-4055

Yolanda Doitteau Ruiz, Judge
Superior Court de San Juan
Post Office Box 190887
San Juan, Puerto Rico 00919-0887
(787) 641-6167 FAX: (787) 641-6102

Miguel J. Fabre Ramírez, Judge
Superior Court de San Juan
Post Office Box 190887
San Juan, Puerto Rico 00919-0887
(787) 641-6163

Ramón E. Febus Bernardini, Judge
Superior Court de Aguadilla
Post Office Box 1010
Aguadilla, Puerto Rico 00605-1010
(787) 891-3629

José M. Fernández Luis, Judge
Superior Court de Caguas
Post Office Box 491
Caguas, Puerto Rico 00726
(787) 743-5535

Rafael A. Flores Diaz, Judge
Superior Court de Arecibo
Post Office Box 6005
Arecibo, Puerto Rico 00613-6005
(787) 878-0346

Eliseo Gaetán y Mejías, Judge
Superior Court de Bayamón
Post Office Box 600619
Bayamón, Puerto Rico 00960-0619
(787) 785-3597

Cristóbal Gallardo Rodríguez, Judge
Superior Court de Arecibo
Post Office Box 6005
Arecibo, Puerto Rico 00613-6005
(787) 880-3185

David García Medina, Judge
Superior Court de Arecibo
Post Office Box 6005
Arecibo, Puerto Rico 00613-6005
(787) 878-0344

Isidro García Pesquera, Judge
Superior Court de Aibonito
Post Office Box 1449
Aibonito, Puerto Rico 00705-1449
(787) 735-7121

Julia Garriga Trillo, Judge
Superior Court de San Juan
Post Office Box 190887
San Juan, Puerto Rico 00919-0887
(787) 641-6151 FAX: (787) 641-6102

Fernando Gierbolini Borelli, Chief Judge
Superior Court de Caguas
Post Office Box 491
Caguas, Puerto Rico 00726
(787) 743-8707 FAX: (787) 743-3500

José L. Gierbolini Rosa, Judge
Superior Court de Ponce
Post Office Box 331791
Ponce, Puerto Rico 00733-1791
(787) 841-3822

María del C. Gómez Córdova, Judge
Superior Court de San Juan
Post Office Box 190887
San Juan, Puerto Rico 00919-0887
(787) 641-6166 FAX: (787) 641-6102

Ricardo J. González Porrata-Doria, Judge
Superior Court de Arecibo
Post Office Box 6005
Arecibo, Puerto Rico 00613-6005
(787) 878-0374

Aldo J. González Quesada, Judge (Regional)
Superior Court de Guayama
Post Office Box 300
Guayama, Puerto Rico 00785-0300
(787) 864-1420

Velma I. González Rivera, Judge
Superior Court de Caguas
Post Office Box 491
Caguas, Puerto Rico 00726
(787) 743-5200 FAX: (787) 743-3500

Aurelio Gracia Morales, Chief Judge
Superior Court de Aibonito
Post Office Box 1449
Aibonito, Puerto Rico 00705-1449
(787) 735-5073

Eduardo Grau Acosta, Judge
Superior Court de Guayama
Post Office Box 300
Guayama, Puerto Rico 00785-0300
(787) 864-0578

José A. Gutiérrez Núñez, Judge
Superior Court de Caguas
Post Office Box 491
Caguas, Puerto Rico 00726
(787) 744-3665 FAX: (787) 743-3500

Magalia Hosta Modestti, Chief Judge
Superior Court de Fajardo
Post Office Box 70009
Fajardo, Puerto Rico 00738-7009
(787) 860-3455

Gloria M. Iagrossi Brenes, Judge
Superior Court de San Juan
Post Office Box 190887
San Juan, Puerto Rico 00919-0887
(787) 641-6177 FAX: (787) 641-6102

Concepción del P. Igartúa, Judge
Superior Court de Bayamón
Post Office Box 600619
Bayamón, Puerto Rico 00960-0619
(787) 785-7350

Awilda Irizarry Pardo, Judge
Superior Court de San Juan
Post Office Box 190887
San Juan, Puerto Rico 00919-0887
(787) 641-6161 FAX: (787) 641-6102

Myrta Irizarry Rios, Judge
Superior Court de San Juan
Post Office Box 190887
San Juan, Puerto Rico 00919-0887
(787) 641-6155 FAX: (787) 641-6102

Charles Jiménez Nettleship, Judge
Superior Court de Bayamón
Post Office Box 600619
Bayamón, Puerto Rico 00960-0619
(787) 785-7617

Nydia Z. Jiménez Sánchez, Judge
Superior Court de San Juan
Post Office Box 190887
San Juan, Puerto Rico 00919-0887
(787) 641-6169 FAX: (787) 641-6102

Nélida Jiménez Velázquez, Judge
Superior Court de San Juan
Post Office Box 190887
San Juan, Puerto Rico 00919-0887
(787) 641-6163

Ramiro Lladó Martínez, Judge
Superior Court de Mayagüez
Post Office Box 1210
Mayagüez, Puerto Rico 00681-1210
(787) 832-3302

Héctor Lajara Alvarez, Judge
Superior Court de Ponce
Post Office Box 331791
Ponce, Puerto Rico 00733-1791
(787) 841-3420

Héctor López García, Judge
Superior Court de San Juan
Post Office Box 190887
San Juan, Puerto Rico 00919-0887
(787) 641-6196 FAX: (787) 641-6102

Danny López Soto, Judge
Superior Court de Humacao
Post Office Box 885
Humacao, Puerto Rico 00792-0885
(787) 852-0200

José M. Lorié Velasco, Judge
Superior Court de San Juan
Post Office Box 190887
San Juan, Puerto Rico 00919-0887
(787) 641-6185 FAX: (787) 641-6102

José E. Loubriel Vázquez, Chief Judge
Superior Court de Utuado
Post Office Box 2555
Utuado, Puerto Rico 00641-2555
(787) 894-2276

Herman Lugo del Toro, Judge
Superior Court de Carolina
Post Office Box 267
Carolina, Puerto Rico 00986-0267
(787) 276-7545

Berta Mainardi Peralta, Judge
Superior Court de San Juan
Post Office Box 190887
San Juan, Puerto Rico 00919-0887
(787) 641-6186 FAX: (787) 641-6102

Melvin Maldonado Colón, Judge
Superior Court de Ponce
Post Office Box 331791
Ponce, Puerto Rico 00733-1791
(787) 841-4336

Wilfredo Maldonado Colón, Judge
Superior Court de Humacao
Post Office Box 885
Humacao, Puerto Rico 00792-0885
(787) 852-3052

Juan Maldonado Torres, Judge
Superior Court de Bayamón
Post Office Box 600619
Bayamón, Puerto Rico 00960-0619
(787) 785-1275

María T. Mandry Pagán, Judge
Superior Court de Arecibo
Post Office Box 6005
Arecibo, Puerto Rico 00613-6005
(787) 878-0374

María del C. Martínez Lugo, Judge
Superior Court de Carolina
Post Office Box 267
Carolina, Puerto Rico 00986-0267
(787) 752-8830

Amneris Martínez Sánchez, Judge
Superior Court de San Juan
Post Office Box 190887
San Juan, Puerto Rico 00919-0887
(787) 641-6353 FAX: (787) 641-6102

Marilyn Martir Gayá, Judge
Superior Court de Carolina
Post Office Box 267
Carolina, Puerto Rico 00986-0267
(787) 757-2920

Samuel Mártir Santiago, Judge
Superior Court de Aguadilla
Post Office Box 1010
Aguadilla, Puerto Rico 00605-1010
(787) 891-3633

Juan R. Melecio Machuca, Judge
Superior Court (General)
Post Office Box 190887
San Juan, Puerto Rico 00919-0887
(787) 641-6619

Roberto Miranda Rivera, Judge
Superior Court de Carolina
Post Office Box 267
Carolina, Puerto Rico 00986-0267
(787) 752-6245

Fernando Montañez Delerme, Judge
Superior Court de Ponce
Post Office Box 331791
Ponce, Puerto Rico 00733-1791
(787) 841-3780

Hernán Morales Alvarez, Judge
Superior Court de Mayaguez
Post Office Box 1210
Mayaguez, Puerto Rico 00681-1210
(787) 833-8133

Ivelisse Moyano Ares, Judge
Superior Court de San Juan
Post Office Box 190887
San Juan, Puerto Rico 00919-0887
(787) 641-6152 FAX: (787) 641-6102

Yazmín Nadal Arroyo, Judge
Superior Court de Bayamón
Post Office Box 600619
Bayamón, Puerto Rico 00960-0619
(787) 785-7617

Carlos M. Nieves Ortiz, Judge
Superior Court de Ponce
Post Office Box 331791
Ponce, Puerto Rico 00733-1791
(787) 841-4055

Jorge Orama Monroig, Judge
Superior Court de San Juan
Post Office Box 190887
San Juan, Puerto Rico 00919-0887
(787) 641-6174 FAX: (787) 641-6102

Manuel Orriola Pérez, Judge
Superior Court de Arecibo
Post Office Box 6005
Arecibo, Puerto Rico 00613-6005
(787) 878-0626

Eladís Orsini Zayas, Judge
Superior Court de Ponce
Post Office Box 331791
Ponce, Puerto Rico 00733-1791
(787) 841-3490

Ramón Orta Berríos, Chief Judge
Superior Court de Guayama
Post Office Box 300
Guayama, Puerto Rico 00785-0300
(787) 864-1120

Lilia Ortiz Puig, Judge
Superior Court de Carolina
Post Office Box 267
Carolina, Puerto Rico 00986-0267
(787) 769-0106

Francisco Ortiz Rivera, Judge
Superior Court de Ponce
Post Office Box 331791
Ponce, Puerto Rico 00733-1791
(787) 841-3911

Juan Ortiz Rodríguez, Judge
Superior Court de Aibonito
Post Office Box 1449
Aibonito, Puerto Rico 00705-1449
(787) 735-7120

Dimas G. Padilla Bruno, Judge
Superior Court de Carolina
Post Office Box 267
Carolina, Puerto Rico 00986-0267
(787) 752-1304

Wilfredo Padilla Soto, Chief Judge
Superior Court de Carolina
Post Office Box 267
Carolina, Puerto Rico 00986-0267
(787) 257-0245

Carmen H. Pagani Padró, Judge
Superior Court de San Juan
Post Office Box 190887
San Juan, Puerto Rico 00919-0887
(787) 641-6184 FAX: (787) 641-6102

José R. Parés Martinez, Judge
Superior Court de Bayamón
Post Office Box 600619
Bayamón, Puerto Rico 00960-0619
(787) 785-3530

Dora T. Peñagarícano Soler, Judge
Superior Court de San Juan
Post Office Box 190887
San Juan, Puerto Rico 00919-0887
(787) 641-6181

Gloria I. Pérez Maury, Judge
Superior Court de San Juan
Post Office Box 190887
San Juan, Puerto Rico 00919-0887
(787) 641-6160 FAX: (787) 641-6102

Felícita Pérez Rivera, Judge
Superior Court de San Juan
Post Office Box 190887
San Juan, Puerto Rico 00919-0887
(787) 641-6183 FAX: (787) 641-6102

Rita L. Pruetzel González, Judge
Superior Court de Caguas
Post Office Box 491
Caguas, Puerto Rico 00726
(787) 746-5579 FAX: (787) 743-3500

Sylvette A. Quiñones Mari, Judge
Superior Court de Mayaguez
Post Office Box 1210
Mayaguez, Puerto Rico 00681-1210
(787) 833-3280

Luis G. Quiñones Martínez, Judge
Superior Court de Bayamón
Post Office Box 600619
Bayamón, Puerto Rico 00960-0619
(787) 787-7205

Angel D. Ramírez Ramírez, Judge
Superior Court de Carolina
Post Office Box 267
Carolina, Puerto Rico 00986-0267
(787) 752-2940

Maritza I. Ramos Mercado, Judge
Superior Court de Carolina
Post Office Box 267
Carolina, Puerto Rico 00986-0267
(787) 752-7085

Sonsire Ramos Soler, Judge
Superior Court de Carolina
Post Office Box 267
Carolina, Puerto Rico 00986-0267
(787) 752-0922

Misael Ramos Torres, Judge
Superior Court de Bayamón
Post Office Box 600619
Bayamón, Puerto Rico 00960-0619
(787) 785-7980

José O. Resto Huertas, Judge
Superior Court de Caguas
Post Office Box 491
Caguas, Puerto Rico 00726
(787) 743-8100 FAX: (787) 743-3500

Juan Reyes Caraballo, Judge
Superior Court de Arecibo
Post Office Box 6005
Arecibo, Puerto Rico 00613-6005
(787) 878-2544

Eddie A. Ríos Benitez, Judge
Superior Court de San Juan
Post Office Box 190887
San Juan, Puerto Rico 00919-0887
(787) 641-6305 FAX: (787) 641-6102

Osvaldo Rivera Cianchini, Judge
Superior Court de Carolina
Post Office Box 267
Carolina, Puerto Rico 00986-0267
(787) 750-6265

Victor M. Rivera González, Judge
Superior Court de San Juan
Post Office Box 190887
San Juan, Puerto Rico 00919-0887
(787) 641-6302 FAX: (787) 641-6102

Milagros Rivera Guadarráma, Judge
Superior Court de San Juan
Post Office Box 190887
San Juan, Puerto Rico 00919-0887
(787) 641-6179 FAX: (787) 641-6102

Carlos de Jesús Rivera Marrero, Judge
Superior Court de Bayamón
Post Office Box 600619
Bayamón, Puerto Rico 00960-0619
(787) 785-7910

Carlos Rivera Martínez, Chief Judge
Superior Court de San Juan
Post Office Box 190887
San Juan, Puerto Rico 00919-0887
(787) 641-6374 FAX: (787) 641-6102

Luis Rivera Román, Judge
Superior Court de Mayagúez
Post Office Box 1210
Mayagúez, Puerto Rico 00681-1210
(787) 265-8510

Isidro Rivera Sánchez, Judge
Superior Court de Guayama
Post Office Box 300
Guayma, Puerto Rico 00785-0300
(787) 864-2622

Wilfredo Robles Carrasquillo, Judge
Superior Court de Ponce
Post Office Box 331791
San Juan, Puerto Rico 00733-1791
(787) 841-4380

José A. Rodríguez Arenas, Judge
Superior Court de Carolina
Post office Box 267
Carolina, Puerto Rico 00986-0267
(787) 257-0135

Wilfredo Rodríguez Figueroa, Judge
Superior Court de Humacao
Post Office Box 885
Humacao, Puerto Rico 00792-0885
(787) 852-2190

Elba R. Rodríguez Fuentes, Judge
Superior Court de San Juan
Post Office Box 190887
San Juan, Puerto Rico 00919-0887
(787) 641-6192 FAX: (787) 641-6102

José M. Rodríguez Viejo, Judge
Superior Court de San Juan
Post Office Box 190887
San Juan, Puerto Rico 00919-0887
(787) 641-6176 FAX: (787) 641-6102

Ramón Rojas Peña, Judge
Superior Court de Humacao
Post Office Box 885
Humacao, Puerto Rico 00792-0885
(787) 852-0110

Emilia Román Nevárez, Judge
Superior Court de Bayamón
Post Office Box 600619
Bayamón, Puerto Rico 00960-0619
(787) 785-7617

Luis E. Roque Colón, Judge
Superior Court de San Juan
Post Office Box 190887
San Juan, Puerto Rico 00919-0887
(787) 641-6170 FAX: (787) 641-6102

Aixa Rosado Pietri, Judge (Regional)
Superior Court de Caguas
Post Office Box 491
Caguas, Puerto Rico 00726
(787) 543-2182 FAX: (787) 743-3500

Miguel A. Rosario Reyes, Judge
Superior Court de Guayama
Post Office Box 300
Guayama, Puerto Rico 00785-0300
(787) 864-6566

Luis Rosario Villanueva, Judge
Superior Court de Bayamón
Post Office Box 600619
Bayamón, Puerto Rico 00960-0619
(787) 780-2609

Edwin Ruiz González, Judge
Superior Court de Bayamón
Post Office Box 600619
Bayamón, Puerto Rico 00960-0619
(787) 785-6408

Carmen D. Ruiz López, Judge
Superior Court de San Juan
Post Office Box 190887
San Juan, Puerto Rico 00919-0887
(787) 641-6301 FAX: (787) 641-6102

Luis A. Ruiz Malavé, Judge
Superior Court de Bayamón
Post Office Box 600619
Bayamón, Puerto Rico 00960-0619
(787) 785-7920

Josè A. Ruiz Rivera, Judge
Superior Court de Ponce
Post Office Box 331791
Ponce, Puerto Rico 00733-1791
(787) 841-4605

Mabel Ruiz Soto, Judge
Superior Court de Arecibo
Post Office Box 6005
Arecibo, Puerto Rico 00613-6005
(787) 878-2466

Angel L. Saavedra De Jesús, Judge
Superior Court de Utuado
Post Office Box 2555
Utuado, Puerto Rico 00641-2555
(787) 894-2476

Luis G. Saavedra Serrano, Judge
Superior Court de Carolina
Post Office Box 267
Carolina, Puerto Rico 00986-0267
(787) 276-7510

Olivette Sagebién Raffo, Judge
Superior Court de San Juan
Post Office Box 190887
San Juan, Puerto Rico 00919-0887
(787) 641-6163 FAX: (787) 641-6102

Ricardo Santana Ramos, Judge
Superior Court de Mayagüez
Post Office Box 1210
Mayagüez, Puerto Rico 00681-1210
(787) 832-5033

Rosaline Santana Ríos, Judge
Superior Court de Ponce
Post Office Box 331791
Ponce, Puerto Rico 00733-1791
(787) 841-3545

Sonia Santana Sepúlveda, Judge
Superior Court de Humacao
Post Office Box 885
Humacao, Puerto Rico 00792-0805
(787) 852-0150

Miguel A. Santiago Gómez, Judge
Superior Court de Ponce
Post Office Box 331791
Ponce, Puerto Rico 00733-1791
(787) 841-4230

Miriam Santiago Guzmán, Judge
Superior Court de Aguadilla
Post Office Box 1010
Aguadilla, Puerto Rico 00605-1010
(787) 819-3631 FAX: (787) 819-3641

Wilfredo Santos López, Chief Judge
Superior Court de Ponce
Post Office Box 331791
Ponce, Puerto Rico 00733-1791
(787) 841-3715

Heriberto Sepúlveda Santiago, Chief Judge
Superior Court de Bayamón
Post Office Box 600619
Bayamón, Puerto Rico 00960-0619
(787) 787-8040

Katheryne Silvestry Hernández, Judge
Superior Court de San Juan
Post Office Box 190887
San Juan, Puerto Rico 00919-0887
(787) 641-6158 FAX: (787) 641-6102

Julio Soto Ríos, Judge
Superior Court de Bayamón
Post Office Box 600619
Bayamón, Puerto Rico 00960-0619
(787) 785-7539

Yamil Suárez Marchan, Chief Judge
Superior Court de Aguadilla
Post Office Box 1010
Aguadilla, Puerto Rico 00605-1010
(787) 819-3608

Mildred Surén Fuentes, Judge (Regional)
Superior Court de Humacao
Post Office Box 885
Humacao, Puerto Rico 00792-0805
(787) 850-0180

Jeannette Tomasini Gómez, Judge
Superior Court de Bayamón
Post Office Box 600619
Bayamón, Puerto Rico 00960-0619
(787) 785-1231

Gladys Torregrosa de la Rosa, Judge
Superior Court de Aguadilla
Post Office Box 1010
Aguadilla, Puerto Rico 00605-1010
(787) 819-3634

Rubén Torres Dávila, Judge
Superior Court de Caguas
Post Office Box 491
Caguas, Puerto Rico 00726
(787) 744-8441 FAX: (787) 743-3500

Aurea Torres Hernández, Judge
Superior Court de San Juan
Post Office Box 190887
San Juan, Puerto Rico 00919-0887
(787) 641-6166 FAX: (787) 641-6102

Edwin Torres Nazario, Judge
Superior Court de Guayama
Post Office Box 300
Guayama, Puerto Rico 00785-0300
(787) 864-1790

Fernando L. Torres Ramírez, Judge
Superior Court de Aguadilla
Post Office Box 1010
Aguadilla, Puerto Rico 00605-1010
(787) 891-5555 Ext. 2001 FAX: (787) 819-3641

Norah E. Vallejo Cruz, Judge
Superior Court de Caguas
Post Office Box 491
Caguas, Puerto Rico 00726
(787) 743-2102 FAX: (787) 743-3500

Carmen Vargas Medina, Judge
Superior Court de Caguas
Post Office Box 491
Caguas, Puerto Rico 00726
(787) 743-3333 FAX: (787) 743-3500

Lourdes Velázquez Cajigas, Judge
Superior Court de San Juan
Post Office Box 190887
San Juan, Puerto Rico 00910-0887
(787) 641-6303 FAX: (787) 641-6102

Sonia I. Vélez Colón, Judge
Superior Court de San Juan
Post Office Box 190887
San Juan, Puerto Rico 00919-0887
(787) 641-6191 FAX: (787) 641-6102

Manuel J. Vera Vera, Judge
Superior Court de Mayagüez
Post Office Box 1210
Mayagüez, Puerto Rico 00681-1210
(787) 832-9700

Mirinda Y. Vicenty Nazario, Judge
Superior Court de Carolina
Post Office Box 267
Carolina, Puerto Rico 00986-0267
(787) 752-7321

Awilda Vilches Reyes, Judge
Superior Courd de Carolina
Post Office Box 267
Carolina, Puerto Rico 00986-0267
(787) 276-7630

Jimmy Villalobos González, Judge
Superior Court de Arecibo
Post Office Box 6005
Arecibo, Puerto Rico 00613-6005
(787) 880-3334

Rafael L. Vissepó Vázquez, Judge
Superior Court de Carolina
Post Office Box 267
Carolina, Puerto Rico 00986-0267
(787) 752-7230

Superior Courts in Districts

José A. Bagué Ramos, Judge
Superior Court
Post Office Box 860
Manati, Puerto Rico 00674-0860
(787) 854-2715

María del C. Berríos Flores, Judge
Superior Court
Post Office Box 3042
Yauco, Puerto Rico 00698-3042
(787) 856-1800

Héctor Brull Cestero, Judge
Post Office Box 190887
San Juan, Puerto Rico 00919-0887
(787) 641-6165

Eduardo Busquets Pesquera, Judge
Superior Court
Post Office Box 2119
Orocovis, Puerto Rico 00720-2119
(787) 867-3930 FAX: (878) 867-2620

Luisa M. Colom García, Judge
Superior Court
Post Office Box 1185
Guaynabo, Puerto Rico 00970
(787) 720-2382

Héctor Cordero Vázquez, Judge
Superior Court
Post Office Box 1185
Guaynabo, Puerto Rico 60970
(787) 720-6500

Lydia E. Couvertier Martínez, Judge
Post Office Box 190887
San Juan, Puerto Rico 00919-0887
(787) 641-6165

Angela L. De Jesús Collazo, Judge
Post Office Box 868
Vieques, Puerto Rico 00765-0868
(787) 863-1314

Luis G. De Jesús Rivera, Judge
Superior Court
Post Office Box 4158
Vega Baja, Puerto Rico 00693
(787) 858-2015

Edgar Delgado García, Judge
Superior Court
Post Office Box 1405
Añasco, Puerto Rico 00616
(787) 826-2606

Juan Hernández Sánchez, Judge
Superior Court
Post Office Box 835
Río Grande, Puerto Rico 00745
(787) 887-0677

Miguel A. Magraner Lizardi, Judge
Post Office Box 927
Cabo Rojo, Puerto Rico 00623-0927
(787) 851-1055

Luis Márquez Torres, Judge
Post Office Box 223
San Germán, Puerto Rico 00683-0223
(787) 892-4333

Myrta M. Montes Villalobos, Judge
Superior Court
Post Office Box 659
Camuy, Puerto Rico 00627-0659
(787) 898-3375

Mario Morales Rosario, Judge
Superior Court
Post Office Box 1113
Comerio, Puerto Rico 00782-1113
(787) 875-3330

Leticia Ortiz Feliciano, Judge
Superior Court
Post Office Box 1160
Salinas, Puerto Rico 00751-1160
(787) 824-2260

Laura I. Ortiz Flores, Judge
Superior Court
Post Office Box 1336
Toa Alta, Puerto Rico 00954
(787) 870-2560

Juan Ortiz Torrales, Judge
Post Office Box 1336
Toa Alta, Puerto Rico 00954
(787) 870-3171

Luis A. Pérez Caraballo, Judge
Post Office Box 190887
San Juan, Puerto Rico 00919-0887
(787) 641-6157

José A. Ramos Aponte, Judge
Superior Court
Post Office Box 48
Adjuntas, Puerto Rico 00601-0048
(787) 829-2630

Mabel Ramón Milián, Judge
Superior Court
Post Office Box 1340
Ciales, Puerto Rico 00638-1340
(787) 871-2400

Felipe Rivera Colón, Judge
Superior Court
Post Office Box 1293
San Lorenzo, Puerto Rico 00754-1293
(787) 736-6216

Carmen V. Rivera de Saldaña, Judge
Post Office Box 600619
Bayamón, Puerto Rico 00960-0619
(787) 785-1208

Lucy I. Rivera Doncell, Judge
Superior Court
Post Office Box 1571
San Sebastian, Puerto Rico 00685-1571
(787) 896-1669

Glorimel Rivera Irizarry, Judge
Superior Court
Post Office Box 1923
Coamo, Puerto Rico 00769-1923
(787) 825-1614

Edmeé Rodríguez Fontánez, Judge
Post Office Box 26
Yabucoa, Puerto Rico 00767-0026
(787) 893-2290

Rafael Rodríguez Olmo, Judge
Superior Court
Post Office Box 1419
Juana Díaz, Puerto Rico 00795-1419
(787) 837-2626

Agapito Rosa Martínez, Judge
Post Office Box 491
Caguas, Puerto Rico 00726
(787) 743-1221

Edison R. Sanabría Pérez, Judge
Superior Court
Post Office Box 560277
Guayanilla, Puerto Rico 00656-0277
(787) 835-3360

Oscar Sánchez Lamboy, Judge
Superior Court
Post Office Box 1249
Lares, Puerto Rico 00669-1249
(787) 897-2395

Gloria M. Soto Burgos, Judge
Superior Court
Post Office Box 373457
Cayey, Puerto Rico 00737-3457
(787) 738-2771
Municipal Court Judges

Aracelia Acevedo Cruz, Judge
Municipal Court
Post Office Box 267257-3430
Carolina, Puerto Rico 00986-0267
(787) 752-1505

Waleska Aldebol Mora, Judge
Municipal Court (General)
Post Office Box 190887
Rincón, Puerto Rico 00919-0887
(787) 641-6103

Abelardo Bermudez Torres, Judge
Municipal Court
Post Office Box 300
Guayama, Puerto Rico 00785-0300
(787) 864-0484

Rosemary Borges Capó, Judge
Municipal Court
Post Office Box 331791
Ponce, Puerto Rico 00733-1791
(787) 841-2605

José O. Burgos Mendez, Judge
Municipal Court
Post Office Box 1449
Aibonito, Puerto Rico 00705-1449
(787) 735-5598

Maria J. Busó Aboy, Judge
Municipal Court
Post office Box 1293
San Lorenzo, Puerto Rico 00754-1293
(787) 736-6093 FAX: (787) 744-8510

Juan A. Calero del Valle, Judge
Municipal Court
Post Office Box 994
Juncos, Puerto Rico 00777-0994
(787) 734-3391 FAX: (787) 734-7701

Sylkia Carballo Nogueras, Judge
Municipal Court
Post Office Box 313
Cidra, Puerto Rico 00739-0313
(787) 739-2886

Sonia L. Cardona Pérez, Judge
Municipal Court
Post Office Box 267257-3430
Carolina, Puerto Rico 00986-0267
(787) 752-1505

Nylda Castro Colón, Judge
Municipal Court (General)
Post Office Box 190887
San Juan, Puerto Rico 00919-0887
(787) 641-6103

Hernán Chico Fuertes, Judge
Municipal Court
Post Office Box 860
Manatí, Puerto Rico 00674-0860
(787) 854-5225

Eric Colón Colón, Judge
Municipal Court
Post Office Box 600619
Bayamón, Puerto Rico 00960-0619
(787) 785-0067

Juan Correa Rodríguez, Judge
Municipal Court
Post Office Box 1571
San Sebastian, Puerto Rico 00685-1571
(787) 896-1140

Nilda I. Cruz Aponte, Judge
Municipal Court
Post Office Box 239
Gurabo, Puerto Rico 00778-0239
(787) 737-2136

Mariluz Cruz Morales, Judge
Municipal Court
Post Office Box 26
Yabucoa, Puerto Rico 00767-0026
(787) 893-2290 FAX: (787) 893-4100

Eugenia M. Cruz Sánchez, Judge
Municipal Court
Post Office Box 659
Camuy, Puerto Rico 00627-0659
(787) 262-9368

Ramiro Cruz Santiago, Judge
Municipal Court
Post Office Box 1336
Toa Alta, Puerto Rico 00954-1336
(787) 870-3171

Víctor M. De Jesús González, Judge
Municipal Court
Post Office Box 346
Florida, Puerto Rico 00650-0346
(787) 822-2450

Angel De Jesús Sepúlveda, Judge
Municipal Court
Post Office Box 411
Trujillo Alto, Puerto Rico 00977-0411
(787) 761-2100

José A. Díaz Espinosa, Judge
Municipal Court
Post Office Box 6005
Arecibo, Puerto Rico 00613-6005
(787) 870-0544

Sheila Díaz García, Judge
Municipal Court
Post Office Box 331791
Ponce, Puerto Rico 00733-1791
(787) 841-4440

Armando Escabí Ramírez, Judge
Municipal Court (General)
Post Office Box 190887
San Juan, Puerto Rico 00919-0887
(787) 641-6103

Cynthia Espéndez Santisteban, Judge
Municipal Court
Post Office Box 1923
Coamo, Puerto Rico 00769-1923
(787) 825-1030

José Feliciano Feliciano, Judge
Municipal Court
Post Office Box 2555
Utuado, Puerto Rico 00641-2555
(787) 897-2325

Nereidá Feliciano Ramos, Judge
Municipal Court
Post Office Box 420
Ceiba, Puerto Rico 00735-0420
(787) 863-1314 FAX: (787) 885-2490

Roger Ferrán Quintana, Judge
Municipal Court
Post Office Box 600619
Bayamón, Puerto Rico 00960-0619
(787) 785-0067

David García Medina, Judge
Guayama Municipal Court
Post Office Box 300
Guayama, Puerto Rico 00785-0300
(787) 864-0045

María S. Gil Delgado, Judge
Municipal Court
Post Office Box 130
Peñuelas, Puerto Rico 00624-0130
(787) 836-1147

Alida Gil Rivera, Judge
Municipal Court
Centro Comercial - Levitt Plaza I
URB Levittown
Toa Baja, Puerto Rico 00949
(787) 784-2504 FAX: (787) 261-6610

Jeannette González Acevedo, Judge
Municipal Court
Post Box Box 269
Isabela, Puerto Rico 00662-0269
(787) 868-4503

Ricardo J. González Porrata-Doria, Judge
Bayamón Municipal Court
Post Office Box 600619
Bayamón, Puerto Rico 00960-0619
(787) 785-0067

Aldo J. González Quesada, Judge
Cayey Municipal Court
Post Office Box 373457
Cayey, Puerto Rico 00737-3457
(787) 738-6633

José A. Grajales González, Judge
Municipal Court
Post Office Box 262
Vega Alta, Puerto Rico 00692-0262
(787) 883-4350

Leyla T. Graulau Igartúa, Judge
Municipal Court
Post Office Box 1449
Aibonito, Puerto Rico 00705-1449
(787) 735-7122

Rocío del C. Hernández, Judge
Municipal Court
Post Office Box 491
Caguas Puerto Rico 00726-0491
(787) 744-8510

Ann M. Higginbotham Arroyo, Judge
Municipal Court
Post Office Box 1160
Salinas, Puerto Rico 00751-1160
(787) 824-7586

Liria Irimia Lliteras, Judge
Municipal Court
Post Office Box 1008
Luquillo, Puerto Rico 00773-1008
(787) 889-3340

Nydza Irizarry Algarín, Judge
Municipal Court
Post Office Box 479
Canóvanas, Puerto Rico 00729-0479
(787) 876-2805

Angela T. Irizarry Irizarry, Judge
Municipal Court
Post Office Box 3042
Yauco, Puerto Rico 00698-3042
(787) 856-8033

María M. Jordán Mir, Judge
Municipal Court
Post Office Box 1210
Mayagúez, Puerto Rico 00681
(787) 265-2280

Ada R. Juarbe Guzmán, Judge
Municipal Court (General)
Post Office Box 190887
San Juan, Puerto Rico 00919-0887
(787) 641-6103

Elizabeth Linares Santiago, Judge
Municipal Court (General)
Post Office Box 190887
San Juan, Puerto Rico 00919-0887
(787) 641-6103

Penny T. López Cordero, Judge
Bayamón Municipal Court
Post Office Box 600619
Bayamón, Puerto Rico 00960-0619
(787) 785-7970

Daniel R. López González, Judge
Municipal Court
Post Office Box 885
Humacao, Puerto Rico 00792-0885
(787) 850-7336

Gricelle Lugo Santiago, Judge
Municipal Court
Post Office Box 267257-3430
Carolina, Puerto Rico 00986-0267
(787) 257-4160

Edgardo Maldonado Maldonado, Judge
Municipal Court
Post Office Box 600619
Bayamón, Puerto Rico 00960-0619
(787) 785-0067

Marcos E. Marcucci Sobrado, Judge
Municipal Court
Post Office Box 560277
Guayanilla, Puerto Rico 00656-0277
(787) 835-3644

Suzette Márquez Valeddón, Judge
Municipal Court
Post Office Box 373457
Cayey, Puerto Rico 00737-3457
(787) 738-6633

Fernando G. Marrero Coll, Judge
Municipal Court
Post Office Box 182
Naguabo, Puerto Rico 00718-0812
(787) 874-2105

Walter Marrero Meléndez, Judge
Municipal Court
Post Office Box 951
Barceloneta, Puerto Rico 00617
(787) 846-5598

Pedro J. Martínez González, Judge
Municipal Court (General)
Post Office Box 190887
San Juan, Puerto Rico 00919-0887
(787) 641-6103

Teresa Medina Monteserín, Judge
Bayamón Municipal Court
Post Office Box 6000619
Bayamón, Puerto Rico 00960-0619
(787) 785-0067

Margarita Medina Sotomayer, Judge
Municipal Court
Post Office Box 393
Lajas, Puerto Rico 00667-0393
(787) 899-1490

José V. Meléndez González, Judge
Municipal Court
Post Office Box 4158
Vega Baja, Puerto Rico 00694-4158
(787) 855-6934

Rafael A. Menéndez Caballero, Judge
Municipal Court
Post Office Box 322
Aguas Buenas, Puerto Rico 00703-0322
(787) 743-6065

José A. Millán Ortiz, Judge
Municipal Court
Post Office Box 65
Culebra, Puerto Rico 00775-0065
(787) 742-3505 FAX: (787) 863-1100

Evelyn Morales Rosario, Judge
Municipal Court
Post Office Box 334
Cataña, Puerto Rico 00963-0334
(787) 788-1739

Emilio Mulero Arruza, Judge
Municipal Court
Post Office Box 1210
Mayagúez, Puerto Rico 00681
(787) 832-4240

Aileen Navas Auger, Judge
Municipal Court
Post Office Box 190887
San Juan, Puerto Rico 00919-0887
(787) 641-6103

Manuel Nieves Torres, Judge
Municipal Court
Post Office Box 2555
Utuado, Puerto Rico 00641-2555
(787) 894-4280

Jorge Nuñez Burgos, Judge
Muncipal Court
Post Office Box 331791
Ponce, Puerto Rico 00733-1791
(787) 841-2665

Francisco Ocasio Ortiz, Judge
Municipal Court
Post Office Box 788
Arroyo, Puerto Rico 00714 -0788
(787) 839-4475

Roxana O'Farril Garcia, Judge
Municipal Court
Post Office Box 491
Caguas, Puerto Rico 00726-0491
(787) 743-6065

Leticia Ortiz Feliciano, Judge
Cidra Municipal Court
Post Office Box 313
Cidra, Puerto Rico 00739-0313
(787) 739-2886

Roberto Ortiz Hernández, Judge
Municipal Court
Post Office Box 491
Caguas, Puerto Rico 00726-0491
(787) 743-8490

Angel R. Pagán Ocasio, Judge
Municipal Court
Post Office Box 1419
Juana Diaz, Puerto Rico 00795-1419
(787) 837-9318

Karen Pagán Pagán, Judge
Municipal Court
Post OfficeBox 1010
Aguadilla, Puerto Rico 00605-1010
(787) 819-3609

Mercedes Peguero Moronta, Judge
Municipal Court
Post Office Box 972
Quebradillas, Puerto Rico 00678-0972
(787) 895-2720

José E. Pérez Marrero, Judge
Municipal Court
Post Office Box 600619
Bayamón, Puerto Rico 00960-0619
(787) 785-0067

Alberto Pérez Ocasio, Judge
Municipal Court
Post Office Box 1189
Guaynabo, Puerto Rico 00970-1189
(787) 720-3251

Ingrid Pierluisi Isern, Judge
Municipal Court
Post Office Box 600619
Bayamón, Puerto Rico 00960-0619
(787) 798-7325

Orlando Puldón Gómez, Judge
Municipal Court (General)
Post Office Box 190887
San Juan, Puerto Rico 00919-0887
(787) 641-6103

Sonia Ralat Pérez, Judge
Municipal Court
Post Office Box 456
Jayuya, Puerto Rico 00664-0456
(787) 828-4060

María E. Ramos Ortiz, Judge
Municipal Court
Post Office Box 6005
Arecibo, Puerto Rico 00613-6005
(787) 878-0544

Angel R. Ramos Otero, Judge
Municipal Court
Post Office Box 905
Corozal, Puerto Rico 00783-0905
(787) 859-3652

Corrally Ramos Prado, Judge
Municipal Court
Post Office Box 190887
San Juan, Puerto Rico 00919-0887
(787) 641-6103

Carmen J. Rivera Marrero, Judge
Municipal Court
Post Office Box 644
Dorado, Puerto Rico 00646-0644
(787) 796-1260

Albis C. Rivera Medero, Judge
Municipal Court
Post Office Box 600619
Bayamón, Puerto Rico 00960-0619
(787) 785-0067

Juan Rivera Otero, Judge
Municipal Court
Post Office Box 635
Morovis, Puerto Rico 00687-0635
(787) 862-0490

Luis B. Rivera Velázquez, Judge
Municipal Court
Post Office Box 885
Humacao, Puerto Rico 00792-0885
(787) 852-6161

Ana M. Rivera Vincenti, Judge
Municipal Court
Post Office Box 602
Barranquitas, Puerto Rico 00794-0602
(787) 857-3000

Rosa M. Rodríguez Cabrera, Judge
Municipal Court
Post Office Box 600619
Bayamón, Puerto Rico 00960-0619
(787) 785-0067

Roberto Rodríguez Casillas, Judge
Municipal Court
Post Office Box 267
Carolina, Puerto Rico 00986-0267
(787) 257-4160

Iris S. Rodríguez López, Judge
Municipal Court
Post Office Box 1210
Mayagüez, Puerto Rico 00681
(787) 265-1497

Edwin Rodríguez Montalvo, Judge
Municipal Court
Post Office Box 433
Hatillo, Puerto Rico 00659-0433
(787) 898-4230

Yolanda Rodríguez Torres, Judge
Municipal Court
Post Office Box 835
Río Grande, Puerto Rico 00745-0835
(787) 888-4405

Raphael G. Rojas Fernández, Judge
Municipal Court
Post Office Box 44
Sabana Grande, Puerto Rico 00637-0044
(787) 873-2190

Edgardo E. Rosarío Cabrera, Judge
Municipal Court
Post Office Box 927
Cabo Rojo, Puerto Rico 00623-0927
(787) 255-3325

Rosalinda Ruiz Ruperto, Judge
Municipal Court
Post Office Box 1010
Aguadilla, Puerto Rico 00605-1010
(787) 819-3610

Elba I. Santiago Rodríguez, Judge
Municipal Court
Post Office Box 331791
Ponce, Puerto Rico 00733-1791
(787) 841-2605

Frank Serrano Bonilla, Judge
Municipal Court
Post Office Box 275
Maunabo, Puerto Rico 00707-0275
(787) 861-2540

Rubén A. Serrano Santiago, Judge
Municipal Court
Post Office Box 300
Guayama, Puerto Rico 00785-0300
(787) 864-0045

Wanda I. Soler Fernández, Judge
Municipal Court
Post Office Box 744
Aguada, Puerto Rico 00602-0744
(787) 868-6205

Mildred I. Surén Fuentes, Judge
Municipal Court (General)
Post Office Box 190887
San Juan, Puerto Rico 00919-0887
(787) 641-6103

Marina Suria Aguiar, Judge
Municipal Court
Loiza, Puerto Rico 00772
(787) 876-2795

Eloína Torres Cancel, Judge
Municipal Court (General)
Post office Box 190887
San Juan, Puerto Rico 00919-0887
(787) 641-6103

Zahira I. Torres Moro, Judge
Municipal Court
Post Office Box 847
Guanica, Puerto Rico 00653-0847
(787) 821-2215

Miguel Trabal Cuevas, Judge
Municipal Court
200 Calle Blanca Chico
Moca, Puerto Rico 00676-2316
(787) 819-3609

Sonia Trujillo Rebollo, Judge
Municipal Court
Post Office Box 168
Las Piedras, Puerto Rico 00771-0168
(787) 733-2741

Hèctor Velázquez Hernández, Judge
Municipal Court
Post Office Box 600619
Bayamón, Puerto Rico 00960-0619
(787) 785-0067

Alicia Velázquez Piñol, Judge
Municipal Court
Post Office Box 1336
Fajardo, Puerto Rico 00738-1336
(787) 863-1100

Borges Vélez Collado, Judge
Municipal Court
Post Office Box 223
San Germán, Puerto Rico 00683-0223
(787) 892-0040

Hiram Vélez Velázquez, Judge
Municipal Court
Post Office Box 48
Adjunctas, Puerto Rico 00601-0048
(787) 829-2126

Ivelísse Zapata Toro, Judge
Municipal Court
Post Office Box 191
Hormígueros, Puerto Rico 00660-0191
(787) 849-2560

Juvenile Court Judges

Francisco R. Agrait Lladó, Judge
Carolina Juvenile Court
Post Office Box 267
Carolina, Puerto Rico 00986-0267
(787) 276-7525

Lirio Bernal Sánchez, Judge
San Juan Juvenile Court
Post Office Box 190887
San Juan, Puerto Rico 00919-0887
(787) 641-6110

Rubén D. Bonilla Martínez, Judge
Humacao Juvenile Court
Post Office Box 8508
Humacao, Puerto Rico 00792-8508
(787) 850-5092 FAX: (787) 852-3270

Carmen A. Bravo Cerezo, Judge
San Juan Juvenile Court
Post Office Box 190887
San Juan, Puerto Rico 00919-0887
(787) 641-6146

Reinaldo Catinchi Padilla, Judge
Bayamón Juvenile Court
Post Office Box 600619
Bayamón, Puerto Rico 00960-0619
(787) 785-4493

Rafael Guzmán Alicea, Judge
Aguadilla Juvenile Court
Post Office Box 718
Aguadilla, Puerto Rico 00605-0718
(787) 819-3627

Evelyn Hernández Sanabria, Judge
Bayamón Juvenile Court
Post Office Box 600619
Bayamón, Puerto Rico 00960-0619
(787) 269-5530

Carlos Ojeda González, Judge
Ponce Juvenile Court
Post Office Box 331826
Ponce, Puerto Rico 00733-1826
(787) 841-5140

Carlos Q. Ramírez Ríos, Judge
Mayagüez Juvenile Court
Post Office Box 472
Mayagüez, Puerto Rico 00681-0472
(787) 832-4254

Dory J. Robles Rívera, Judge
Guayama Juvenile Court
Post Office Box 300
Guayama, Puerto Rico 00785-0300
(787) 866-5904

Raymond J. Russo Correa, Judge
Caguas Juvenile Court
Post Office Box 1196
Caguas, Puerto Rico 00726-1196
(787) 743-6062

Manuel A. Santiago Tirado, Judge
San Juan Juvenile Court
Post Office Box 190887
San Juan, Puerto Rico 00919-0887
(787) 641-6148

Rubén Vélez Torres, Judge
Arecibo Juvenile Court
Post Office Box 1736
Arecibo, Puerto Rico 00613-1736
(787) 817-2717

Municipal Juvenile Courts

Waleska Aldebol Mora, Judge
San Juan Municipal Juvenile Court
Post Office Box 190887
San Juan, Puerto Rico 00919-0887
(787) 641-6147

Ana M. Colón Soto, Judge
Ponce Municipal Juvenile Court
Post Office Box 331826
Ponce, Puerto Rico 00733-1826
(787) 841-5044

Zandra Cordero Rodríguez, Judge
Caguas-Guayama Municipal Juvenile Court
Post Office Box 1196
Caguas, Puerto Rico 00726-1196
(787) 745-5535

Elba I. Martínez Torres, Judge
Carolina Municipal Juvenile Court
Post Office Box 267
Carolina, Puerto Rico 00986-0267
(787) 752-9250

Teresa Medina Monteserin, Judge
Arecibo Municipal Juvenile Court
Post Office Box 1736
Arecibo, Puerto Rico 00613-1736
(787) 878-3820

Norma Morales Báez, Judge
Bayamón Municipal Juvenile Court
Post Office Box 600619
Bayamón, Puerto Rico 00960-0619
(787) 780-1744

Administrative Law Judges and Administrative Judges

Mayda Gilde La Madrid
Administrative Law Judge
Industrial Commission of Puerto Rico
Post Office Box 3344
Arecibo, Puerto Rico 00613
(787) 898-5602

RHODE ISLAND: (0)

SOUTH CAROLINA: (1)

FEDERAL

Edwin W. Tyler, Administrative Law Judge
Office of Hearings and Appeals
Social Security Administration
300 University Ridge, Suite 116
Greenville, South Carolina 29601-3698
(864) 242-9154 FAX: (864) 467-1690

SOUTH DAKOTA: (0)

TENNESSEE: (1)

FEDERAL

Administrative Law Judge

Eduardo Soto, Administrative Law Judge
Office of Hearings and Appeals
Social Security Administration
Uptain Building
5751 Uptain Road - Suite 300
Chattanooga, Tennessee 37411-5673
(423) 855-6409 FAX: (855) 6407

TEXAS: (428)

FEDERAL

Fortunato P. Benavidez, U. S. Circuit Judge
U. S. Court of Appeals for the Fifth Circuit
450 Homer Thornberry Judicial Building
903 San Jacinto Boulevard
Austin, Texas 78701-2449
(512) 916-5796 FAX: (512) 589-4620

Emilio M. Garza, U. S. Circuit Judge
U. S. Court of Appeals for the Fifth Circuit
501 Fountainhead One Building
8200 Interstate 10 West
San Antonio, Texas 78230
(210) 525-2950 FAX: (210) 525-2961

Reynaldo G. Garza, U. S. Circuit Sr., Judge
U. S. Court of Appeals for the Fifth Circuit
Post Office Box 1129
Brownsville, Texas 78522-1129
(956) 548-2592

David Briones, Judge
U. S. District Court
for the Western District of Texas
U. S. Courthouse
511 East San Antonio Avenue
El Paso, Texas 79901-2401
(915) 534-6744 FAX: (915) 534-6881
E-mail: david_briones@txwd.uscourts.gov

H. F. Garcia, Judge
U. S. District Court
for the Western District of Texas
John H. Wood, Jr. U. S. Courthouse
655 East Durango Boulevard
San Antonio, Texas 78206-1198
(210) 472-6575 FAX: (210) 472-6577

Orlando L. Garcia, Judge
U. S. District Court
for the Western District of Texas
John H. Wood, Jr. U. S. Courthouse
655 East Durango Boulevard
San Antonio, Texas 78206-1198
(210) 472-6565 FAX: (210) 472-6568

Ricardo H. Hinojosa, Judge
U. S. District Court
for the Southern District of Texas
Post Office Box 5007
McAllen, Texas 78502-5007
(956) 618-8100 FAX: (956) 618-8068

Edward C. Prado, Judge
U. S. District Court
for the Western District of Texas
John H. Wood, Jr. U. S. Courthouse
655 East Durango Boulevard
San Antonio, Texas 78206-1198
(210) 472-4060 FAX: (210) 472-4063

Jorge A. Solis, Judge
U. S. District Court
for the Northern District of Texas
13B31 Earle Cabell Federal Building
and U. S. Courthouse
1100 Commerce Street
Dallas, Texas 75242-1003
(214) 753-2342 FAX: (214) 753-2352

Filemon B. Vela, Judge
U. S. District Court
for the Southern District of Texas
Post Office Box 1072
Brownsville, Texas 78522-1072
(956) 548-2595 FAX: (956) 548-2598

Alia Moses Ludlum, Magistrate Judge
U. S. District Court for the
Western District of Texas
A-202 U. S. Courthouse
111 East Broadway
Del Rio, Texas 78840-5573
(830) 703-2038 or 703-2039 FAX: (830) 703-2159

Richard P. Mesa, Magistrate Judge
U. S. District Court for the
Western District of Texas
409 U. S. Courthouse
511 East San Antonio Avenue
El Paso, Texas 79901-2401
(915) 534-6732 FAX: (915) 534-6714

Manuel D. Leal, Bankruptcy Judge
U. S. District Court
for the Southern District of Texas
6202 Bob Casey U. S. Courthouse
515 Rusk Avenue
Houston, Texas 77002
(713) 250-5780 FAX: (713) 250-5871

Dorina Ramos, U. S. Magistrate Judge
U. S. District Court
for the Southern District of Texas
Post Office Box 4569
McAllen, Texas 78502-4569
(956) 618-8060 FAX: (956) 928-8247

Administrative Law Judges

Jamis Estrada, Administrative Law Judge
Office of Hearings and Appeals
Social Security Administration
6800 West Loop South, Suite 300
Bellaire, Texas 77401
(713) 349-7300 FAX: (713) 349-7380

Oscar A. Galvan, Administrative Law Judge
Office of Hearings and Appeals
Social Security Administration
Trinity Building
4204 Woodcock, Suite 100
San Antonio, Texas 78229-3593
(210) 731-3301 FAX: (210) 731-3325

Alvaro Garza, Administrative Law Judge
Office of Hearings and Appeals
Social Security Administration
Trinity Building
4204 Woodcock Drive, Suite 100
San Antonio, Texas 78228
(210) 731-3301 FAX: (210) 731-3325

Gerardo Mariani, Administrative Law Judge
Office of Hearings and Appeals
Social Security Administration
Trinity Building
4204 Woodcock Drive, Suite 100
San Antonio, Texas 78228
(210) 731-3301 FAX: (210) 731-3325

Ruth Tentori-Vila, Administrative Law Judge
Office of Hearings and Appeals
Social Security Administration
12770 Merit Drive
Park Central VIII 8th Floor
Dallas, Texas 75251
(972) 341-5123 FAX: (972) 341-5153

Adolfo J. Vila III, Administrative Law Judge
Social Security Administration
Plaza of The Americas
South Tower
600 North Pearl Street, Suite 300
Dallas, Texas 75201
(214) 880-9870 FAX: (214) 880-9869

David Ayala, U. S. Immigration Judge
201 East Jackson Street
Harlingen, Texas 78550
(956) 427-8582 FAX: (956) 427-8905

John D. Carté, U. S. Immigration Judge
615 East Houston Street, Room 598
San Antonio, Texas 78205-2040
(210) 472-6637 FAX: Call on phone first

Susan E. Castro, U. S. Immigration Judge
615 East Houston Street, Room 598
San Antonio, Texas 78205-2040
(210) 472-6637 FAX: Call on phone first

Eleazar Tovar, U. S. Immigration Judge
201 East Jackson Street
Harlington, Texas 78550
(956) 427-8582 FAX: (956) 427-8905

Bertha A. Zuniga, U. S. Immigration Judge
1545 Hawkins Boulevard, Suite 205
El Paso, Texas 79925
(915) 540-1910 FAX: (915) 540-1922

STATE

Alfonso Chapa, Chief Justice (Retired)
Supreme Court of Texas
Heard, Goggan, Blair and Williams
Tower Life Building, Tenth Floor
San Antonio, Texas 78205-3171
(210) 225-6763 FAX: (210) 225-6410

District Court of Appeals

Richard Barajas, Chief Justice
8th District Court of Appeals
500 East San Antonio Street, Suite 1203
El Paso, Texas 79901-2421
(915) 546-2040 FAX: (915) 546-2252

Errlinda Castillo, Justice
13th District Court of Appeals
Courthouse, 901 Leopard Street - 10th Floor
Corpus Christi, Texas 78401
(361) 888-0416 FAX: (361) 888-0794

Federico Gilbert Hinojosa, Justice
13th District Court of Appeals
100 East Cano - 5th Floor
Edinburg, Texas 78539
(956) 318-2405 FAX: (361) 318-2403

Alma Lopez, Justice
4th District Court of Appeals
Bexar County Justice Center
300 Dolorosa Street, Suite 3200
San Antonio, Texas 78205-3037
(210) 335-2658 FAX: (210) 335-2762

Nelda V. Rodriguez, Justice
13th District Court of Appeals
Courthouse, 901 Leopard Street, 10th Floor
Corpus Christi, Texas 78401
(361) 888-0416 FAX: (361) 888-0794

Rogelio (Roy) Valdez, Chief Justice
13th District Court of Appeals
100 East Cano - 5th Floor
Edinburg, Texas 78539
(956) 318-2405 FAX: (956) 318-2403

Linda Reyna Yanez, Justice
13th District Court of Appeals
100 East Cano - 5th Floor
Edinburg, Texas 78539
(956) 318-2405 FAX: (956) 318-2403

Carlos C. Cadena, Chief Justice (Retired)
4th District Court of Appeals
Bexar County Justice Center
300 Dolorosa Street, Suite 3200
San Antonio, Texas 78205
(210) 220-2589

Antonio Gallardo Cantu, Justice (Retired)
4th District Court of Appeals
106 Dogwood Lane
San Antonio, Texas 78213
(210) 349-0987

Melchor Chavez, Justice (Retired)
13th District Court of Appeals
901 Leopard Streeet - 10th Floor
Corpus Christi, Texas 78401
(956) 318-2405

Peter Tijerina, Justice (Retired)
4th District Court of Appeals
Bexar County Justice Center
300 Dolorosa Street, Suite 3200
San Antonio, Texas 78205
(210) 226-7392 Ext. 2589

District Courts

Amado Abascal, III, Judge
365th District Court
Post Office Box 4129
Eagle Pass, Texas 78853-4129
(830) 773-1151 FAX: (830) 757-2720

Dick Alcala, Judge
340th District Court
112 West Beauregard Avenue
San Angelo, Texas 76903-5850
(915) 658-1915 FAX: (915) 658-8046

Elsa Alcala, Judge
338th District Court
1201 Franklin Street
Houston, Texas 77002
(713) 755-7774 FAX: (713) 368-9205

Edward G. Aparicio, Judge
92nd District Court
100 North Closner, 2nd Floor
Edinburg, Texas 78539
(956) 318-2250 FAX: Call on phone first

José J. Baca, Judge
346th District Court
500 East San Antonia Street, Room 902
El Paso, Texas 79901-2457
(915) 546-2119 FAX: (915) 546-2233

J. Manuel Banales, Judge
105th District Court
901 Leopard Street, Room 802
Corpus Christi, Texas 78401
(361) 888-0510 FAX: (361) 888-0779

Adolph Canales, Judge
298th District Court
County Courthouse
600 Commerce Street
Dallas, Texas 75202-4606
(214) 653-6779 FAX: (214) 653-7155

Terry A. Canales, Judge
79th District Court
Post Office Box 482
Falfurrias, Texas 78355
(361) 325-5604 Ext. 242 FAX: (361) 325-5679

Kathleen Cardone, Judge
388th District Court
500 East San Antonio
El Paso, Texas 79901
(915) 543-3850 FAX: Call on phone first

Alfredo Chavez, Judge
65th District Court
500 East San Antonio Street, Room 1105
El Paso, Texas 79901-2496
(915) 546-2149 FAX: (915) 546-8157

Rodolfo (Rudy) Delgado, Judge
93rd District Court
Courthouse, 100 Closner Street
Edinburg, Texas 78539
(956) 318-2255 FAX: (956) 318-2552

Elma Teresa Salinas Ender, Judge
341st District Court
1110 Victoria Street, Room 302
Laredo, Texas 78040
(956) 721-2625 FAX: (956) 718-8558

Benjamin Euresti, Jr., Judge
107th District Court
974 East Harrison
Brownsville, Texas 78520
(956) 544-0845 FAX: (956) 544-0803

Manuel R. Flores, Judge
49th District Court
1110 Victoria Street - Suite 304
Laredo, Texas 78040
(956) 721-2660 FAX: (956) 718-8560

Alex W. Gabert, Judge
229th District Court
Post Office Box 726
Rio Grande City, Texas 78582
(956) 487-2636 FAX: (956) 487-4093

Lee Gabriel, Judge
367th District Court
1450 East McKinney Street
Denton, Texas 76201
(940) 565-8546 FAX: (940) 565-5626

Ernest C. Garcia, Judge
126th District Court
Post Office Box 1748
Austin, Texas 78767
(512) 473-9313 FAX: (512) 473-9332

Patrick Michael Garcia, Judge
384th District Court
500 East San Antonio Street, Room 906
El Paso, Texas 79901-2457
(915) 546-2134 FAX: (915) 543-3882

Robert Garza, Judge
138th District Court
974 East Harrison Street
Brownsville, Texas 78520
(956) 544-0877 FAX: (956) 544-0881

Alexander R. Gonzalez, Judge
83rd District Court
Post Office Box 1777
Fort Stockton, Texas 79735-1777
(915) 336-3361 FAX: (915) 336-3554

Nelva Gonzalez-Ramos, Judge
347th District Court
901 Leopard Street
Corpus Christi, Texas 78401
(361) 888-0593 FAX: (361) 888-0798

Noe Gonzalez, Judge
370th District Court
100 North Closner, 1st Floor
Edinburg, Texas 78539
(956) 318-2280

David C. Guaderrama, Judge
243rd District Court
500 East San Antonio Street, Room 901
El Paso, Texas 79901-2457
(915) 546-2168 FAX: (915) 246-8107

Eva M. Guzman, Judge
309th District Court
1115 Congress Avenue, 7th Floor
Houston, Texas 77002
(713) 755-6234 FAX: (713) 755-3688

Nanette Hasette, Judge
28th District Court
901 Leopard Street
Corpus Christi, Texas 78401
(361) 888-0506 FAX: (361) 888-0634

Leticia Hinojosa, Judge
139th District Court
100 North Closner, 2nd Floor
Edinburg, Texas 78539
(956) 318-2260 FAX: (956) 383-7608

Martha Huerta, Judge
319th District Court
Courthouse, 901 Leopard Street, Room 801
Corpus Christi, Texas 78401
(361) 888-0533 FAX: (361) 888-0644

Abel Limas, Judge
404th District Court
974 East Harrison Street
Brownsville, Texas 78520
(956) 544-0827 FAX: (956) 550-1373

José Longoria, Judge
214th District Court
901 Leopard Street
Corpus Christi, Texas 78401
(361) 888-0463 FAX: (361) 888-0795

Abelardo Lopez, Judge
108th District Court
501 South Fillmore Street, Suite 4-A
Amarillo, Texas 79101
(806) 379-2355 FAX: (806) 379-6517

Midgalia Lopez, Judge
197th District Court
974 East Harrison Street
Brownsville, Texas 78520
(956) 574-8150 FAX: (956) 574-8128

Fernando Mancias, Judge
93rd District Court
100 North Closner, 2nd Floor
Edinburg, Texas 78539
(956) 318-2255 FAX: (956) 318-2552

Phillip R. Martinez, Judge
327th District Court
500 East San Antonio Street, Room 60
El Paso, Texas 79901-2496
(915) 546-2032 FAX: 546-2131 or 545-1403

Sam Medina, Judge
237th District Court
Post Office Box 10536
Lubbock, Texas 79408-3536
(806) 775-1019
FAX: (806) 775-1629 or 775-1196

Andy Mireles, Judge
73rd District Court
Courthouse, Main Plaza
100 Dolorosa Street, Room 410
San Antonio, Texas 78205-3028
(210) 335-2523 FAX: (210) 335-2843

Frank Montalvo, Judge
288th District Court
Courthouse, Main Plaza
100 Dolorosa Street
San Antonio, Texas 78205-3028
(210) 335-2663 FAX: (210) 335-2843

Cynthia L. Muniz, Judge
293rd District Court
Post Office Drawer 4360
Eagle Pass, Texas 78852
(830) 758-1730 FAX: (830) 758-1775

Kathleen H. Olivares, Judge
205th District Court
500 East San Antonio Street, Room 1002
El Paso, Texas 79901-2457
(915) 546-2107 FAX: (915) 546-2013

Juan R. Partida, Judge
275th District Court
100 North Closner Street, 2nd Floor
Edinburg, Texas 78519
(956) 318-2270 FAX: Call on phone first

Mario E. Ramirez, Jr., Judge
332nd District Court
100 North Closner Street, 2nd Floor
Edinburg, Texas 78539
(956) 318-2275 FAX: (956) 318-2698

Rose Guerra Reyna, Judge
206th District Court
100 North Closner, 2nd Floor
Edinburg, Texas 78359
(956) 318-2265 FAX: (956) 318-2005

Guadalupe Rivera, Judge
168th District Court
500 East San Antonio Street, Room 602
El Paso, Texas 79901-2457
(915) 546-2141 FAX: (915) 546-2142

Alonzo T. Rodriguez, Judge
343rd District Court
Post Office Box 700
Sinton, Texas 78387-0700
(361) 364-6202 FAX: Call on phone first

Mary R. Roman, Judge
175th District Court
300 Dolorosa Street, Room 2199
San Antonio, Texas 78205-3028
(210) 335-2527 FAX: (210) 335-2793

Jerry A. Sandel, Judge
278th District Court
1100 University Avenue, Suite 304
Huntsville, Texas 77340-4642
(936) 436-4916

Charles F. Sandoval, Judge
380th District Court
200 South McDonald, Suite 425
McKinney, Texas 75069
(972) 548-4762 FAX: Call on phone first

Raul Vasquez, Judge
111th District Court
1110 Victoria Street, Room 301
Laredo, Texas 78040
(956) 721-2671 FAX: (956) 718-8559

Rose Vela, Judge
148th District Court
901 Leopard Street, Room 903
Corpus Christi, Texas 78401-3688
(361) 888-0333 FAX: (361) 888-0798

District Court Associate Judges, Masters and Referees

Pat Garza, Associate Judge/Referee
289th District Court
600 Mission Road
San Antonio, Texas 78210-3851
(210) 531-1054

Irma Hernandez, Associate Judge/Referee
289th District Court
600 Mission Road
San Antonio, Texas 78210-3851
(210) 681-7017

Iris A. Dominguez, MasterTitle IV
229th District Court
Fifth Administrative Judicial Region
100 North Closner Street
Edinburg, Texas 78539
(956) 318-2452 FAX: (956) 381-4269

David Longoria, Master
314th District Court
1115 Congress, 4th Floor
Houston, Texas 77002
(713) 755-6470 FAX: (713) 755-1110

Patricia Macias, Master
65th District Court
500 East San Antonio, Suite 1104
El Paso, Texas 79901-2457
(915) 546-2147 FAX: (915) 543-3811

J. M. **Ramirez**, Child Support Master Title IV
229th District Court
Fifth Administrative Judicial Region
100 North Closner Street
Edinburg, Texas 78539
(956) 318-2398 FAX: (956) 381-4269

County Courts

Wilfred R. Aguilar, Judge
County Court at Law No. 5, Travis County
Post Office Box 1748
Austin, Texas 78759-1748
(512) 473-9676 FAX: (512) 473-9226

José Aliseda, County Judge
Bee County
105 West Corpus Christi Street, Suite #105
Beeville, Texas 78102
(361) 362-3260 FAX: (361) 362-3270

Alfonso E. Alonso, Jr., Judge
Count Court at Law No. 1 and Probate Court
Bexar County
300 Dolorosa Street, Room 206
San Antonio, Texas 78205
(210) 335-2571 FAX: (210) 335-3211

Javier Alvarez, Judge
County Court at Law No. 3
El Paso County
500 East San Antonio Street
El Paso, Texas 79901-2496
(915) 546-2183 FAX: (915) 546-2184

Jesús M. Alvarez, Judge
County Court at Law, Starr County
501 North Britton
Rio Grande City, Texas 78582
(956) 487-4871 FAX: (956) 487-7521

Pablo Avila, Judge
County Court, Zavala County
Post Office Box 688
Crystal City, Texas 78839
(830) 374-3810 FAX: (830) 374-3007

Dolores Briones, County Judge
County Court, El Paso County
500 East San Antonio, Room 301
El Paso, Texas 79901
(915) 546-2098 FAX: (915) 543-3888

H. Paul Canales, Judge
County Court at Law No. 2, Bexar County
100 Dolorosa Street, Room 206
San Antonio, Texas 78205
(210) 335-2573 FAX: (210) 335-2649

Elia Cornejo-Lopez, Judge
County Court at Law No. 2, Cameron County
974 East Harrison Street
Brownsville, Texas 78520
(956) 544-0856 FAX: (956) 504-3678

Hector DePena, Jr., Judge
County Court at Law No. 2, Nueces County
Courthouse, 901 Leopard Street, Room 702
Corpus Christi, Texas 78401-3693
(361) 888-0596

Rogelio Escobedo, County Judge
County Court, Maverick County
Post Office Box 955
Eagle Pass, Texas 78853
(830) 773-3824 FAX: (830) 773-6450

Manuel ("Mike") L. Fernandez, County Judge
County Court
Val Verde County
Post Office Box 4250
Del Reio, Texas 78841
(830) 774-7501 FAX: (830) 775-9406

Jimmy B. Galindo, County Judge
Reeves County
100 East 4th, 3rd Floor
Pecos, Texas 79772
(915) 445-5418 FAX: (915) 445-7285

Nicholas Gallegos, County Judge
Edwards County
Post Office Box 348
Rocksprings, Texas 78880-0348
(830) 683-6122

Carlos A. Garcia, County Judge
Frio County
500 East San Antonio Street #7
Pearsall, Texas 78061-3145
(830) 334-2154 FAX: (830) 334-0010

David Garcia, Judge
County Criminal Court #3 Denton County
1450 East McKinney Street
Denton, Texas 76202
(940) 320-4801 FAX: (940) 565-5547

Edmundo B. Garcia, Jr., County Judge
County Court, Duval County
Post Office Box 189
San Diego, Texas 78384
(361) 279-3322 FAX: (361) 279-3310

Joseph A. Garcia, Jr., County Judge
County Court, Kenedy County
Post Office Box 37
Sarita, Texas 78385
(361) 294-5224 FAX: (361) 294-5218

Federico (Fred) Garza, Jr., Judge
County Court at Law No. 4
Hidalgo County
Courthouse, 100 North Closner Street, 3rd Floor
Edinburg, Texas 78539
(210) 318-2390 FAX: (210) 380-2247

G. Jaime Garza, Judge
County Court at Law No. 2
Hidalgo County
Courthouse, 100 North Closner Street, 3rd Floor
Edinburg, Texas 78539
(210) 318-2380 FAX: (210) 380-2247

Homero Garza, Judge
County Court at Law No. 3
Hidalgo County
Courthouse, 100 North Closner Street, 3rd Floor
Edinburg, Texas 78539
(210) 318-2385 FAX: (210) 380-2247

Jesús Garza, Judge
County Court at Law No. 2
Webb County
1110 Victoria Street, Room 404
Laredo, Texas 78040
(956) 718-8640 FAX: (956) 718-8556

Julie Gonzalez, Judge
County Court at Law No. 2
El Paso County
500 East San Antonio Street, Room 801
El Paso, Texas 79901
(915) 546-2145 FAX: (915) 543-3866

Sergio J. Gonzalez, Judge
County Court at Law
Val Verde County
Post Office Box 1431
Del Rio, Texas 78841-1431
(830) 774-7575 FAX: (830) 778-7440

Alex R. Hernandez, Judge
County Court at Law
Calhoun County
211 South Ann
Port Lavaca, Texas 77979
(361) 553-4640

Ricardo Herrera, Judge
County Court at Law No. 1
El Paso County
500 East San Antonio Street, Room 802
El Paso, Texas 79901-2496
(915) 546-2011 FAX: (915) 546-8156

Gilberto Hinojosa, County Judge
County Court, Cameron County
964 East Harrison Street
Brownsville, Texas 78520
(956) 544-0830 FAX: (956) 544-0801

M. Sue Kurita, Judge
County Court at Law No. 6
El Paso County
500 East San Antonio Street, Room 1106
El Paso, Texas 79901
(915) 543-3868

Janet Leal, Judge
County Court at Law No. 1
Cameron County
974 East Harrison Street
Brownsville, Texas 78520
(956) 544-0855 FAX: (956) 548-9542

Mercurio Martinez, Jr., County Judge
County Court
Webb County
Post Office Box 29
Laredo, Texas 78042
(956) 721-2500 FAX: (956) 726-6906

Agapito Molina, Jr., County Judge
County Court, Jim Hogg County
Post Office Box 729
Hebbronville, Texas 78361
(361) 527-3015 FAX: (361) 527-5843

Homer Mora, County Judge
County Court
Brooks County
Post Office Box 515
Falfurrias, Texas 78355-0515
(361) 325-5064 FAX: (361) 325-9065

Alvino (Ben) Morales, Judge
County Court at Law
Webb County
1110 Victoria Street, Room 303
Laredo, Texas 78040
(956) 721-2630 FAX: (956) 718-8557

David Morales, County Judge
County Court
Zapata County
Post Office Box 99
Zapata, Texas 78076-0099
(956) 765-9920 FAX: (956) 765-9926

Orlinda L. Naranjo, Judge
County Court at Law No. 2
Travis County
Post Office Box 1748
Austin, Texas 78767-1748
(512) 473-9248 FAX: (512) 473-9226

José Eloy Pulido, County Judge
County Court
Hidalgo County
Post Office Box 1356
Edinburg, Texas 78539
(956) 318-2600 FAX: (956) 318-2699

Daniel T. Robles, Judge
County Court at Law No. 3
Cameron County
974 East Harrison Street
Brownsville, Texas 78520
(956) 574-8137 FAX: Call on phone first

Linda Ann Rodriguez, Judge
County Court at Law No. 2, Hays County
Hays County Justice Center
110 East MLK Drive, Room 177
San Marcos, Texas 78666-5541
(512) 353-7625 FAX: (512) 393-7633
E-mail: linda@co.hays.tx.us

L. Arnoldo Saenz, County Judge
Jim Wells County
200 North Almond Street
Alice, Texas 78332
(361) 668-5706 FAX: (361) 668-8671

Marisela G. Saldana, Judge
County Court at Law No. 3
Nueces County
Courthouse, 901 Leopard Street, Room 703
Corpus Christi, Texas 78401-3693
(361) 888-0466 FAX: (361) 888-0250
E-mail: mgsaldana@nueces.esc2.net

Patrick Edward Sebesta, Judge
County Court at Law No. 2 and Probate Court
Brazoria County
111 East Locust
Angleton, Texas 77515
(979) 864-1256 FAX: (979) 864-1056

Robert J. Vargas, Judge
County Court at Law No. 1, Nueces County
Courthouse, 901 Leopard Street, Room 701
Corpus Christi, Texas 78401-3693
(361) 888-0344 FAX: (361) 888-0253

Juan Velasquez, II, Judge
County Court at Law No. 2
Victoria County
208 West Constitution
Victoria, Texas 77901-6544
(361) 575-7195 FAX: (361) 575-7195
(Fax Number same as Phone Number)

Eloy Vera, County Judge
County Court
Starr County
County Courthouse, Room 203
Rio Grande City, Texas 78582
(956) 487-2307 FAX: (956) 487-4250

Sr. and Retired County Judges

Carlos Cadena, Sr., Judge
Bexar County
203 Belvidere
San Antonio, Texas 78212
(210) 822-1526

John F. Dominguez, Sr., Judge
Hidalgo County
218 South Texas Avenue
Mercedes, Texas 78570
(210) 565-2182

Juan F. Gallardo, Judge (Retired)
Travis County
4032 South Lamar Boulevard, #500-106
Austin, Texas 78704
(512) 972-2884

Sergio Gonzalez, Jr., Judge (Retired)
Val Verde County
Post Office Box 275
Del Rio, Texas 78840-0275
(210) 774-3611

Joaquin Villareal, III, Judge (Retired)
347th District Court
Corpus Christi, Texas 78401

Justices of the Peace Courts - (Under Texas Law, they are ranked above Municipal Courts and their Judges have broader jurisdiction - civil actions under $5,000, small claims, criminal misdemeanors with fine-only offenses, and magistrate functions. Municipal Courts have jurisdiction over criminal misdemeanors with fine-only offenses, exclusive jurisdiction over municipal ordnance violations with fines up to $2,000, limited civil penalties in cases involving dangerous dogs, and magistrate functions).

Saul Acevedo, Justice of the Peace
Precinct 1, Place 1, Bexar County
218 S Laredo Street, 1st Floor
San Antonio, Texas 78207
(210) 335-2803

Mauro B. Adamez, Justice of the Peace
Precinct 2, Place 1
San Patricio County
Post Office Box 73
Odem, Texas 78370
(361) 368-4311

A. (Butch) Aguilar, Justice of the Peace
Countywide, Menard County
Post Office Box 1107
Menard, Texas 76859-1107
(915) 396-2239 FAX: (915) 396-2047

Adelita Lozano Alvarez, Justice of the Peace
Countywide, Sutton County
Post Office Box 165
Sonora, Texas 76950
(915) 387-3322

Guadalupe Aponte, Justice of the Peace
Precinct 3, Place 1
El Paso County
500 East San Antonio, Room 803
El Paso, Texas 79901
(915) 546-2170

Mike Arevalo, Justice of the Peace
Precinct 2, Place 1, Brooks County
Route 1, Box 59-A
Falfurrias, Texas 78355
(361) 325-5604

Felix R. Barrera, Justice of the Peace
Precinct 1, Place 1, Val Verde County
Post Office Box 1144
Del Rio, Texas 78841-1144
(830) 774-7545

Santos Benavides, Justice of the Peace
Precinct 2, Place 1, Webb County
720 South Smith Street
Milmo, Texas 78043
(956) 721-2502

Melissa Bernal, Justice of the Peace
Precinct 4, Place 1, Refugio County
Post Office Box 446
Tivoli, Texas 77990
(361) 286-3401

Nancy Bosquez, Justice of the Peace
Precinct 2, Place 1, Potter County
500 South Fillmore, Room 502
Amarillo, Texas 79101-2437
(806) 379-2390

John Cabaniss, Justice of the Peace
Precinct 1, Place 1, McLennan County
501 Washington, Suite 108
Waco, Texas 76701
(254) 757-5040

Loretta G. Cabrera, Justice of the Peace
Precinct 4, Place 1, Brooks County
Route 2, Box 164-H
Falfurrias, Texas 78355
(361) 325-3757

Edelmira Calzada, Justice of the Peace
Precinct 2, Place 1, Terrell County
Post Office Box 52
Sanderson, Texas 79848
(915) 345-2341

Diana Guerrero Campos, Justice of the Peace
Precinct 1, Place 1, Comal County
100 Main Plaza, Suite # 303
New Braunfels, Texas 78130
(830) 620-5547

Celestino Canales, Justice of the Peace
Precinct 4, Place 1, Jim Hogg County
201 North Oak, Suite 1
Hebbronville, Texas 78361
(361) 527-5830

José Benito Canales, Justice of the Peace
Precinct 4, Place 1, Duval County
Post Office Box 841
Freer, Texas 78357-0841
(361) 394-6011

Abel Cantu, Justice of the Peace
Precinct 1, Place 1, Starr County
4192 West Highway 83
Rio Grande City, Texas 78582
(956) 849-4558

Amada V. Cardenas, Justice of the Peace
Precinct 5, Place 1, San Patricio County
619 North Frio
Mathis, Texas 78368
(361) 547-2244

Rosendo Carrasco, Justice of the Peace
Precinct 3, Place 1, Reeves County
Post Office Box 104
Balmorhea, Texas 79718-0104
(915) 375-2663

Raul G. Casarez, Justice of the Peace
Precinct 2, Bee County
105 West Corpus Christi St. #104
Beeville, Texas 78102
(361) 362-3233

Edmundo Castellanos, Justice of the Peace
Precinct 2, Place 1, Guadalupe County
2611 North Guadalupe Street
Seguin, Texas 78155-7396
(830) 379-2214

Martha V. Chacon, Justice of the Peace
Precinct 2, Place 1, Maverick County
Post Office Box 1768
Eagle Pass, Texas 78853
(830) 757-1699

Aurora Chaides-Hernandez
Justice of the Peace
Precinct 3, Place 1, Lubbock County
Post Office Box 10536
Lubbock, Texas 79408-3536
(806) 775-1326 FAX: (806) 775-1327

Endercio Chapa, Jr., Justice of the Peace
Precinct 4, Place 1, Live Oak County
Post Office Box 535
George West, Texas 78022
(361) 449-2733

Fred Chavez, Justice of the Peace
Precinct 5, Place 1, El Paso County
8080 Gateway East
El Paso, Texas 79908
(915) 593-1349

M. Louis Cisneros, Justice of the Peace
Precinct 1, Place 1, Caldwell County
Post Office Box 58
Lockhart, Texas 78644
(512) 398-1810

Bertha Ramirez Clark, Justice of the Peace
Precinct 1, Place 1, Hudspeth County
Post Office Box 40
Sierra Blanca, Texas 79851-0040
(915) 369-4141

David M. Cobos, Justice of the Peace
Precinct 2, Midland County
400 South Main
Midland, Texas 79701-5223
(915) 688-1127

Arnaldo Corpus, Justice of the Peace
Precinct 3, Place 1, Hidalgo County
1401 East Griffin Parkway
Mission, Texas 78572
(956) 585-4528

Ramon de la Cruz, Justice of the Peace
Precint 6, Place 1, Starr County
Post Office Box 33
Garciasville, Texas 78547
(956) 487-7180

Oscar De La Fuente, Justice of the Peace
Precinct 3, Place 1, Cameron County
181 West Rowson Street
San Benito, Texas 78586
(956) 399-1387

Esequiel (Cheque) DeLaPaz, Justice of the Peace
Precinct 4, Place 1, Kleberg County
622 North 14th Street
Kingsville, Texas 78363
(361) 595-8586

Catalina De Leon, Justice of the Peace
Precinct 4, Place 1, Dimmit County
Post Office Box 377
Asherton, Texas 78827-0377
(830) 468-3530

Martin De Leon, Justice of the Peace
Precinct 1, Aransas County
301 North Live Oak, Room 111
Rockport, Texas 78382-2798
(361) 790-0130

Mario A. Delgado, Justice of the Peace
Precinct 2, Place 1, Kleberg County
620 North 3rd Street
Kingsville, Texas 78363
(361) 595-8571

Elena Diaz, Justice of the Peace
Precinct 4 Place 1, Travis County
2201 Post Road, Room 101
Austin, Texas 78704-4390
(512) 473-9479

John F. Donaho, Justice of the Peace
Precinct 3, Place 1, Kleberg County
Post Office Box 214
Riviera, Texas 78379
(361) 296-3214

Timmy Drapela, Justice of the Peace
Precinct 4, Wharton County
605 East Calhoun Street
El Campo, Texas 77437
(409) 543-4322

Charlie Espinoza, Justice of the Peace
Precinct 4, Place 1, Hidalgo County
1212 South 25th Street, Suite B
Edinburg, Texas 78539
(956) 380-4473

Josie Espinoza, Justice of the Peace
Precinct 2, Place 1, Zavala County
County Courthouse
Crystal City, Texas 78839
(830) 374-2116

Oscar Espinoza, Sr., Justice of the Peace
Precinct 1, Place 1, Culberson County
Post Office Box 367
Van Horn, Texas 79855
(915) 283-2609

Eloy Flores, Justice of the Peace
Precinct 8, Place 1, Starr County
H/C Box 53 J.P.
Rio Grande City, Texas 78582
(956) 849-7450

Emilio Flores, Justice of the Peace
Precinct 1, Place 1, Wilson County
Post Office Box 472
Floresville, Texas 78114
(830) 393-5112

Esmeralda Frausto, Justice of the Peace
Precinct 3, Place 1, La Salle County
204 NE Lane, Suite 9
Cotulla, Texas 78014-2545
(830) 879-2568

Alfredo Garcia, Jr., Justice of the Peace
Precinct 3, Place 1, Webb County
Post Office Box 55
Oilton, Texas 78371
(361) 747-5481

Esteban Garcia, Jr., Justice of the Peace
Precinct 3, Place 1, Brooks County
Post Office Box 541
Falfurrias, Texas 78355-0541
(361) 325-9432

Benny V. Garza, Justice of the Peace
Precinct 3, Place 1, Duval County
Post Office Box 756
Benavides, Texas 78341-0756
(361) 256-3449

David Garza, Justice of the Peace
Precinct 3, Place 2, Cameron County
195 East Robertson
San Benito, Texas 78586
(956) 399-3525

David B. Garza, Justice of the Peace
Precinct 1, Bee County
105 West Corpus Christi Street #109
Beeville, Texas 78102
(361) 362-3235

Gilbert Garza, Justice of the Peace
Precinct 4, Karnes County
Post Office Box 26
Runge, Texas 78151-0026
(830) 239-4459

Sabas Garza, Jr., Justice of the Peace
Precinct 3, Place 1, Willacy Conty
757 East Kimball
Raymondville, Texas 7850
(956) 689-2265

Teresa M. Gomez, Justice of the Peace
Precinct 4, Place 1, Maverick County
267 North Monroe Street
Eagle Pass, Texas 78852
(830) 773-9616

Edward L. Gonzales, Justice of the Peace
Precinct 4, Place 1, Kenedy County
Post Office Box 8
Sarita, Texas 78385
(361) 294-5785

Robert N. Gonzales, Justice of the Peace
Precinct 1, Place 1, Pecos County
Post Office Box 1647
Fort Stockton, Texas 79735
(915) 336-3281

Beatriz Q. Gonzalez, Justice of the Peace
Precinct 3, Victoria County
111-A North Glass Street
Victoria, Texas 77901 6544
(361) 575-0246 FAX: (361) 575-6276

Cinderela Rice Gonzalez, Justice of the Peace
Precinct 1, Place 1, Presidio County
Post Office Box 481
Marfa, Texas 79843
(915) 729-4831

Sallie A. Gonzalez, Justice of the Peace
Precinct 5, Place 1, Cameron County
608 East Harrison
Harlington, Texas 78550
(956) 427-8056

José Clemente Gutierrez, Justice of the Peace
Precinct 4, Place 1, Zapata County
Post Office Box 2310
Zapata, Texas 78076-2310
(956) 765-9945

Lamberto T. Herrera, Justice of the Peace
Precinct 4, Place 1, Reeves County
Post Office Box 1894
Pecos, Texas 79772-1894
(915) 415-2628

Cesar Iracheta, Justice of the Peace
Precinct 3, Place 1, Maverick County
1609 Del Rio Boulevard
Eagle Pass, Texas 78852
(830) 773-2493

Juan Jasso, Justice of the Peace
Precinct 6, Place 2, Dallas County
410 South Beckley
Dallas, Texas 75203
(214) 943-5981

Frank Leal, Justice of the Peace
Precinct 1, Atascosa County
1420 2nd Street
Pleasanton, Texas 78064
(830) 569-2801

Hector Javier Liendo, Justice of the Peace
Precinct 1, Place 1, Webb County
Post Office Box 29
Laredo, Texas 78040
(956) 721-2570

Darrell Longino, Justice of the Peace
Precinct 1, Place 1, Polk County
101 West Church Street
Livingston, Texas 77351
(409) 327-6841

Olga Longoria, Justice of the Peace
Precinct 1, Place 1, Brooks County
Post Office Box 513
Falfurrias, Texas 78355
(361) 325-5604

Felicitas S. Lopez, Justice of the Peace
Precinct 1, Place 1, Kleberg County
Kingsville, Texas 78363
(512) 596-8586

Hector F. Lopez, Justice of the Peace
Precinct 1, Place 1, Zapata County
Post Office Box 2310
Zapata, Texas 78076-2310
(956) 765-9945

Lorraine M. Lopez, Justice of the Peace
Precinct 1, Place 1, Refugio County
808 Commerce, Room 111
Refugio, Texas 78377
(361) 526-4877

Arnulfo C. Luna, Justice of the Peace
Precinct 3, Place 1, Frio County
411 North Willow Street
Pearsall, Texas 78061
(830) 334-8386

Virgilio Luna, Justice of the Peace
Precinct 4, Place 1, Val Verde County
Post Office Box 482
Del Rio, Texas 78840
(830) 774-7581

Frank Macias, Justice of the Peace
Precinct 6, Place 1, El Paso County
Post Office Box 597
Clint, Texas 79836-0597
(915) 851-2019

Dario L. Martinez, Justice of the Peace
Precinct 2, Place 1, Hidalgo County
1899 North Cage, Suite J
Pharr, Texas 78577-2563
(956) 702-4178

Heriberto Martinez, Justice of the Peace
Precinct 3, Place 1, Jim Hogg County
201 North Oak, Suite 1
Hebbronville, Texas 78361
(361) 527-5830

Oscar O. Martinez, Justice of the Peace
Precinct 4, Place 1, Webb County
610 Del Mar Boulevard
Laredo, Texas 78041
(956) 721-2510 FAX: (956) 718-8561

Rodrigo T. Martinez, Justice of the Peace
Precinct 4, Place 1, Uvalde County
111 1/2 Grove Street
Uvalde, Texas 78801
(830) 278-3904

Emilia G. Medellin, Justice of the Peace
Precinct 3, Place 1, Kenedy County
Post Office Box 8
Sarita, Texas 78385
(361) 294-5786

Celestine V. Menchaca, Justice of the Peace
Precinct 1, Place 1, Calhoun County
201 West Austin, Room 12
Port Lavaca, Texas 77979
(361) 553-4621

Jesús E. Morales, Justice of the Peace
Precinct 1, Place 2, Hidalgo County
303 East Highway 83
Weslaco, Texas 78596
(956) 968-0707

Ophelia Moreno, Justice of the Peace
Precinct 2, Goliad County
700 East End Street
Goliad, Texas 77963
(361) 645-3320

Pablo V. Moreno, Justice of the Peace
Precinct 4, Place 1, Jim Wells County
Post Office Box 668
Premont, Texas 78375
(361) 348-2092

Rey Munoz, Justice of the Peace
Precinct 1 Place 1, Kleberg County
700 East Kleberg
Kingsville, Texas 78363
(361) 595-8505

Rosalio Munoz, Jr., Justice of the Peace
Precinct 4, Place 1, El Paso County
3160 Lee Trevino Drive, No. 110B
El Paso, Texas 79936
(915) 594-1143

Bennie Ochoa, III, Justice of the Peace
Precinct 1, Place 1, Cameron County
Post Office Box 1563
Port Isabel, Texas 78578-1563
(956) 943-2520

Ismael (Melo) Ochoa, Justice of the Peace
Precinct 3, Place 2, Hidalgo County
118 East 11th Street
Mission, Texas 78572
(956) 581-2124

Pascual G. Olibas, Justice of the Peace
Precinct 1, Place 1, Ward County
1900 South Stockton
Monahans, Texas 79756-6500
(915) 943-7227

Diana Marie Orozco, Justice of the Peace
Precinct 6, Place 1, Dallas County
410 South Beckley
Dallas, Texas 75203
(214) 943-6980

David Ortiz, Justice of the Peace
Precinct 1, Place 1, Dimmit County
County Courthouse
Carrizo Springs, Texas 78834
(830) 876-5486

David William Pareya, Justice of thePeace
Precinct 3, Place 1, McLennan County
Post Office Box 495
West, Texas 76691
(254) 826-3341

Mariano Pargas, Justice of the Peace
Precinct 6, Place 1, Uvalde County
Courthouse Plaza, Box 12
Uvalde, Texas 78801
(830) 278-8123

Hermilo Pena, Jr., Justice of the Peace
Precinct 5, Place 2, Nueces County
Post office Box 133
Aqua Dulce, Texas 78380
(361) 998-2231

Leonardo Perez, Jr., Justice of the Peace
Precinct 1, Place 1, Jim Hogg County
111 East Beasley
Hebbronville, Texas 78361
(361) 527-3122

Rosa Quijano, Justice of the Peace
Precinct 4, Place 1, Zavala County
Post Office Box 36
La Pryor, Texas 78872
(830) 365-4276

Ramiro Quintero, Justice of the Peace
Precinct 5, Place 1, Brazos County
202 East 27th Street, Suite 103B
Bryan, Texas 77803
(409) 361-4402

Hector E. Ramirez, Justice of the Peace
Precinct 2, Place 1, Jim Hogg County
210 Viggie
Hebbronville, Texas 78361
(361) 527-3165

Amonario P. Ramon, Justice of the Peace
Precinct 1, Place 1, Reeves County
Post Office Box 913
Pecos, Texas 79772-0913
(915) 445-2619

Annie Ramos, Justice of the Peace
Precinct 1, Victoria County
2203 Lone Tree Road
Victoria, Texas 77901-7227
(361) 573-0836

José Antonio Ramos, Justice of the Peace
Precinct 3, Place 1, Zapata County
Falcon Box 102
Lopeno, Texas 78564-0102
(956) 848-5848

Gabriel E. Reci, Justice of the Peace
Precinct 2, Place 1, Starr County
Post Office Box 939
Roma, Texas 78584
(956) 849-1253

Armando V. Rodriguez, Justice of the Peace
Precinct 6, Place 2, Harris County
1001 Macario-Garcia Drive
Houston, Texas 77011
(713) 921-6141

Diana Rodriguez, Justice of the Peace
Precinct 2, Place 1, La Salle County
Post Office Box 67
Encinal, Texas 78019
(512) 948-5222

José L. Rodriguez, Justice of the Peace
Precinct 6, Place 1, Jim Wells County
Post Office Box 434
Ben Bolt, Texas 78342
(361) 664-9987

Luis Romero, Justice of the Peace
Precinct 6, Place 1, Cameron County
Post Office Box 1410
Los Fresnos, Texas 78566-1410
(956) 233-4073

Catarino Ruiz, Jr., Justice of the Peace
Precinct 3, Place 1, Dimmit County
Post Office Box 340
Big Wells, Texas 78830-0340
(830) 457-2643

Gilbert Saenz, Justice of the Peace
Precinct 1, Place 1, Hidalgo County
326 South Texas
Mercedes, Texas 78570
(956) 565-0100

Auturo Salas, Sr., Justice of the Peace
Precinct 7, Place 1, Cameron County
Post Office Box 672
La Feria, Texas 78559-0672
(956) 797-1887

Santiago A. Saldano, Justice of the Peace
Precinct 4, Place 1, Cameron County
Post Office Box 1087
Rio Hondo, Texas 78583
(956) 748-4233

Lilia G. Salinas, Justice of the Peace
Precinct 1, Place 1, Duval County
Post Office Box 429
San Diego, Texas 78384
(361) 279-3322

Henry A. Santana, Justice of the Peace
Precinct 1, Place 2, Nueces County
901 Leopard Street, Room 208
Corpus Christi, Texas 78401
(361) 888-0210

Leonardo Santoya, Justice of the Peace
Precinct 1, Place 1, Maverick County
885 Tampico Circle
Eagle Pass, Texas 78852
(830) 773-5887

Bennie Ray Sebesta, Justice of the Peace
Precinct 2, Place 1, Burleson County
Post Office Box 250
Snook, Texas 77878-0250
(409) 272-3656

Guillermo C. Serna, Justice of the Peace
Precinct 1, Place 1, Tom Green County
122 West Harris
San Angelo, Texas 76903-5839
(915) 659-6493

Becky V. Sierra, Justice of the Peace
Precinct 1, Place 2, Hays County
110 East MLK Drive
San Marcos, Texas 78666-5541
(512) 393-7636

Feliz Tamez Silva, Justice of the Peace
Precinct, Place 1, Willacy County
Route 2, Box 627
Raymondville, Texas 78580-9645
(956) 642-3542

Jesús (Chuy) Solis, Justice of the Peace
Precinct 4, Places1 and 2, Starr County
County Courthouse - 3rd Floor
Rio Grande City, Texas 78582
(956) 487-5401

Jerry Sotello, Justice of the Peace
Precinct 1, Place 1, Brewster County
Post Office Box 1074
Alpine, Texas 79831-0174
(915) 837-3912

Richard Teniente, Justice of the Peace
Precinct 1, Place 1, Bexar County
2185 Laredo Street - 1st Floor
San Antonio, Texas 78207
(210) 335-2803 FAX: (210) 335-2780

René O. Torres, Justice of the Peace
Precinct 4, Place 2, Hidalgo County
1212 South 25th Avenue
Edinburg, Texas 78539-7208
(956) 383-0921

Tony Torres, Justice of the Peace
Precinct 2, Place 1, Cameron County
974 East Harrison Street
Brownsville, Texas 78520
(956) 544-0857 FAX: (956) 548-9573

Antonia Trevino, Justice of the Peace
Precinct 5, Place 1, Starr County
Route 1, Box 79 G
Rio Grande City, Texas 78582
(956) 481-3476

Rosa E. Trevino, Justice of the Peace
Precinct 2, Place 2, Hidalgo County
122 East Park Avenue
Pharr, Texas 78577
(956) 787-1986

Teresa G. Trevino, Justice of the Peace
Precinct 4, Place 1, Willacy County
Post Office Box 118
Sebastian, Texas 78594-0118
(956) 347-3011

Oscar Tullos, Justice of the Peace
Precinct 2, Place 2, Cameron County
974 East Harrison Street
Brownsville, Texas 78520
(956) 544-0858 FAX: (956) 550-1467

Gisela Triana, Justice of the Peace
Precinct 5, Place 1
Travis County
Post Office Box 1748
Austin, Texas 78767-1748
(512) 473-9049

Mary Davis Valadez, Justice of the Peace
Precinct 2, Place 1, Duval County
Post office Box 1065
San Diego, Texas 78384
(361) 279-3322

Danny Valdez, Justice of the Peace
Precinct 1, Place 2, Webb County
1110 Victoria Street, Room 103
Laredo, Texas 78042-0715
(956) 721-2580

Manuel T. Valdez, Justice of the Peace
Precinct 5, Place 1, Tarrant County
350 West Belknap, Room 112C
Fort Worth, Texas 76196-0247
(817) 884-1438

Richard C. Vara, Justice of the Peace
Precinct 6, Place 1, Harris County
333 Lockwood Street
Houston, Texas 77011
(713) 921-1576

Emilio Vargas, Justice of the Peace
Precinct 1, Goliad County
Post Office Box 678
Goliad, Texas 77963
(361) 645-3310

Pilo Vasquez, Justice of the Peace
Precinct 3, Place 1, Zavala County
602 South Seventh Avenue
Crystal City, Texas 78839
(830) 374-3812

Rodolfo Vasquez, Justice of the Peace
Precinct 1, Place 1, Zavala County
Post Office Box 332
Batesville, Texas 78829
(830) 376-4747

Mona Velasquez, Justice of the Peace
Precinct 2, Place 1, Uvalde County
Post Office Box 177
Sabinal , Texas 78881
(830) 988-2461

Ismael Villalobos, Justice of the Peace
Precinct 2, Place 1
Post Office Box 83
Van Horn, Texas 79855
(915) 283-2059

Delia (Daisy) Villanueva, Justice of the Peace
Precinct 3, Karnes County
120 West Calvert
Karnes City, Texas 78118-3119
(830) 780-4373

Fernando M. Villareal, Justice of the Peace
Precinct 8, Place 1, McLennan County
1001 South 18th Suite A
Waco, Texas 76706
(254) 752-4242

Gabriel Villareal, Justice of the Peace
Precinct 2, Place 1, Zapata County
Post Office Box 116
San Ygnacio, Texas 78067-0116
(956) 765-5333

Victor Villareal, Justice of the Peace
Precinct 1, Place 1, La Salle County
Courthouse Square, Suite 205
Cotulla, Texas 78014
(830) 879-2112

Gualberto Weaver, Justice of the Peace
Precinct 7, Place 2, Cameron County
Route 4 - Box 137
San Benito, Texas 78586
(956) 428-7362

Sexto William Wolff, Justice of the Peace
Precinct 2, Place 1, El Paso County
4994 Hondo Pass
El Paso, Texas 79924
(915) 751-7575

Edmundo M. Zaragoza, Justice of the Peace
Precinct 5, Place 1, Bexar County
1313 Southeast Military Drive, Suite 114
San Antonio, Texas 78214
(210) 333-9373

Salvador Zarate, Jr., Justice of the Peace
Precinct 3, Place 1, Starr County
Post Office Box 276
Grulla, Texas 78548
(956) 487-7049

Juan Zavala, Justice of the Peace
Precinct 2, Place 1, Willacy County
294 East Yturria
Raymondville, Texas 78580-2101
(956) 689-3746

Matt Zepeda, Justice of the Peace
Precinct 3, Place 2, Brazoria County
3801 East Pear
Pearland, Texas 77581
(281) 485-1528

Municipal Courts Presiding Judges - The Asterisk (*) indicates those individuals who serve in more than one judgeship position, where the positions are part-time, and the individuals sits in more than one specific court. An Asterisk (*) also designates those individuals who may serve both as a municipal court judge and a justice of the peace judge at the same time. In the aggregate counting of number of judges, the asterick designations have not been counted, to assure accuracy in the counting of the total number of minority judges.

Robert Steven Anchondo, Presiding Judge
El Paso Municipal Court
810 East Overland Street
El Paso, Texas 79901-2560
(915) 546-2901 FAX: (915) 546-2939

Leopoldo Aviles, Jr., Presiding Judge
Uvalde Municipal Court
Post Office Box 799
Uvalde, Texas 78802-0799
(830) 275-9147

Angie Juarez Barill, Judge
El Paso Municipal Court
810 East Overland Street
El Paso, Texas 79901-2560
(915) 546-2901 FAX: (915) 546-2939

Gina M. Benavides, Presiding Judge
Palm Valley Municipal Court
1313 Stuart Place Road
Palm Valley, Texas 78552
(956) 423-8384 FAX: (956) 423-6324

Mary Berreia, Presiding Judge
Robstown Municipal Court
Post Office Box 872
Robstown, Texas 78380
(361) 387-9558 FAX: (361) 767-0082

Edward P. Cano, Presiding Judge
Elmendorf Municipal Court
Post Office Box 247
Elmendorf, Texas 78112-0247
(210) 635-8210 FAX: (210) 635-8221

Enrique Cantu, Presiding Judge
La Joya Municipal Court
Post Office Box H
La Joya, Texas 78560
(956) 581-7095 FAX: (956) 584-6677

Rosalinda De La Fuente, Presiding Judge
Poteet Municipal Court
Post Office Box 967
Poteet, Texas 78065-0967
(830) 742-3564 FAX: (830) 742-8607

Gloria Espinosa, Presiding Judge
Ralls Municipal Court
800 Avenue I
Ralls, Texas 79357-9700
(806) 253-2558 FAX: (806) 253-2550

Alvaro (A.P.) Flores, Presiding Judge
Van Horn Municipal Court
Post Office Box 517
Van Horn, Texas 79855-0517
(915) 283-2050 FAX: (915) 283-2839

Ernesto Flores, Presiding Judge
Mercedes Municipal Court
323 South Ohio Street
Mercedes, Texas 78570
(956) 565-3102 FAX: (956) 565-3114

Frances M. Flores, Presiding Judge
San Benito Municipal Court
485 North Sam Houston Boulevard
San Benito, Texas 78586-1870
(956) 361-3831 FAX: (956) 361-3805

G. R. (Lupe) Flores, Presiding Judge
Beaumont Municipal Court
Post Office Box 3827
Beaumont, Texas 77704-3827
(409) 880-3885 Ext. 211 or 835-3325
FAX: (409) 833-6414

Lauro Flores, Presiding Judge
Dilley Municipal Court
Post Office Box 230
Dilley, Texas 78017
(830) 965-1733 FAX: (830) 965-4012

Eustacio A. Galvan, Presiding Judge
Kyle Municipal Court
Post Office Box 40
Kyle, Texas 78640
(512) 268-5341 FAX: (512) 268-0675

Luis Ricardo Galvan, Presiding Judge
Gregory Municipal Court
Post Office Box 297
Gregory, Texas 78359-0297
(361) 643-6562 FAX: (361) 643-1335

Rose Mary Galvan-Schulze, Presiding Judge
Meadows Municipal Court
One Troyan Drive
Meadow Place, Texas 77477-2108
(281) 983-2950 FAX: (281) 983-2940

Albert Garcia, Presiding Judge
Alamo Municipal Court
840 West Austin Street, Suite 1-B
Alamo, Texas 78516
(956) 787-8689 FAX: (956) 787-8500

Alberto Garcia, Presiding Judge
Harlingen Municipal Court
Post Office Box 3562
Harlingen, Texas 78551
(956) 427-8759 FAX: (956) 427-8747

Esmerlda Garcia, Presiding Judge
Alton Municipal Court
Post Office Drawer 9004
Alton, Texas 78572
(956) 581-2733 FAX: (956) 581-2253

Richard Garcia, Presiding Judge
Pearsall Municipal Court
411 North Willow #8
Pearsall, Texas 78061
(830) 334-4160 FAX: (830) 334-4750

Dora P. Garza, Presiding Judge
Crystal City Municipal Court
101 East Dimmitt Street
Crystal City, Texas 78839
(830) 374-2923 FAX: Call on phone first

Elvira Garza, Presiding Judge
Rio Grande City Municipal Court
203 West Water Street
Rio Grande City, Texas 78582
(956) 487-8889 FAX: (956) 716-6007

Fred Garza, Presiding Judge
Beesville Municipal Court
402 North Washington Street
Beesville, Texas 78102
(361) 354-5337 FAX: (361) 362-1889

Javier S. Garza, Presiding Judge
Donna Municipal Court
207 South 10th Street
Donna, Texas 78537-3337
(956) 464-6942 FAX: (956) 464-6933

Rudy R. Garza, Presiding Judge
Floresville Municipal Court
1120 D Street
Floresville, Texas 78114-0845
(830) 393-4232 FAX: (830) 393-2056

Gustavo Gonzales, Judge
Dallas Municipal Court
2014 Main Street, Room 210
Dallas, Texas 75201
(214) 670-5573 FAX: (214) 670-6947

Edelia Gonzalez-Lemon, Presiding Judge
Alice Municipal Court
415 East Main Street
Alice, Texas 78332
(361) 668-7285 FAX: (361) 668-6829

Luis Rey Guerra, Presiding Judge
Premont Municipal Court
Post Office Box Drawer 340
Premont, Texas 78375-0340
(361) 348-2022 FAX: (361) 348-2196

Janie Guerra, Presiding Judge
Cactus Municipal Court
Post Office Box 365
Cactus, Texas 79013
(806) 966-5458 FAX: (806) 966-5771

Eutimio Guterrez, Jr., Presiding Judge
Lyford Municipal Court
Post Office Box 310
Lyford, Texas 78569
(956) 347-3512 FAX: (956) 347-5434

Hector M. Hernandez, Administrative Judge
Houston Municipal Court
1400 Lubbock Street - 2nd Floor
Houston, Texas 77002-1526
(713) 247-5464 or 247-8791 FAX: (713) 247-8747
E-mail: hhernand@mca.ci.houston.tx.us

Joe Hernandez, Presiding Judge
Combes Municipal Court
Post Office Box 280
Combes, Texas 78535
(956) 425-7131 FAX: (956) 412-6795

Pat Hernandez, Presiding Judge
Plainview Municipal Court
901 Broadway Street
Plainview, Texas 79072
(806) 296-1177 FAX: (806) 296-1125

Hector E. Huerta, Presiding Judge
Raymondville Municipal Court
523 West Hidalgo Avenue
Raymondville, Texas 78580
(956) 689-6449 FAX: (956) 689-2811

Jesse Lerma, Jr., Presiding Judge
Palmview Municipal Court
Route 11, Box 1000
Palmview, Texas 78572
(956) 581-7411 FAX: (956) 581-7494

Joe L. Lopez, Presiding Judge
Rio Hondo Municipal Court
Post Office Box 389
Rio Hondo, Texas 78583
(956) 748-2102 FAX: (956) 748-4394

Juan A. Lopez, Presiding Judge
Eagle Pass Municipal Court
Post Office Box 4019
Eagle Pass, Texas 78853-4019
(830) 773-1111 FAX: (830) 773-9170

Sylvia Marie Lopez-Beaver, Presiding Judge
Waxahachie Municipal Court
401 South Rogers
Waxahachie, Texas 75165
(972) 937-7330 Ext. 261 FAX: (972) 935-9835

David Maldonado, Presiding Judge
Cockrell Hill Municipal Court
4125 West Clarendon Drive
Dallas, Texas 75211
(214) 330-6333 FAX: (214) 330-5483

Ninfa L. Mares, Presiding Judge
Fort Worth Municipal Court
1000 Throckmorton Street
Fort Worth, Texas 76102-6382
(817) 871-6715 or 817-6716 FAX: (817) 871-6723

Rodolfo G. Mares, Presiding Judge
La Feria Municipal Court
115 E Commerical Avenue
La Feria, Texas 78559-5002
(956) 797-2261 FAX: (956) 797-1898

Anastacio (Rocky) Martinez, Jr.
Presiding Judge
Richwood Municipal Court
215 Halbert Street
Richwood, Texas 77531
(979) 265-8157 FAX: (979) 265-7345

Arturo Martinez, Presiding Judge
San Juan Municipal Court
2301 A North Raul Longoria Road
San Juan, Texas 78589
(956) 783-3505 FAX: (956) 783-3503

Catarino Martinez, Presiding Judge
Loraine Municipal Court
Post Office Box 7
Loraine, Texas 79532
(915) 737-2222 FAX: (915) 737-2452

Dario Martinez, Presidng Judge
Pharr Municipal Court
202 East Clark
Pharr, Texas 78577
(956) 783-7859 FAX: (956) 702-2259

Roxane E. Martinez, Judge
Houston Muncipal Court
1400 Lubbock, Basement
Houston, Texas 77002
(713) 247-5464 or 247-5760 FAX: (713) 247-8747

Berta A. Mejia, Director and Presiding Judge
City of Houston Municipal Courts
Harris County
1400 Lubbock - Room 214
Houston, Texas 77002
(713) 247-5464 FAX: (713) 247-8747

Rosalinda M. Mendiola, Presiding Judge
Carrizo Springs Municipal Court
Post Office Box 329
Carrizo Springs, Texas 78834
(830) 876-2476 FAX: (830) 876-3127

Lali Minjarez, Presiding Judge
Fort Stockton Municipal Court
116 West Second Street
Fort Stockton, Texas 79735
(915) 336-8525 FAX: (915) 336-6273

Lawrence Morales, Presiding Judge
Leon Valley Municipal Court
6400 El Verde Road
San Antonio, Texas 78238-2399
(210) 684-1391 FAX: (210) 684-4476

Fred Nieto, Jr., Presiding Judge
Moulton Municipal Court
Post Office Box 369
Moulton, Texas 77975
(361) 596-4621 FAX: (361) 596-7075

Tony Kosturakis Oaxaca, Presiding Judge
Anthony Municipal Court
Post Office Box 1269
Anthony, Texas 79821
(915) 886-3272 FAX: (915) 886-3115

Ruben Ochoa, Jr., Presiding Judge
Santa Rosa Municipal Court
Post Office Box 326
Santa Rosa, Texas 78593-0326
(956) 636-1064 FAX: (956) 636-2044

Ruben Ochoa, Jr. *, Presiding Judge
Primera Municipal Court
Route 1, Box 176
Primera, Texas 78552
(956) 423-9654 FAX: (956) 423-2166

Filemon Ortiz, Jr., Presiding Judge
Del Rio Municipal Court
109 West Broadway
Del Rio, Texas 78840
(830) 774-8506 FAX: (830) 774-8542

Toribio (Terry) Palacios, Presiding Judge
Edinburg Municipal Court
100 East Freddy Gonzalez Drive
Edinburg, Texas 78539-4339
(956) 388-0500 FAX: (956) 386-0667

Horacio Pena, Jr., Presiding Judge
Mission Muncipal Court
200 East Tom Landry
Mission, Texas 78572
(956) 580-8800

Alicia Perez, Presiding Judge
Freer Municipal Court
Post Office Drawer N
Freer, Texas 78357
(361) 394-6612 FAX: (361) 394-6326

Normalinda Perez, Presiding Judge
Muleshoe Municipal Court
215 East Avenue B
Muleshoe, Texas 79347
(806) 272-7586 FAX: (806) 272-5260

Ricardo A. Perez, Presiding Judge
Roma Municipal Coiurt
Post Office Box 947
Roma, Texas 78584
(956) 849-1915 FAX: (956) 849-1333

Ray M. Quintanilla, Presiding Judge
Galveston Municipal Court
Post Office Box 687
Galveston, Texas 77553
(409) 797-3885 or 762-6553 FAX: (409) 797-3881

Minerva R. Ramirez, Presiding Judge
Mathis Municipal Court
214 North Nueces Street
Mathis, Texas 78368
(361) 547-4205 FAX: (361) 547-4209

Maggie Ribera, Presiding Judge
Hamlin Municipal Court
Post Office Box 157
Hamlin, Texas 79520-0157
(915) 576-3634 FAX: (915) 576-3635

Daniel Robledo, Presiding Judge
Horizon City Municipal Court
14999 Darrington Road
Horizon City, Texas 79928-7348
(915) 852-1048 FAX: (915) 852-1005

Javier Rodriguez, Presiding Judge
Elsa Municipal Court
216 East Fourth Street
Post Office Box 427
Elsa, Texas 75843
(956) 262-2127 FAX: (956) 262-5050

Javier Rodriguez*, Judge
La Villa Municipal Court
Post Office Box 60
La Villa, Texas 78562
(956) 262-2122 FAX: (956) 262-2516

Olivero Rosas, Presiding Judge
Falfurrias Municipal Court
205 East Allen Street
Post Office Drawer E
Falfurrias, Texas 78355
(361) 325-5039 FAX: (361) 325-9784

Robert P. de Saglio, Presiding Judge
Fairview Municipal Court
Post Office Box 855
Rhome, Texas 76078
(800) 631-4257

Daniel F. Solis, Judge
Dallas Municipal Court
2014 Main Street, Suite 210
Dallas, Texas 75201
(214) 670-5573 FAX: (214) 670-6947

Rodolfo G. Tamez, Presiding Judge
Corpus Christi Municipal Court
120 North Chaparral Street
Corpus Christi, Texas 78401-2802
(361) 886-2520 FAX: (361) 886-2560

Alfredo M. Tavera, Presiding Judge
San Antonio Municipal Court
Frank Wing Municipal Court Building
401 South Frio Street
San Antonio, Texas 78207
(210) 207-7130 FAX: (210) 207-4259
E-mail: atavera@ci.sat.tx.us

Rosaura (Wawi) Tijerina, Presiding Judge
Laredo Municipal Court
Post Office Box 579
Laredo, Texas 78042
(956) 795-2300 FAX: (956) 717-3407

Vivian Torres, Presiding Judge
Hondo Municipal Court
1600 Avenue M
Hondo, Texas 78861
(830) 426-3370 FAX: (830) 426-5189

Mario Alberto Trevino, Presiding Judge
Hill Country Village Municipal Court
116 Aspen Lane
San Antonio, Texas 78232
(210) 494-3671 FAX: (210) 490-8645

Manuel T. Valdez, Presiding Judge
Rhome Municipal Court
Post Office Box 228
Rhome, Texas 76078
(817) 636-2462 FAX: (817) 636-2465

Manuel T. Valdez*, Presiding Judge
Newark Municipal Court
Post Office Box 156
Newark, Texas 76071
(817) 489-2274 FAX: (817) 884-3323

Eliseo B. Vega, Presiding Judge
Port Isabel Municipal Court
110 West Hickman Street
Port Isabel, Texas 78578-0146
(956) 943-1242 FAX: (956) 943-6011

Joe Gilbert Vera, Presiding Judge
Lamesa Municipal Court
601 South First Street
Lamesa, Texas 79331-6247
(806) 872-4343

Cynthia Villarreal, Presiding Judge
Bishop Municipal Court
500 East Texas Avenue
Bishop, Texas 78335
(361) 584-2567 FAX: (361) 584-3253

Joseph H. Vives, Presiding Judge
Alamo Heights Municipal Court
6116 Broadway
San Antonio, Texas 78209-4545
(210) 822-3331 FAX: (210) 822-8197

Municipal Court Associate Judges

Bernardo Aldape, Associate Judge
South Houston Municipal Court
Post Office Box 238
South Houston, Texas 77587-0238
(713) 947-7700 FAX: (713) 947-2213

Auturo Alvarez, Associate Judge
Austin Municipal Court
Post Office Box 2135
Austin, Texas 78768-2135
(512) 433-4841 FAX: (512) 433-4837

Yolanda A. Bernal, Associate Judge
Fort Worth Municipal Court
1000 Throckmorton
Fort Worth, Texas 76102-6382
(817) 871-6715 FAX: (817) 871-6723

David Bonilla, Associate Judge
El Paso Municipal Court
810 East Overland Street
El Paso, Texas 79901-2560
(915) 546-2901 FAX: (915) 546-2939

Gloria Cabrera, Associate Judge
San Antonio Municipal Court
Frank Wing Municipal Court Building
401 South Frio Street
San Antonio, Texas 78207
(210) 207-7130 FAX: (210) 207-4259
E-mail: gcabrera@ci.sat.tx.us

Maria E. Casanova, Judge
Houston Municipal Court
1400 Lubbock, 2nd Floor
Houston, Texas 77002
(713) 247-5464 or 247-8063
FAX: (713) 247-8747

Celia Castro, Associate Judge
Austin Municipal Court
Post Office Box 2135
Austin, Texas 78768-2135
(512) 433-4841 FAX: (512) 433-4837

Ouifa Davis, Associate Judge
El Paso Municipal Court
810 East Overland Street
El Paso, Texas 79901-2560
(915) 546-2901 FAX: (915) 546-2939

Carla De Leon, Associate Judge
San Antonio Municipal Court
Frank Wing Municipal Court Building
401 South Frio Street
San Antonio, Texas 78207
(210) 207-7130 FAX: (210) 207-4259
E-mail: cmdeleon@ci.sat.tx.us

Patricia Diaz-Hartline, Associate Judge
Dallas Municipal Court
2014 Main Street, Room 210
Dallas, Texas 75201
(214) 670-5573 FAX: (214) 670-6947

Elihu H. Dodler, Associate Judge
Houston Municipal Court
1400 Lubbock - Room 214
Houston, Texas 77002
(713) 247-5464 FAX: (713) 247-8747

Candelario Elizondo, Associate Judge
West University Place Municipal Court
3800 University Boulevard
West University Place, Texas 77005
(713) 662-5825

Roland Esparza, Associate Judge
San Antonio Municipal Court
Frank Wing Municipal Court Building
401 South Frio Street
San Antonio, Texas 78207
(210) 207-7130 FAX: (210) 207-4259

Alfred Flores, Jr., Associate Judge
Houston Municipal Court
1400 Lubbock - Room 214
Houston, Texas 77002
(713) 247-5464 FAX: (713) 247-8747

Paulo Flores, Associate Judge
Dallas MunicipalCourt
2014 Main Street, Room 210
Dallas, Texas 75201
(214) 670-5573 FAX: (214) 670-6947

David O. Fraga, Associate Judge
Houston Municipal Court
1400 Lubbock - Room 214
Houston, Texas 77002
(713) 247-5464 FAX: (713) 247-8747

Mary Elizabeth Fuentes-Valdez
Associate Judge
San Antonio Municipal Court
Frank Wing Municipal Court Building
401 South Frio Street
San Antonio, Texas 78207
(210) 207-7130 FAX: (210) 207-4259

Ramon Gallegos, Associate Judge
Lubbock Municipal Court
Post Office Box 2000
Lubbock, Texas 79457
(806) 775-2462 FAX: (806) 775-2468

Esmeralda Peña Garcia, Judge
Houston Municipal Court
3203 South Dairy Ashford
Houston, Texas 77082-2320
(281) 584-4889 or (713) 247-5464
FAX: (713) 247-8747

Ralph Garcia, Associate Judge
El Paso Municipal Court
810 East Overland Street
El Paso, Texas 79901-2560
(915) 546-2901 FAX: (915) 546-2939

Robert Garcia, Associate Judge
Lake Dallas Municipal Court
Post Office Box 368
Lake Dallas, Texas 75065
(940) 497-2227 FAX: (940) 497-4485

Joe D. Gonzales, Associate Judge
San Antonio Municipal Court
Frank Wing Municipal Court Building
401 South Frio Street
San Antonio, Texas 78207
(210) 207-7130 FAX: (210) 207-4259

Mario Gonzalez, Associate Judge
El Paso Municipal Court
810 East Overland Street
El Paso, Texas 79901-2560
(915) 546-2901 FAX: (214) 546-2939

Monica A. Gonzalez, Associate Judge
San Antonio Municipal Court
Frank Wing Municipal Court Building
401 South Frio Street
San Antonio, Texas 78207
(210) 207-7130 FAX: (210) 207-4259
E-mail: monicagonz@ci.sat.tx.us

Simon C. Gonzalez, Associate Judge
Hudson Oaks Municipal Court
150 North Oakridge Drive
Hudson Oaks, Texas 76087
(817) 594-0302

Tim Gonzalez, Associate Judge
Dallas Municipal Court
2014 Main Street, Room 210
Dallas, Texas 75201
(214) 670-5573 FAX: (214) 670-6947

Juventino Guerra, Associate Judge
San Antonio Municipal Court
Frank Wing Municipal Court Building
401 South Frio Street
San Antonio, Texas 78207
(210) 207-7130 FAX: (210) 207-4259

Daniel Guerrero, Associate Judge
San Antonio Municipal Court
Frank Wing Municipal Court Building
401 South Frio Street
San Antonio, Texas 78207
(210) 207-7130 FAX: (210) 207-4259

A. Robert Hinojosa, Associate Judge
Houston Municipal Court
1400 Lubbock - Room 214
Houston, Texas 77002
(713) 247-5464 FAX: (713) 247-8747

Lori A. Jasso, Associate Judge
Monahans Municipal Court
114 South Bruce Avenue
Monahans, Texas 79756
(915) 943-6361 FAX: (915) 943-7388

Enrique Martinez, Associate Judge
Lubbock Municipal Court
Post Office Box 2000
Lubbock, Texas 79457
(806) 775-2473 FAX: (806) 775-2468

Roxane E. Martinez*, Associate Judge
Kendleton Municipal Court
Post Office Box 809
Kendleton, Texas 77451
(409) 532-8240

Carmen Medrano, Associate Judge
Elgin Municipal Court
Post Office Box 591
Elgin, Texas 78621-0599
(512) 285-5721

Alex Melendez, Associate Judge
El Paso Municipal Court
810 East Overland Street
El Paso, Texas 79901-2560
(915) 546-2901 FAX: (915) 546-2939

Margaret A. Muñoz, Associate Judge
Houston Municipal Court
1400 Lubbock - Room 214
Houston, Texas 77002
(713) 247-5464 FAX: (713) 247-8747

Adelaida Murillo, Associate Judge
Hereford Municipal Court
Post Office Box 2277
Hereford, Texas 79045-2277
(806) 363-7127

A. Josefina "Jo" Nelson, Associate Judge
Houston Municipal Court
1400 Lubbock - Room 214
Houston, Texas 77002
(713) 247-5464 FAX: (713) 247-8747

Ana M. Otero, Associate Judge
Houston Municipal Court
1400 Lubbock - Room 214
Houston, Texas 77002
(713) 247-5464 FAX: (713) 247-8747

Daniel Perez, Jr., Judge
Houston Municipal Court
1400 Lubbock, Basement
Houston, Texas 77002
(713) 247-5464 or 247-5760 FAX: (713) 247-8747

Richard Porras, Associate Judge
El Paso Municipal Court
810 East Overland Street
El Paso, Texas 79901-2560
(915) 546-2901 FAX: (915) 546-2939

Daniel Ramirez, Associate Judge
Laredo Municipal Court
Post Office Box 579
Laredo, Texas 78042
(956) 795-2300 FAX: (956) 717-3407

Maria Ramirez, Associate Judge
El Paso Municipal Court
810 East Overland Street
El Paso, Texas 79901-2560
(915) 546-2901 FAX: (915) 546-2939

Marco Ramirrez, Associate Judge
La Joya Municipal Court
Post Office Box H
La Joya, Texas 78560
(956) 581-7095 FAX: (956) 584-6677

Samuel Ramos, Associate Judge
Rio Grande City Municipal Court
203 West Water Street
Rio Grande City, Texas 78582
(956) 487-8889 FAX: (956) 716-6007

Josefina M. Rendon, Associate Judge
Houston Municipal Court
1400 Lubbock - Room 214
Houston, Texas 77002
(713) 247-5465 FAX: (713) 247-8747

Jo Ann Reyes, Associate Judge
Fort Worth Municipal Court
1000 Throckmorton
Fort Worth, Texas 76102-6382
(817) 871-6715 FAX: (817) 871-6723

Mauro Longino Reyna, Associate Judge
Mission Municipal Court
200 East Tom Landry
Mission, Texas 28572
(956) 584-7822

Julianna Siracus Rivera, Associate Judge
Corpus Christi Municipal Court
120 North Chaparral
Corpus Christi, Texas 78401-2802
(361) 886-2520 FAX: (361) 886-2560

David Rodriguez, Associate Judge
San Antonio Municipal Court
Frank Wing Municipal Court Building
401 South Frio Street
San Antonio, Texas 78207
(210) 207-7130 FAX: (210) 207-4259

Roberto Salazar, Associate Judge
McAllen Municipal Court
1501 West Pecan Boulevard
McAllen, Texas 78501
(956) 682-1291

Roberto Sandoval, Associate Judge
El Paso Municipal Court
810 East Overland Street
El Paso, Texas 79901-2560
(915) 546-2901 FAX: (915) 546-2939

Herman Segovia, Associate Judge
Leon Valley Municipal Court
6400 El Verde Road
San Antonio, Texas 78238-2399
(210) 684-1391

Roger Segura, Associate Judge
San Antonio Municipal Court
Frank Wing Municipal Court Building
401 South Frio Street
San Antonio, Texas 78207
(210) 207-7125 FAX: (210) 207-4259
E-mail: rsegura@ci.sat.tx.us

Rebecca A. Terrazas, Associate Judge
Clint Municipal Court
Post Office Box 350
Clint, Texas 79836
(915) 851-3146 FAX: (915) 851-0040

Catherine Torres-Stahl, Associate Judge
San Antonio Municipal Court
Frank Wing Municipal Court Building
401 South Frio Street
San Antonio, Texas 78207
(210) 207-7130 FAX: (210) 207-4259
E-mail: ctorstahl@ci.sat.tx.us

Michael Ugarte, Associate Judge
San Antonio Municipal Court
Frank Wing Municipal Court Building
401 South Frio Street
San Antonio, Texas 78207
(210) 207-7130 FAX: (210) 207-4259

Edward B. Valverde, Associate Judge
Fort Worth Municipal Court
1000 Throckmorton
Fort Worth, Texas 76102-6382
(817) 871-6715 FAX: (817) 871-6723

Joseph W. Varela, Associate Judge
Houston Municipal Court
1400 Lubbock - Room 214
Houston, Texas 77002
(713) 247-5465 FAX: (713) 247-8747

Roberto Vargas, Associate Judge
San Antonio Municipal Court
Frank Wing Municipal Court Building
401 South Frio Street
San Antonio, Texas 78207
(210) 207-7130 FAX: (210) 207-4259
E-mail: RobertoV@ci.sat.tx.us

John R. Vasquez, Associate Judge
Austin Municipal Court
Post Office Box 2135
Austin, Texas 78768-2135
(512) 443-4841 FAX: (512) 433-4837

Sr. and Retired Municipal Judges

Harold L. Valderas, Sr.,Judge
Sutton County
3133 Wabash Avenue
Fort Worth, Texas 76109
(817) 292-5241

Judicial Masters and Referees

Ida Hernandez Brazell, Master Title IV-D
Nueces County
901 Leopard Street, Room 404
Corpus Christi, Texas 78401-3693
(512) 888-0292 FAX: (512) 888-0234

Juan A. Chavira, Master Title IV
Bexar County
Fourth Administrative Judicial Region
Bexar County Courthouse, Room 300-A
San Antonio, Texas 78205
(210) 220-2706 FAX: (210) 220-3900

George Martinez, Master Title IV
Dallas County
First Administrative Judicial Region
6733 Keswick Street
Dallas, Texas 75232-2314
(214) 337-6395

Angelita Mendoza-Waterhouse,
Master Title IV
Travis County
Third Administrative Judicial Region
2515 South Congress
Austin, Texas 78704
(512) 448-7000

James Coronado, Master
District Court
Travis County
Post Office Box 1748
Austin, Texas 78767
(512) 473-9897 FAX: (512) 473-9140

G. R. (Lupe) Flores*, Master
County Court, Jefferson County
1149 Pearl Street
Beaumont, Texas 77701
(409) 835-8466 FAX: (409) 833-6414

M. Dolores Abalos, Referee
Criminal District Court #5
Dallas County
600 Commerce Street
Dallas, Texas 75020
(214) 653-5940 FAX: (214) 653-7155

Magistrates

Julie Gonzalez, Criminal Magistrate
El Paso County
500 East San Antonio Street
El Paso, Texas 79901-2496
(915) 546-2181 FAX: (915) 546-2184

Sam Medrano, Magistrate
Juvenile Probation Court
500 East San Antonio Street
El Paso, Texas 79901-2496
(915) 772-2133 FAX: (915) 775-4777

UTAH: (4)

FEDERAL

Samuel Alba, U. S. Magistrate Judge
U. S. District Court for the District of Utah
350 South Main Street, Suite 260
Salt Lake City, Utah 84101
(801) 524-6155 FAX: (801) 526-1171

Administrative Law Judge

Gilbert A. Martinez, Administrative Law Judge
Office of Hearings and Appeals
Social Security Administration
American Plaza II, Suite 201
57 West 200 South Street
Salt Lake City, Utah 84101
(801) 524-5315 FAX: (801) 524-3348

STATE

Denise P. Lindberg, District Judge
Salt Lake County - Third District Court
210 West 10000 South
Sandy, Utah 84070
(801) 565-5722 FAX: (801) 565-5747
E-mail: dlinber@email.utcourts.gov

Andrew A. Valdez, Judge
Third District Juvenile Court
450 South State Street, 2nd Floor
Salt Lake City, Utah 84114
(801) 238-7787 FAX: (801) 238-7771
E-mail: Jvaldez@email.utcourts.gov

VERMONT: (0)

VIRGIN ISLANDS: (0)

VIRGINIA: (5)

FEDERAL

Jose R. Davila, Chief Administrative Law Judge
Office of Hearings and Appeals
Social Security Administration
Main Street Center, Suite 1720
600 East Main Street
Richmond, Virginia 23219-2406
(804) 771-2977 FAX: (804) 771-2405

Carlos Garza, Administrative Law Judge (Retired)
Member, Board of Directors
State Justice Institute
1650 King Street, Suite 600
Alexandria, Virginia 22314
(703) 684-6100

Elias C. Rodriguez
Administrative Law Judge (Retired)
9300 Santayana Drive
Fairfax, Virginia 22031
(703) 591-6258

Gustavo D. Villageliu, Member
Board of Immigration Appeals
Executive Office of Immigration Review
5107 Leesburg Pike, Suite 1711
Falls Church, Virginia 22041
(703) 305-1194 FAX: Call on phone first

Wayne R. Iskra, U. S. Immigration Judge
901 North Stuart Street, Suite 1300
Arlington, Virginia 22203
(703) 235-2307

WASHINGTON: (7)

FEDERAL

Ricardo S. Martinez, U. S. Magistrate Judge for the Western District of Washington
304 U. S. Courthouse
1010 Fifth Avenue
Seattle, Washington 98104-1130
(206) 553-1396 FAX: (206) 553-4054

STATE

Charles Z. Smith, Justice
Supreme Court of Washington
Temple of Justice
Post Office Box 40929
Olympia, Washington 98504-0929
(360) 357-2053 FAX: (360) 357-2103

Sergio Armijo, Judge
Pierce County Superior Court
County-City Building
930 Tacoma Avenue South
Tacoma, Washington 98402-2102
(206) 591-3655 FAX: (206) 591-7214

Carmen Otero, Judge (Retired)
King County Superior Court
Seattle, Washington 98104

Michael S. Hurtado, Judge
Seattle Municipal Court
Public Safety Building
610 Third Avenue
Seattle, Washington 98104
(206) 684-8709 FAX: (206) 233-0056

Terry L. Jurado, Presiding Judge
Renton Municipal Court
1005 S. Grady Way
Renton, Washington 98005
(425) 430-6550 FAX: (425) 430-6544

Administrative Law Judges

Deborah Lazaldi, Administrative Law Judge
Board of Industrial Insurance Appeals
Post Office Box 42401 FL-13
Olympia, Washington 98504-2402
(360) 753-6823 FAX: (360) 586-5611

WEST VIRGINIA: (0)

WISCONSIN: (3)

STATE

Ramona A. Gonzalez, Judge
La Crosse County Circuit Court
400 North Fourth Street, Suite 305
La Crosse, Wisconsin 54601
(608) 785-9570 FAX: (608) 785-7821

Elsa C. Lamelas, Judge
Milwaukee County Circuit Court #23
901 North Ninth Street, Suite 104
Milwaukee, Wisconsin 53233
(414) 278-4554

Alice De La O, Administrative Law Judge
Wisconsin Department of Industry,
Labor and Human Relations
Equal Rights Division
819 North Sixth Street, Room 255
Milwaukee, Wisconsin 53203
(414) 227-4393 FAX: (414) 227-4084

Wyoming: (0)

U. S. Armed Forces: (0)

Section IV
Native American Judges of the United States

Prepared by
Honorable Arthur L. Burnett, Sr.

ALABAMA: (1)

FEDERAL

Robert Gary Goosens,
Administrative Law Judge
Office of Hearings & Appeals
Social Security Administration
3605 Springhill Business Park
Mobile, Alabama 36608
(334) 441-5441 FAX: (334) 441-5993

ALASKA: (0)

ARIZONA: (5)

STATE

Gloria J. Kindig, Judge
Superior Court of Navajo County
County Courthouse
Post Office Box 668
Holbrook, Arizona 86025
(520) 524-4213 FAX: (520) 524-4246

Eveyln Bradley, Justice of the Peace
Post Office Box 38
Kayenta, Arizona 86033
(520) 697-3522 FAX: (520) 697-3528

Merwin Lynch, Justice of the Peace
Post Office Box 610
Sanders, Arizona 86512
(520) 688-2954 FAX: (520) 688-2244

Ronnie O. McDaniel, Justice of the Peace
714 South Beeline - Suite 103
Payson, Arizona 85541
(520) 474-5267 FAX: (520) 474-6214

Glenn E. Stoner, Justice of the Peace
Post Office Box 888
Chinle, Arizona 86503
(520) 674-4922 FAX: (520) 674-5926

ARKANSAS: (0)

CALIFORNIA: (6)

FEDERAL

Maria-Elena James, Magistrate Judge
U. S. District Court
for the Northern District of California
450 Golden Gate Avenue
San Francisco, California 94102
(415) 522-4708 FAX: (415) 522-2140

Administrative Law Judge

Earl J. Waits, Chief Administrative Law Judge
Office of Hearings & Appeals
Social Security Administration
City National Bank Building
606 South Olive - Room 1200
Los Angeles, California 90014
(213) 894-2669 FAX: (213) 894-2595

STATE

Gary Strankman, Presiding Justice
Court of Appeal, Fourth District, Division One
Marathon Plaza, South Tower
303 Second Street, Suite 600
San Francisco, California 94107
(619) 645-2760

Marilyn Miles, Judge
Superior Court
State of California
825 Fifth Street
Eureka, California 95501
(707) 445-7620

Abby Abinanti, Commissioner
Superior Court
State of California, County of San Francisco
Juvenile Division
375 Woodside Avenue
San Francisco, California 94127-1298
(415) 753-7753 FAX: (415) 753-7888

Fred W. Gabourie, Sr., Judge (Retired)
Los Angeles Municipal Court
Chief Judge Kootnia Tribe
Post Office Box 369
Plummer, Idaho 83851
(208) 667-3836 or (509) 927-9900

Colorado: (0)

Connecticut: (0)

Delaware: (0)

District of Columbia: (0)

Florida: (1)

Lawrence Kirkwood, Judge
Circuit Court of Orange County
9th Judicial Circuit
Orange County Courthouse
425 North Orange Avenue
Orlando, Florida 32801
(407) 836-2018 E-mail: ctjulk1@ocnjcc.org

Georgia: (1)

State

James W. Oxendine, Judge
Superior Court
Gwinnett Justice Administration Center
75 Langley Drive
Lawrenceville, Georgia 30245
(770) 822-8613 FAX: (770) 822-8637

Guam: (0)

Hawaii: (0)

Idaho: (0)

Illinois: (0)

Indiana: (0)

Iowa: (0)

Kansas: (0)

Kentucky: (1)

Federal

Lawrence E. Shearer,
Chief Administrative Law Judge
Office of Hearings & Appeals
Social Security Administration
Gene Snyder U. S.Courthouse
601 West Broadway, Suite 300
Louisville, Kentucky 40202
(502) 582-6446 FAX: (502) 582-6819
E-mail: Lawrence.E.Shearer@ssa.gov

Louisiana: (1)

Federal

Administrative Law Judge

Sally N. Willett, Administrative Law Judge
Office of Hearings & Appeals
Social Security Administration
1515 Poydras Street, Suite 1600
New Orleans, Louisiana 70112
(504) 589-2418 FAX: (504) 589-4585

Maine: (0)

Maryland: (0)

Massachusetts: (0)

Michigan: (0)

Minnesota: (1)

Robert A. Blaeser, Judge
Fourth Judicial District
Hennepin County Government Building
Minneapolis, Minnesota 55487-0421
(612) 348-4964 FAX: (612) 348-2131

MISSISSIPPI: (0)

MISSOURI: (0)

MONTANA: (1)

J. A. Turnage, Chief Justice (Retired)
Montana Supreme Court
Justice Building, Room 416
Helena, Montana 59620
(406) 444-3858

NEBRASKA: (0)

NEVADA: (2)

STATE

Howard Huttman, Jr., Justice of the Peace
McDermitt Township Justice Court
Post Office Box 381
McDermott, Nevada 89421
(775) 532-8292

Randy P. Varain, Justice of the Peace
Schurz Township Justice Court
Post Office Box 89427
Schurz, Nevada 89427
(775) 773-2241

NEW HAMPSHIRE: (0)

NEW JERSEY: (2)

John A Casarow, Jr., Judge
Deerfield Township Municipal Court
Post Office Box 350
Rosenhayn, New Jersey 08352
(609) 455-3200 FAX: (856) 455-0025
and Judge Downe Township Municipal Court
Route 553 and Sharp Lane
Post Office Box 569
Newport, New Jersey 08345-0569
(856) 447-3501 FAX: (856) 447-3533
and Judge Greenwich Municipal Building
590 Shiloh Pike
Bridgeton, New Jersey 08302
(856) 453-1523 FAX: (856) 455-3080

Russell G. Cheek, Judge
Howell Township Municipal Court
300 Old Tavern Road
Post Office Box 580
Howell, New Jersey 07731-0580
(732) 938-4848 FAX: (732) 938-7054

NEW MEXICO: (3)

FEDERAL

Carol A. Connor, Administrative Law Judge
Office of Hearings and Appeals
Social Security Administration
American Financial Center
Building #1, Suite 300
2400 Louisiana Boulevard, N.E.
Albuquerque, New Mexico 87110-4338
(505) 346-7823 FAX: (505) 346-7862

STATE

Teresa Ann Gomez, Judge
Metropolitan Court
Post Office Box 133
Albuquerque, New Mexico 87103-0133
(505) 841-8196 FAX: (505) 222-4814

Carol J. Vigil, Judge
First Judicial District
Division III
Post Office Box 2268
Santa Fe, New Mexico 87504
(505) 827-5083 FAX: (505) 827-5055

NEW YORK: (0)

NORTH CAROLINA: (4)

Dexter Brooks,
Senior Resident Superior Court Judge
16B Judicial District
Post Office Box 730
Pembroke, North Carolina 28372
(910) 671-3325 FAX: (910) 671-3113

Bradley B. Letts, Judge
30th District Court
Post Office Box 23
Sylvia, North Carolina 28779
(828) 456-3796 FAX: (828) 452-2510

Gary Locklear, Chief Judge
16B District Court
Robeson County Courthouse
Lumberton, North Carolina 28358
(910) 671-3335 FAX: (910) 671-3113

William Jeffrey Moore, Judge
16B District Court
Robeson County Courthouse
Lumberton, North Carolina 28358
(910) 671-3335 FAX: (910) 671-3113

NORTH DAKOTA: (1)

STATE

Donovan Foughty, Judge
District Court
Post Office Box 70
Devil's Lake, North Dakota 58301
(701) 662-1308 FAX: (701) 662-8539

NORTH MARIANNA ISLANDS: (0)

OHIO: (0)

OKLAHOMA: (4)

FEDERAL

Michael Burrage, Judge
U. S.District Court
for the Northern District of Oklahoma
U. S.Courthouse, Room 411
333 West Fourth Street
Tulsa, Oklahoma 74103
(918) 687-2405 FAX: (918) 687-2630

James D. Jordan, Administrative Law Judge
Office of Hearings and Appeals
Social Security Administration
51 Yale Building, Suite 204
5110 South Yale Street
Tulsa, Oklahoma 74135
(918) 496-6700 FAX: (918) 496-6725

STATE

Douglas L. Combs, Special District Court Judge
Pottawatomie County
Shawnee, Oklahoma 74801
(405) 273-0971 FAX: (405) 878-5525

Administrative Law Judge

Mary A. Black, Administrative Law Judge
Workers' Compensation Court
1915 North Stiles
Oklahoma City, Oklahoma 73105-4904
(405) 557-8760 FAX: (405) 552-8760

OREGON: (3)

STATE

Richard B. Rambo, Judge
District Court
Klamath County Courthouse
316 Main Street
Klamath Falls, Oregon 97601
(503) 883-5560

Administrative Law Judges

Murray MacNeill, Administrative Law Judge
Employment Department, Hearings Section
800 N.E. Oregon Street #6, Suite 225
Portland, Oregon 97232
(503) 731-4588 FAX: (503) 731-4042

Weisha Mize, Administrative Law Judge
State Water Resources Department
158 12th Street, N.E.
Salem, Oregon 97304
(503) 378-8455 FAX: (503) 378-2496

PENNSYLVANIA: (1)

Henry Oliver, Chief Administrative Law Judge
Office of Hearings and Appeals
Social Security Administration
8380 Old York Road, Suite 250
Elkins Park, Pennsylvania 19027
(215) 887-2191 FAX: (215) 887-0541

PUERTO RICO: (0)

RHODE ISLAND: (0)

SOUTH CAROLINA: (0)

SOUTH DAKOTA: (0)

TENNESSEE: (1)

FEDERAL

Administrative Law Judge

William F. Taylor, Administrative Law Judge
Office of Hearings and Appeals
Social Security Administration
221 Cumberland Bend, Room 221
Nashville, Tennessee 37228-1803
(615) 736-5384 FAX: (615) 736-2175

TEXAS: (7)

STATE

Cynthia Marie Crowe, Judge
County Civil Court at Law No. 4
1115 Congress, 2nd Floor
Houston, Texas 77002
(713) 755-5791 FAX: (713) 755-4674
E-mail: Cynthia_Crowe@ccl.co.harris.tx.us

J. David Phillips, Judge
County Court at Law No. 1, Travis County
Post Office Box 1748
Austin, Texas 78767
(512) 473-9241 FAX: (512) 708-4724

Ray M. Truelove, Judge
Justice of the Peace Court
Precinct 3, Place 1
8991 East SH 21
Bryan, Texas 77803
(979) 589-2073

James A. Crow, Jr., Presiding Judge
Big Sandy Municipal Court
Post Office Box 568
Big Sandy, Texas 75755
(903) 636-4343

Dottie Nation, Presiding Judge
Lake Tanglewood Municipal Court
Route 8, Box 35-15
Amarillo, Texas 79118
(806) 378-3014622-1242

Pat M. Rosebud, Presiding Judge
Surfside Beach Municipal Court
1304 Monument Drive
Surfside Beach, Texas 77541
(979) 233-1597 FAX: (979) 239-1334

Steve Russell, Judge (Retired)
Travis County Court at Law #2
College of Social & Behavioral Sciences
Division of Social and Policy Science
University of Texas - San Antonio
MS 4.03.10
6900 North Loop 1604 West
San Antonio, Texas 78249-0655
(210) 691-5626, E-mail: Srussell@utsa.edu

UTAH: (1)

STATE

William A. Thorne, Jr., Judge
Salt Lake County - Salt Lake City District Court
450 South State Street
Salt Lake City, Utah 84114
(801) 238-7134 FAX: (801) 238-7137

VERMONT: (0)

VIRGIN ISLANDS: (0)

VIRGINIA: (1)

STATE

Charles R. Cloud, Judge
Norfolk General District Court
811 East City Hall Avenue, Room 265
Norfolk, Virginia 23510
(757) 664-4932 FAX: (757) 664-4901

WASHINGTON: (4)

FEDERAL

Administrative Law Judges

Arnold S. Battise, Administrative Law Judge
Office of Hearings & Appeals
Social Security Administration
2201 Sixth Avenue, Suite 500
Seattle, Washington 98121-2312
(206) 615-3700 FAX: (206) 615-3731

Douglas W. Luna, Administrative Judge
U. S.Equal Employment
Opportunity Commission
2815 Second Avenue, Suite 800
Seattle, Washington 98121
(206) 553-2441 FAX: (206) 553-1308

STATE

Nile E. Aubrey, Judge
Pierce County Superior Court
County-City Building
930 Tacoma Avenue South
Tacoma, Washington 98402
(206) 591-7564 FAX: (206) 591-7509

Mary Wicks Brucker, Judge (Retired)
King County Superior Court
King County Courthouse
9111 Southeast 44th Street
Mercer Island, Washington 98040

WEST VIRGINIA: (0)

WISCONSIN: (3)

STATE

Jacqueline D. Schellinger, Judge
Circuit Court of Milwaukee County, Branch 34
901 North Ninth Street
Milwaukee, Wisconsin 53233-1425
(414) 278-5316 FAX: (414) 223-1242

James Taylor, Judge
Circuit Court of Burnett County
7410 County Road K, Box 115
Siren, Wisconsin 54872-9043
(715) 349-2147

Robert A. Gardner
Special District Court Judge (Retired)
Caddo County District Court
319B 8th Street, South
Wisconsin Rapids, Wisconsin 54494
(715) 424-1100 FAX: (715) 423-5070

WYOMING: (1)

STATE

Allen Wald, Judge
Municipal Court
Post Office Box 75
Granger, Wyoming 82934
(307) 872-9272

U. S. ARMED FORCES: (0)

Section V

NATIVE AMERICAN TRIBAL COURT JUDGES OF THE UNITED STATES

Initially prepared by
Prepared by Arvo Q. Mikkanen, Esq.

ALABAMA: (2)

Samuel M. Hill, Tribal Judge
Mowa Band of Choctaw
Mt. Vernon, Alabama 36580
(334) 829-5500 or (205) 930-5331
FAX: (205) 930-5101

Earnest Ray White, Tribal Judge
Poarch Band of Creek Indians
5811 Jackspring Road
Atmore, Alabama 36502
(334) 368-9136 FAX: (334) 444-8086

ALASKA: (3)

Edward Littlefield, Appellate Judge
Northwest Intertribal Court System
Post Office Box 586
Metlakatla, Alaska 99926-0586

Casey Nelson, Sr., Chief Magistrate Judge
Metlakatla Tribal Court
Post Office Box 8
Metlakatla, Alaska 99926-0008
(907) 886-4021 FAX: (907) 886-4022

Pamela D. McGilton, Magistrate Judge
Metlakatla Tribal Court
Post Office Box 8
Metlakatla, Alaska 99926
(907) 886-4021 FAX: (907) 886-4022

ARIZONA: (46)

Supreme Court Justices

Raymond D. Austin, Associate Justice
Courts of the Navajo Nation
Post Office Box 520
Window Rock, Arizona 86515-0520
(520) 871-6762 or 871-6763
FAX: (520) 871-6761 or 871-7016

Wayne A. Cadman, Sr., Associate Justice
Courts of the Navajo Nation
Post Office Box 520
Window Rock, Arizona 86515-0520
(520) 871-6762 or 871-6763 FAX: (520) 871-7016

Robert Yazzie, Chief Justice
Courts of the Navajo Nation
Post Office Box 520
Window Rock, Arizona 86515-0520
(520) 871-6763 or 871-2216 FAX: (520) 871-7016

Appellate Judges

Jay Abbey, Justice
Hopi Appellate Court
Post Office Box 156
Keams Canyon, Arizona 86034-0156
(520) 738-2288 or 738-2289 FAX: (520) 738-5589

Fred Lomagesva, Justice
Hopi Appellate Court
Post Office Box 156
Keams Canyon, Arizona 86034-0156
(520) 738-2288 or 738-2289 FAX: (520) 738-5589

Emery Sekaquaptewa, Justice
Hopi Appellate Court
Post Office Box 156
Keams Canyon, Arizona 86034-0156
(520) 738-2288 FAX: (520) 738-5589

Trial Judges

Rachel Arnold, Tribal Judge
Colorado River Tribal Court - Box BH
Parker, Arizona 85344
(520) 669-9211 FAX: (520) 669-5675

Regan Armstong, Jr., Associate Judge
White Mountain Apache Tribe
Post Office Box 700
Whiteriver, Arizona 85941
(520) 338-4346 FAX: (520) 388-1514

Wesley W. Atakai, District Court Judge
Navajo Nation - Chinle District
Post Office Box 547
Chinle, Arizona 86503-0725
(520) 674-2070 or 674-2071 FAX: 674-2089

Leroy S. Bedonie, District Judge
Navajo Nation, Kayenta District Court
Post Office Box 1248
Kayenta, Arizona 86033
(520) 697-5549 or 697-5550 FAX: (520) 697-5546

Jennifer D. Benally, District Court Judge
Tuba City Judicial District, District/Family Court
Post Office Box 725
Tuba City, Arizona 86046
(520) 283-3140 FAX: (520) 283-3156

Cornelia Cruz, Chief Tribal Judge
Pascua Yaqui Tribe
7474 S. Camino De Oeste
Tucson, Arizona 85746
(520) 883-5000 FAX: (520) 883-5014

Richard Engler, Tribal Judge
Fort Yuma - Quechan Indian Tribe
Post Office Box 1899
Yuma, Arizona 85366-1899
(760) 572-0544

Malcolm Escalante, Tribal Judge
Tohono O'odham Tribal Court
Post Office Box 761
Sells, Arizona 85634-0761
(520) 383-6300 FAX: (520) 383-3500

Neil T. Flores, Sr., Chief Tribal Judge
Colorado River Indian Tribal Court
Route 1, Box 23-B
Parker, Arizona 85344
(520) 669-9211 FAX: (520) 669-5675

Ray Gilmore, Family Court Judge
Chinle Judicial District
Post Office Box 547
Chinle, Arizona 86503
(520) 674-2071 or 674-2084 FAX: (520) 674-2089

Kathleen Gratz, Tribal Judge
Ak-Chin Indian Community
42507 West Peters & Nall Road
Maricopa, Arizona 85239
(520) 568-2618 FAX: (520) 568-4566

Marjorie Grimes, Chief Judge
White Mountain Apache Tribe
Post Office Box 700
Whiteriver, Arizona 85941
(520) 338-4346 or 338-4872 FAX: (520) 388-1514

Joseph C. Hibbard, Tribal Judge
Yavapai-Apache Tribal Court
Post Office Box 1188
Camp Verde, Arizona 86322-1188
(520) 567-3649 FAX: (520) 567-3994

Thomas J. Holgate, Family Court Judge
Window Rock Judicial District
Post Office Box 5520
Window Rock, Arizona 86515
(520) 674-2071 or 674-7562
FAX: (520) 674-2089 or 871-7560

Evelyn B. Juan, Chief Judge
Tohono O'odham Nation Judiciary
Post Office Box 761
Sells, Arizona 86534-0761
(520) 383-2221 FAX: (520) 383-3379

LaVerne A. Johnson, District Court Judge
Window Rock Judicial District
Post Office Box 5520
Window Rock, Arizona 86515
(520) 871-6962 or 871-6984 FAX: (520) 871-7560

Robert Kuebler, Jr., Tribal Judge
530 East Merritt
Prescott, Arizona 86301
(520) 445-8790 FAX: (520) 778-9445

Edwin Lawrence, Tribal Judge
Tonto Apache Tribe
#30 Tonto Apache Reservation
Payson, Arizona 85541
(520) 474-5000 FAX: (520) 474-9125

Kerstin LeMaire, Tribal Judge
Cocopah Tribe
Avenue G & Co. 15th
Somerton, Arizona 85350
(520) 627-2061 or 627-2102 FAX: (520) 627-1617

Delfred Leslie, Acting Chief Judge
Hopi Tribal Court
Post Office Box 123
Kykotsmovi, Arizona 86039
(520) 734-2441 or 734-3000 FAX: (520) 738-5589

Nicholas Lewis, Associate Judge
Tohono O'odham Nation
Post Office Box 761
(520) 383-3500 FAX: (520) 383-3500

William L. McCulley, Associate Judge
Hopi Tribal Court
Post Office Box 156
Keams Canyon, Arizona 86034
(520) 738-5171 FAX: (520) 738-5561

Darlina Milda-Mercado, Associate Judge
Gila River Indian
Community Tribal Court
Post Office Box 97
Sacaton, Arizona 85247
(520) 562-6000 FAX: (520) 562-3422

Lucilda Norris, Judge
Tohono O'Odham Judiciary
Post Office Box 761
Sells, Arizona 85634
(520) 383-3193 FAX: (520) 383-3500

Christine Owens, Associate Judge
Salt River Pima-Maricopa
Community Court
10005 East Osborn Road
Scottsdale, Arizona 85256
(602) 874-8115 FAX: (602) 874-8132

Delmar Pablo, Tribal Judge
Hualapai Tribal Court
Post Office Box 179 - Peach
Spings, Arizona 86434
(520) 769-2216 FAX: (520) 769-2343

William Roy Rhodes, Chief Tribal Judge
Gila River Indian Community
Post Office Box 97
Sacaton, Arizona 85247
(520) 562-6000 FAX: (520) 562-3422

Robert A. Scott, Associate Judge
Colorado River Indian Tribal Court
Post Office Box BH
Parker, Arizona 85344
(520) 669-1355 FAX: (520) 669-9273

Amelia Segundo, Tribal Judge
Kaibab Band of Pauite Indians
HC 65, Box 2
Fedonia, Arizona 86022
(520) 643-7245 FAX: (520) 643-7260

Allen Sloan, District Court Judge
Navajo Nation - Window Rock
Judicial District
Post Office Box 5520
Window Rock, Arizona 86516-5520
(520) 871-6962, 871-6984 or 871-6471
FAX: (520) 871-7560

Gary Thomas, Chief Judge
Hopi Tribe
Post Office Box 123
Kykotsmovi, Arizona 86039
(520) 734-2441 or 734-3000 FAX: (520) 734-2435

Spencer Thomas, Chief Judge
Ak-Chin Indian Community
42507 West Peters & Nall Road
Maricopa, Arizona 85239
(520) 568-2618 FAX: (520) 568-4566

Tamoan F. Tsosie, Tribal Judge
Havasupai Tribe
Post Office Box 10
Supai, Arizona 86435
(520) 448-2731 FAX: (520) 448-2551

Tammy Walker, Associate Judge
Hualapai Tribal Court
Post Office Box 179
Peach Springs, Arizona 86434-0179
(520) 769-2216 FAX: (520) 769-2343

Manuel Watchman, District Court Judge
Tuba City Judicial District
District/Family Court
Post Office Box 725
Tuba City, Arizona 86045
(520) 283-3140 FAX: (520) 283-3158

Ben Wood, Jr., Tribal Judge
Salt River Pima-Maricopa Indian
Community Court
10005 East Osborn Road
Scottsdale, Arizona 85256
(480) 850-8000 FAX: (480) 850-8014

Juvenile Courts

Alene Delgarito, Associate Judge
Children's Court
Hopi Tribal Court
Post Office Box 156
Keams Canyon, Arizona 86034
(520) 738-5171 FAX: (520) 738-5561

Ramona Loring, Juvenile Judge
Salt River Pima-Maricopa
Community Court
10005 East Osborn Road
Scottsdale, Arizona 85256
(602) 874-8115 FAX: (602) 874-8132

Alberta Mercado, Juvenile Judge
Salt River Pima-Maricopa Community Court
10005 East Osborn Road
Scottsdale, Arizona 85256
(602) 874-8115 FAX: (602) 874-8132

Jay Pedro, Associate Judge
Children's Court
Gila River Indian Community Tribal Court
Post Office Box 368
Sacaton, Arizona 85247-0368
(520) 562-3530 FAX: (520) 562-3525

ARKANSAS: (0)

CALIFORNIA: (6)

John L. Macarro, Appellate Judge
Northwest Intertribal Court System
Post Office Box 1477
Temecula, California 92593

John James, Chief Judge
Cabazon Band of Mission Indians Tribal Court
84-245 Indio Spring Drive
Indio, California 92203
(760) 342-2593 FAX: (760) 347-7880

Kaye Lewis, Chief Judge
Fort Mohave Indian Tribal Court
500 Merriman Avenue
Needles, California 92363
(760) 629-4591 FAX: (760) 629-2468 or 629-4323

Raqueilo Myers, Chief Judge
Inter-Tribal Court of Northern California
Mendoncino County (6 Tribes)
(Lytton, Redwood, Coyote Valley, Laytonville, Pinoleville, Hopland)
#7 Fourth Street, Suite #46
Petaluma, California 94952
(707) 762-8113 FAX: (707) 762-7681

Byron Nelson, Jr., Chief Judge
Hoopa Valley Tribal Court
Highway 96
Post Office Box 1389
Hoopa, California 95546
(530) 625-4305 FAX: (530) 625-4307

Mike Ross, Chief Judge
Yurok Tribal Court
15900 Highway 101 North
Klamath, California 95548
(707) 482-2841 FAX: (707) 482-0384

COLORADO: (3)

Elizabeth Cullued, Associate Judge
Ute Mountain Ute Tribal Court
Justice Complex
Post Office Box 737
Ignacio, Colorado 81137-0737
(970) 563-0240 FAX: (970) 563-0357

Elaine Newton, Chief Judge
Southern Ute Tribal Court
Justice Complex
Post Office Box 737
Ignacio, Colorado 81137-0737
(970) 563-0240 FAX: (970) 563-0357 or 563-0241
E-mail: enewton@Southern-ute.nsn.us

Michael Stancampiano, Associate Judge
Southern Ute Tribal Court
Justice Complex
Post Office Box 737
Ignacio, Colorado 81137-0737
(970) 563-0240 FAX: (970) 563-0357

CONNECTICUT: (3)

Thomas J. Londregan, Judge
Mashantucket Pequot Tribal Court
38 Huntington Street
Post Office Box 1351
New London, Connecticut 06320
(860) 447-3171 FAX: (860) 444-6103

Edward B. O'Connell, Judge
Mashantucket Pequot Tribal Court
52 Eugene O'Neill Drive
Post Office Box 88
New London, Connecticut 06320
(860) 422-0367 FAX: (860) 447-9915
E-mail: wspandpail@uconnect.net

Lawrence Otway, Tribal Judge
Golden Hill Paugeesukq
Pauqussett Tribal Nation
95 Stanavage Road
Colchester, Connecticut 06415-2032
(860) 537-8527 FAX: (860) 537-8527 (call first)
E-mail: inobu@aol.com

DELAWARE: (0)

DISTRICT OF COLUMBIA: (0)

FLORIDA: (3)

Minnie Bert, Judge
Miccosukee Tribal Court
Post Office Box 440021 Tamiami Station
Miami, Florida 33144
(305) 223-8380 Ext. 310 FAX: (305) 894-2391

Andy Buster , Judge
Miccosukee Tribal Court
Post Office Box 440021 Tamiami Station
Miami, Florida 33144
(305) 223-8380 Ext. 310 FAX: (305) 894-2391

Bernie Roman, Judge
Miccosukee Tribal Court
Post Office Box 440021 Tamiami Station
Miami, Florida 33144
(305) 223-8380, Ext. 310
FAX: 223-1011 or (305) 894-2391

GEORGIA: (0)

GUAM: (0)

HAWAII: (0)

IDAHO: (11)

Appellate Judges

Thomas Keefe Jr., Appellate Judge
Northwest Intertribal Court System
Post Office Box 1401
Kamiah, Idaho 83536

Earl L. McGeoghegan, Associate Justice
Colville Tribal Court of Appeals
1301 G Street
Lewiston, Idaho 83501
(208) 746-4333 FAX: (208) 746-8533

Trial Court Judges

Fred W. Gabourie, Sr., Chief Judge
Kootenai Tribal Court
North 1011 Virginia Road
Spokane, Washington 99216
(509) 927-9900 FAX: (509) 922-0814
E-mail: whitedeer@sprynet.com
(Note: Also sits in Idaho)

Robert Gonzales, Chief Judge
Shonshone-Bannock Tribal Court
Post Office Box 306
Fort Hall, Idaho 83203
(208) 238-4069 FAX: (208) 238-4076

Glenn E. Hardin, Chief Judge
ShoshonePaiute Tribe of the
Duck Valley Reservation
Post Office Box 219
Owyhee, Nevada 89832-0219
(702) 757-2227 FAX: (702) 575-2078
(Note: Also sits in Idaho)

David L. Harding, Associate Judge
Coeur d'Alene Tribal Court
RR 11CDA
Plummer, Idaho 83851
(208) 686-1777 FAX: (208) 686-1289

Marina Fast Horse, Associate Judge
Shoshone-Bannock Tribal Court
Post Office Box 306
Fort Hall, Idaho 83203
(208) 238-4069 FAX: (208) 238-4076

Earl L. McGeoghegan *, Associate Judge
Coeur d'Alene Tribal Court
RR 11CDA
Plummer, Idaho 83851
(208) 686-0177 FAX: (208) 686-1289
also Associate Judge
Nez Perce Tribal Court
Post Office Box 305
Lapwai, Idaho 83540-0305
(208) 843-7338 FAX: (208) 843-7337

Corrine Pocatilla, Associate Judge
Shoshone-Bannock Tribal Court
Post Office Box 306
Fort Hall, Idaho 83203
(208) 238-4069 FAX: (208) 238-4076

David R. Risley, Associate Judge
Nez Perce Tribal Court
Post Office Box 305
Lapwai, Idaho 83540
(208) 843-7338 FAX: (208) 843-7337

** Some individuals serve as a judge in more than one judicial position. The asterisk assures that the person is not counted more than once.*

Eva J. White, Chief Judge
Nez Perce Tribal Court
Post Office Box 305
Lapwai, Idaho 83540-0305
(208) 843-7338 FAX: (208) 843-7337
E-mail: evaw@nezperce.org

ILLINOIS: (3)

John C. Huffer, Judge
Central Illinois Chippewa Tribal Court
Post Office Box 131
Tuscola, Illinois 61953-0131
(217) 253-2959 FAX: (217) 253-2959
E-mail: caj@advancenet.net

James Shephard, Judge
Central Illinois Chippewa Tribal Court
Post Office Box 131
Tuscola, Illinois 61953-0131
(217) 253-2959 FAX: (217) 253-2959
E-mail: caj@advancenet.net

Elliott J. Stein, Judge
Central Illinois Chippewa Tribal Court
Post Office Box 131
Tuscola, Illinois 61953-0131
(217) 253-2959 FAX: (217) 253-2959
E-mail: varlawyer@hotmail.com

INDIANA: (0)

IOWA: (0)

KANSAS: (0)

KENTUCKY: (0)

LOUISIANA: (4)

C. Thomas Bievenue, Associate Judge
Chitimacha Tribal Court of Appeals
Post Office Box 610
Charenton, Louisiana 70523-610
(318) 923-7806 FAX: (318) 923-7806

Edward delaHoussaye, Chief Judge
Chitimacha Tribal Court of Appeals
Post Office Box 790
Franklin, Louisiana 70538
(318) 923-7806 FAX: (318) 923-7889

Trial Judges

Cameron B. Simmons, Chief Judge
Chitimacha Tribal Court
Post Office Box 610
Charenton, Louisiana 70544
(318) 923-7806 FAX: (318) 923-7889

Kathyrn Fowler Van Hoof, Tribal Judge
Tunica-Biloxi Tribal Court
Post Office Box 331
Marksville, Louisiana 71351
(318) 253-9033 FAX: (318) 253-0408

MAINE: (0)

MARYLAND: (0)

MASSACHUSETTS: (0)

MICHIGAN: (19)

Court of Appeals

Catherine Castagne, Chief Judge
Court of Appeals
Sault Ste. Marie Tribe of Chippewa Indians
Post Office Box 343
2175 Shunk Road
Sault Ste. Marie, Michigan 49783
(906) 635-4963 FAX: (906) 635-4952

Janine Gable, Associate Judge
Court of Appeals
Sault Ste. Marie Tribe of Chippewa Indians
Post Office Box 343
2175 Shunk Road
Sault Ste. Marie, Michigan 49783
(906) 635-4963 FAX: (906) 635-4952

Doncida Harper, Associate Judge
Court of Appeals
Sault Ste. Marie Tribe of Chippewa Indians
Post Office Box 343
2175 Shunk Road
Sault Ste. Marie, Michigan 49783
(906) 635-4963 FAX: (906) 635-4952

Julie Timmer, Appellate Judge
Chippewa-Ottawa Conservation Court
12140 West Lakeshore Drive, Route 1
Brimley, Michigan 49715
(906) 248-3241 or 248-3243 FAX: (906) 248-3283

Trial Court Judges

Carol S. Andary, Chief Judge
Chippewa-Ottawa Conservation Court
Bay Mills Tribal Center
Post Office Box 313
12140 West Lakeshore Drive, Route 1
Brimley, Michigan 49715
(906) 248-3241 or 248-3243 FAX: (906) 248-3283

Roxann Bain, Chief Judge
Lac Vieux Desert Band of Lake
Superior Chippewa Indians
Box 446
Choate Road
Watersmeet, Michigan 49969
(906) 358-4585

Barry Brown, Associate Judge
Civil Division
Sault Ste. Marie Chippewa Tribal Court
Sault Ste. Marie Tribe of Chippewa Indians
Post Office Box 343
2175 Shunk Road
Sault Ste. Marie, Michigan 49783
(906) 635-4963 FAX: (906) 635-4952

Corrine A. Cameron, Chief Judge
Bay Mills Tribal Court
Bay Mills Indian Community
12140 West Lakeshore Drive
Brimley, Michigan 49715
(906) 248-3243 FAX: (906) 248-3283

Bradley Dakota, Chief Judge
Keweenaw Bay
Indian Community Tribal Court
Tribal Center Building
107 Beartown Road
Baraga, Michigan 49908
(906) 353-6623 Ext. 234 or 353-8124
FAX: (906) 353-7540

Douglas B. Gurski, Chief Judge
Hannahville Indian Community
N 14911 Hannah B-1 Road
Wilson, Michigan 49896
(906) 466-2342 Ext. 106 FAX: (906) 466-7377

Michelle Hank, Associate Judge
Sault St. Marie Chippewa Tribal Court
Sault Ste. Marie Tribe of Chippewa Indians
Post Office Box 343
2428 Shunk Road
Sault St. Marie, Michigan 49783
(906) 635-4963 FAX: (906) 635-4952

Bruce Himmon, Judge
Saginaw-Chippewa Tribal Court
7070 East Broadway
Mount Pleasant, Michigan 48858
(517) 772-1964 FAX: (517) 772-3508

William Jondreau, Judge
Keweenaw Bay Tribal Court
Tribal Center Building - Route 1
Baraga, Michigan 49908
(906) 353-6623 Ext. 234 FAX: (906) 353-7540

Anthony Nertoli, Associate Judge
Sault St. Marie Chippewa Tribal Court
Post Office Box 343
2175 Shunk Road
Sault St. Marie, Michigan 49783
(906) 635-4963 FAX: (906) 635-4952

George Nolan, Chief Judge
Sault St. Marie Chippewa Tribal Court
Sault Ste. Marie Tribe of Chippewa Indians
Post Office Box 343
2428 Shunk Road
Sault St. Marie, Michigan 49783
(906) 635-4963 FAX: (906) 635-4952

Michael Petoskey, Chief Judge
Grand Traverse Band of
Ottawa and Chippewa Indians
2605 North West Bayshore Drive
Suttons Bay, Michigan 49682
(231) 947-6382 or 271-3538 FAX: (231) 947-3204
E-mail: mpetoskc@nmc.edu
also Chief Judge
Little Traverse Bay Bands
Of Odawa Indians, Inc.
Box 246
1150 Bayview Road
Petoskey, Michigan 49770
(231) 439-3828 FAX: (231) 439-3885

Kandra Robbins, Judge
Sault Ste. Marie Chippewa Tribal Court
Sault Ste. Marie Tribe of Chippewa Indians
Post Office Box 343
2175 Shunk Road
Sault Ste. Marie, Michigan 49783
(906) 635-4963 FAX: (906) 635-4952
E-mail: qlaw7@northernway.net

Jonnie J. Sam II, Associate Judge
Little River Band of Ottawa Indians
1762 U.S. 31 South
Manistee, Michigan 49660-0314
(231) 723-8288 FAX: (231) 723-8020

Patrick M. Shannon, Chief Judge
Saginaw Chippewa Indian Tribe
6954 East Broadway
Mt. Pleasant, Michigan 48858
(517) 775-4800

MINNESOTA: (8)

Kurt V. BlueDog, Judge
Fon Du Lac Tribal Court
105 University Road
Cloquet, Minnesota 55720
(218) 879-1494

John Herrera, Judge
Leech Lake Tribal Court
RR 3 Box 100
Cass Lake, Minnesota 56633
(218) 335-8240

Wanda L. Lyons, Judge
Red Lake Tribal Court
Post Office Box 572
Red Lake, Minnesota 56671
(218) 679-3303 FAX: (218) 679-2683

Phillip Smith, Judge
Red Lake Tribal Court
Box 572
Red Lake, Minnesota 56671
(218) 679-3303 FAX: (218) 679-2683

Richard Tanner, Judge
White Earth Tribal Court
Box 418
White Earth, Minnesota 56591
(218) 983-3285 FAX: (218) 983-3641

Margaret Treuer, Chief Judge
Leach Lake Tribal Court
1001 Farmstead Lane, N.E.
Bemidji, Minnesota 56601
(218) 335-8200 FAX: (218) 335-8309

Natalie Weyaus, Judge
Mille Lacs Tribal Court
Non Removable Chippewa Indians
HCR 67, Box 1940
Namia, Minnesota 56359
(612) 532-4181

Dan Charnoski, Special Judge
Red Lake Tribal Court
Box 572
Red Lake, Minnesota 56671
(218) 679-3303 FAX: (218) 679-2683

MISSISSIPPI: (4)

Roy Jim, Judge
Mississippi Choctaw Tribal Court
Post Office Box 6012 - Choctaw Branch
Philadelphia, Mississippi 39350
(601) 656-5352 FAX: (601) 656-1992

Donna Morris, Judge
Mississippi Choctaw Tribal Court
Post Office Box 6012 - Choctaw Branch
Philadelphia, Mississippi 39350
(601) 656-5352 FAX: (601) 656-1992

Hilda Nickey, Associate Judge
Youth Court
Mississippi Choctaw Tribal Court
Post Office Box 6010
Philadelphia, Mississippi 39350
(601) 663-0013 FAX: (601) 663-4240

Rae N. Vaughn, Judge
Youth Court
Mississippi Choctaw Tribal Court
Post Office Box 6010
Philadelphia, Mississippi 39350
(601) 663-0013 FAX: (601) 663-4240

MISSOURI: (0)

MONTANA: (34)

Appellate Judges

Claudia Bear, Appellate Judge
Fort Belknap Tribal Court
RR #1 Box 62
Harlem, Montana 59526
(406) 353-2206 (406) 353-2286

Gary M. Beaudry, Associate Justice
Fort Peck Court of Appeals
Assiniboine & Sioux Tribes
Fort Peck Indian Reservation
Post Office Box 1027
Poplar, Montana 59255
(406) 766-5557 FAX: (406) 768-3710

Theodora Cochran, Appellate Judge
Fort Belknap Tribal Court
RR #1 Box 62
Harlem, Montana 59526
(406) 353-2205 FAX: (406) 353-2205

Carrol James DeCoteau, Associate Justice
Fort Peck Court of Appeals
Associate Justice
Assiniboine & Sioux Tribes
Fort Peck Indian Reservation
Post Office Box 1027
Poplar, Montana 59255
(406) 768-5557 FAX: (406) 768-3710

Brenda C. Desmond, Associate Justice
Confederated Salish and
Kootenai Court of Appeals
1301 South Fifth, West
Missoula, Montana 59801
(406) 523-4728 or 523-4773 FAX: (406) 523-4739
E-mail: the3@mt-usa.com

Gregory T. Dupuis, Associate Justice
Confederated Salish and
Kootenai Court of Appeals
Post Office Box 415
Pablo, Montana 59855
(406) 883-7960 or 675-7900 FAX: (406) 883-5235
E-mail: kikuum@digisys.net

Michael Eakin, Associate Justice
Confederated Salish and
Kootenai Court of Appeals
2035 Park Hill Drive
Billings, Montana 59102
(406) 248-7113 FAX: (406) 252-7113

Clayton Matt, Associate Justice
Confederated Salish and
Kootenai Court of Appeals
Post Office Box 374
Pablo, Montana 59855
(406) 675-2700 Ext. 1230 FAX: (406) 675-2743
E-mail: yollie@ronan.net

Patricia Quisno, Appellate Judge
Fort Belknap Tribal Court
RR #1 Box 62
Harlem, Montana 59526
(406) 353-2205 FAX: (406) 353-2386

Patrick L. Smith, Chief Justice
Confederated Salish and
Kootenai Court of Appeals
815 East Front, Suite 3
Missoula, Montana 59802
(406) 721-1070 FAX: (406) 721-1799
E-mail: Eagleview@aol.com

Duane L. Stiffarm, Appellate Judge
Fort Belknap Tribal Court
RR #1 Box 62
Harlem, Montana 59526
(406) 353-2205 FAX: (406) 353-2386

Gary Sullivan, Chief Justice
Fort Peck Court of Appeals
Assiniboine & Sioux Tribes
Fort Peck Indian Reservation
Post Office Box 1027
Poplar, Montana 59255
(406) 768-5557 FAX: (406) 768-3710

Jerry M. Schuster, Associate Justice (Alternate)
Fort Peck Court of Appeals
Assiniboine & Sioux Tribes
Fort Peck Indian Reservation
Post Office Box 1027
Poplar, Montana 59225
(406) 768-5557 FAX: (406) 768-3710

Alma Young, Appellate Judge
Fort Belknap Tribal Court
RR #1 Box 62
Harlem, Montana 59526
(406) 353-2205 FAX: (406) 353-2387

Trial Judges

Gary L. Acevedo, Associate Judge
Confederated Salish and
Kootenai Tribal Court
Post Office Box 278
Pablo, Montana 59855
(406) 675-2700 FAX: (406) 675-4704
E-mail: tcourt@ronan.net

Catherine A. Aragon, Judge
Fort Belknap Tribal Court
Route 1, Box 62
Harlem, Montana 59526
(406) 353-2205 Ext. 413 FAX: (406) 353-2797

James Arnold, Associate Judge
Blackfeet Tribal Court
Post Box 1200
Browning, Montana 59417
(406) 338-5061 FAX: (406) 338-2722

Barry C. Bighom, Sr., Associate Judge
Fort Peck Tribal Court
Assiniboine & Sioux Tribes
Fort Peck Indian Reservation
Post Office Box 1027
Poplar, Montana 59225
(406) 768-5558 or (406) 768-5155 Ext. 338 or 401
FAX: (408) 768-3710
E-mail: tribalcrt@nemontel.net

Louise C. Burke, Chief Judge
Confederated Salish and Kootenai Tribal Court
Post Office Box 278
Pablo, Montana 59855
(406) 675-2700 FAX: (406) 675-4704
E-mail: tcourt@ronan.net

Juanita M. Cantrell, Associate Judge
Fort Peck Tribal Court
Assiniboine & Sioux Tribes
Fort Peck Indian Reservation
Post Office Box 1027
Poplar, Montana 59255
(406) 768-5558 or 768-5155 Ext. 338 or 401
FAX: (406) 768-3710
E-mail: tribalcrt@nemontel.net

John D. Christian, Associate/Juvenile Judge
Fort Peck Assiniboine & Sioux Tribal Court
Post Office Box 1027
Poplar, Montana 59255
(406) 768-5557 FAX: (406) 768-3710

Howard Door, Associate Judge
Blackfeet Tribal Court
Post Office Box 1200
Browning, Montana 59417
(406) 338-5061 FAX: (406) 338-2722

Kenny Gardipee, Judge
Chippewa Cree Tribal Court
Box 544, Rocky Boy
Box Elder, Montana 59521
(406) 395-4735 FAX (406) 395-4375 or 395-5184

Terry P. Healy, Associate Judge
Fort Belknap Tribal Court
RR #1 Box 62
Harlem, Montana 59526
(406) 353-2205 Ext. 414 FAX: (406) 353-2797

Bradley A. Pluff, Associate Judge
Confederated Salish and Kootenai Tribal Court
Post Office Box 278
Pablo, Montana 59855
(408) 675-2700 FAX: (406) 675-4704
E-mail: tcourt@ronan.net

Leland J. Pond, Sr., Chief Judge
Fort Belknap Tribal Court
RR #1 Box 62
Harlem, Montana 59526
(406) 353-2205 FAX: (406) 353-2386

John Robinson, Judge
Northern Cheyenne Tribal Court
Post Office Box 128
Lame Deer, Montana 59043
(406) 477-8340 FAX: (406) 477-6210

Don Sollars, Chief Judge
Blackfeet Tribal Court
Post Office Box 1200
Browning, Montana 59417
(406) 338-5061 FAX: (406) 338-2722

A. T. Stafne, Chief Judge
Fort Peck Tribal Court
Assiniboine & Sioux Tribes
Fort Peck Indian Reservation
Post Office Box 1027
Poplar, Montana 59255
(406) 768-5558 or 768-5155 Ext. 338 or 401
FAX: (406) 768-3710
E-mail: tribalcrt@nemontel.net

Donald Stewart, Sr., Judge
Crow Tribal Court
Box 489
Crow Agency, Montana 59022
(406) 638-2681 FAX: (406) 638-2459

Winona Tanner, Associate Judge
Confederated Salish and
Kootenai Tribal Court
Post Office Box 278
Pablo, Montana 59855
(406) 675-2700 FAX: (406) 675-4704
E-mail: tcourt@ronan.net

Charleen Yellow Kidney, Associate Judge
Confederated Salish & Kootenai Tribal Court
Post Office Box 278
Pablo, Montana 59855
(406) 675-2700 Ext. 598 FAX: (406) 675-4704
E-mail: tcourt@ronan.net

Marvin K. Youpee, Associate Judge
Fort Peck Tribal Court
Assiniboine & Sioux Tribes
Fort Peck Indian Reservation
Post Office Box 1027
Poplar, Montana 59255
(406) 768-5558 or 768-5155 Ext. 338 or 401
FAX: (406) 768-3710
E-mail: tribalcrt@nemontel.net

Juvenile Judge

Virginia Cochran, Children's Court Judge
Fort Belknap Children's Court
RR #1 Box 62
Harlem, Montana 59526
(406) 353-2205 FAX: (406) 353-2637

NEBRASKA: (9)

Supreme Court Justices

James Botsford, Associate Justice
Winnebago Supreme Court
Post Office Box 626
Winnebago, Nebraska 68071
(402) 878-2570 FAX: (402) 878-2540

Robert N. Clinton, Chief Justice
Winnebago Supreme Court
Post Office Box 626
Winnebago, Nebraska 68071
(402) 878-2570 FAX: (402) 878-2540

Mary Jo Hunter, Associate Justice
Winnebago Supreme Court
Post Office Box 626
Winnebago, Nebraska 68071
(402) 878-2570 FAX: (402) 878-2540

Trial Judges

Peter B. Beekman, Judge
Iowa Nation Native American Court
3218 Center Street
Omaha, Nebraska 68105-2527
(402) 345-0499
FAX: 402-345-1720 or (785) 595-5995
E-mail: hizzoner@home.com
(Rides Circuit - for Iowa Nation in
Kansas & Nebraksa
Kickapoo Nation in Kansas
Omaha Nation Sac & Fox Nation
of Missouri, and Northern Ponca Housing
Authority Tribunal
different days of the week, as needed).

Heidi Drobnick, Presiding Judge
Winnebago Tribal Court
Post Office Box 626
Winnebago, Nebraska 68071
(402) 878-2570 FAX: (402) 878-2540

Barbara Kueny, Judge
Winnebago Nation Native American Court
Post Office Box 68071
Winnebago, Nebraska 68071
(402) 878-2570 FAX: (402) 878-2540

JWilliam Moreland, Judge
Omaha Nation Native American Court
Post Office Box 508
Macy, Nebraska 68039
(402) 837-5814 FAX: (402) 837-4045

Stephen Jay Smith, Judge
Omaha Court of Indian Offenses
Post Office Box 508
Macy, Nebraska 68039
(402) 837-5814 FAX: (402) 837-5308

Kenneth J. Vampola, Associate Judge
Winnebago Tribal Court
Post Office Box 626
Winnebago, Nebraska 68071
(402) 878-2570 FAX: (402) 878-2540

NEVADA: (23)

Court of Appeals

Elbridge Coochise, Associate Justice
Inter-Tribal Court of Appeals of Nevada
98 Colony Road
Reno, Nevada 89502
(775) 785-8775 FAX: (775) 329-8153

Arthur A. Gladstone, Associate Justice and CFR Magistrate
Inter-Tribal Court of Appeals of Nevada
98 Colony Road
Reno, Nevada 89502
(775) 785-8775 FAX: (775) 329-8153

Clarence McDade, Chief Justice
Inter-Tribal Court of Appeals of Nevada
98 Colony Road
Reno, Nevada 89502
(775) 785-8775 FAX: (775) 329-8153

Virginia R. Shane, Associate Justice and CFR Magistrate
Inter-Tribal Court of Appeals of Nevada
98 Colony Road
Reno, Nevada 89502
(775) 785-8775 FAX: (775) 329-8153

F. Woodside Wright, Associate Justice and CFR Magistrate
Inter-Tribal Court of Appeals of Nevada
98 Colony Road
Reno, Nevada 89502
(775) 785-8775 FAX: (775) 329-8153

Mitchell C. Wright, Associate Justice
Inter-Tribal Court of Appeals of Nevada
98 Colony Road
Reno, Nevada 89502
(775) 785-8775 FAX: (775) 329-8153

Rebecca A. Harold, CFR Magistrate
Inter-Tribal Court of Appeals of Nevada
98 Colony Road
Reno, Nevada 89502
(775) 785-8775 FAX: (775) 329-8153

Peter J. Sferrazza, CFR Magistrate
Inter-Tribal Court of Appeals of Nevada
98 Colony Road
Reno, Nevada 89502
(775) 785-8775 FAX: (775) 329-8153

Trial Court Judges

James Anderson, Chief Judge
Yoma Tribal Court
HC61 - Box 6275
Austin, Nevada 89310
(775) 964-2463 FAX: (775) 964-2443

Philip Becker, Chief Judge
Shoshone-Paiute Tribal Court
Post Office Box 219
Owyhee, Nevada 89832
(775) 757-2741 FAX: (775) 757-2078

Elbridge Cochise*, Associate Judge
Washoe Tribal Court
919 U.S. Highway 395 South
Gardnerville, Nevada 89140
(775) 583-1446 FAX: (775) 265-9101

Terry A. Coffing, Trial Judge
Las Vegas Paiute Tribal Court
#1 Paiute Drive
Las Vegas, Nevada 89106
(702) 386-3926 FAX: (702) 383-4019

Arthur Gladstone*, Tribal Associate Court Judge
Reno-Sparks Tribal Court
98 Colony Road
Reno, Nevada 89502
(775) 785-8775 FAX: (775) 329-8153
also Tax Judge
Pyramid Lake Tribal Court
Post Office Box 257
Nixon, Nevada 89424
(775) 574-1094 or 574-1095 FAX: (775) 574-1096

Ronald E. Johnny, Chief Judge
Duckwater Shoshone Tribal Court
Post Office Box 140068
Duckwater, Nevada 89314
(775) 863-0227 FAX: (775) 863-0301

Sheila G. McCord, Chief Judge
Moapa Paiute Tribal Court
Post Office Box 187
Moapa, Nevada 89025
(760) 865-2845 FAX: (760) 865-2865

Clarence McDade*, Chief Judge
Reno-Sparks Tribal Court
98 Colony Road
Reno, Nevada 89502
(775) 735-8775 FAX: (775) 329-8153
also Associate Judge
Washoe Tribal Court
919 U.S. Highway 395 South
Gardnerville, Nevada 89410
(775) 883-1446 FAX: (775) 265-9101

Gene O'Brien, Chief Judge
Walker River Tribal Court
Post Office Box 225
Schurz, Nevada 89427
(775) 773-2232 FAX: (775) 773-2333

Peter J. Sferrazza*, Chief Judge
Fallon Tribal Court
8955 Mission Road
Fallon, Nevada 89406
(775) 423-8883 FAX: (775) 423-7395
also Chief Judge
Pyramid Lake Tribal Court
Post Office Box 257
Nixon, Nevada 89424
(775) 574-1094 or 574-1095 FAX: (775) 574-1096
also Chief Judge
Yerington Tribal Court
171 Campbell Lane
Yerington, Nevada 89447
(775) 463-3301 FAX: (775) 463-1372

Theresa D. Sprouse, Chief Judge
Ely Shoshone Tribal Court
16 Shoshone Circle
Ely, Nevada 89301
(775) 289-2700 FAX: (775) 289-3156

Carolyn Seneca Steele, Chief Judge
Fort McDermitt Tribal Court
Post Office Box 397
McDermitt, Nevada 89421
(775) 532-8402 FAX: (775) 532-8202

Kyle B. Swanson, Tribal Judge
Winnemucca Tribal Court
Post Office Box 1370
Winnemucca, Nevada 89446

F. Woodside Wright *, Chief Judge
Lovelock Paiute Tribal Court
Post Office Box 2023
Lovelock, Nevada 89419
(775) 273-9039 FAX: (775) 273-3802
also Associate Judge
Fallon Tribal Court
8955 Mission Road
Fallon, Nevada 89406
(775) 423-8883 FAX: (775) 423-7395
also Associate Judge
Pyramid Lake Tribal Court
Post Office Box 257
Nixon, Nevada 89424
(775) 574-1094 or 574-1095 FAX: (775) 574-1096
also Associate Judge
Shoshone-Paiute Tribal Court
Post Office Box 219
Owyhee, Nevada 89832
(775) 757-2741 FAX: (775) 757-2078
also Magistrate
Te-Moak Western Shoshone CFR Court
1523 Shoshone Circle
Elko, Nevada 89801
(775) 738-7042 FAX: (775) 738-6047

Mitchell C. Wright*, Chief Judge
Washoe Tribal Court
919 U.S. Highway 395 South
Gardnerville, Nevada 89410
(775) 883-1446 FAX: (775) 265-9101

NEW HAMPSHIRE: (0)

NEW JERSEY: (0)

** Some individuals serve as a judge in more than one judicial position. The asterisk assures that the person is not counted more than once.*

New Mexico: (35)

Appellate Judges

Cheryl D. Fairbanks, Appellate Judge
Northwest Intertribal Court System
Post Office Box 707
Cedar Crest, New Mexico 87008

James M. Abeita, Chief Judge
Isleta Pueblo Tribal Court
Post Office Box 729
Isleta, New Mexico 87022
(505) 869-6510 FAX: (505) 869-8138

Marilou B. Begay, District Family Court Judge
Navajo Nation - Shiprock District Tribal Court
Post Office Box 1168
Shiprock, New Mexico 87420
(505) 368-1287 FAX: (505) 368-1288

Raymond Begaye, District Court Judge
Navajo Nation - Shiprock District Tribal Court
Post Office Box 1168
Shiprock, New Mexico 87420
(505) 368-1270 FAX: (505) 368-1288

Stanley A. Bird, Chief Judge
San Juan Pueblo Tribal Court
Post Office Box 1128
San Juan Pueblo, New Mexico 87566
(505) 852-4475 FAX: (505) 852-4820

Keith Bohren, Chief Judge
Publeo of Taos Tribal Court
Post Office Box 1846
Taos Pueblo, New Mexico 87566
(505) 751-0488 FAX: (505) 751-3552

Clarice Calricerocha, Associate Judge
Mescalero Apache Tribal Court
Post Office Box 176
Mescalero, New Mexico 88340
(505) 671-4489 FAX: (505) 761-4863

Frank Cerno, Jr., Chief Judge
Pueblo of Laguna Tribal Court
Post Office Box 194
Laguna, New Mexico 87026
(505) 552-6687 or 552-6688 FAX: (505) 552-7186

Jimmy Cimarron, Judge
Pueblo of San Felipe
Post Office Box 4339
San Felipe Pueblo, New Mexico 87001
(505) 867-3381 FAX: (505) 887-3383

Joe Cordero, Judge
Pueblo of Cochiti
Post Office Box 70
Cochiti Pueblo, New Mexico 87072
(505) 465-2244 FAX: (505) 465-2245

Frank DeMolli, Judge
Pueblo of Pojoaque Tribal Court
Route 11, Box 71
Santa Fe, New Mexico 87501
(505) 455-2271 FAX: (505) 455-2950

Roman Duran, Judge
Pueblo of Tesuque
Route 5, Box 360-H
Santa Fe, New Mexico 87501
(505) 989-4969 FAX: (505) 989-5037

Lorene B. Ferguson*, Circuit Court Judge
Post Office Box 3101
Canoncito, New Mexico 87026
(505) 836-1642 FAX: (505) 836-6431
also District Judge/Family Court Judge
Navajo Nation - Ramah Judicial District
Post Office Box 291
Ramah, New Mexico 87321
(505) 775-3218 FAX: (505) 775-3399

Raymond Gachupin, Associate Judge
Pueblo of Jemez Tribal Court
Post Office Box 100
Jemez Pueblo, New Mexico 87024
(505) 834-7369 FAX: (505) 834-7331

Beth Gallia, Associate Judge
Pueblo of Isleta Tribal Court
Post Office Box 729
Isleta, New Mexico 87022
(505) 869-6510 FAX: (505) 869-8138

Marcia Green, Associate Judge
Pueblo of Laguna
Post Office Box 194
Laguna, New Mexico 87026
(505) 552-6688 FAX: (505) 552-7186

Sharon M. Johnson, District Judge
Judicial Branch of the Navajo Nation
Post Office Box 6
Crownpoint, New Mexico 87313
(505) 786-2072 FAX: (505) 786-2086
also Ramah Judicial District
Post Office Box 291
Ramah, New Mexico 87321
(505) 775-3215 FAX: (505) 775-3399
also Alamo Circuit Court
Post Office Box 163
(505) 854-2888 FAX: (505) 854-2860
also Canoncito Circuit Court
Post Office Box 3101
Canoncito, New Mexico 87026
(505) 836-1642 FAX: 836-6431

Floyd J. Kezele, Chief Judge
Pueblo of Santa Ana Tribal Court
2 Dove Road
Bernalillo, New Mexico 87004
(505) 867-3394 Ext. 311 FAX: (505) 867-3395

Joseph Leonard Loretto, Judge
Publeo of Jemez
Post Office Box 100
Jemez Pueblo, New Mexico 87024
(505) 834-7359 FAX: (505) 834-7331

Angela R. Lujan, Chief Tribal Court Judge
Pueblo De Acoma Tribal Courts
Post Office Box 347
Pueblo De Acoma, New Mexico 87034
(505) 552-5144 or 552-6604 Ext. 51
FAX: (505) 552-6600 or 552-7394

Raquel Montoya, Associate Judge
Pueblo of Isleta Tribal Court
Post Office Box 729
Isleta, New Mexico 87022
(505) 869-6510 FAX: (505) 869-8138

Victor Montoya, Judge
Pueblo of Sandia Tribal Court
Post Office Box 6008
Bernalillo, New Mexico 87004
(505) 867-3317 FAX: (505) 867-9235

Loretta A. Morris, District Court Judge
Navajo Nation - Crownpoint District Tribal Court
Post Office Box 6
Crownpoint, New Mexico 87313
(505) 786-2072 FAX: (520) 786-2086

Valentino Pino, Judge
Pueblo of Zia Tribal Court
135 Capitol Square Drive
Zia Pueblo, New Mexico 87053-6013
(505) 867-3304 FAX: (505) 867-3308

Edie Quintana, Chief Judge
Pueblo of Pojoaque Tribal Court
Route 11, Box 71
Santa Fe, New Mexico 87501
(505) 455-2271 FAX: (505) 455-2950 or 455-0102

Clarise Rocha, Judge
Mescalaro Apache Tribal Court
Children's Court
Post Office Box 176
Mescalero, New Mexico 88340
(505) 671-4489 FAX: (505) 671-4863

Dennis Silva, Chief Judge
Pueblo of Santa Clara Tribal Court
Post Office Box 580
Espanola, New Mexico 87532
(505) 753-7326 FAX: (505) 753-0466
also Pueblo of Picuris Tribal Court
Post Office Box 127
Penasco, New Mexico 87553
(505) 587-2519 FAX: (505) 587-1071

Melvin R. Stoof, Chief Judge
Jicarilla Apache Tribal Court
Post Office Box 221
Dulce, New Mexico 87528
(505) 759-3366 FAX: (505) 759-3005

David Toledo, Associate Judge
Pueblo of Zia Tribal Court
135 Capitol Square Drive
Zia Pueblo, New Mexico 87053-6013
(505) 867-3304 FAX: (505) 867-3308

** Some individuals serve as a judge in more than one judicial position. The asterisk assures that the person is not counted more than once.*

Irene M. Toledo
District Judge/ Family Court Judge
Navajo - Nation Crownpoint District Tribal Court
Post Office Box 6
Crownpoint, New Mexico 87313
(505) 786-2072 FAX: (505) 786-2086

Tony Tortalita, Judge
Pueblo of Santo Domingo Tribal Court
Post Office Box 99
Santo Domingo Pueblo, New Mexico 87052
(505) 465-2214 FAX: (505) 465-2688

William Tsikewa, Chief Judge
Pueblo of Zuni Tribal Court
Post Office Box 339
Zuni, New Mexico 87237
(505) 782-4501 FAX: (505) 782-2250 or 782-5715

H. Paul Tsosie, Chief Judge
Pueblo of Ildefonso Tribal Court
Route 5, Box 315A
Santa Fe, New Mexico 87501
(505) 455-7500 or 455-2036
FAX: (505) 455-7942 or 455-2038

Roland Vigil, Judge
Pueblo of Nambe Tribal Court
Route 1, Box 117 BB
Santa Fe, New Mexico 87501
(505) 455-2036 FAX: (505) 455-2038

Steve Wahl, Chief Judge
Mescalero Apache Tribal Court
Post Office Box 176
Mescalero, New Mexico 88340
(505) 671-4494 Ext. 315 FAX: (505) 671-4863

NEW YORK: (4)

Charles Nephew, Judge
Court of Appeals
Seneca Nation of Indians
1508 Route 438
Irving, New York 14081
(716) 532-0024 FAX: (716) 532-0400

Rhonda Porter, Judge
Court of Appeals
Seneca Nation of Indians
1508 Route 438
Irving, New York 14081
(716) 532-0024 FAX: (716) 532-0400

Trial Judges

Maxine Black, Judge
Seneca Nation Peacemakers & Surrogate Courts
Judicial Court Office
Post Office Box 231
Salamanca, New York 14779
(716) 945-1790 FAX: (716) 945-3917

Angelia Johns, Judge
Seneca Nation Peacemakers
& Surrogate Courts
Judicial Court Office
Post Office Box 231
Salamanca, New York 14779
(716) 945-1790 FAX: (716) 945-3917

NORTH CAROLINA: (7)

Supreme Court

Terry Henry, Associate Justice
Cherokee Supreme Court
Eastern Band of Cherokee Indians
Post Office Box 455
Cherokee, North Carolina 28719
(828) 497-7874 FAX: (828) 497-5705

Harry C. Martin, Chief Justice
Cherokee Supreme Court
Eastern Band of Cherokee Indians
Post Office Box 455
Cherokee, North Carolina 28719
(828) 497-7874 FAX: (828) 497-5705

Brenda Toineeta, Associate Justice
Cherokee Supreme Court
Eastern Band of Cherokee Indians
Post Office Box 455
Cherokee, North Carolina 28719
(828) 497-7874 FAX: (828) 497-5705

Trial Court

Steven E. Philo, Chief Judge
Cherokee Tribal Court
Eastern Band of Cherokee Indians
1 Acquoni Road
Post Office Box 455
Cherokee, North Carolina 28719
(828) 497-7874 or 497-7720 FAX: (828) 497-5705

Kirk G. Saunooke, Associate Judge
Cherokee Tribal Court
Eastern Band of Cherokee Indians
1 Acquoni Road
Post Office Box 455
Cherokee, North Carolina 28719
(828) 497-7874 FAX: (828) 497-5705

George S. Wolfe, Jr., Associate Judge
Cherokee Tribal Court
Eastern Band of Cherokee Indians
1 Acquoni Road
Post Office Box 455
Cherokee, North Carolina 28719
(828) 497-7874 or 497-7720 FAX: (828) 497-5705

Magistrate

Selena Pheasant, Magistrate
Cherokee CFR Court
Bureau of Indian Affairs, Cherokee Agency
Post Office Box 66
Cherokee, North Carolina 28719
(828) 497-7874 FAX: (828) 497-5705

NORTH DAKOTA: (4)

Mary Cavanaugh, Chief Judge
Spirit Lake Nation Tribal Court
Post Office Box 30
Fort Totten, North Dakota 58335

P. Diane Johnson, Chief Judge
Standing Rock Sioux Tribal Court
Post Office Box 363
Fort Yates, North Dakota 58538-0363

Albert Jones, Chief Judge
Three Affiliated Tribes Tribal Court
Post Office Box 969
New Town, North Dakota 58763

Francis Morin, Chief Judge
Turtle Mountain Band of Phippewa
Post Office Box 900
Relcourt, North Dakota 58316

NORTH MARIANNA ISLANDS: (0)

OHIO: (0)

OKLAHOMA: (8)

Supreme Court Justices

Michael Flud, Supreme Court Justice
Muscogee (Creek) Nation Judicial System
Post Office Box 652
Okmulgee, Oklahoma 74447
(918) 758-1439 FAX: (918) 758-1440

Richard Lerblance, Supreme Court Justice
Muscogee (Creek) Nation Judicial System
Post Office Box 652
Okmulgee, Oklahoma 74447
(918) 758-1439 FAX: (918) 758-1440

Amos McNac, Chief Supreme Court Justice
Muscogee (Creek) Nation Judicial System
Post Office Box 652
Okmulgee, Oklahoma 74447
(918) 758-1439 FAX: (918) 758-1440

Larry Oliver, Supreme Court Justice
Muscogee (Creek) Nation Judicial System
Post Office Box 652
Okmulgee, Oklahoma 74447
(918) 758-1439 FAX: (918) 758-1440

Houston Shirley, Supreme Court Justice
Muscogee (Creek) Nation Judicial System
Post Office Box 652
Okmulgee, Oklahoma 74447
(918) 758-1439 FAX: (918) 758-1440

Roger Wiley, Vice-Chief Supreme Court Justice
Muscogee Creek Nation Judicial System
Post Office Box 652
Okmulgee, Oklahoma 74447
(918) 758-1439 FAX: (918) 758-1440

Trial Judges

Patrick Moore, District Judge
Muscogee Creek Nation Judicial System
Post Office Box 652
Okmulgee, Oklahoma 74447
(918) 758-1400 FAX: (918) 758-1413

James R. Wolfe, Tribal Court Judge
Choctaw Nation of Oklahoma
Court of Indian Offenses
HC64, Box 3270
Tuskahoma, Oklahoma 74574-9758
(918) 569-4465 FAX: (918) 569-7675
E-mail: chatacourt@pisp.net

OREGON: (22)

Appellate Court Judges

George Clements, Sr.
Chief Appellate Court Judge
Warm Springs Tribal Court
The Confederated Tribes of Warm Springs
Post Office Box 850
Warm Springs, Oregon 97761
(541) 553-3450 FAX: (541) 553-2257

Gerald Danzuka, Appellate Court Judge
Warm Springs Tribal Court
The Confederated Tribes of Warm Springs
Post Office Box 850
Warm Springs, Oregon 97761
(541) 553-3450 FAX: (541) 553-2257

Mary Danzuka, Appellate Court Judge
Warm Springs Tribal Court
The Confederated Tribes of Warm Springs
Post Office Box 850
Warm Springs, Oregon 97761
(541) 553-3450 FAX: (541) 553-2257

Robert Dickinson, Appellate Judge
Siletz Appellate Court
Post Office Box 549
Siletz, Oregon 97380

Eunice Esquiro, Appellate Court Justice
Warm Springs Tribal Court
The Confederated Tribes of Warm Springs
Post Office Box 850
Warm Springs, Oregon 97761
(541) 553-3450 FAX: (541) 553-2257

Hamilton Greeley, Appellate Court Judge
Warm Springs Tribal Court
The Confederated Tribes of Warm Springs
Post Office Box 850
Warm Springs, Oregon 97761
(541) 553-3450 FAX: (541) 553-2257

Kirby Heath, Sr., Appellate Court Judge
Warm Springs Tribal Court
The Confederated Tribes of Warm Springs
Post Office Box 850
Warm Springs, Oregon 97761
(541) 553-3450 FAX: (541) 553-2257

Leo Hellon, Appellate Court Judge
Warm Springs Tribal Court
The Confederated Tribes of Warm Springs
Post Office Box 850
Warm Springs, Oregon 97761
(541) 553-3450 FAX: (541) 553-2257

Buford Johnson, Jr., Appellate Court Judge
Warm Springs Tribal Court
The Confederated Tribes of Warm Springs
Post Office Box 850
Warm Springs, Oregon 97761
(541) 553-3450 FAX: (541) 553-2257

Redine Kirk, Appellate Court Judge
Warm Spring Tribal Court
The Confederated Tribes of Warm Springs
Post Office Box 850
Warm Springs, Oregon 97761
(541) 553-3450 FAX: (541) 553-2257

Robert Miller, Appellate Court Judge
Northwest Intertribal Court System
10015 S.W. Terwilliger Boulevard
Portland, Oregon 97219
(503) 768-6821 FAX: (503) 768-6671
E-mail: miller@clark.edu

Ginger Smith, Appellate Court Judge
Warm Springs Tribal Court
The Confederated Tribes of Warm Springs
Post Office Box 850
Warm Springs, Oregon 97761
(541) 553-3450 FAX: (541) 553-2257

Cathern Tufts, Chief Appellate Judge
Siltez Appellate Court
Post Office Box 549
Siletz, Oregon 97380

Perthina White, Appellate Court Judge
Warm Springs Tribal Court
The Confederated Tribes of Warm Springs
Post Office Box 850
Warm Springs, Oregon 97761
(541) 553-3450 FAX: (541) 553-2257

Trial Court Judges

Katherine English, Chief Judge
Grand Ronde Tribal Court
9615 Grand Ronde Road
Grand Ronde, Oregon 97347

Calvin Gantebien, Chief Judge
Siletz Tribal Court
Post Office Box 549
Siletz, Oregon 97380

William Johnson, Chief Judge
Umatilla Tribal Court
73303 July Gronds Lane
Pendleton, Oregon 97801

Mark Kemp, Chief Judge
Burns Piaute Tribal Court
HC-71, 100 Pasigo Street
Burns, Oregon 97720
(503) 573-2793

Walter Langnese III, Associate Judge
Warm Springs Tribal Court
The Confederated Tribes of Warm Springs
Post Office Box 850
Warm Springs, Oregon 97761
(541) 553-3454 FAX: (541) 553-3281

Wilma Picard, Associate Judge
Warm Springs Tribal Court
The Confederated Tribes of Warm Springs
Post Office Box 850
Warm Springs, Oregon 97761
(541) 553-3454 FAX: (541) 553-3281

Lola Sohappy, Chief Judge
Warm Springs Tribal Court
Post Office Box 850
Warm Springs, Oregon 99761
(541) 553-3454 FAX: (541) 553-3281

Donna J. Goldsmith, Presiding Judge
North Coast Intertribal Children's Court
2365 N.W. Irving #8
Portland, Oregon 97210
(503) 223-4169 FAX: (503) 227-6847

PENNSYLVANIA: (0)

PUERTO RICO: (0)

RHODE ISLAND: (0)

SOUTH CAROLINA: (0)

SOUTH DAKOTA: (8)

Trial Court Judges

Viola Burnete, Judge
Rosebud Sioux Tribal Court
Post office Box 129
Rosebud, South Dakota 57570
(605) 747-2278 FAX: (605) 747-2832 or 747-2279

Patrick Lee, Judge
Oglala Sioux Tribal Court
Post Office Box 280
Pine Ridge, South Dakota 57770-0289
(605) 867-5151 or 867-5821 FAX: (605) 867-1549

Sherman J. Marshall, Chief Judge
Rosebud Sioux Tribal Court
Post Office Box 129
Rosebud, South Dakota 57570-0129
(605) 747-2278 FAX: (605) 747-2832
also Judge Crow Creek Sioux Tribal Court
Post Office Box 247
Fort Thompson, South Dakota 57339-0247
(605) 245-2325 FAX: (605) 245-2216 or 245-2326

Rose McCauley, Judge
Lower Brule Sioux Tribal Court
Post Office Box 187
Lower Brule, South Dakota 57548-0187
(605) 473-5529 FAX: (605) 473-5606

Bette Iron Moccasin, Judge
Oglala Sioux Tribal Court
Post Office Box 280
Pine Ridge, South Dakota 57770
(605) 867-5151 FAX: (605) 867-1549

Charles T. Montileaux, Sr., Judge
Oglala Sioux Tribal Court
Post Office Box 280
Pine Ridge, South Dakota 57770
(605) 867-5151 FAX: (605) 867-1549

Cheryl Three Stars Valandra, Judge
Rosebud Sioux Tribal Court
Post Office 129
Rosebud, South Dakota 57570-0129
(605) 747-2278 FAX: (605) 747-2832

Sidney T. Witt, Judge
Oglala Sioux Tribal Court
Post Office Box 159
Kyle, South Dakota 57752
(605) 455-2316 FAX: (605) 455-2197

TENNESSEE: (0)

TEXAS: (0)

UTAH: (4)

George Tah Bone, Chief Judge
Ute Tribal Court
Post Office Box 190
Ft. Duchesane, Utah 84028
(435) 722-3633 FAX: (435) 722-3637

Leon Perank, Associate Judge
Ute Tribal Court
Post Office Box 190
Ft. Duchesane, Utah 84026
(435) 722-3633 FAX: (435) 722-3637

Debra Ridley, Juvenile Judge
Ute Tribal Court
Post office Box 190
Ft. Duchesane, Utah 84028
(435) 722-2314 FAX: (435) 722-3086

James Underwood, Chief Judge
Goshute Tribal Court
Post Office Box 6104
Ibapah, Utah
(435) 234-1136

VERMONT: (0)

VIRGIN ISLANDS: (0)

VIRGINIA: (0)

WASHINGTON: (43)

Appellate Judges

David Bonga, Justice
Colville Court of Appeals
Post Office Box 150
Nespelem,Washington 99155
(509) 634-2507 FAX: 509) 634-2513

Michelle Demmert, Justice
Northwest Intertribal Court System
144 Railroad Avenue
Edmonds, Washington 98020
(425) 778-7704 FAX: (425) 774-5808
E-mail: mmdemmert@aol.com

Anita Dupris, Chief Justice
Colville Tribes Court of Appeals
Post Office Box 150
Nespelem, Washington 99155
(509) 634-2507 FAX: (509) 634-2513
E-mail: ctappadm@aol.com

Katherine Eldemar, Appellate Judge
Northwest Intertribal Court System
3942 Cliffside Drive
Bellingham, Washington 98226
(360) 676-2758 FAX: (360) 392-8266

Elizabeth Fry, Justice
Colville Court of Appeals
Post Office Box 150
Nespelem,Washington 99155
(509) 634-2507 FAX: (509) 634-2513
also Justice, Spokane Tribe
Post Office Box 949
Omak, Washington 98841
E-mail: Efry@televar.com

Cynthia Ann Jordan, Appellate Judge
Nez Perce Tribal Appellate Court
921 West Broadway, Suite 201
Spokane, Washington 99201

Darwin S. Long Fox, Appellate Judge
Northwest Intertribal Court System
3006 31st Avenue
Seattle, Washington 98199
(206) 285-1622

Douglas Luna, Appellate Judge
Northwest Intertribal Court System
121 Fifth Avenue North, Suite 305
Edmonds, Washington 98020
(206) 774-5808 FAX: (206) 778-7704

Wanda L. Miles, Justice
Colville Court of Appeals
Post Office Box 150
Nespelem, Washington 99155
(509) 634-2507 FAX: (509) 634-2513

Earl McGeoghegan*, Associate Justice
Colville Tribes Court of Appeals
Post Office Box 150
Nespelem, Washington 99155
(509) 634-2507 FAX: (509) 634-2513

Dennis Nelson, Justice
Colville Court of Appeals
Post Office Box 150
Nespelem, Washington 99155
(509) 634-2507 FAX: (509) 634-2513

Conrad Pascal, Associate Judge
Appellate Court
Spokane Indian Tribe
Post Office Box 225
Wellpinit, Washington 99040
(509) 258-7717 FAX: (509) 258-9223

Patricia Paul, Appellate Judge
Northwest Intertribal Court System
619 Commercial Avenue
Room 26, 3rd Floor
Anacortes, Washington 98221
(360) 299-2346 FAX: (360) 466-3906

Mary Linda Pearson, Chief Judge
Appellate Court
Spokane Indian Tribe
Post Office Box 225
Wellpinit, Washington 99040
(509) 258-7717 FAX: (509) 258-9223

Julian Pinkham, Appellate Judge
Northwest Intertribal Court System
760 North Olden Way Road
Toppenish, Washington 98948
(509) 877-5861

Rose Purser, Appellate Judge
Northwest Intertribal Court System
Post Office Box 280
Kingston, Washington 98346-0280
(360) 297-6246 FAX: (360) 297-7521

Jerrie Simmons, Appellate Judge
Northwest Intertribal Court System
Post Office Box 13223
Mill Creek, Washington 98082

Howard E. Stewart, Justice
Colville Court of Appeals
Post Office Box 150
Nespelem, Washington 99155
(509) 634-2507 FAX: (509) 634-2513

Lovina Washines, Appellate Judge
Yakima Tribal Court of Appeals
Post Office Box 151
Toppenish, Washington 98948

Mary T. Wynne, Justice
Spokane Tribe
Post Office Box 1218
Okanogan, Washington 98840
E-mail: Wynne_law@hotmail.com

Trial Judges

Steven D. Aycock, Chief Judge
Coville Tribal Court
Post Office Box 150
Nespelem, Washington 99155
(509) 634-8880 FAX: (509) 634-8566

Martin Bohl, Chief Judge
Upper Skagit Tribal Court
2284 Community Plaza
Sedro Woolley, Washington 98280
(360) 856-4200

Randy Brown, Chief Judge
Suquamish Tribal Court
Post Office Box 1209
Suquamish, Washington 98392-1209
(360) 589-3311 FAX: (360) 598-5333

Edythe Chenois, Chief Judge
Quinault Tribal Court
Post Office Box 99
Taholah, Washington 98587-0099
(206) 276-8211 Ext. 223 FAX: (206) 276-4606

Les Ching, Chief Judge
Nisqually Tribal Court
4820 She-Nah-Num Drive S.E.
Olympia, Washington 98513

Emma Dulik, Chief Judge
Makah Tribal Court
Post Office Box 192
Neah Bay, Washington 98357-0192
(360) 645-3302 FAX: (360) 645-2760

Katherine Eldemar*, Associate Judge
Colville Tribal Court
3942 Cliffside Drive
Bellingham, Washington 98226
(360) 676-2758 FAX: (360) 392-8260

Rory SnowArrow Flint Knife, Judge
Yakima Indian Nation Tribal Court
Post Office Box 151
Toppenish, Washington 98948-0151
(509) 865-5121 FAX:(509) 865-2794

Frank LaFountaine, Associate Judge
Colville Tribal Court
Post Office Box 150
Nespelem, Washington 99155
(509) 634-8880 FAX: (509) 634-8566

Douglas Luna*, Judge
Northwest Intertribal Court Systems
121 Fifth Avenue, North, Suite 305
Edmonds, Washington 98020
(206) 774-5808 FAX: 9206) 778-7704

Bertha M. Miller, Judge
Yakima Indian Nation Tribal Court
Post Office Box 151
Toppenish, Washington 98948-0151
(509) 865-5121 FAX: (509) 865-2794

Lawrence Numkena, Chief Judge
Puyallup Tribal Court
2002 East 28th Street
Tacoma, Washington 98404
(253) 953-0212 FAX: (253) 272-9299

Conrad Pascal, Associate/Family Court Judge
Spokane Tribal Court
Post Office Box 225
Wellpinit, Washington 99040
(509) 258-7717, FAX: 258-9223 or 258-7718

Mary Linda Pearson, Chief Judge
Spokane Tribal Court
Post Office Box 225
Wellpinit, Washington 99040
(509) 258-7717 FAX: (509) 258-9223
E-mail: Mlpearsonl@juno.com

Theresa Pouley, Chief Judge
Lummi Tribal Court
2616 Kwina Road
Bellingham, Washington 98226

Rose Purser*, Judge
Port Gamble Klallam Tribal Court
Post Office Box 280
Kingston, Washington 98346-0280
(360) 297-6246 FAX: (360) 297-7521

Francis Rosander, Judge
Quinault Tribal Court
Post Office Box 99
Taholah, Washington 98587-0099
(206) 276-8211 Ext. 223, FAX: (206) 276-4191

Tamara Saluskin, Juvenile Judge
Yakima Tribal Court
Post Office Box 151
Toppenish, Washington 98948

Reuben Sandoval, Associate Judge
Yakima Tribal Court
Post Office Box 151
Toppenish, Washington 98948

Cindy Smith, Associate Judge
Suquamish Tribal Court
Post Office Box 1209
Suquamish, Washington 98392-1209
(360) 598-3311 FAX: (360) 598-5333

Jean Vitalis, Chief Judge
Quileute Tribal Court
Post Office Box 297
La Push, Washington 98350-0297
(206) 374-9020
also Judge Makah Tribal Drug Court
Post Office Box 192
Neah Bay, Washington 98357-0192
(206) 645-2727 FAX: (206) 645-2411

Lorintha Warwick, Associate Judge
Puyallup Tribal Trial Court
2002 East 28th Street
Tacoma, Washington 98404
(253) 573-7824 FAX: (253) 272-9299

Mary T. Wynne, Chief Judge
Colville Tribal Court
Post Office Box 150
Nespelem, Washington 99155
(509) 634-8880 FAX: (509) 634-8566

Note: Those individuals indicated with an asterisk (*) serve both as appellate and as trial judges. They are only counted once in our total number of Native American Judges serving as Tribal Judges. We also note that a number of Non-Native Americans serve as Tribal Judges. To the extent that our sources have identified them, we have not included them in this Directory.

WEST VIRGINIA: (0)

WISCONSIN: (31)

Supreme Court Justices

Mary Jo Brooks Hunter, Chief Justice
Ho-Chunk Nation Supreme Court
Post Office Box 70
Black River Falls, Wisconsin 54615
(715) 284-2722 FAX: (715) 284-3136
E-mail: henuj2@aol.com

Rita Cleveland, Justice
Ho-Chunk Nation Supreme Court
Post Office Box 70
Black River Falls, Wisconsin 54615
(715) 284-2722 FAX: (715) 284-3136

Debra Greengrass, Justice
Ho-Chunk Nation Supreme Court
Post Office Box 70
Black River Falls, Wisconsin 54615
(715) 284-2722 FAX: (715) 284-3136

Robert Kittecon, Chief Justice
Menominee Supreme Court
Post Office Box 429
Keshena, Wisconsin 54135

Trial Judges

Fred A. Ackley, Jr., Chief Judge
Sokaogon Tribal Court
Route 1, Box 625
Crandon, Wisconsin 54520
(715) 478-2604 Ext. 15 FAX: (715) 478-5275

Harriet Balber, Associate Judge
Red Cliff Tribal Court
Post Office Box 529
Bayfield, Wisconsin 54814
(715) 779-3725 FAX: (715) 779-3704

Louis Bearheart, Chief Judge
St. Croix Tribal Court
Post Office Box 287
Hertel, Wisconsin 54845
(715) 349-2195 FAX: (715) 349-2975

Luke Beauprey, Judge
Menominee Tribal Court
Post Office Box 429
Keshena, Wisconsin 54135
(715) 799-3348 FAX: (715) 799-4061

Jean Buffalo-Reyes, Chief Judge
Red Cliff Tribal Court
Post Office Box 529
Bayfield, Wisconsin 54814
(715) 779-3725 or 779-3726
FAX: (715) 779-3704 or 779-3724

Mark Butterfield, Chief Trial Judge
Ho-Chunk Nation Tribal Court
Post Office Box 70
Black River Falls, Wisconsin 54615
(715) 284-2722 or 1-800 434-4070
FAX: (715) 284-3136

Joe Corbine, Associate Judge
Bad River Tribal Court
Post Office Box 39
Odanah, Wisconsin 54861
(715) 682-7111 FAX: (715) 682-7118

Betty Graveen, Judge
Lac Du Flambeau Tribal Court
Post Office Box 67
Lac du Flambeau, Wisconsin 54538
(715) 588-3303 FAX: (715) 588-7930

Joan Greendeer-Lee
Associate Trial Court Judge
Ho-Chunk Nation Tribal Court
Post Office Box 70
Black River Falls, Wisconsin 54615
(715) 284-2722 or 1-800-434-4070
FAX: (715) 284-3136

Louis Hawpetoss, Judge
Menominee Tribal Court
Post Office Box 429
Keshena, Wisconsin 54135
(715) 799-3348 FAX: (715) 799-4061

Floyd Hipsher, Associate Trial Court Judge
Red Cliff Tribal Court
Post Office Box 529
Bayfield, Wisconsin 54814
(715) 779-3725, FAX: (715) 779-3724 or 779-3704

Robert Kittecon, Chief Judge
Menominee Tribal Court
Post Office Box 429
Keshena, Wisconsin 54135
(715) 799-3348 FAX: (715) 799-4061

Todd Matha, Associate Judge
Ho-Chunk Nation Tribal Court
Post Office Box 70
Black River Falls, Wisconsin 54615
(715) 284-2722 FAX: (715) 284-3136

Gloria Merrill, Alternate Judge
St. Croix Tribal Court
Post office Box 287
Hertel, Wisconsin 54845
(715) 349-2195 FAX: (715) 349-2975

Robert Miller, Jr., Associate Judge
Stockbridge-Munsee Tribal Court
N8476 Moh He Con Nuck Road
Bowler, Wisconsin 54416
(715) 793-4111 or 793-4397 FAX: (715) 793-4880

David R. Raasch, Chief Judge
Stockbridge-Munsee Tribal Court
N8476 Moh He Con Nuck Road
Bowler, Wisconsin 54416
(715) 793-4111 or 793-4397, FAX: (715) 793-4880

Alton Smart, Associate Judge
Bad River Tribal Court
Post Office Box 39
Odanah, Wisconsin 54861
(715) 682-7111 FAX: (715) 682-7118

Alice Soulier, Judge
Lac Du Flambeau Tribal Court
Post Office Box 67
Lac du Flambeau, Wisconsin 54538
(715) 588-3303 FAX: (715) 588-7930

Ervin Soulier, Chief Judge
Bad River Tribal Court
Post Office Box 39
Odanah, Wisconsin 54861
(715) 682-7111 FAX: (715) 682-7118

Ernest St. Germaine, Chief Judge
Lac Du Flambeau Tribal Court
Post Office Box 67
Lac du Flambeau, Wisconsin 54538
(715) 588-3303 FAX: (715) 588-7930
also Judge Lac Courte Oreilles Tribal Court
Route 2, Box 2700
Hayward, Wisconsin 54843
(715) 634-8934 FAX: (715) 634-4797

Debra VanZile, Judge
Sokaogon Tribal Court
Route 1, Box 625
Crandon, Wisconsin 54520
(715) 478-2604 Ext. 15 FAX: (715) 478-5275

Kimberly Vele, Associate Judge
Stockbridge-Munsee Tribal Court
N8476 Moh He Con Nuck Road
Bowler, Wisconsin 54416
(715) 793-4111 or 793-4397 FAX: (715) 793-4880

James Washinawatok, Judge
Menominee Tribal Court
Post Office Box 429
Keshena, Wisconsin 54135
(715) 799-3348 FAX: (715) 799-4061

Eugene L. White-Fish, Tribal Court Judge
Forest County Potawatorni Community
Tribal Court
Post Office Box 340
Crandon, Wisconsin 54520
(715) 478-5850 FAX: (715) 478-5805

Phyllis White, Judge
Lac du Flambeau Tribal Court
Post Office Box 67
Lac du Flambeau, Wisconsin 54538
(715) 588-3303 FAX: (715) 588-7930

Magistrates

Robert Buffalo, Magistrate
Red Cliff Tribal Court
Post Office Box 529
Bayfield, Wisconsin 54814
(715) 779-3725 FAX: (715) 779-3704

Robert Goslin, Magistrate
Red Cliff Tribal Court
Post Office Box 529
Bayfield, Wisconsin 54814
(715) 779-3725 FAX: (715) 779-3704

WYOMING: (3)

Vida Haukas, Judge
Shoshone and Arapahoe Tribal Court
109 Norkok Road
Post Office Box 608
Ft. Washakie, Wyoming 82514
(307) 332-6702

John St. Clair, Chief Judge
Shoshone and Arapahoe Tribal Court
109 Norkok Road
Post Office Box 608
Ft. Washakie, Wyoming 82514
(307) 332-6702

John Warren, Judge
Shoshone and Arapahoe Tribal Court
109 Norkok Road
Post Office Box 608
Ft. Washakie, Wyoming 82514
(307) 332-6702

U.S. ARMED FORCES: (0)

MINORITY JUDGES OF THE UNITED STATES